The Memory of Judgment

The Memory *of* Judgment

. . .

Making Law and History in the Trials of the Holocaust

LAWRENCE DOUGLAS

Yale University Press

New Haven and London

Designed by Nancy Ovedovitz and set in Galliard Oldstyle
type by The Composing Room of Michigan, Inc. Printed
in the United States of America by Edwards Brothers, Inc.

Library of Congress Cataloging-in-Publication Data
Douglas, Lawrence.
The memory of judgment : making law and history
in the trials of the holocaust /
Lawrence Douglas.
p.   cm.
Includes index.
ISBN 0-300-08436-6 (alk. paper)
1. War crimes trials.   2. World War, 1939–1945 —
Atrocities.   I. Title.
KZ1174. .D68   2001
341.6′9 — dc21   00-043967

A catalogue record for this book is available from the
British Library.
The paper in this book meets the guidelines for permanence
and durability of the Committee on Production Guidelines
for Book Longevity of the Council on Library Resources.

10   9   8   7   6   5   4   3   2   1

For my parents

Is it possible that the antonym of "forgetting" is
not "remembering," but *justice*?
— Yosef Hayim Yerushalmi

Contents

Part Three Zundel

Acknowledgments

I am extremely grateful to the following people whose guidance, support, and assistance have made this book possible. In particular, I would like to acknowledge the unstinting support of Owen Fiss, mentor and friend. The following persons offered critical advice on the manuscript in part or whole: Robert Burt, Geoffrey Hartman, Michael Marrus, Robert Post, Mark Osiel, James Young, Shoshana Felman, Sue Vice, Jeff Rubin, Lawrence Langer, Martha Minow, Dana Villa, and Berel Lang.

I greatly benefited from the support of colleagues at Amherst, in particular, from the tireless and penetrating advice of Austin Sarat. I was also helped by Nasser Hussain, Frank Couvares, David Delaney, Martha Umphrey, Tom Kearns, and Alexander George. President Tom Gerety and Dean of Faculty Lisa Raskin also offered valuable support, and the research and writing of this book was aided by three generous grants from Amherst: a Loewenstein fellowship, a Wilson fellowship, and a Faculty Research Award.

For research on Nuremberg, I would like to thank Bill Connelly and Alexander Rossino, United States Holocaust Research Institute; Rosemary Haines, Library of Congress; Robert Wolfe (retired), National Archives; Jonathan Bush; and David Luban, Georgetown University School of Law.

For material on the Eichmann and Demjanjuk trials, I am grateful to Justice Gabriel Bach, Supreme Court of Israel (retired); Chief Justice Aaron Barak, Supreme Court of Israel; Haim Gouri; Judith Levin, Yad Vashem;

Hannah Yablonka, Ben-Gurion University; Andrew Ingall, Jewish Museum Film Department; Joanne Rudof, Fortunoff Video Archive for Holocaust Testimonies, Yale University; and Tom Segev.

For material concerning the Barbie trial, I am grateful to Henri Rousso and Annette Wieviorka, both of the Centre National de la Recherche Scientifique, Paris. For material on Holocaust denial litigation in Germany, I am indebted to Ulrich Preuss, Free University, Berlin; Juliane Wetzel, Zentrum für Antisemitismusforschung, Berlin; Ken Rudolf, Yale International Law Library; and Eric Stein, University of Michigan Law School. For help on the Zundel trial, I am grateful to Christopher Browning, University of North Carolina, Chapel Hill; Crown Prosecutors Peter Griffiths and John Pearson, Sol Litman of the Simon Wiesenthal Center, Toronto; Robert Kahn; and Steven Shulman of the Canadian Jewish Congress.

I am grateful for the expert editorial advice and sharp reading of my wife, Nancy Pick, Rand Cooper, and my student assistants, Ethan Katz and Laura Moser. Two other students, Stephen Porder and Jarkko Cain, provided helpful research and assistance. Frank Ward helped prepare the still photographs and Karen Underwood helped ready the manuscript.

At Yale University Press, I greatly benefited from the superior editing of Jonathan Brent, John Covell, and Lawrence Kenney.

Jacob and Milo simply helped. Barry, too. And Nancy, well—but for, not.

I am also grateful to the following persons and institutions for inviting me to present earlier versions of material in this book. Florent Brayard, Centre Marc Bloch, Berlin; Gary Smith, the Einstein Forum and the American Academy, Potsdam; Joël Kotek, le Centre Européen d'Études sur Shoah, l'Antisémitisme et le Génocide, Brussels; Leora Bilsky, the Cegla Center for Comparative and Private International Law, University of Tel Aviv Law School; Michael Freeman, Bentham House, University College London; Janice Stein, Munk Centre for International Studies, University of Toronto; The Getty Research Institute for the History of Art and the Humanities, Los Angeles; Sylvia Fuks Fried, the Tauber Institute for the Study of European Jewry, Brandeis University; and the Schell Center for International Human Rights, Yale Law School.

Portions of this book have appeared in substantially different form in the following publications. Chapter 1 appeared as "Film as Witness: Screening *Nazi Concentration Camps* Before the Nuremberg Tribunal," *Yale Law Jour-*

nal 105, no. 2 (1995): 449–81. A small section of chapter 3 appeared as "The Shrunken Head of Buchenwald: Icons of Atrocity at Nuremberg," *Representations* 63 (1998): 39–64. Parts of chapters 7 and 8 appeared as "The Memory of Judgment: The Law, the Holocaust and Denial," *History & Memory* 7, no. 2 (1996): 100–20; and, in expanded and altered form, as "Policing the Past: Holocaust Denial and the Law," in Robert Post, ed., *Censorship and Silencing: Practices of Cultural Regulation* (Getty Research Institute Press, 1998), 66–87.

The Memory of Judgment

Introduction

The dead, Elias Canetti observed, "are nourished by judgment." Canetti's words conjure a provocative image of the criminal law: as a means of recompensing the slain through a deliberative act. But when the dead number untold thousands how can such nourishment be provided? This question presses upon the world as forensic teams sift through evidence and prosecutors prepare cases against the perpetrators of atrocity in Bosnia, Kosovo, and Rwanda. The problems facing these prosecutors are great — but not without precedent. For it is impossible to imagine Slobodan Milosevic standing trial without bringing to mind pictures of Hermann Göring in the defendants' dock at Nuremberg and Adolf Eichmann in the glass booth in Jerusalem. Indeed, it is the memory of these earlier trials that creates the hope, if not the expectation, that today's perpetrators will be forced to answer to the law.

This book asks readers to remember the law's first great efforts to submit mass atrocity to principled judgment. In these pages, I will examine fifty years of legal struggle with the crimes of the Holocaust through the record of four principal trials of perpetrators: the Nuremberg trial of the major Nazi war criminals in 1945–46, the Israeli trials of Eichmann in 1961 and John (Ivan) Demjanjuk in 1987, and the French trial of Klaus Barbie, also in 1987. In addition, I will look at the two trials of a Holocaust denier, Ernst Zundel, before Canadian courts in 1985 and 1988. Most studies of the great perpetrator trials have sought to resolve whether these proceedings fulfilled their requirement to do justice to the defendants. My book will be largely devoted to answering a different question: Did the trials do justice to the unprecedented crimes of the Holocaust? Did they present a responsible portrait of a horrific subject? To answer this question, one must examine how a specialized legal instrument, the criminal trial, was used as a tool of collective pedagogy and as a salve to traumatic history.

Such a study may seem to deflect attention from the more orthodox issues of legal justice raised by these cases. In her controversial book *Eichmann in Jerusalem,* Hannah Arendt argued that "the purpose of a trial is to render justice, and nothing else; even the noblest of ulterior purposes — 'the making of a record of the Hitler regime which would withstand the test of history' . . . — can only detract from the law's main business: to weigh the charges brought against the accused, to render judgment, and to mete out due punishment."[1] Arendt's argument presupposed a strict separation between the legal and the extralegal, between the rule of law and the interests of collective instruction. One must resist, Arendt insisted, subjecting the trial to pressures that may distort the solemn dictates of justice.[2] The danger of turning a trial into a pedagogic spectacle is that it becomes a legal farce, a fear that finds expression in Ian Buruma's claim that "when the court of law is used for history lessons, then the risk of show trials cannot be far off."[3]

Arendt's concerns serve as a critical foil for this book. No one, I believe, would deny that the primary responsibility of a criminal trial is to resolve questions of guilt in a procedurally fair manner. And certainly one must appreciate the potential tension between the core interests of justice and the concerns of didactic legality. To insist, however, as Arendt does, that the *sole* purpose of a trial is to render justice and nothing else, presents, I will argue, a crabbed and needlessly restrictive vision of the trial as legal form.

All the trials that are the subject of this book were staged with an eye toward satisfying the requirements of both principled judgment and historical tutelage.[4] Robert M. W. Kempner, a junior prosecutor at Nuremberg, called the Nuremberg trials the "the greatest history seminar ever held in the history of the world."[5] Sir Hartley Shawcross, the British chief prosecutor, echoed this idea, declaring that the Nuremberg tribunal would "provide . . . an authoritative and impartial record to which future historians may turn for truth."[6] Many important histories of the Holocaust, such as Raul Hilberg's *The Destruction of the European Jews,* could not have been written without the massive archive of documentary material assembled through Nuremberg's act of legal discovery.

The Eichmann trial, even more explicitly than Nuremberg, was staged to teach history and shape collective memory. Gideon Hausner, the Israeli attorney general who led the prosecution, believed that a courtroom re-creation of the "Great Catastrophe" would "bring the youth closer to the nation's past"—and specifically help young Israelis answer the question, "How did they allow themselves to be led like lambs to the slaughter?"[7] By bringing the public into contact with the demeanor and stories of the sur-vivors, the trial, he believed, would serve the ends of responsible memory. It would turn the public into witnesses of the witnesses—thereby creating a vital organic link to the past.[8] This mindfulness of the past was meant, in turn, to support the Zionist politics of the present.

Likewise, the Barbie and Demjanjuk trials were staged as exercises in di-dactic legality, prosecutions shaped to build upon the lessons of Nurem-berg and Eichmann. Finally, the Zundel trial offers perhaps the most un-usual instance of prosecution as a pedagogic exercise. In trying a Holocaust denier, the Zundel prosecutors sought to enlist the coercive power of the law to protect historical truth and sacral memory from hateful distortion.

Thus to call Holocaust trials show trials—the term used by Arendt to dis-parage the Eichmann proceeding—is to state the obvious. After all, that is what these trials were—orchestrations designed to show the world the facts of astonishing crimes and to demonstrate the power of law to reintroduce order into a space evacuated of legal and moral sense. As dramas of didactic legality, the trials of the Holocaust blurred, then, the very boundary be-tween the legal and extralegal upon which Arendt's critique was based.

Of course, Arendt meant the term "show trial" to raise the specter of a Stalinist fraud, and it is here, on the normative level, that Arendt's argu-ment shows its deeper insufficiencies. Although each of these trials tested the plasticity of the trial form, they preserved, I will argue, the integrity of the system of justice. Indeed, the notion that a trial can succeed as peda-gogy yet fail to do justice is crucially flawed. To succeed as a didactic specta-cle in a democracy, a trial must be justly conducted insofar as one of the principal pedagogic aims of such a proceeding must be to make visible and public the sober authority of the rule of law.

A number of scholars, however, have recently expressed a critique of the law that is the obverse of Arendt's. Concerned less that law's tutelary role will distort its responsibility to the accused, these scholars argue that the procedural norms that govern a criminal trial render it a flawed tool for comprehending traumatic history.[9] In the first edition of his influential study *After Auschwitz: Radical Theology and Contemporary Judaism,* Richard Rubenstein dismissed the pedagogic value of the Eichmann trial with the observation that "once the defendant's legal sanity was established, psychological considerations were precluded by the nature of the judicial process."[10] This sentiment is echoed by Buruma, who writes that a trial "can only be concerned with individual crimes," and as a result, "history is reduced to criminal pathology and legal argument."[11] More recently, and with greater attention to the peculiarities of specific Holocaust trials, Michael Marrus has urged that "we should not look to trials to validate our general understanding of the Holocaust or to provide a special platform for historical interpretations."[12] These critiques insist that the judicial process inevitably fails to grasp the most disturbing and fundamental issues raised by traumatic history, issues more satisfactorily explored through history, literature, or psychoanalysis — or perhaps through such instruments as a South African–style truth and reconciliation commission.

This critique also represents a grave attack on the logic of didactic legality, but it too, as we shall see, does not fully capture the reality of the trials of the Holocaust. While much of this book will probe the limits of these proceedings, it will also reveal the intense, creative labors of the law to master the problems of representation and judgment posed by the Holocaust. Against those who contend that the trial's need to reach a verdict indicates the law's hostility to a spirit of open-ended historical inquiry, I will show that this requirement in fact supports the power of the criminal trial to galvanize collective interest in the past. The Nuremberg and Eichmann trials, for example, received extraordinary attention not simply because evidence of unprecedented crimes was publicly aired, but because this airing was framed against the backdrop of the gallows. Against the view that legal discourse is too formal and anchored in precedent to make sense of unprecedented crimes, I will examine how the law struggled to master the radicalness of Nazi atrocity through the creation of novel concepts of criminality — most important, genocide and the crime against humanity. And against the view that contrasts the fixedness of legal judgment with the fluidity of historical inquiry, I seek to demonstrate how legal understandings can be revised through a process of juridical restagings, in which a latter-day trial (for example, the Barbie proceeding) revisits and revises the issues considered in its precursor (Nuremberg). Individual trials must be staged to reach closure; yet, the discourse of legal judgment and the historical understanding it contains remain fluid and can be complexly revised.

Otto Kirchheimer identified a quality of "irreducible risk" as the sine qua non of the just trial. This quality of risk means that every decision to submit traumatic history to the criminal law is, in a sense, a double wager — not only might the defendant prevail, but even if the trial ends in a conviction, it might fail in its didactic aim. In the chapters that follow, we shall see how the law at times succeeded and at times failed in winning this wager. Specifically, the Nuremberg and Eichmann trials will, missteps notwithstanding, emerge as powerful, imaginative, and socially necessary responses to extreme crimes. The Demjanjuk and Zundel trials, in contrast, present disasters of didactic legality — proceedings that obfuscated the very history they were intended to enlighten. But even in its losses, the law, formally conceived, emerged victorious: for the great Holocaust trials never betrayed their primary obligation to render legal justice to those who stood trial. If the law's struggle to master the trauma of the Holocaust proved at times provocatively insufficient, it was precisely because the core requirements of legal justice often trumped the demands of didactic legality.

To judge the wisdom of using the criminal trial as a response to traumatic history, it will be necessary to study the law's struggle to locate terms of representation and judgment adequate to the task of doing justice to the Holocaust. To do this, one must attend to the particular problems that the Holocaust posed to the legal imagination.

Distinct from literature, history, and other discourses concerned with locating terms and tones adequate to the task of capturing "the unrepresentable" nature of the Holocaust, the law, as a matter of institutional imperative, has been confronted with a dual burden. It has had to find a way both to represent *and* judge the Holocaust's horror.[13] By offering a vision of atrocity that seemed to defy rational and juridical explanation, the Holocaust threatened to expose law's limits, challenging the law to create a coherent, judicially manageable response to unprecedented crimes.[14] To study the great Holocaust trials is, then, to examine how the law has struggled to locate an idiom adequate to the task of representing and judging traumatic history — events so disruptive to structures of collective cultural and social meaning that they resist being assimilated into conventional vernaculars of memory and understanding.[15]

Each of the trials studied in this book offers its own distinct response to the traumatic history of the Holocaust, and, by extension, raises its own problems. For each trial, then, I will consider its specific didactic paradigm — its method of transforming an unspeakable event into evidence for a trial staged to serve both conventionally juridical and pedagogic ends. I will then consider how this didactic proof was enlisted to support the idiom of judgment used in the case, the jurisdictional and doctrinal standards through which unprecedented crimes were to be named and condemned.

The trials that are the focus of this book are, I believe, paradigmatic of the range of efforts to solve the problems of representation and judgment posed by the Holocaust through the instrument of the criminal law.[16] As trials staged at discrete historical moments — the Nuremberg trial followed directly on the heels of Germany's unconditional surrender, the Eichmann trial followed Nuremberg by half a generation, and Zundel followed a full quarter century after Eichmann — each stands as a landmark of a moment in the struggle, now more than half a century old, to comprehend the Holocaust through the medium of the law.

The Nuremberg and Eichmann trials rank among the most spectacular trials of the century in terms of the anomaly of the proceedings, the gravity of the crimes prosecuted, and the intensity of global attention directed upon them. To treat the Nuremberg trial as a Holocaust trial, however, is not uncontroversial. The prosecution's case was not primarily occupied with trying the defendants for the extermination of the Jews of Europe but instead focused on the accuseds' roles in launching and waging an aggressive war. Still, the extermination of the Jews was importantly explored and condemned at Nuremberg, especially as it was filtered through the freshly minted legal category of crimes against humanity.

The Eichmann trial, by contrast, remains the Great Holocaust Trial — the legal proceeding in which the tasks of doing justice to unprecedented crimes, clarifying a tortured history, and defining the terms of collective memory conjoined and collided in the most provocative fashion. Indeed, the Eichmann trial served to *create* the Holocaust: it helped remove an episode of unprecedented atrocity from the silences of shame, unexamined horror, and purposeful avoidance and transform it into an episode of world historical significance and collective meaning.

The Klaus Barbie trial in Lyon in 1987 and the John (Ivan) Demjanjuk trial that began in Jerusalem the same year were juridically structured, like Nuremberg and Eichmann, around the issue of accountability. At the same time, however, these trials marked a gradual passing of the era of prosecuting those responsible for Nazi atrocities — for reasons less moral than actuarial.[17] As such, the Barbie and Demjanjuk trials served as moments of legal transition, at once harking back to Nuremberg and Eichmann while also establishing a conceptual bridge to the Zundel trial.

Compared to Nuremberg and Eichmann, or even the Barbie and Demjanjuk trials, the trial of Ernst Zundel seems like a minor affair. Yet the Zundel trial powerfully captured the changing terms of the law's engagement with the Holocaust. For the Zundel trial was not occupied with trying an aging war criminal. Instead, its concern was safeguarding the historical record from the arguments of a negationist. As such, the Zundel case illustrates the law's continuing engagement with the Holocaust, even as the perpetrators gradually die off. The advent of criminal trials of Holocaust deniers signals that the principal challenge now facing the law is how to protect the terms of responsible collective memory as the Holocaust slowly passes into history.

Together these trials reveal the imaginative range of legal efforts directed toward mastering the problems of representation and judgment posed by the Holocaust—and the shortcomings of these efforts. As prosecutors presently struggle to submit mass atrocities in Bosnia, Kosovo, and Rwanda to legal judgment, my study of the trials of the Holocaust aims to remind readers of the strength of the legal will and of the difficulty of mastering the lessons and meanings of traumatic history through acts of legal will alone.

Part One

. . .

Nuremberg

I

. . .

Film as Witness: Screening
Nazi Concentration Camps Before the
Nuremberg Tribunal

And then they showed that awful film,
and it just spoiled everything.
— Hermann Göring, quoted in *Nuremberg Diary*

The Tedium and the Spectacle

The courtroom at Nuremberg held the largest group of journalists ever gathered to cover a single event,[1] yet the "most significant criminal action in history" surprised reporters with its dullness.[2] Rebecca West, who reported on the trial for the *New Yorker,* described the courtroom as "a citadel of boredom."[3] This was no run-of-the-mill boredom, West argued; it was "boredom on a huge historic scale":[4]

> The eight judges on the bench . . . were plainly dragging the proceedings over the threshold of their consciousness by sheer force of will; the lawyers and the secretaries . . . sat sagged in their seats at the tables in the well of the court; the interpreters twitter[ed] unhappily in their glass box like cage-birds kept awake by a bright light . . . ; the guards . . . stood with their arms gripping their white truncheons behind their backs, all still and hard as metal save their childish faces, which were puffy with boredom.[5]

As the trial meandered toward its conclusion, Norman Birkett, the British alternate member of the International Military Tribunal who would later draft the judgment of the court, noted in his diary, "When I consider the utter uselessness of acres of paper and thousands of words and that life is slipping away, I moan for this shocking waste of time"[6] (fig. 1.1).

Granted: the trial was long—eleven months would pass from the reading of the indictment on November 21, 1945, until the tribunal pronounced judgment on October 1, 1946. All told, the court presided over 403 open sessions, during which it received testimony from 94 witnesses. The trial was also enormously complex, both as a logistical and legal matter. Befitting a trial convened by conquering powers, the proceeding itself came to resemble a military maneuver. At its peak, the American staff alone numbered 654 persons—lawyers, secretaries, interpreters, translators, and clerical help. More than one hundred thousand captured German documents were examined for use at the trial, and around four thousand were entered as trial exhibits. Millions of feet of film were examined for their evidentiary value. Twenty-five thousand captured still photographs were reviewed, of which eighteen hundred were prepared as trial exhibits.[7]

Fig. 1.1. "A citadel of boredom." *From left to right:* Judge Norman Birkett and Lord Justice Sir Geoffrey Lawrence (Great Britain), Judge Francis Biddle and Judge John J. Parker (U.S.A.), and Judge Donnedieu de Vabre (France) struggle to endure the tedium of the trial. Courtesy National Archives.

Once the proceedings had begun, the trial posed additional complexities. The court had to cope with the unprecedented media attention, as 250 members of the press and radio were dispatched to report the proceedings around the world. In addition, more than 60,000 visitors' permits were issued to observers.[8] As Robert H. Jackson, a sitting justice of the U.S. Supreme Court and the chief counsel for the Allied prosecution, noted, "It is safe to say that no litigation approaching this magnitude has ever [before] been attempted."[9]

The logistical complexity of the case echoed its legal intricacy. The 21 defendants in the dock comprised, to quote the Moscow Declaration of 1943 that announced the Allies' intention of submitting the "brutalities of Hitlerite domination" to legal judgment, "the major criminals whose offenses have no particular geographical location"[10] (fig. 1.2). These included such leading Nazi functionaries as Reichsmarschall Hermann Göring, who, despite having lost weight, cut a redoubtable figure as he followed the proceedings with a conspicuous display of boredom and contempt. Joining Göring was the former Nazi party boss Rudolf Hess. In British custody since his notorious *Alleinflug* (solo flight) to Scotland in 1941 and of questionable mental health, Hess provided a source of morbid fascination for many of the trial's observers. (West found herself drawn to Hess's "odd faculty, peculiar to lunatics, of falling into strained positions . . . and staying fixed in contortion for hours.")[11] Also in the dock were such leading government administrators as Hans Frank, the wartime governor general of Poland, and Wilhelm Frick, the Reich's minister of the interior; and prominent officers of the military, including, most notably, Wilhelm Keitel, chief of the German high command (Oberkommandos der Wehrmacht — OKW). Other leading defendants in the dock were Ernst Kaltenbrunner, who had succeeded to the leadership of the Reichssicherheithauptamt (Reich main security office, or RSHA) after the assassination of Reinhard Heydrich (and whom West memorably likened to a "vicious horse"); and Albert Speer, Hitler's architect and the Reich's minister for armaments and war production.[12]

The detailed indictment, a hybrid of the typically laconic Anglo-American charging instrument and the more elaborate continental version, powerfully revealed the ambitions of the prosecution. In the sixty-five page document, the defendants were charged with a spectacular range of offenses, committed over the course of a decade and spread over the space of a continent. Formally, the indictment listed four separate, though related,

Fig. 1.2. The defendants in the dock. Courtesy of USHMM.

crimes.[13] As a substantive matter, the defendants were accused of having committed three offenses: crimes against peace, war crimes, and crimes against humanity. Fourth and finally, the indictment also accused the defendants of engaging in a "common plan or conspiracy" to perpetrate these substantive offenses. Dramatically adding to the complexity of the case, the prosecution also asked the tribunal to declare six groups, including the entire ss (Schutzstaffel) and Gestapo, "criminal organizations" (*IMT* 1:100). Although such a declaration would carry no punishment in the case of the major war criminals, it was intended to expedite the subsequent trials of thousands of other suspected offenders detained by the Allies.

Yet neither length nor complexity adequately explains why the trial was so widely perceived as tedious. After all, the O. J. Simpson murder trial, with its single defendant and straightforward charge, managed to take nearly as long as the Nuremberg trial without boring a watchful world. Given the enormous complexity of the case, the Nuremberg proceeding was in many ways an exercise in concision, a point captured in Jackson's prideful statement to President Harry Truman, "If it were not that the comparison might be deemed invidious, I could cite many anti-trust actions, rate cases . . . and other large litigations that have taken much longer to try."[14] If anything, one might have feared that the notorious personages in the dock and the sensational charges brought against them would have threatened to turn the trial into a circus; one would not have predicted the trial to leave its spectators puffy with boredom.

The court's impatience, then, had more to do with certain concrete aspects of the case. The trial was at its most excruciating during the lengthy presentations of the defense. The prosecution had called 33 witnesses compared to the defense's 61, and an additional 143 witnesses testified for the defense through written interrogatories. Much of the testimony offered by the witnesses was of questionable relevance: rambling disquisitions on German history or platitudinous endorsements of the character of the defendants.[15] The president of the tribunal, Sir Geoffrey Lawrence, Britain's lord justice of appeal, labored, in the words of one observer, to explain to the defense attorneys "what the word 'relevant' has meant for centuries in law."[16] Yet the tribunal, eager to rebut the charges voiced in certain legal and political circles that the trial was no more than an exercise of victors' justice, "bent over backward to let the defense handle the witnesses . . . in any way it chose."[17] Although the American and Soviet judges pressured Lawrence to put an end to the defense's interminable "hogwash," the lord justice, supported by his French colleague, refused.[18] Also contributing mightily to the "water torture" of boredom was the structure of the prosecution's case. The indictment, as noted, charged the defendants both with substantive crimes, such as war crimes, and with partaking in a conspiracy or common plan to commit such offenses. Drafted into the indictment by the Americans, the conspiracy charge was never popular with the French members of the Allied prosecutorial team, as the crime of conspiracy lacked a clear analog in continental law. Assailed even in American legal circles as "a doctrine as anomalous and provincial as it is unhappy in its results,"[19] the crime of conspiracy had never been recognized as an international crime.[20] Moreover, as we shall see, the tribunal itself was discomfited by the charge, dramatically limiting its reach in its final judgment. Yet the jurisprudential problems notwithstanding, the prosecution's reliance on a conspiracy charge had an even more troubling effect on its case. Following a Soviet recommendation, the prosecution agreed to divide the material among the four teams by offense: the Americans would present the conspiracy charge, the British would deal with crimes against the peace, and the French and Soviets would present evidence relating to war crimes and crimes against humanity (in the west and east, respectively). However tidy on paper, this scheme caused regrettable prosecutorial overlap as the handling of the conspiracy charge inevitably required presentation of evidence relating to the substantive charges underlying it (for example, in order to prove a conspiracy to wage an aggressive war, the American prosecution had to offer evidence of the aggressive war itself). Consequently, the same documents were often read twice into the record, and some subjects, such as the economic aspects of the attack on the Soviet Union, were treated three times.[21]

Although the conspiracy charge contributed to the tedium, it was still another decision of the prosecution that most drastically drained the proceeding of its expected drama. Following the strategy outlined by Chief of Counsel Jackson, the Allies structured their case around captured documentary evidence, material considered harder and more reliable than eyewitness testimony (fig. 1.3). Jackson's strategy was not uncontroversial: Allied prosecutors, principally some on the American team, had expressed

Fig. 1.3. Trial by document: members of the American team sifting through material to be used at the trial. Jackson's decision to structure the prosecution around documentary evidence served to drain the trial of drama.
Courtesy of USHMM.

contrasting ideas about how the prosecution should present its case. Anticipating the position of Israeli prosecutors years later in the Eichmann trial, William J. Donovan, the former head of the Office of Strategic Services and Jackson's first deputy, argued in favor of structuring the prosecution's case around eyewitness testimony. Such an approach, Donovan argued, would give the trial "an affirmative human aspect" and better enable it to serve its broadly pedagogic end.[22] Having already begun the process of screening potential witnesses, the Americans had no want of victims of Nazi aggression eager to take the stand. But despite the abundance of potential witnesses, Jackson insisted on relying on the document as the prosecution's didactic paradigm.[23] As a result, Donovan, who continued to disparage the strategy as foolish, was unceremoniously removed from the case after the first week of the trial.[24]

Although Donovan's reservations proved prescient, Jackson's approach was backed by sound thinking. The closest precedents to the Nuremberg trial were the war crimes trials staged in Leipzig after World War I. As James Willis has demonstrated, the initial impetus for staging war crimes trials came as a response to news reports of the "rape of Belgium."[25] These rumors, widely circulated in French, British, and American newspapers covering the Great War, had described in lurid detail German acts of civilian slaughter, well poisoning, and infanticide. Repeated, in part, in the solemn report of the Commission on the Responsibility of the Authors of the War (1919) that endorsed the idea of a war crimes trial,[26] these stories were later exposed largely as prevarications.[27] The failure of the complaining parties to support their allegations with credible evidence had dramatically eroded the legitimacy of the beleaguered Leipzig proceedings.[28]

Jackson was justifiably concerned that allegations of Nazi atrocity would be likewise dismissed as propaganda — particularly in light of the staggering magnitude of the crimes. The Nazis themselves had recognized that the incredible nature of their atrocities would cast long shadows of doubt upon any eyewitness reports. Primo Levi described how inmates at concentration camps heard the frequent taunt from their captors that should they survive, their stories would not be believed: "And even if some proof should remain and some of you survive, people will say that the events you describe are too monstrous to be believed: they will say that they are the exaggerations of Allied propaganda and will believe us, who will deny everything, and not you."[29] As if responding to Levi's evidentiary plight, Jackson, in a report sent to President Truman in June 1945, wrote, "We must establish incredible events by credible evidence."[30] While eyewitness and survivor testimony might offer a human dimension to the suffering caused by Nazi atrocity, such testimony, Jackson feared, would be vulnerable to charges of hyperbole, especially if the witnesses could be brought "by defense lawyers to waver in their statements."[31]

Jackson's logic supported, then, the didactic ends of the trial. In the words of a memorandum to President Franklin Roosevelt from Henry Stimson, the secretary of war, and Edward Stettinius, the secretary of state, on January 22, 1945, "The use of the judicial method will . . . make available for all mankind to study in future years an authentic record of Nazi crimes and criminality."[32] The documentary method was seen, then, as critical to the tutelary end of the trial. Proudly quoting the International Military Tribunal's own judgment, Jackson was able to report to President Truman in 1947 that "the case . . . against the defendants rests in large measure on documents of their own making, the authenticity of which has not been challenged."[33]

Unfortunately, this sound strategy began to backfire early in the trial. Overwhelmed by the flood of documents with which the American prosecution inundated the court—many of which had not even been supplied to the defense (or, for that matter, to the other prosecutorial teams) in translation—the defense began lodging objections. While the Americans argued that the sheer volume of records made prompt translation extremely difficult, the tribunal arrived at a solution that was at once brilliant and disastrous. As the trial ended its first week, the judges announced that "only such parts of documents as are read in court by the Prosecution shall in the first instance be part of the record" (*IMT* 2:255–56). Because the trial was simultaneously conducted in four languages thanks to IBM's ingenious interpretation system (fig. 1.4), the reading of a document in open court would automatically solve the translation problem. Yet as Bradley Smith has observed, "Once the prosecutors were required to read every single passage into the record . . . much of the documentary trove had to be discarded, and [the] lengthy prosecution readings that resulted . . . were boring and, often, anticlimactic."[34]

Much of the Nuremberg trial was consequently devoted to a numbing protocol that seemed to highlight less the malignancy of the defendants than the ingenuity of IBM. As one American observer noted, even President Lawrence "was driven to protest that the trial would never end if our lawyers continued to read aloud documents that had already been read aloud twice before."[35] Jackson's comparison of the trial to an antitrust litigation became inadvertently apt.

Fig. 1.4. IBM's ingenious interpretation machine, designed
specifically for the trial, permitted the four-way
simultaneous interpretation of the proceedings.
Courtesy of Wide World Photo.

Nuremberg was not, however, without its moments of high drama. It
offered numerous instances of memorable oratory, including Jackson's
opening statement for the prosecution, a speech that continues to be regarded as one of the great courtroom addresses of the century. Also of note
was the lengthy summation of Sir Hartley Shawcross, the British attorney
general and lead prosecutor at Nuremberg, who, as we shall see, succeeded
in giving legal shape and moral weight to the complex case — above all as it
involved the crimes of the final solution. Other moments of high drama
were adversarial, most notably Jackson's cross-examination of Göring. Ea-
gerly anticipated, in the words of one British lawyer, as "a duel to the death
between all that is worthwhile in civilization and the last surviving protago-

nist of all that was evil," the cross-examination turned into something of a disaster for the prosecution in general and for Jackson in particular. Displaying "a phenomenal memory and a remarkable gift for casuistic maneuver," Göring parried Jackson's questions with clever, indignant, time-consuming responses that left the chief of counsel visibly rattled.[36] Though a reading of the transcript of the examination does not, from today's perspective, make clear the disaster that unfolded in the Nuremberg courtroom, Jackson's sense of desperation became so great that he appealed to the tribunal to command the accused to answer his questions without engaging in patronizing lectures. The tribunal, concerned with maintaining its neutrality, refused to save Jackson from his own bungled examination, and it was not until the British prosecutor, Sir David Maxwell-Fyfe, took over the questioning of Göring that the prosecution was able to corner the former Reichsmarschall into any damaging admissions.

In addition to adversarial drama, the trial offered sensational testimony. Although the paradigm of proof at Nuremberg was largely documentary, the testimony of the witnesses who did take the stand was often gripping and added precisely the "human aspect" so often missing from the trial. The defendants themselves provided moments of testimonial spectacle, although their words on the stand tended to fascinate simply because of the shameless transparency of their efforts at self-exculpation. About the final solution, the defendants' ignorance was most pronounced. Arthur Seyss-Inquart, who served as Reich commissioner in the Netherlands, testified that "I had people sent to Auschwitz. . . . The people were comparatively well off there. For example they had an orchestra of 100 men" (*IMT* 15:668). Kaltenbrunner, whose brazen lies on the stand led one prosecutor annoyedly to ask, "Is it not a fact that you are simply lying?" (11:348), testified that the term *Sonderbehandlung* (the code word for extermination, literally, "special treatment") meant that persons so designated "were allowed to receive visits on several occasions, their wishes were cared for wherever they were" (11:339).

Yet the Nuremberg trial's most spectacular moments were neither oratorical, adversarial, nor testimonial — but documentary. If the prosecution's embattled paradigm of proof often contributed to the trial's dullness, it also made possible its moments of most extraordinary spectacle. One such moment occurred as the trial entered its second week. Following Jackson's outstanding opening address, the American prosecution had quickly bogged down. A lengthy and disorganized presentation of evidence concerning the *Anschluß* of Austria had resulted in the tribunal's ruling requiring the prosecution to read documents into the record. Sensing the need to reinfuse drama into the proceeding, the prosecution ended its discussion of the Austrian annexation on the afternoon of November 29, 1945, with an announcement of its intent to interject a brief cinematic interlude: "At this point it is planned by our staff to show a motion picture" (2:431) (fig. 1.5).

After a short recess, Thomas Dodd, executive counsel to the American prosecutorial team, described the purpose of the screening: "This film which we offer represents in a brief and unforgettable form an explanation of what the words 'concentration camp' imply" (2:431). Jackson had mentioned the film during his opening statement, as he offered the first description of the evidence that would introduce Nazi mass atrocity to the law's ken: "We will show you these concentration camps in motion pictures, just as the Allied armies found them when they arrived. . . . Our proof will be disgusting and you will say I have robbed you of your sleep. . . . I am one who received during this war most atrocity tales with suspicion and skepti-

Fig. 1.5. The screening of *Nazi Concentration Camps:* the Nuremberg courtroom showing the screen upon which the Signal Corps' documentary was shown. Courtesy of USHMM.

cism. But the proof here will be so overwhelming that I venture to predict not one word I have spoken will be denied" (2:130).

News of the camps had broken months before the trial; indeed, British and American newspaper reports from Buchenwald and Bergen-Belsen in late April and early May 1945 had created a sensation. "It is my duty," one British journalist had begun his dispatch, "to describe something beyond the imagination of mankind."37 Edward R. Murrow concluded his famous CBS radio broadcast of April 15, 1945, with the words, "I pray you to believe what I have said about Buchenwald. I have reported what I saw and heard, and only part of it. For most of it, I have not words."38 Generals Patton and Eisenhower, as was well publicized, had ordered every soldier not committed to the front line to visit the camps.39 Eisenhower himself had issued a terse statement (now etched into slabs of gray granite at the rear entrance to the U.S. Holocaust Memorial Museum in Washington, D.C.): "The things I saw beggar description. . . . I made the visit deliberately, in order to be in a position to give *first-hand* evidence of these things if ever, in the future, there develops a tendency to charge these allegations merely to 'propaganda.'"40

Of course, even these news reports were less than new. Accounts of the Nazi camps had been published in the American press and circulated in government circles long before the appalling stories began to emerge from the liberated camps. These early reports had already begun to galvanize American support of a juridical response to Nazi atrocities. On March 9, 1943, more than two years before the liberation of the camps in the west (but still well after accurate and detailed reports of the extermination process had reached government circles), Congress had passed a concurrent resolution condemning the "mass murder of Jewish men, women, and children" and demanding that this "inexcusable slaughter . . . [be] punished in a manner commensurate with offenses." Attached to this resolution was a report released by the State Department describing "cold-blooded extermination" of the Jewish population of Europe.41

Still, there remained a crucial gap between the circulation of such reports and the comprehension of a staggering reality. Apparently many of the Nuremberg prosecutors came to grasp the dimensions of the crimes against the Jews only as they readied their case for trial. Telford Taylor, in his outstanding memoir of the trial, in which he served as an associate counsel, observed, "Like so many others, I remained ignorant of the mass extermination camps in Poland, and the full scope of the Holocaust did not dawn on me until several months later, at Nuremberg."42 To combat this ignorance, the prosecution decided not to call Eisenhower to the stand, or any of the other thousands of soldiers who had been commanded to bear witness to Nazi atrocities. Instead, the Nuremberg prosecution turned to a novel witness — a documentary film laconically entitled *Nazi Concentration Camps*.

This use of film in a juridical setting was unprecedented.[43] Crime scene photography was well established in Anglo-American courts; but while the turn to filmic proof was perhaps a logical extension of available technology, it nevertheless marked a wholly new method of documenting criminality. Although motion pictures had been submitted as trial evidence as early as 1915, prior to Nuremberg one can find no records of any court using graphic film of atrocities as proof of criminal wrongdoing.[44] As the prosecution readied the army's documentary for screening, James Donovan, an assistant trial counsel, expressed succinctly the logic behind the turn to the filmic witness. "These motion pictures," he announced, "speak for themselves in evidencing life and death in Nazi concentration camps" (*IMT* 2:433). As a visual artifact, the film could offer undeniable proof of a reality that might seem invented or exaggerated if recounted through written or spoken testimony.[45]

As the first evidence of extermination and of the larger "concentrationary universe" presented to the Nuremberg courtroom, *Nazi Concentration Camps* tells a great deal about how the Nuremberg trial sought to locate an idiom adequate to the task of representing and judging the extermination of European Jewry.[46] Indeed, a study of what the court saw in this startling documentary, and how the evidence it supplied was assimilated into the prosecution's case and the court's judgment, reveals in exemplary fashion how imperfectly evidence of Nazi genocide was presented and digested at Nuremberg.

The Screening of *Nazi Concentration Camps*

What exactly did the tribunal see when the prosecution screened *Nazi Concentration Camps?* This seemingly straightforward question is critical if one is to understand how the prosecution attempted to translate images of atrocity into a coherent legal idiom. The official transcript of the proceedings before the International Military Tribunal records James Donovan's announcement that the footage had been "compiled from motion pictures taken by Allied military photographers as the Allied armies in the West liberated the areas in which these camps were located" (*IMT* 2:432–33). Some eighty thousand feet of tape had been edited into about six thousand feet of film with a running time of a little more than an hour (2:434). The accompanying narration, Donovan noted, had been "taken directly from the reports of the military photographers who filmed the camps" (2:433).

According to the official transcript, "photographs were then projected on the screen showing the following affidavits while at the same time the voices of the respective affiants were reproduced reading them" (2:433). The first affidavit belonged to Lt. Col. George C. Stevens, already a well-known Hollywood director before he joined the Army Signal Corps and destined in the 1950s to reach great fame through such films as *Shane, A Place in the Sun,* and, more provocatively, *The Diary of Anne Frank*. Responsible for the "photographing of the Nazi concentration camps and prison camps as liberated by Allied Forces," Stevens certified that "these motion pictures constitute a true representation of the individuals and scenes photographed" (2:433). The second affidavit, that of E. R. Kellog, a "director of film effects," certified that "the images of these excerpts from the original negative have not been retouched, distorted or otherwise altered in any respect" (2:434) (fig. 1.6).

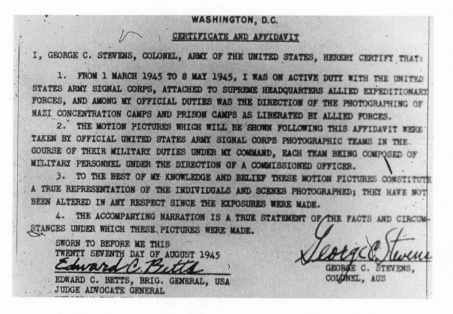

Fig. 1.6. "A True Representation of the Individuals and Scenes Photographed." Still from the beginning of *Nazi Concentration Camps* showing Stevens's affidavit. Courtesy of Library of Congress.

Yet after the dramatic buildup preparing the court for the documentary, the trial transcript suddenly turns laconic:

[The film was then shown.]
COL. STOREY: That concludes the presentation.
[The Tribunal adjourned until 30 November 1945 at 1000 hours.] [2:434][47]

The morning session on Friday, November 30, began without any mention of the film, as the prosecution turned from its meandering discussion of the Anschluß to an equally unfocused presentation of the seizure of the Sudetenland. Yet the absence of any mention of the film should not be taken as a sign that the documentary had left the court unmoved. On the contrary. As one news account filed from the trial makes clear, the spectators were so disturbed that "the presiding judges retired without a word and without announcing as usual the time set for the next session."[48] Echoing this, the *New York Times* ran an article on November 30 under the title "War-Crimes Court Sees Horror Films":

The coolest and most collected spectators were the prisoners, whose rapt expressions were illuminated by the dimmed lights along the front of the dock. All but Schacht followed every scene of the film, leaning forward to get a better view. . . . The only other prisoner affected . . . was von Ribbentrop, who watched the first third of the film and then turned away and closed his eyes for most of the remainder, taking only an occasional glance at the screen as if urged to it by some horrible fascination.[49]

A rather different account of the screening is offered by G. M. Gilbert, who served as the prison psychologist at Nuremberg and who noted in his famous diary,

Funk covers his eyes . . . Sauckel mops brow . . . Frank swallows hard, blinks eyes, trying to stifle tears . . . Frank mutters "Horrible!" . . . Rosenberg fidgets, peeks at screen, bows head, looks to see how others are reacting . . . Seyss-Inquart stoic throughout . . . Speer looks very sad, swallows hard . . . Defense attorneys are now muttering, "for God's sake-terrible." . . . Fritzsche, pale, biting lips, really seems in agony . . . Doenitz has head buried in his hands . . . Keitel now hanging head.[50]

In his memoir of 1978, Airey Neave, who as a twenty-nine-year-old Oxford lawyer assisted the British prosecutorial staff at Nuremberg, described the impact of the screening in still different terms:

Several in the darkened courtroom were faint or sobbed quietly at the scenes described by a burly British lieutenant-colonel as he stood among the dead and dying of Belsen. . . .

. . . During the showing of the film, the dock, as a measure of security, was picked out by small spotlights. Few of the defendants could bear to watch the whole film. . . .

I cannot forget the sudden vision of those twisted guilty faces . . . with tears on their cheeks. I sometimes dream of it.[51]

More recently, Taylor remembered the screening in his memoir *The Anatomy of the Nuremberg Trials* (1992): "Dr. von der Lippe recorded that the film would rob its viewers of sleep and that he had heard one of the defense counsel say it had become intolerable to sit in the same room with men like Kaltenbrunner and Frank. Schacht turned his back on the screen to show that he had had no connection with such bestiality; Goering tried to brazen it out; the weaker ones like Ribbentrop, Frank, and Funk appeared shattered."[52]

The four accounts, despite their differences, share an interesting rhetorical feature. Hardly mentioning the images in the film, they ask us to see the film voyeuristically through the eyes not of just any viewers, but of those allegedly responsible for the very atrocities captured on film. The technique itself partakes of a cinematic logic, as the spectators, caught between voyeurism and revulsion, break their gaze away from the images of atrocity and turn toward the perpetrators. The agitation of the defendants seems baffling: One is left wondering whether they had never before seen or imagined the atrocities they had orchestrated, as the realism of the film's representations produced an awareness among the defendants greater than that gained through their engagement as Nazi functionaries.[53] The melodrama of the scene is underscored by Neave's description of the defendants' dock discreetly illuminated by small spotlights. And while Taylor recalls that an assistant to the defense, Dr. Viktor von der Lippe, feared the film would deprive its viewers of sleep, it is not the images from the documentary that recur in Neave's dreams, but the expressions on the defendants' faces.

In focusing on the Nazi defendants, the memoirs leave one in the dark about what the tribunal actually saw in *Nazi Concentration Camps*. This was not accidental, as the authors of the memoirs do not investigate the defendants' legal culpability as much as presuppose it: they ask readers to see the defendants through the reflection of atrocities in their eyes. By neglecting to make clear what the court saw in *Nazi Concentration Camps,* the journalists and memoirists only reinforce an understanding that the images "speak for themselves" as to the defendants' guilt.

Yet guilty of what? If the question seems grotesque given our knowledge of Nazi atrocities, it is worth recalling that the Nuremberg trial was dedicated to proving, not assuming, that the accused had engaged in criminal acts as defined by relevant law. As Taylor himself has observed, "The public showing of the film certainly hardened sentiment against the defendants generally, but it contributed little to the determination of their individual guilt."[54] Less diplomatically, Janet Flanner, who along with Rebecca West reported on the trial for the *New Yorker,* referred to the screening as providing "the irrelevant diversion of horror movies."[55] Yet however minor its explicit evidentiary value, *Nazi Concentration Camps* was hardly a diversion. Indeed, Flanner's criticism overlooks the crucial function of the film in a trial designed as an exercise in didactic legality. By presenting the tribunal with images of organized atrocity, the film confronted the court with the chief challenge of the trial: to submit unprecedented horror to principled legal judgments.

The Film as Witness: The Plight of the Camera

To view *Nazi Concentration Camps* today gives an imperfect idea of what the tribunal saw fifty years ago. The horror captured in *Nazi Concentration Camps* is by now so familiar that it is difficult to imagine an *original* screening — that is, a screening that shocks not simply because of the barbarity of the images, but also because of their novelty. By familiar, however, I do not mean to suggest that the images shown in the film trigger the same specific visual recognition of, for example, the Zapruder film of the Kennedy assassination (though the scenes of British soldiers bulldozing heaps of corpses into mass graves at Bergen-Belsen certainly remain among the most harrowing and recognizable documentary footage associated with the war). Rather, I mean to suggest that the filmic landscape we inhabit is very much the visual legacy of films like *Nazi Concentration Camps,* a cultural universe defined by the production and circulation of graphic images of extreme violence.

Film had, of course, discovered the allure of warfare on the battlefields of World War I. Yet even when battle sequences were shown in weekly British and American newsreels, these films rarely showed graphic shots of the war dead.[56] As George Roeder has observed, because of "the technical limitations of early twentieth century photography, the most striking images to come out of World War I were written ones."[57] Here one thinks of such important novelistic treatments as Erich Maria Remarque's *All Quiet on the Western Front* and Ernest Hemingway's *A Farewell to Arms*, the autobiographies of Robert Graves and Siegfried Sassoon, and the shattering poetry of Wilfred Owens.[58]

Earlier still, Mathew Brady's photography of the Civil War had demonstrated the special relation between photography and death: how the stillness of the image demonstrates formal affinities with death's repose.[59] Indeed, in an age of slow shutter speeds, the dead struck the most cooperative poses. Perhaps not coincidentally, Stevens was a great admirer of Mathew Brady's work, and he owned, at the end of his life, a large collection of the Unionist's photographs.[60] But by ushering film into a new, and at the time unknown, terrain of violence and horror, Stevens's *Nazi Concentration Camps* did less to extend Brady's legacy than to make it obsolete.

That Stevens should be credited with this shocking documentary is itself ironic. Esteemed for his romantic comedies, Stevens's prewar work united an occasionally edgy critical eye with a fundamentally benign outlook on the nation. If Stevens searched for fresh and entertaining twists on the romantic struggle between individual and society, the range of reality present in his movies largely typified the world known to American film: images of frustrated courtship and working-class hardship absorbed in a larger mosaic of honest individuals searching for meaning among local attachments. Although *Nazi Concentration Camps* displays many of the virtues that distinguished Stevens's filmmaking — classically framed panoramas that dissolve into fastidiously composed close-ups, arresting stills, unsettling juxtapositions — this technique found itself enlisted to create a work that exploded the very filmic universe his Hollywood career had served to build.[61]

Just as *Nazi Concentration Camps* marked a novel use of film in a courtroom, the magnitude of the atrocities it depicted as well as the immediacy of its representations also was without precedent.[62] Commenting on photographic stills from the camps, Susan Sontag writes, "Nothing I have seen — in photographs or in real life — ever cut me as sharply, deeply, instantaneously. Indeed, it seems plausible to me to divide my life into two parts, before I saw those photographs (I was twelve) and after. . . . When I looked at those photographs, something broke. Some limit had been reached, and not only that of horror."[63]

The representational limit that Sontag describes in the photographic stills finds its filmic analog in *Nazi Concentration Camps*. By providing a visual register of extreme atrocity, the film crossed a threshold of representation from which there was no turning back. But if our presence in a culture saturated with images of both the Holocaust and the graphic violence of Hollywood makes it difficult to view the documentary through the eyes of the contemporaneous spectator, it also makes it easier, less sacrilegious, to consider critically what we have seen. Because we have viewed these images before, we are free, as the first observers were not, to examine their structure, meaning, and uses as representations within the context of the Nuremberg trial.

Nazi Concentration Camps begins by testifying to its own authenticity. The trial transcript, as I mentioned, notes that pictures of various affidavits supporting the film's accuracy were projected before the Nuremberg court. What the transcript fails to make clear, however, is that these affidavits are part of the film itself, and the voice that reads them aloud is part of the sound track. This gesture of self-authentication supports a novel understanding of the documentary as a privileged witness independently competent to swear to the truth of its own images.

On a procedural level, this unorthodox submission of affidavits draws attention to the relaxed rules of proof that governed the tribunal's proceedings and permitted the prosecution to introduce the film as evidence.[64] The standard of admissibility of filmic proof, at least in Anglo-American jurisprudence, centered on the doctrine of the authenticating witness.[65] This doctrine, which continued to control in certain jurisdictions until well after Nuremberg, maintained that "the motion picture does not of itself prove an actual occurrence but the thing reproduced must be established by the testimony of witness."[66] Because film was conceptualized as being dependent upon the corroboration of eyewitness testimony,[67] it was often barred not because of its inaccuracy, but because of its redundancy: it offered no more than a needless repetition of information already supplied by the eyewitness.[68] Furthermore, the failure to support filmic evidence with eyewitness testimony was also fatal, as the film would then be barred as hearsay. Without in-court corroboration, such evidence would provide no more than a declaration of material fact made by an out-of-court witness unavailable for adversarial cross-examination — the very definition of hearsay. Finally, and crucially to the Nuremberg tribunal, certain American jurisdictions had barred photographic proof not because it was cumulative or hearsay, but because it was "gruesome": graphic pictures of injuries had been declared inadmissible in certain suits because their relevance as evidence was outweighed by their potential for prejudicing a jury.[69]

The enabling charter of the International Military Tribunal solved these evidentiary problems by the simplest means possible: it declared that the trial would "not be bound by technical rules of evidence." The tribunal, the charter declared, "shall adopt and apply to the greatest possible extent expeditious and non-technical procedure, and shall admit any evidence which it deems to have probative value."[70] The application of these relaxed evidentiary conventions was tested early in the trial when the defense took exception to the prosecution's strategy—consonant with its documentary approach—of relying on sworn affidavits of persons who could have been called to testify in court. Responding to the defense's objection, Jackson argued, "This Tribunal sits under a Charter which recognized the impossibility of covering a decade of time, a continent of space, a million acts, by ordinary rules of proof, and at the same time finishing this case within the lives of living men" (*IMT* 3:543). The absence of a jury, Jackson argued, also supported the idea that the war crimes trial was "no occasion for applying jury rules" (3:543); judges, as distinct from laypersons, could weigh the relevance of hearsay testimony and would be less susceptible to being swayed by tendentious arguments or prejudicial material. The very idea of convening a military tribunal "instead of an ordinary court of law," he argued, "was in order to avoid the precedent-creating effect of what is done here on our own law and the precedent control which would exist if this were an ordinary judicial body" (3:543). While the trial itself was meant to supply a critical precedent for the articulation and defense of principles of international law, the procedures that governed the conduct of the trial were bound by neither the past nor the future. Finally, Jackson suggested that ordinary evidentiary conventions both slow a trial and render it a blunter instrument for securing historical truth. By permitting evidence such as that supplied by *Nazi Concentration Camps,* the tribunal acted in the interest not only of efficiency, but also of securing the most reliable and complete representations of unspeakable atrocities.

As noted, the film begins by swearing to its own authenticity and representational completeness. The stentorian voices that read aloud the two affidavits lead one to assume that one is hearing George Stevens and E. R.

Kellog in person, until the documentary's narration begins, speaking in the same professional voice. It is only then that one realizes the transcript's error in reporting that "the voices of the respective affiants were reproduced reading them" (2:433). In fact, we are listening to an unnamed narrator, who, by standing in for Stevens and Kellog, claims a central omniscience as the speaker of what the camera sees. The narrator supplies the voice not of a military historian or soldier witnessing the liberation of the camps, but of the camera itself. As such, it seems to speak with the same objectivity that the images claim for themselves.[71]

The film fades to a map of Europe, marked by its prewar borders, upon which appear, in rapid proliferation, the names not of nations and capitals, but of obscure locales, until the center of the continent is crowded with the names of concentration camps. During the course of its presentation, the documentary visits a dozen of these *Lagers,* each of which is treated discretely and introduced with its name presented in bold block letters: PENIG CONCENTRATION CAMP, OHRDRUF CONCENTRATION CAMP, NORDHAUSEN CONCENTRATION CAMP, BUCHENWALD CONCENTRATION CAMP, DACHAU CONCENTRATION CAMP. Although shot entirely in that finely shaded black and white that has powerfully overdetermined our images of the period, *Nazi Concentration Camps* could have been a color film. Technicolor, an expensive process, was available at the time of the liberation of the camps, and Stevens filmed much of the footage from Dachau with the same handheld color camera with which he had kept a personal filmic diary of the making of his popular *Gunga Din.*[72] The army, however, fearing that the three-track projectors necessary for showing Technicolor films would be unavailable in courtrooms and movie houses, decided to rely exclusively on monochrome for its documentaries, a decision that proved instrumental in shaping persistent cultural images of the Holocaust as an event that unfolded in black and white. (Steven Spielberg, for example, describing his choice to film *Schindler's List* in black and white, stated, "I knew *Schindler's List* had to be black and white the moment I decided to make the movie.")[73]

The film begins with the camp in Leipzig, where shortly before the liberation hundreds of prisoners were locked in a barrack and torched alive by the retreating Nazis. The camera shows the scar of the building upon the blackened earth surrounded by dirty snow, and then draws close, examining the brittle remains of burnt corpses. It is an image that defines the visual legend of the film, which captures not the active commission of atrocities but the wounds they leave behind — upon the earth, the dead, and the survivors. Such images powerfully suggest belatedness: The liberators have arrived, but they have come too late. No specific regimen of punishments could have reduced the victims to this horrific state, the film seems to say. Only a vast and systematic pattern of perverse cruelty could account for the magnitude of the death and affliction seen by the camera.

While it is commonplace today to speak of the camera's exclusions and aggressions, in *Nazi Concentration Camps* the viewer catches glimpses of a more unusual phenomenon: the camera's confusion and embarrassment.[74] Its efforts to occupy a position of detached neutral observation — the putatively privileged position of the realist documentary — merely call attention to a central confusion that leaves its traces throughout the film.[75] The camera functions, then, less as the invisible witness imagined by the members of the Nuremberg prosecution than as a flummoxed provocateur — spectators learn of the survivors' world through their reactions (or lack thereof) to the lens's awkward probings. Even those moments when the survivors treat the camera as invisible are unnerving, as we are so accustomed to posing for a photograph that the subjects' capacity to stare past the camera's gaze becomes revealing. Close-ups of former inmates show the twisted facial geometries and afflicted eyes of the demented. Their very obliviousness to the filming eye, the absence of any defense against the camera's intrusions, makes their isolation and despair manifest.

At other times, the survivors' awareness of the camera presents moments of inadvertent revelation. In one peculiar shot, three former inmates are caught posing not for the filmmaker, but for a still photographer also captured within the documentary's frame (fig. 1.7). According to the accompanying soundtrack, these "photographs are [being] made for further documentation of the horrors committed at the Hannover camp" (*IMT* 30:466). Yet in the shot within the shot, we see the three survivors — two emaciated men, stripped to their waists, seated on either side of a third, standing, clothed in layers of rags — directing gaunt, macabre smiles toward the photographer, like three members of a grotesque reunion. Here it is the absurdity of their efforts to satisfy the roseate expectations of the camera that creates a haunting image.

In another shot, a young woman lifts her skirt to reveal puncture wounds upon her buttocks inflicted by Nazi torturers. She is filmed, for reasons unknown, standing on the rooftop of an apartment building, and as she stares over her shoulder back at the camera, her skirt gathered at her waist, we can

Fig. 1.7. Three smiling survivors of the Hannover Concentration Camp pose for
a photograph. Still from *Nazi Concentration Camps*.
Courtesy of Library of Congress.

see, stretching behind her, the ruins of a bombed and ravaged city (fig. 1.8).
The film connects the woman's body to the cityscape as if to suggest that for
the Nazis both were forms of property to be violated. Yet the very effort to
document the Nazis' sexual cruelty inadvertently creates a pornographic
moment, as the film offers her body as an object to be voyeuristically sur-
veyed.[76]

A remarkable instance of filmic posturing occurs in a sequence in which
the camera interrogates a former American prisoner of war at the Mauthausen camp. Up to this point, the film has been guided exclusively by the
voice-over of the invisible narrators. Now, as the camera focuses upon a
ruggedly handsome American who towers above the other liberated prisoners of war (POWs) crowding about him, one hears, for the first time, the
voice of a person *in* the film. Compared to the walking corpses and bedrid-
den patients that largely people the documentary, the American soldier
makes a healthy, even robust, impression (fig. 1.9). As he stands before the
camera, he begins his grim narrative with an odd introduction: "I am Lt.
(senior grade) Jack H. Taylor, U.S. Navy, from Hollywood, California. Be-

Fig. 1.8. Torture and the townscape: A woman lifts her skirt to disclose "the results of a beating." Still from *Nazi Concentration Camps*. Courtesy of Library of Congress.

lieve it or not, this is the first time I have ever been in the movies" (*IMT* 30:462, 467). The burden of credibility falls, then, not upon his enumeration of the various forms of execution used at the Mauthausen camp — "by gas, by shooting, by beating, that is beating with clubs, by exposure, that is standing out in the snow naked for 48 hours and having cold water thrown on them in the middle of winter, starvation, dogs, and pushing over a hundred-foot cliff" (30:468) — but rather upon the fortuity of his appearance on the big screen. And as the camera moves from his sturdy frame to mass graves, the viewer glimpses the perverse logic behind his ironic celebration of his filmic debut.

The horrors mount and intensify as the film journeys to Buchenwald, Dachau, and Bergen-Belsen. The camera lingers upon naked, emaciated bodies strewn upon a barrack floor. Suddenly, one twitches, and one realizes that unlike the other mounds of corpses, these people are alive. It is a jarring moment, as what appears to be a still turns into a moving image. The camera then shifts to a shot of emaciated men moving like phantoms. "These are the survivors" (30:470), comments the narrator tersely (fig. 1.10). The documentary concludes with the now-famous footage of British

Fig. 1.9. "Believe it or not, this is the first time I have ever been in the movies": Lt. (senior grade) Jack H. Taylor, U.S. Navy, from Hollywood at Mauthausen. Still from *Nazi Concentration Camps*. Courtesy of Library of Congress.

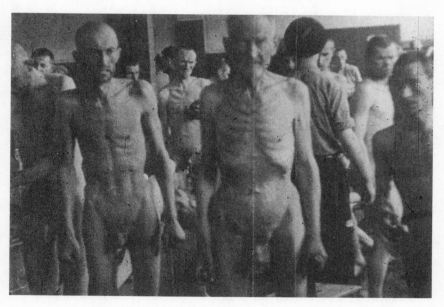

Fig. 1.10. "These are the survivors." Photographic still from *Nazi Concentration Camps*. Courtesy of Library of Congress.

bulldozers pushing a veritable mountain of bodies into a mass grave. As the dead and dirt cascade down the deep pit, the narrator ends with the flat declaration, "This was Bergen-Belsen" (30:472). The horrific images render any additional commentary superfluous.

Yet just as the documentary calls attention, however inadvertently, to the camera's intrusions, it relies upon a final, notable technique to authenticate what it has seen: it offers shot after shot of eyewitnesses viewing the very legacy of atrocities that the film records. One watches Generals Eisenhower, Bradley, and Patton grimly examining the camps; one tracks the journey of a delegation of congressmen; one follows the footsteps of GI's filing past rows of bodies. Here, again, the documentary supplies within its own frame witnesses to corroborate the truth of its representations.

The spectacle of witnessing the act of witnessing serves, however, an end distinct from evidentiary interests. Many of the film's most powerful images are shots of Germans forced to bear witness to Nazi barbarity. From a

Fig. 1.11. "Twelve hundred civilians walked from the neighboring city of Weimar to begin a forced tour of [Buchenwald]. There are many smiling faces and, according to observers, at first the Germans act as though this were something being staged for their benefit." Still from *Nazi Concentration Camps*. Courtesy of Library of Congress.

field of rotting exhumed corpses, the film cuts suddenly to a promenade of smiling Weimar women, dressed in their Sunday best, strolling along a tree-lined road, on their way to view the camps by "invitation" of the Americans (fig. 1.11). Compelled to witness the legacy of Nazi atrocities, the "good" German citizens are later captured stifling sobs or nausea by burying their faces in handkerchiefs.[77] These scenes reappear throughout the film. The memoirists' device of depicting the screening of the film at the trial through a description of the reaction of the defendants thus powerfully echoes the visual structure of the film itself. In his opening statement, Jackson declared that the prosecution did not seek to condemn a nation in its entirety: "We have no purpose to incriminate the whole German people" (*IMT* 2:102); the film, by contrast, offers no such assurances. It disperses responsibility to those who, through the tacit and cowardly tolerance of places they chose to know nothing about, became complicitous in the crimes that surrounded them.[78]

Yet by dispersing responsibility so broadly, the film gives little insight as to who is responsible for the atrocities in a more conventionally legal sense. The camera focuses briefly on the face of Josef Kramer, the former commandant of Belsen, whose unusually brutal appearance — small eyes cast to the side; thick neck; beefy cheeks ribboned with, to all appearances, dueling scars — makes him a helpful exemplar of the kind of person responsible for such crimes.[79] Yet notwithstanding its brief focus upon this specimen of evil, the film fails to clarify more specific questions of legal responsibility.

But the problems are deeper still. For if the film fails to identify who was responsible for the atrocities it has documented, it also fails to name the crimes whose legacy the viewer has witnessed. Though the film provides a picture of a crime scene so extreme that its horrors have unsteadied the camera's idiom of representation, it does not translate its images into a conventional vocabulary of wrongdoing. Instead, the very extremity of the atrocity captured on film challenges one to locate terms capable of naming and condemning these crimes. How, then, was the prosecution able to assimilate evidence of unprecedented atrocity into a legal category of criminality?

The answer to this question lies in the novel category of criminality through which the prosecution sought to name and condemn the atrocities on the screen: the crime against humanity.

2

. . .

The Idiom of Judgment: Crimes
Against Humanity

Since forgetting the laws of humanity . . .
could prove to be even more murderous than their
transgression, it was necessary to confer upon those
laws a mode of existence henceforth unforgettable.
— Alain Finkielkraut, *Remembering in Vain*

An undisputed gain coming out of Nuremberg
is the formal recognition that there
are crimes against humanity.
— Harry Truman

Atrocity and the Limits of Law

Even in the waning moments of the war, it was far from clear that the Allies
would use the arm of the law to punish the Nazi leadership. The British, in
particular, resisted the idea of trying the various heads of the Nazi state, fa-
voring instead a political solution. Recalling the "Napoleonic precedent" —
the banishment of the French emperor to the forlorn island of Saint He-
lena by the Grand Alliance in 1815 — the British supported the summary execution of a dozen or so leading members of the Nazi apparatus. Such an
act, Lord Chancellor John Simon argued, would be a symbolic yet tangible
punishment of a criminal state's most visible functionaries.[1] The British

proposal enjoyed early Soviet support; indeed, Stalin, in a "half-serious recommendation," suggested that 50,000 German general staff officers be shot.[2] Such proposals arose from American circles as well: Joseph Pulitzer, the newspaper tycoon, advocated in May 1945 the shooting of 1.5 million Nazis. Henry Morgenthau, the secretary of the Treasury, also prominently recommended that major war criminals be summarily executed, an idea originally accepted by Roosevelt.

Certainly the British position had its advantages. A political solution enjoyed the virtue of simplicity, as it would spare the Allies the tedious process of quickly organizing a vast amount of material into a legal case. Moreover, it would deprive the guilty of an opportunity to vex prosecutors through dilatory tactics and the presentation of evidence inconvenient to the Allies, such as the details of the German-Soviet Nonaggression Pact of August 1939 that paved the way for the Wehrmacht's invasion of Poland. Finally, as the jurisdictional basis of any formal action against former heads of state would be vulnerable to challenge, summary execution also had the added attraction of candor: The victors would not attempt to rationalize or disguise an act of vengeance exacted by one sovereign upon another by appeal to the neutral instrument of the law.

The British position implicitly found support among various thinkers who expressed deeper doubts about the efficacy of relying upon a legal response to atrocities perpetrated on such a vast scale. Commenting on the Nuremberg proceedings in a letter to the philosopher Karl Jaspers, Hannah Arendt observed, "The Nazi crimes, it seems to me, explode the limits of the law; and that is precisely what constitutes their monstrousness. For these crimes, no punishment is severe enough. It may well be essential to hang Göring, but it is totally inadequate. That is, this guilt, in contrast to all criminal guilt, oversteps and shatters any and all legal systems. That is the reason why the Nazis in Nuremberg are so smug. . . . We are simply not equipped to deal, on a human, political level, with a guilt that is beyond crime."[3]

Although Arendt's statement begs the question—she never offers a definition of normal criminal guilt and as a consequence fails to specify the manner in which the Nazis' crimes "explode the limits of the law" — it gives voice to the important insight that the Nazis' crimes threatened to unsettle the most fundamental conceptions of personal responsibility, moral progress, and the normativity of rule-governed social life upon which Western jurisprudential understandings are predicated. Years later Arendt returned to this idea when, borrowing from Kant, she described her understanding of "radical evil": "All we know is that we can neither punish nor forgive such offenses and that they therefore transcend the realm of human affairs and the potentialities of human power, both of which they radically destroy wherever they make their appearance."[4] By the time she wrote her controversial book *Eichmann in Jerusalem* (which I consider closely in part 2), Arendt's characterization of Nazi evil had moved from an emphasis on its radicalness to a description of its banality; still, her notion of an offense beyond punishment powerfully calls into question the value and efficacy of a juridical response to Nazi atrocity.

The controlling trope of Anglo-American law is the scales of justice, a device meant not only to measure the formal proof in a given case, but also to strike a balance between the wrong committed and the sanction imposed.[5] The common challenge to legal justice comes from the failure to strike this balance in a fair manner: the requirements of a just resolution are not satisfied when the scales are tipped in the direction of force imposed in the law's name. The Nazis' crimes, by contrast, offered a more extraordinary challenge to this concept of legal justice, as no amount of juridically authorized violence could ever balance the scales against the impossible burden of such atrocities. This dilemma was inadvertently captured by the language of the Concurrent Resolution of Congress passed in 1943 that I quoted in the first chapter: "Those guilty [of "this inexcusable slaughter"] . . . shall be . . . punished in a manner commensurate with the offense."[6] What punishment, however, was "commensurate" with the offense of extermination? The problem, as Arendt conceived it, was not that the law would fail to do justice to the defendants; rather, the crimes of the defendants had so distorted the meaning of legal justice that the law could not possibly do justice to *itself*.

While Arendt's critique was metadoctrinal, her argument implicitly found its corollary on a doctrinal level. For among those who questioned the wisdom of a trial were those who doubted the capacity of the law to assimilate the kind of offenses captured in *Nazi Concentration Camps* into any available category of criminal wrongdoing. In this regard, another register of the radical nature of Nazi evil was its power to resist being pegged into a conventional denomination of criminality. Here again the British worried that many of the atrocities committed against the Jews — in particular, those perpetrated before the beginning of the war and those directed against German Jews — were not, in the words of one aide-mémoire, "war crimes in the ordinary sense, nor is it at all clear that they can properly be described as crimes under international law."[7] Because international law did not ordinarily concern itself with a sovereign's treatment of its own nationals, atrocities against the Jews of Germany did not seem to constitute a crime in international law. Summary execution would at least cover the law's impotence to name and condemn such extreme offenses.

Jackson and the Prosecution's Idiom of Judgment

The insistence upon a juridical response to Nazi crimes issued largely from the Americans. Those who most adamantly supported a legal response, including Henry Stimson and John McCloy of the War Department, argued that political execution would, in McCloy's words, represent "a descent to the methods of the Axis" and in so doing would damage "democratic principles of justice."[8] Moreover, summary execution would "encourage the Germans to turn these criminals into martyrs."[9] A legal response, by contrast, would represent a valuable opportunity to apply, extend, and enforce principles of international law. A trial would also perform an important pedagogic function for both the victors and the vanquished. It would, in the words of the historian Bradley Smith, "provide the victorious peoples with a feeling that their cause was just and their prodigious sacrifices worthwhile," at the same time that it would teach the German people about the atrocities perpetrated in their name.[10]

Many of the Americans who supported a legal solution—including Murray Bernays, who, as a legal specialist working in the personnel branch of the War Department, largely shaped the case's jurisdictional and substantive framework; and Justice Jackson, who, in a confidential letter to President Truman on April 29, 1945, agreed to lead the effort to prepare a prosecution of major Nazi war criminals—were sensitive to the claim that the Nazis' crimes threatened to expose law's limits.[11] Yet for strategists like Bernays and Jackson, it was the very seriousness of the challenges that intensified the need for a legal response. The trial was understood as an exercise in the reconstitution of the law, an act staged not simply to punish extreme crimes but to demonstrate visibly the power of the law to submit the most horrific outrages to its sober ministrations. In this regard, the trial was to serve as a spectacle of legality, making visible both the crimes of the Germans and the sweeping neutral authority of the rule of law.

The resolve of Jackson and his colleagues made itself clear in the "London Agreement of 8 August 1945," and the accompanying charter of the In-

Fig. 2.1. The members of the London Conference preparing the Charter of the International Military Tribunal. Robert Jackson, in bow tie, sits at the right of the table examining documents. Courtesy of USHMM.

ternational Military Tribunal (IMT) (fig. 2.1). In these documents, hammered out after a long summer of direct negotiations under Jackson's auspices, representatives from England, France, the Soviet Union, and the United States officially laid out the structure and jurisdiction of an international military tribunal established for the "just and prompt punishment of the major war criminals of the European Axis" (*IMT* 1:10). Although the language of "prompt punishment" was perhaps unfortunate, as it sounded more like the endorsement of summary execution than the embrace of a juridical response, the charter unmistakably contemplated a legal solution in the form of an international trial.[12] The famous article 6 of the charter specifically enumerated the "crimes coming within the jurisdiction of the Tribunal for which there shall be *individual responsibility*" (emphasis added). The charter embraced the critical, though not uncontroversial, principle that international law authorizes a court to hold heads of state and other functionaries personally responsible for certain of its violations.[13]

First among the substantive crimes for which the defendants would have to answer was 6(a) crimes against the peace: "namely, planning, preparation, initiation or waging of a war of aggression, or a war in violation of international treaties, agreements or assurances, or participation in a Common Plan or Conspiracy for the accomplishment of any of the foregoing" (*IMT* 1:11). The source of grave controversy, this charge represented a debatable extension of principles of international law at the same time that it emerged as the gravamen of the prosecution's case at Nuremberg. By contrast, the second offense, 6(b) war crimes, "namely, violations of the laws or customs of war," enjoyed a relatively secure legal basis. In the charter's understanding, war crimes included offenses that had been officially condemned in conventional international law, and consequently the language of 6(b) closely tracked the language of the Hague convention of 1907: "Such violations shall include, but not be limited to, murder, ill-treatment or deportation to slave labor or for any other purpose of civilian population of or in occupied territory, murder or ill-treatment of prisoners of war or persons on the seas, killing of hostages, plunder of public or private property, wanton destruction of cities, towns, or villages, or devastation not justified by military necessity" (1:11). If 6(b) summarized offenses proscribed in the Hague convention, the last two crimes named in the charter—the conspiracy charge and crimes against humanity—seemed specifically created to deliver an idiom of judgment capable of naming and, by extension, condemning the evidence of atrocity so graphically captured in *Nazi Concentration Camps*.

As I noted in chapter 1, the prosecution's decision to include a conspiracy charge was unpopular even among the Allies. The charter of the IMT enumerated crimes against the peace, war crimes, and crimes against humanity as separate justiciable offenses, whereas the status of the conspiracy charge remained less than clear—apparently as a result of the continuing disagreements between the American and French representatives.[14] Yet putting aside for the moment the complex legal haggling over the scope of conspiracy, one must bear in mind that, as originally conceived, the charge was meant to create a legal instrument capable of reaching Nazi atrocities against the Jews. When American legal experts first considered the case against the major Nazi functionaries, they shared the British fear that available concepts in international law furnished no definite basis for holding Germans responsible for atrocities committed before the beginning of the war against German Jews. As a solution to this problem, Bernays pioneered the use of the concept of criminal conspiracy as the organizing principle of the prosecution. In Bernays's original proposal, Nazi organizations would be charged "with conspiracy to commit murder, terrorism, and the destruction of peaceful populations in violation of the laws of War."[15] Though

Bernays's plan was to undergo serious revision, the original impulse was to create a legal instrument that could serve the interests of formal justice and didactic legality. In the language of the memorandum to President Roosevelt of January 22, 1945, Bernays's plan would "permit full proof of the entire Nazi Plan . . . including prewar atrocities and those committed against their own nationals, neutrals, and stateless persons"[16] — that is, principally crimes against the Jews.

More radical still was the third and final offense formally enumerated in article 6 of the charter of the IMT. Bearing an appellation suggested by Hersh Lauterpacht, a British expert in international law,[17] 6(c) authorized the tribunal to sit in judgment on "crimes against humanity": "namely, murder, extermination, enslavement, deportation, and other inhumane acts committed against any civilian population, before or during the war, or persecutions on political, racial, or religious grounds in execution of or in connection with any crime within the jurisdiction of the Tribunal, whether or not in violation of domestic law of the country where perpetrated" (*IMT* 1:11). The degree of innovation contained in 6(c) has been the subject of some disagreement: in her influential study *Legalism: Law, Morals and Political Trials* (1964), Judith Shklar claimed that "there was not even a pseudo-legal basis" for the charge.[18] Yet in certain respects, the concept of crimes against humanity predated Nuremberg. The preamble to the First Hague Convention of 1899 on the laws and customs of war declared, for example, that even in the absence of specific regulations "populations and belligerents remain under the protection and empire of the principles of international law, as they result from the usages established between civilized nations, from the laws of humanity, and the requirements of the public conscience." This language, in turn, was repeated in the preamble to the Hague Convention of 1907, which contained the famous Martens clause, a rule of interpretation that permitted appeal to "general principles" to fill the gaps in the language of international conventions.

Yet Shklar's assessment was not altogether incorrect. As noted by M. Cherif Bassiouni, a leading expert on international criminal law, prior to the Nuremberg charter, the words in the preambles of the two Hague conventions were "the only reference in conventional international law which approach[ed] the term 'crimes against humanity.'"[19] Indeed, the effort to prosecute for violations of such crimes after War World I stumbled badly — largely as a result of American objections. As previously noted, the reports of German atrocities during World War I motivated members of the Great

Powers (Britain, France, Italy, Japan, and the United States) to seek legal redress for these reputed crimes. Charged by the Great Powers to explore the legal basis for a possible trial, "the Commission on Responsibility of Authors of the War," an advisory body formed in 1919 and composed of representatives from the five victorious nations, reached several conclusions critical to the study of Nuremberg. First, after considering the legal basis for crimes against peace, the commission regretfully reached the conclusion that although the "public conscience reproves" a war of aggression, such an act "may not be considered an act directly contrary to positive law."[20] Presciently, the commission cast its doubts about the concept of crimes against peace by voicing larger concerns about the institutional limitations of a trial as a forum for history lessons: "Any inquiry into the authorship of the war," the commission reported, "must . . . raise difficult and complex problems which might be more fitly investigated by historians and statesmen than by a tribunal."[21]

At the same time that it refused to recognize the illegality of a war of aggression, the majority of the members of the commission strongly endorsed a "trial of outrages" conducted by an international tribunal authorized to apply "the law of nations as they [*sic*] result from the usages established among civilized peoples, from the laws of humanity and from the dictates of public conscience."[22] This, of course, was the language from the preamble to the two Hague conventions, now treated as legal authority. According to the commission's report, to conclude that international law did not authorize trying heads of state for such crimes was tantamount to declaring that "the greatest outrages against . . . the laws of humanity . . . could in no circumstances be punished." Such a conclusion, the report proclaimed, "would shock the conscience of civilized mankind."[23]

Yet such was the conclusion reached by the two American members of the Great Powers' commission. Secretary of State Robert Lansing and James Brown Scott, a former delegate to the Hague Conference of 1907 and a leading scholar on international law, both voiced similar objections to any trial based on the "laws of humanity." Scott and Lansing acknowledged that it made perfect sense to punish war crimes, as "the laws and customs of war are a standard, certain to be found in books of authority and in the practice of nations." The laws of humanity, however, "vary with the individual, which if for no other reason, should exclude them from consideration in a court of justice." Not only are the laws and principles of humanity "not certain, varying with time, place, and circumstance," they may also vary "according . . . to the conscience of the individual judge." Concerned by the specter of judicial subjectivity, Lansing and Scott echoed the famous words of the "wise and cautious" John Selden, the great seventeenth-century English jurist and legal scholar: the law of humanity, like the law of equity, "is a roguish thing."[24]

Roguish and incoherent. For as Lansing and Scott pointed out, if by humanity one means "humaneness" (as a opposed to, say, some notion of humankind as a whole),[25] then the very idea of criminalizing such violations seems ridiculous, for what could be more inhumane than war, a practice whose legality, as the other members of the commission themselves acknowledged, was not open to serious question.

As a final matter, Lansing and Scott vehemently objected to the idea of treating a violation of the laws of humanity as a crime for which individuals could be held responsible. However ill-defined and incoherent such laws may be, worse was the idea of using an international tribunal to try heads of state as criminals. Such an idea had "no precedents . . . in the modern practice of nations," and, by "subordinating [a head of state] to foreign jurisdictions to which neither he nor his country owes allegiance or obedience," violated "the very conception of sovereignty."[26] In support of this conclusion, Lansing and Scott approvingly cited the Supreme Court case of *Schooner Exchange v. McFadden* (1812), in which Chief Justice John Marshall insisted upon the "perfect equality and absolute independence of sovereigns."[27] Regardless of the merits of their position, the fact that Lansing and Scott would think a century-old American high court decision dispositive of a difficult question in international law affords its own ironic consistency. For implicit in their stance is the suggestion that one of the prerogatives of sovereignty is the right to settle for oneself the substance of these very prerogatives.

The Nuremberg charter's concept of crimes against humanity represented a stunning repudiation of the arguments of Lansing and Scott. As Egon Schwelb, an expert in international law, observed in 1946, the concept of crimes against humanity set forth in 6(c) of the charter at least ostensibly called into existence a radical "set of novel principles of law."[28] Here it is important to recall the exact language of 6(c): "Crimes against humanity: namely, murder, extermination, enslavement, deportation, and other inhumane acts committed against any civilian population, before or during the war, or persecutions on political, racial, or religious grounds in execution of or in connection with any crime within the jurisdiction of the Tribunal, whether or not in violation of domestic law of the country where perpetrated" (*IMT* 1:11). In particular, four critical phrases in 6(c) deserve attention. First, the language "*before* and during the war" (emphasis added) formally separates crimes against humanity from war crimes. In so doing, it implies, as Schwelb noted, the bold proposition that "there is in existence a system of international criminal law under which individuals are responsible to the community of nations," and that this system applies not just in wartime, but at all times. Second, the phrase "any civilian population" seems to contain the idea that international law protects civilians not simply from the violence of a neighboring country (a notion already contained in the standard theory of war crimes), but more provocatively, from "the alleged crimes . . . committed by sovereign states against their own subjects." Third, the clause "whether or not in violation of the domestic law of the country where perpetrated" seems powerfully to expand the protections accorded civilian populations against acts of their leaders by emphatically establishing "the absolute supremacy of international law over municipal law." Finally, the phrase "persecutions on political, racial, or religious grounds" suggests that these offenses now stand as international crimes for which personal criminal responsibility attaches. This seems strikingly original, for while the other crimes named in 6(c), murder and extermination, for example, clearly have their analogs in domestic legal systems, "persecution" makes its appearance as an international offense sui generis.

Novel in their own right, these four principles seem on their face truly stunning when taken together. As Schwelb observed, "A radical inroad has been made into the sphere of the domestic jurisdiction of states."[29] If Lansing and Scott once vigorously resisted the idea that international law provided any enforceable principles of humanity, the charter now claimed that international law authorized foreign states to impose criminal penalties upon heads of state for actions directed against their own domestic population — even for acts *permitted* by local law. By radically limiting sovereign prerogatives and by ostensibly embracing a robust concept of humanity, 6(c) can be grasped as the legal imagination's attempt to respond to the unprecedented nature of Nazi crimes against the Jews.[30] In crimes against humanity, it seems, the legal imagination had found the legal category capable of naming and condemning the atrocities so graphically depicted in *Nazi Concentration Camps*.

LIMITATIONS AND LEGITIMACY

Appearances, however, can be deceiving. For if one reads 6(c) in light of the limitations placed upon it by its authors, the Nuremberg prosecutors, and the judges of the IMT, one realizes that a great deal of its radical potential was restrained by more conservative aspects of the text. To appreciate this point one must reexamine the often tortured language of the charter. One's attention is drawn, first, to a short phrase of legalese in 6(c) that declares that murder, extermination, persecution, and so on are to be considered crimes against humanity provided they were "in execution of or in connection with any crime within the jurisdiction of the Tribunal."[31] Whatever else this might mean, it seems to serve as limiting language and, as such, raises an immediate and critical question: what crimes are "within the jurisdiction of the Tribunal"? Article 6 ostensibly supplies an answer as it lists crimes against peace, war crimes, and crimes against humanity as "crimes coming within the jurisdiction of the Tribunal for which there shall be individual responsibility."

Here one cannot help but be confused. Article 6 says that crimes against humanity constitute "crimes coming within the jurisdiction of the Tribunal," at the same time that the text of 6(c) declares that in order to be justiciable, the various crimes against humanity must be "in execution of or in connection with any crime within the jurisdiction of the Tribunal." But if crimes against humanity are already agreed to be "within the jurisdiction of the Tribunal," then the limiting language in 6(c) seems to be entirely meaningless.

In its final judgment, however, the tribunal concluded that the limiting language was hardly empty of content. Noting that the description of crimes against peace in 6(a) and war crimes in 6(b) contained no analogous language of limitation, the judges concluded that these two offenses alone constituted "crimes coming within the jurisdiction of the Tribunal." As a consequence, the judges read the limiting language in 6(c) to mean that crimes against humanity fell within the jurisdiction of the tribunal if, and only if, they were in "execution of or in connection with" crimes against the peace or war crimes.[32]

If this parsing of the jurisdictional architecture of 6(c) seems numbingly technical, it is nevertheless crucial to understanding the legal idiom shaped at Nuremberg to deal with the Holocaust. As a substantive matter, by holding that only those crimes against humanity committed in connection with a criminal war of aggression or war crimes were justiciable, the tribunal radically restricted the reach of 6(c). Suddenly atrocities committed by the Nazi government against its own civilians — precisely those offenses reached by the charter's seemingly ambitious notion of crimes against humanity — could be brought into the IMT's jurisdiction only if they had been committed in connection with the planning or waging of a war of aggression or other war crimes. And so the tribunal reached the famous conclusion that prewar atrocities against the Jews did not fall within its jurisdictional competence:

> The policy of persecution, repression and murder of civilians in Germany before the war of 1939 . . . was most ruthlessly carried out. The persecution of Jews during the same period is established beyond all doubt. To constitute crimes against humanity, the acts relied on before the outbreak of war must have been in execution of, or in connection with, any crime within the jurisdiction of the Tribunal. The Tribunal is of the opinion that revolting and horrible as many of these crimes were, it has not been satisfactorily proved that they were done in execution of, or connection with, any such crime. The Tribunal therefore cannot make a general declaration that the acts before 1939 were Crimes Against Humanity within the meaning of the Charter. [*IMT* 22:498]

The prosecution was disappointed by the tribunal's conclusion, but only because it thought it had proven that the prewar atrocities against the Jews were connected with war preparations. The one-billion-mark fine imposed upon German Jews after *Kristallnacht* was, the prosecution pointed out, used for the Nazi war coffers. The prosecution did not, however, disagree with the court's parsing of 6(c). Indeed, in his closing argument Sir Hartley Shawcross anticipated the tribunal's position with the words, "So the crime against the Jews, insofar as it is a Crime against Humanity and not a War Crime, is one which we indict because of its association with the Crime Against the Peace. That is, of course, an important qualification, and is not always appreciated by those who have questioned the exercise of this jurisdiction."[33] Jackson himself had made much the same point during his opening address to the tribunal. "Th[e] attack on the peace of the world," he argued, "is the crime against international society which brings into international cognizance crimes in its aid and preparation which otherwise might be only internal concerns" (*IMT* 2:103).

If such a position seemed to abandon the promise of 6(c), it merely

echoed the reasoning of the members of the London Conference responsible for drafting the charter of the IMT. During the conference, Jackson defended restrictions on the reach of the atrocities charge because "ordinarily
we do not consider that the acts of a government toward its own citizens
warrant our interference." Behind Jackson's position lurked a concern that
too robust a concept of crimes against humanity might have supplied a potentially troubling precedent for challenging a sovereign's treatment of its
domestic population. As Jackson acknowledged, "We have some regrettable circumstances at times in our own country in which minorities are un-
fairly treated."[34] He was loathe, then, to create a precedent that would permit these "regrettable circumstances" to be condemned in international law
as crimes against humanity for which, say, the president could be held personally responsible.

Along with Jackson's political concerns, however, were formal legal considerations. For, as one expert in international law put it, "Even if the acts of
nationals of one state against citizens of the same state amounted to the
most flagrant violations of fundamental principles of civilized behavior as
recognized by most nations, it is not certain that this fact alone would constitute sufficient legal basis for holding individuals criminally responsible
for them."[35] A dramatic limitation on sovereign prerogative, then, would
have certainly highlighted the weakness of the charter's foundation in international law, strengthening the charges of "victors' justice."[36] Understandably, both the prosecution and the court were highly sensitive to this
charge — voiced not only by the attorneys for the defense, but within Anglo-American and continental legal circles as well. Jackson, for example,
had been criticized for accepting leadership of the Nuremberg prosecution,
and the sitting chief justice on the Supreme Court, Harlan Fiske Stone, refused to administer the oath to the American members of the IMT, privately
explaining that he "did not wish to appear, even in that remote way to give
. . . [his] blessing" to a trial which, in his mind, was no more than a "high-
grade lynching affair."[37] In the face of these concerns, Jackson tried candidly
to broach the victors' trial charge in his powerful opening address (fig. 2.2).
"Unfortunately," he acknowledged, "the nature of these crimes is such that
both prosecution and judgment must be by victor nations over vanquished
foes" (*IMT* 2:101). While this point was less than persuasive — the Allies
might, for example, have included representatives of neutral nations on the
IMT — Jackson did not shy away from the challenge facing the trial: "We
must never forget that the record on which we judge these defendants to-

Fig. 2.2. Robert Jackson delivers the opening statement for the prosecution, widely considered one of the great courtroom addresses of the century. Courtesy of USHMM.

day is the record on which history will judge us tomorrow. To pass these defendants a poisoned chalice is to put it to our own lips as well" (2:101). Along with the defendants, the very integrity of law as a system of neutral rules was on trial at Nuremberg.

Bearing in mind the prosecution's and the court's concern with securing the trial's legitimacy as a matter of law, one can better understand Jackson's argument at conference concerning the scope of crimes against humanity:

The reason that this program of extermination of Jews and destruction of the rights of minorities becomes an international concern is this: it was part of a plan for making an illegal war. Unless we have a war connection as a basis for reaching them, I would think we have no basis for dealing with atrocities. . . . We see no other basis on which we are justified in reaching the atrocities which were committed inside Germany, under German law, or even in violation of German law, by authorities of the German state.

Here Jackson clearly argues that as a matter of doctrinal legitimacy crimes against humanity must piggyback on crimes against peace. The crimes against peace charge, as noted earlier, emerged as the gravamen of the prosecution's case, though it too aroused controversy before, during, and after the trial. André Gros, the French delegate to the London Conference, insisted that the aggressive war charge "is a creation of four people who are just four people."[38] Many legal critics found the charter's imputation of criminal responsibility for waging war problematic in the extreme, and many now believe the prosecution's greatest misstep was in focusing the Nuremberg trial on crimes against peace rather than crimes against humanity.[39] These arguments, especially in hindsight, enjoy a certain plausibility. If a principal didactic purpose of the trial was to make visible the grand authority of the rule of law, it seems odd that the prosecution structured its case on the anomalous aggressive warfare charge of 6(a).

On another level, however, Jackson's strategy, controversial as it was, can be seen as conservative — designed to legitimate the proceedings by remaining, to the greatest extent possible, within the available strictures of international law. In this regard, Jackson's vision of the case was intended to avoid precisely the kind of radical justice that might have resulted from a prosecution based on a robust concept of crimes against humanity. To appreciate this point, it is helpful to consider Schwelb's observation that notwithstanding the innovative (read ex post facto) aspects of the crimes enumerated in 6(a), "It is by no means a novel principle in international law that the sovereignty of one state does not prevent the punishment of crimes committed against other states and their nationals."[40] The criminalization of aggressive warfare, unusual as it might have been, both respected conventional notions of sovereignty and represented, in certain respects, no more than the attempt to extend available principles of international law through a time-honored Anglo-American method of law making. During his opening statement, Jackson said as much in the analogy that he drew between international and common law: "[International law] grows, as did the common law, through decisions reached from time to time in adapting settled principles to new situations. The fact is that when the law evolves by the case method, as did the common law and as international law must do if it is to advance at all, it advances at the expense of those who wrongly guessed the law and learned too late their error" (*IMT* 2:147). In this elegant statement, Jackson extended the common law method to a meta-doctrinal level: the specific case no longer supplied the precedent to the subsequent holding; now it was the very method of law making through judicial accretion that supplied the precedent for the tribunal's authority to reach a legal decision.[41] By asking his audience to imagine international law as a subspecies of domestic common law (instead of vice versa), Jackson was able to stretch the law's power of legitimate sanction without altering its basic, familiar idiom.

By contrast, the prosecution could not center its case on a robust conception of crimes against humanity without abandoning the legal sanctity of the concept of sovereignty. This the prosecution was not prepared to do — not merely because it was motivated by strategic political concerns or because it was swept away by a "fetish of sovereignty."[42] Rather, the prosecution sought to recuperate its claims to legitimacy by demonstrating that it was not about to destroy in its entirety a classically formalist conception of the legal prerogatives of sovereign states.[43] By focusing the prosecution on the crime of waging aggressive war, Jackson unfortunately failed to quiet the charges of victors' justice. Yet by avoiding a trial based on a robust notion of crimes against humanity, Jackson managed to preserve the legal respect of sovereignty without making altogether futile the effort to introduce law to a domestic context that had never before been subjected to international juridical administration and judgment.

DOCTRINE AND DIACRITICS

As a textual matter, Jackson's restrictive reading of the atrocities charge found confirmation in the famous Semicolon Protocol of October 6, 1945. As originally printed, the charter of the IMT revealed certain discrepancies between the English, French, and Russian versions. The most important difference involved the punctuation of 6(c). In the English and French originals, a semicolon divided the charter's definition of crimes against humanity in the following fashion: "namely, murder, extermination, enslavement, deportation, and other inhumane acts committed against any civilian population, before or during the war; or persecutions on political, racial, or religious grounds in execution of or in connection with any crime within the jurisdiction of the Tribunal, whether or not in violation of domestic law of the country where perpetrated." Seemingly a minor matter of punctuation, the semicolon after "war" was potentially of great significance.[44] With the semicolon, 6(c) seemed to contemplate two very different kinds of offenses for which dramatically disparate jurisdictional principles would apply. The first kind of offense, the murder-like crime, could reach conduct that occurred before and during the war and did not require any connection to crimes against peace or war crimes. Only the second offense, persecution-like crimes, would require the jurisdictional tie.

The Russian version, however, contained a comma after "war." The comma, by contrast, erased the difference between the two kinds of crimes against humanity, tethering both to the same jurisdictional restrictions. The Allies convened to rectify this important textual discrepancy, and in the somber protocol of October 6, 1945, decreed that the "said semi-colon in the English text should be changed to a comma."[45] The triumph of the comma over the semicolon was not, however, the result of behind-the-scenes wrangling. As one student of the protocol observed, despite "the nagging doubt . . . that something more substantive was going on," apparently the mysterious semicolon was the work of "the usual bunch of incompetents,"[46] and the protocol simply restored the charter to the form contemplated by its drafters. The restrictive approach to crimes against humanity now found support in the proper punctuation.

If this parsing of 6(c) weakened the tribunal's authority to punish the crimes against the Jews, then the court's interpretation of the conspiracy charge only further limited its power. The charter did not enumerate the "Common Plan or Conspiracy" charge as a specific crime coming within the jurisdiction of the tribunal; instead the conspiracy language confusingly appeared in two places in the charter, first in 6(a) as an element in crimes against peace, and second as an unenumerated offense at the end of Article 6. The indictment, by contrast, named the conspiracy charge as the first of the four indictable offenses, as it formally accused the defendants of being "leaders, organizers, instigators, or accomplices in the formulation or execution of a common plan or conspiracy to commit . . . Crimes Against Peace, War Crimes, and Crimes Against Humanity" (*IMT* 1:29) (fig. 2.3). The language here is important, as the indictment now created the legal possibility that a defendant could be convicted of a common plan or conspiracy to commit crimes against humanity. Such a construction might, then, have authorized the tribunal to punish prewar atrocities despite the restrictive construction of 6(c).

Again, however, the tribunal offered a restrictive reading. In this case, the court concluded that the indictment had misapplied the charter—the "binding . . . law to be applied to the case" (22:414)—by treating conspiracy as a crime unto itself. Returning to the language of 6(a), the tribunal held that "the Charter does not define as a separate crime any conspiracy ex-

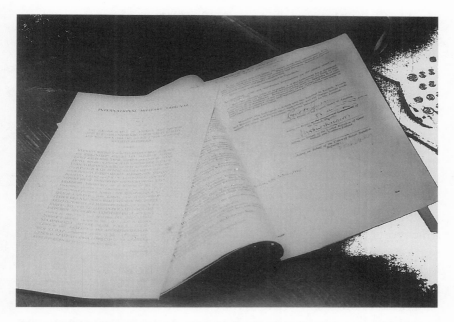

Fig. 2.3. The indictment as signed by the heads of the four prosecutorial teams.
Courtesy of National Archives.

cept the one to commit acts of aggressive war" (22:469). This conclusion
again confirmed the centrality of crimes against peace to the structure of
the trial. More important, the tribunal decided, in light of this conclusion,
"to disregard the charges in Count One that the defendants conspired to
commit War Crimes and Crimes Against Humanity, and . . . [to] consider
only the common plan to prepare, initiate and wage aggressive war"
(22:469).

However technical the court's reasoning may seem, this decision must, I
believe, be seen as another effort on the part of the tribunal to legitimate
the deeply anomalous trial. Aware of the controversy surrounding the conspiracy charge, the tribunal checked its power to punish this offense, but in
so doing secured the legal foundation for its judgment on other matters.
Yet taken together with its restrictive reading of 6(c), the court's decision
significantly limited its authority to receive evidence of crimes against Jews.
On their face, both the conspiracy charge and crimes against humanity appeared as distinct, yet mutually supportive, attempts to stretch available notions of criminality in order juridically to reach Nazi atrocities against the
Jews. Now, however, the conspiracy charge was constructed in such a way

as to *limit,* rather than extend, the reach of crimes against humanity, which, as we have seen, had already been parsed as itself dependent on the aggressive warfare charge. As Telford Taylor has observed, this was a "disastrous blow" to Bernays's original proposal, as the very logic of the conspiracy charge was to criminalize prewar atrocities.[47]

And so the scope of crimes against humanity was now doubly restricted. First, such crimes were made an accessory of crimes against peace. Second, crimes against humanity were treated as an interstitial category, covering a small number of offenses (such as crimes against German Jews) technically left untouched by a traditional notion of war crimes. The crime against humanity did not stand as the great master offense against the very notion of a rule-ordered existence; neither did it provide the overarching rubric under which crimes against peace were also tried. Instead, the crime of aggressive war loomed as the principal charge, and crimes against humanity were legally digested as an accessory and interstitial transgression.

But if this was the case, then one is left with a conundrum—one that harks back to the examination of *Nazi Concentration Camps* in chapter 1. There spectators were asked to bear witness to atrocities so extreme that they challenged the legal imagination to locate a category of criminality capable of naming and condemning such outrages. At first blush, it seemed that crimes against humanity constituted precisely such a juridical term—a radically new legal idiom capable of reaching unprecedented crimes. On closer examination, however, the concept of crimes against humanity made its appearance at Nuremberg in a dramatically compromised form. In light of this, how was the prosecution able to digest the disorienting material screened in *Nazi Concentration Camps?* How was the prosecution able to assimilate this sensational evidence into a case designed to conserve, not radically change, existing principles of legality?

Harmonizing the Evidence with the Argument

Like most documentary films, *Nazi Concentration Camps* was made up of two principal constitutive elements—images and narration. Commenting on the role that captions play in news photography, the French director Jean-Luc Godard once observed, "This photograph, like any photograph, . . . is physically mute. It talks through the mouth of the text written beneath it."[48] By contrast, in the theory of documentary realism, sound is meant to be "merely a supplementary support of representation; it must integrate itself docilely with the mimed object."⁴⁹ Close study of *Nazi Concentration Camps,* however, reveals that the narration does not simply strengthen the verisimilitude of the image; on the contrary, the voice of the commentary comes ultimately to assert control over the film's images. While the pictures captured by the camera's eye produce a "visual impact . . . such as will nullify explanation,"⁵⁰ the narration attempts to restrict and secure the meaning of the evidence that has been presented to the viewers' eyes.

In *Nazi Concentration Camps,* the narrator, as I observed, remains nameless and often seems to do no more than clarify what the camera sees: "They see the woodshed where lime-covered bodies are stacked" (*IMT* 30:463).⁵¹ "Victims bear the marks of violent deaths" (30:466). "Charred remains of several inmates still lay heaped atop the grill" (30:463). "On the ceiling, the dummy shower heads" (30:470). At other times, the narrator's omniscience is greater than the film's, supplying information unavailable to the camera: "The victims are mainly Poles and Russians with considerable numbers of French and other nationalities also included in the camp roster" (30:467). "The Nazis maintained a building at the camp for medical experiments and vivisections with prisoners as guinea pigs" (30:469). The narration is relatively flat and laconic, free of the histrionics and rhetorical flourishes one often finds in wartime weekly newsreels. The entire text of the hour-long film takes up no more than eleven pages of the tribunal's massive eighteen-volume catalogue "Documents and Other Material in Evidence" (30:462–72). Indeed, it is the very flatness and terseness of the commentary that most potently creates the impression that the images, not the words, are speaking.

Yet this terseness, upon closer inspection, calls attention to certain interesting omissions. The word "Jew," for example, is mentioned only once in the entire film, and in such a manner as to obscure any suggestion that Nazi terror was directed against Jews as a group: "The 4,000 Ohrdruf victims are said to include Poles, Czechs, Russians, Belgians, Frenchmen, German Jews and German political prisoners" (30:464). Any further mention of terror directed specifically against Jews is suggested in a highly elliptical manner: "Under the guise of an insane asylum this had been the headquarters for the systematic murder of 35,000 Poles, Russians, and Germans sent here mainly for political and religious considerations" (30:464). The film's understanding of its own images is revealed, then, in a small but telling description. As the camera moves across the corpses littered about Buchen-

Fig. 2.4. "Pictorial evidence of the almost unprecedented crimes perpetrated by the Nazis at Buchenwald Concentration Camp." Still from *Nazi Concentration Camps*. Courtesy of Library of Congress.

wald, the narrator declares, "Pictorial evidence of the *almost* unprecedented crimes perpetrated by the Nazis at Buchenwald Concentration Camp" (30:468) (emphasis added) (fig. 2.4).

Without wishing to overread the significance of this unobtrusive qualifier, I think it is worth pausing over the meaning of "almost" in this context. Whether the final solution was unique or unprecedented has, of course, emerged as one of the most contentious issues in Holocaust studies. While some scholars continue to emphasize the monstrous singularity of the Nazi genocide and question the motives of those who would challenge such an understanding,[52] others have attempted to assimilate the extermination of the Jews into a more "conventional" history of atrocity, one that finds precedents in Stalin's gulags and echoes in Pol Pot's killing fields.[53] However one construes this film's qualification, the narration's use of "almost" to modify "unprecedented" clearly does not mean to acknowledge other instances of extreme organized cruelty. In the film's own parsing, crimes perpetrated by the Nazis at Buchenwald are "almost" unprecedented not because the final solution has its historical antecedents, but

because the film does not understand itself to be a document about genocide against the Jews. At the very least, the modest qualification appeals to
the naturally incredulous mind that associates the rhetoric of the "unprecedented" with the ends of propaganda. But the insertion of "almost" also
suggests that the film does not perceive its images as bearing witness to the
extermination of Europe's Jewish population.[54]

If *Nazi Concentration Camps* does not open a window upon the crimes of
the final solution, then what does it show? As I noted at the end of the first
chapter, the narration offers no unequivocal answers or rigid explanatory
framework to make intelligible its accompanying images. Yet in the terse
words that narrate the camera's entry into each camp, a larger understanding begins to emerge:

> More than 200 political prisoners were burned to death in this concen-
> tration camp near Leipsig [sic].

> At this concentration camp in the Gotha area, the Germans starved,
> clubbed and burned to death more than 4,000 political prisoners over a
> period of 8 months.

> This is Breendonck prison in Belgium. It offers evidence of Nazi brutal-
> ity imposed on Belgian patriots during the period of German occupation.

> The slave labor camp at Nordhausen liberated by the 3rd Armored Divi-
> sion, 1st Army.

> At least 3,000 political prisoners died here at the brutal hands of SS
> troops.

> The report lists the surviving inmates [of Buchenwald] as representing
> every European nationality.

> In the official report, the Buchenwald camp is termed an "extermination
> factory." . . . By these means, the report continues, many tens of thousands
> of the best leadership personnel of Europe have been exterminated. [*IMT*
> 30:462–68]

By its own terms, then, *Nazi Concentration Camps* is a film about political
terror and the excesses of war. It documents a barbaric campaign to eliminate political enemies of a brutal regime. It exposes the horrific mistreatment of prisoners of war and the enslavement of civilians to service a ruth-
less war machine. It bears witness to spectacular excesses of cruelty and
reveals the administrative and technological apparatus that made possible

campaigns of mass murder. It understands mass killing, however, in terms of the harsh logic of political control and military conquest. The crimes it has witnessed are the consequence of aggressive militarism rather than genocide unconnected to the aims of war.

Translating the film into a legal idiom, one would have to conclude that *Nazi Concentration Camps* offers indelible proof of conventional (albeit extreme) war crimes, not crimes against humanity. More precisely, by describing the astonishing mistreatment and murder of political prisoners, the film offers evidence of crimes proscribed under both 6(b) ("murder . . . of civilian population" and "murder or ill-treatment of civilian population") and 6(c) ("murder, extermination . . . against any civilian population"). Thus, insofar as the film offers images of crimes against humanity, these were also war crimes — a telling example of how the ostensibly novel legal category was essentially reabsorbed into existing international law.

Technically, the only moments in the film documenting crimes against humanity as a category unto itself are when the narrator mentions that the four thousand victims at Ohrdruf "are said to include Poles, Czechs, Russians, Belgians, Frenchmen, *German Jews and German political prisoners*" (emphasis added) (30:464) (fig. 2.5); and later when he asserts, "35,000 Poles, Russians, and Germans [were] sent here [to Hadamar] mainly for political and religious considerations" (30:464). The Polish, Russian, and French victims of Ohrdruf and Hadamar can all be considered victims of war crimes; it is only when the film mentions the *German* Jews and *German* political prisoners that it exits the category of war crimes and enters the exclusive terrain of crimes against humanity. But even here the crime against humanity functions in precisely the manner envisioned by the framers of the charter: as an interstitial legal category, filling the small gaps in the conventional category of war crimes.

But if *Nazi Concentration Camps* understands its own documentary footage as evidence of horrific war crimes — and not of the final solution per se — then the question remains: Did the film misinterpret its own images? The question raises interesting issues about the meaning of documentary evidence. Writing about a British film team's documentary covering the liberation of the camps, Neal Ascherson has observed, "The filmmakers had not, in fact, had time to grasp the horror within the horror. The scale of the 'Final Solution of the Jewish Problem' had scarcely dawned on them."[55] Yet this observation does not settle the matter. Certainly the narration was not wrong in its claim that such camps as Dachau and

Fig. 2.5. Witnesses to crimes against humanity. This is the shot that accompanies the narrator's statement that the four thousand victims at Ohrdruf "are said to include Poles, Czechs, Russians, Belgians, Frenchmen, German Jews and German political prisoners." Still from *Nazi Concentration Camps*. Courtesy of Library of Congress.

Buchenwald were used for the internment and killing of political prisoners and prisoners of war. Moreover, the camps liberated by the British and Americans were not, technically speaking, centers of extermination designed for the Jews of Europe. At the same time, however, the Germans' retreat before Soviet advances had led to the liquidation of the death camps in the east, and by the time the Allies reached Bergen-Belsen, for example, the camp was already hideously overcrowded with Jews forcibly marched westward.[56] If *Lagers* such as Bergen-Belsen and Dachau were not death camps per se (Belsen ironically was a "model" camp until late 1944, when it began receiving internees from the east),[57] it is equally certain that the mounds of corpses shown at Belsen were largely of Jews, as were the emaciated survivors at Buchenwald. The documentary's paradoxical relation to its own images is captured, then, in the observation of one scholar who noted that the photos and film of the liberation of these camps "more than any other aspect of the Holocaust imprinted on the Western consciousness the images which have come to characterize the Final Solution."⁵⁸ And as Ascherson has noted, it was not until the Eichmann trial that "the word 'Auschwitz' (implying the gassing of millions), replaced 'Belsen' . . . as the ultimate metaphor of evil."⁵⁹

In light of these considerations, it seems that the film cannot be dismissed as having simply misrepresented or distorted its images. Rather, the film conflated evidence of the final solution with evidence of crimes against political prisoners and prisoners of war. This running together, in turn, echoed Nuremberg's larger conflation of crimes against humanity with war crimes and crimes against peace that I have located on a legal doctrinal level.

Provocatively, subsequent screenings of *Nazi Concentration Camps* attempted to undo this conflation. As I discuss in chapter 4, fifteen years after Nuremberg, an edited version of *Nazi Concentration Camps* was shown at the Eichmann trial. In this courtroom screening, the film, now spliced with footage from Birkenau and Einsatzgruppen (mobile extermination units) actions, was offered as direct evidence of the Holocaust.⁶⁰ At roughly the same time, *Nazi Concentration Camps* made its Hollywood debut, appearing as the film within the film of Stanley Kramer's *Judgment at Nuremberg*.⁶¹ Starring Spencer Tracy and Burt Lancaster, *Judgment at Nuremberg* offered a loose dramatization of the trial not of the major war criminals, but of the *Alstoetter* case, one of the twelve subsequent Nuremberg proceedings tried by American courts. A trial involving defendants in the Reich Ministry of Justice and other legal functionaries,⁶² *Alstoetter* was used, in Kramer's film, as a device to examine how members of a legal apparatus, in particular judges, could come to pervert institutions of justice. *Judgment at Nuremberg* reaches its dramatic climax when the prosecution screens documentary footage of the liberation of the concentration camps. The film within the film is none other than *Nazi Concentration Camps,* and Kramer drives home its power by using precisely the technique employed by the memoirists: he cuts from the film within the film back to the Hollywood drama, revealing the shock and revulsion etched on the faces of the American prosecutor, played by Richard Widmark, and the principal defendant, a prominent German jurist played by a stiff Burt Lancaster. In *Judgment at Nuremberg, Nazi Concentration Camps* is comprehended as it was at the Eichmann trial—as irrefutable evidence of the Holocaust. (Viewers who watched TNT's recent movie original *Nuremberg* [starring Alec Baldwin as Justice Jackson] again witnessed *Nazi Concentration Camps* used as a film within the film, supplying the dramatic core of the movie and irrebuttable proof of crimes against humanity.)

This understanding of *Nazi Concentration Camps* was also at work in the film's most recent use in a trial setting. In 1985, some forty years after the film's first showing at Nuremberg, *Nazi Concentration Camps* was again called to the stand — this time in the criminal trial of Ernst Zundel for denying the Holocaust. As we shall see in greater detail in part 3, Zundel had arranged for the publication of "Did Six Million Really Die?" a tract that claimed the Holocaust was a Zionist swindle. As a consequence, he was charged with violating a little-used portion of the Canadian criminal code prohibiting the publication of false statements "likely to cause injury or mischief to a public interest."[63] Because the indictment charged Zundel with knowingly publishing false statements, the court reasoned that it was incumbent upon the prosecution to prove the falsity of Zundel's Holocaust denials. Toward this end, *Nazi Concentration Camps* was shown to the jury as evidence of precisely those crimes against the Jews that the film largely fails to mention. Indeed, at the film's conclusion, the prosecutor made the bald pronouncement to the court, "That is the case for the Crown, Your Honour."

Ironically, then, *Nazi Concentration Camps* has been used as irrefutable proof of an event the film did not originally see itself as documenting.[64] Though ironic, this is not entirely surprising, as one is reminded of the plasticity of visual evidence, the way identical images can sponsor multiple interpretations and support different legal arguments. Yet regardless of how *Nazi Concentration Camps* was used in the Eichmann and Zundel trials, for present purposes it is important to note how the documentary's narration — the understanding that it supplies of its own images — made the film available for juridical use at Nuremberg. By framing its horrific scenes in a narrative about perverted militarism and the excesses of war and by sweeping together evidence of the final solution with evidence of conventional war crimes, the film delivered a vision of Nazi atrocity fully consonant with the prosecution's case. Just as the final solution was, in the documentary's eye, indistinguishable from atrocities against political prisoners and POWs, so crimes against humanity, as a legal matter, were absorbed into a conventional understanding of war crimes. In this way, the film came to service the prosecution's case.

In *The Reawakening,* Primo Levi describes his first encounter after his liberation from Auschwitz with a man from "the civilized world." Standing before a well-dressed lawyer — an "extremely courteous and benevolent" person — Levi recalls feeling a powerful need to unburden himself of all that he had witnessed:

> I had a torrent of urgent things to tell the civilized world: . . . things which (it seemed to me) ought to shake every conscience to its very foundations. . . . I spoke at dizzy speed of those so recent experiences of mine, of Auschwitz nearby, yet, it seemed, unknown to all, of the hecatomb from which I alone had escaped, of everything. The lawyer translated into Polish for the public. Now I do not know Polish, but I know how one says "Jew" and how one says "political"; and I soon realized that the translation of my account, although sympathetic, was not faithful to it. The lawyer described me to the public not as an Italian Jew, but as an Italian political prisoner.[65]

Astonishing in its own detail, Levi's story brilliantly captures the small strategic distortions that both made possible and resulted from the effort of the Nuremberg prosecution to comprehend the extermination of European Jewry. By conflating, on a doctrinal level, systematic extermination with excesses of war, the prosecution not only protected the jurisdictional reach of the tribunal, but also preserved the underlying jurisprudential vision that sought to extend international law into the conflicts between nations but not into the darkest bowels of a reprobate sovereign. Like the actions of the lawyer whom Levi encounters, the prosecution's efforts remained sympathetic, though less than faithful, to the history its arguments had to defend.

3
. . .

The Father Pointed to the Sky:
Legitimacy and Tortured History

If the floor was given over to the lawyers and
magistrates, it is because it was no more possible
to "write off the death camps as work related
accidents in the victorious advancement
of civilization."
— Alain Finkielkraut, *Remembering in Vain*

Tortured History

In chapter 2 I discussed how the prosecution and the court at Nuremberg
were pulled in opposite directions. On the one hand, the radicalness of
Nazi atrocity created demands for an extraordinary legal response that
would serve the interests of both formal justice and didactic legality. On the
other hand, the very absence of precedents for such an unusual international proceeding created pressures to normalize the trial. Two warring impulses thus shaped the jurisprudential profile of the case: the desire to submit extreme outrages to the rule of law, and the refusal to permit the law to
be misshapen by its contact with atrocity.

This conflict played itself out over the scope and meaning of the new legal category of crimes against humanity. Ostensibly an astonishing doctrinal innovation, this concept was narrowly construed in order to bolster the
legal adequacy of the trial. As a consequence, one's expectation that the ev-

idence captured in *Nazi Concentration Camps* would be condemned by a unique legal category was disappointed. Instead, both the images of atrocity and the legal category meant to name them were conventionalized in accordance with the doctrinal and jurisdictional commitments of the IMT. This gesture was not an isolated or discrete instance of the prosecution conflating the crimes of the final solution with conventional war crimes (excessive as these were) — rather, it was exemplary of a larger understanding of the Holocaust that emerged at the Nuremberg trial.

Not all evidence of the extermination of the Jews was misrepresented at Nuremberg. To their credit, the prosecution and the court both struggled to present a detailed account of the Nazis' campaign of Judeocide. In his opening statement, Jackson devoted a lengthy section to detailing "Crimes against the Jews" (*IMT* 2:118–27) during which he powerfully declared, "It is my purpose to show a plan and design, to which all Nazis were fanatically committed, to annihilate all Jewish people" (2:118). Close to a year later, the IMT echoed Jackson's words in its final judgment, condemning the crimes against the Jews in two separate sections of its decision, one of which was solely devoted to detailing "a record of consistent and systematic inhumanity on the greatest scale" (1:247). Although the court concluded (as discussed in the chapter 2) that prewar atrocities were not justiciable, it emphasized its authority to condemn the greatest crimes against the Jews: "From the beginning of the war in 1939 war crimes were committed on a vast scale, which were also crimes against humanity; and insofar as the inhumane acts charged in the Indictment, and committed after the beginning of the war, did not constitute war crimes, they were all committed in execution of, or in connection with, the aggressive war, and therefore constituted crimes against humanity" (22:498). Evidence of these crimes was in abundant supply. Yet in spite of the prosecution's redoubtable efforts to document the Nazis' campaign to exterminate the Jews of Europe, these pedagogic efforts were importantly compromised by the legal grid in which unprecedented atrocities were framed, contributing to the serious shortcomings in the historical understanding of the Holocaust that emerged from Nuremberg.

The Americans presented evidence concerning the conspiracy count, a capacious charge that required a précis of the full range of Nazi crimes. As a consequence, the Americans had the first opportunity to offer evidence of crimes against the Jews and in certain respects acquitted themselves well.

Assistant Trial Counsel William Walsh began his presentation with the acknowledgment that it was "singularly inappropriate" to refer to the mistreatment of the Jews as a case of persecution. "Academically . . . ," he said, "to persecute is to afflict, harass, and annoy. The term used does not convey, and indeed I cannot conjure a term that does convey the ultimate aim, the avowed purpose to obliterate the Jewish race" (3:519).

Such a term was, however, available. In 1943, Raphaël Lemkin, a legal adviser to the State Department, had coined the term "genocide" in a report prepared for the Carnegie Endowment for International Peace, examining Axis rule in occupied Europe. Famously beginning his discussion with the words, "new conceptions require new terms," Lemkin argued that the neologism was meant "to signify a coordinated plan of different actions aiming at the destruction of essential foundations of life of national groups." Although Lemkin's understanding of Nazi genocide was not limited to the physical extermination of Jews as a racial category, he clearly saw the atrocities against Jews as the paradigmatic offense named by his novel coinage.[1] The prosecution used the term "genocide" in the indictment, though not surprisingly the new offense appeared as a war crime and not as a crime against humanity (*IMT* 1:44).[2] And while both Shawcross and the French prosecutors would use the neologism in their closing arguments, it largely vanished from the trial.

Instead, consistent with Jackson's sober documentary approach, the Americans adopted the perpetrators' term for their crime, *Die Endlösung* — the final solution. The final solution, the American prosecutors argued, was accomplished in three stages—registration, concentration, and extermination—and they presented detailed evidence of each step. Indeed, the organizational approach of the American prosecution found echoes in Raul Hilberg's magisterial *Destruction of the European Jews,* which similarly divided the "destructive process" into several discrete stages: the defining of who counted as a Jew, the expropriation of property, the isolation and concentration of the Jewish population, and the actual killing itself.

The presentation of this evidence by the American team provided the trial with many of its most dramatic moments. In the first chapter I observed that the "trial by document" often undercut the didactic purpose of the proceeding. When it came to offering evidence of the final solution, however, the prosecution relied on a fuller panoply of proof than it did in other areas of the trial.[3] *Nazi Concentration Camps,* for example, was only the first of a number of films used as witnesses. The Americans also screened a silent short unambiguously titled, *Original German 8-millimeter Film of Atrocities Against the Jews*. This film, described by Assistant Prosecutor Walsh as "perhaps one of the most unusual exhibits that will be presented during the trial" (3:535), had been shot with a home camera and had a running time of ninety seconds. Its celluloid partially burned, the film consisted of a rushed and disturbing set of images that were shown in slow motion twice in succession. It revealed, according to Walsh, "the extermination of a ghetto by Gestapo agents, assisted by military units" (3:536). As opposed to *Nazi Concentration Camps,* which traced the scars left upon the living and the dead, *Atrocities Against the Jews* is an active document of violence. In its halting register, naked and half-naked women are seen being chased through cobbled streets littered with fallen bodies. A man bleeding from a head wound is viciously beaten. A woman is dragged by her hair over a curb (fig. 3.1). The shots are skewed and blurred by the motion of the camera, suggesting the agitation of the hand that did the filming, and it is this disturbed quality, along with the images themselves, that accounts for the film's power. Soviet prosecutors also used documentary film in their

Fig. 3.1. Document Number 3052-PS (USA 280): Still from "Original German 8-millimeter Film of Atrocities Against the Jews." ("Number 45: a woman is dragged by her hair across the street.") Courtesy of USHMM.

case, screening *The Atrocities by the German Fascist Invaders in the USSR,* a movie that showed now-famous images of women lying in their bunks at Birkenau and of children framed by barbed wire showing their tattoos to their off-camera liberators.[4] In the words of one stunned journalist, the Russian film showed "piles of corpses dwarfing those in Dachau and Buchenwald."[5]

Representations of the Holocaust also provided the trial with many of its most memorable moments of testimony. On those occasions when the prosecution did call witnesses to the stand, it remained faithful to the strategy of privileging the use of captured material, turning in the first instance not to survivors but to perpetrators. The most spectacular perpetrator-witness, Rudolf Höß, the former commandant at Auschwitz (not to be confused with ex–party boss Hess), appeared before the court not as a witness for the prosecution, but, incredibly, for the defense. Höß had been captured by the British in May 1945 but then released with thousands of other prisoners.[6] Rearrested on March 11, 1946, he was brought to Nuremberg and interrogated at length by Assistant U.S. Prosecutor Whitney Harris. Although Harris recognized the importance of Höß's testimony, the prosecution's case had already ended. Then, in a staggering misjudgment, Kaltenbrunner's defense attorney, Kurt Kauffmann, decided to call Höß to the stand, presumably so the ex-commandant could tell the court that details of the exterminations camps were kept so secret that they were unknown even to Kaltenbrunner, the head of the RSHA. On cross-examination, Höß failed to offer plausible support of this ridiculous claim, and instead the court learned, for example, that Höß took pride in the knowledge that the extermination agent used at Auschwitz, Zyklon B, marked an unmistakable technical improvement over Treblinka's diesel-generated monoxide gas (*IMT* 11:416).

Astonishing perpetrator testimony was, however, also supplied by prosecution witnesses. Most notable was the testimony of SS General Otto Ohlendorf. As the commander of Einsatzgruppe D, Ohlendorf had organized and overseen the killing of ninety thousand Jewish men, women, and children, primarily in the Ukraine and Russia. "Small of stature, young-looking, and rather comely" (in Taylor's description), Ohlendorf had, in the years before orchestrating acts of mass atrocity, earned a doctorate in jurisprudence and worked as a research director in the Institute for World Economy and Maritime Transport in Kiel. Speaking "quietly, with great precision, dispassion, and apparent intelligence,"[7] Ohlendorf expressed his disapproval of the sloppy procedures followed by other Einsatzgruppen and detailed the "humane" principles that controlled the mass killings that took place under his orders: "1. Exclusion of the public; 2. Military execution by a firing-squad; 3. Arrival of the transports and carrying out of the liquidation in a smooth manner to avoid unnecessary excitement; 4. Supervision of the property to prevent looting" (*IMT* 4:331).

Appalled by the irregularities that marred the actions of the other Einsatzgruppen, Ohlendorf revealed a competitive attitude toward his rivals in extermination. When asked to explain why other Einsatzgruppen reported killing figures considerably in excess of his ninety thousand, the ss officer responded with the dismissive claim, "I believe that to a large extent the figures submitted by the other Einsatzgruppen were exaggerated" (4:319) (fig. 3.2). And when asked (on cross-examination) whether the legality of the orders to kill had been explained "under false pretenses" to the members of the Einsatzgruppen, Ohlendorf responded with utter noncomprehension, providing a brilliant and chilling encapsulation of the "Befehl ist Befehl" (An order is an order) mentality: "I do not understand your question; since the order was issued by the superior authorities, the question of legality could not arise in the minds of these individuals, for they had sworn obedience to the people who had issued the orders" (4:354).

Gripping testimony also came from victims and bystanders. The French prosecution, for example, called to the stand a number of victims of Nazi terror, perhaps none more eloquent than Marie Claude Vaillant-Couturier. A Communist and a highly regarded member of the National Assembly, Vaillant-Couturier had been sent to Auschwitz and later to Ravensbrück for her work in the French resistance.[8] At Nuremberg, her powerful testimony made vivid the horrific conditions in the camps, particularly the mistreatment of Jewish children at Auschwitz. Articulate and composed, Vaillant-Couturier described how "after confinement, the babies [of Jewish women] were drowned in a bucket of water" (6:212) and how, once, because the gas supply had run out, the "Sonderkommando . . . had thrown the children into the furnaces alive" (6:216).[9]

This testimony, taken with other evidence, supplied the court with many of the details that were to become central to popular understandings of the Holocaust. Dieter Wisliceny, a *Hauptsturmführer* (captain) in the ss, described the activities of his superior Adolf Eichmann, "in every respect a confirmed bureaucrat" (4:361), who had boasted at the war's conclusion that he "would leap laughing into the grave because . . . he had five million

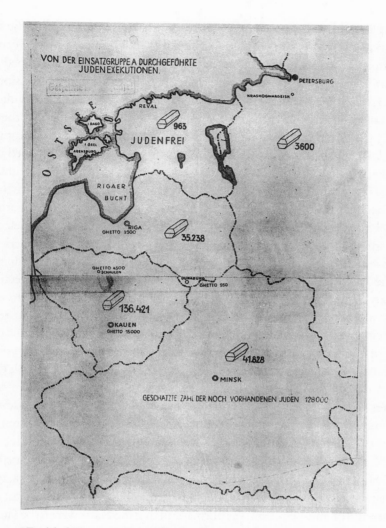

Fig. 3.2. Entitled "Executions of Jews carried out by Einsatzgruppe A," this map
shows the number of Jews killed in the Baltic states and Belorussia by late 1941.
The coffin is a symbol for the number of executed Jews in each area; group A
claims in excess of 200,000 victims. The legend at the bottom reads,
"Estimated number of Jews still on hand: 128,000." In his testimony before
the IMT, Otto Ohlendorf, the commander of *Einsatzgruppe* D, claimed 90,000
deaths for his squad and dismissed the estimations of the other groups
as self-serving exaggerations.Courtesy of USHMM.

people on his conscience" (4:371). Prosecutor Walsh presented to the IMT the notorious Stroop report — describing it as "this finest example of ornate German craftsmanship, leather bound, profusely illustrated, typed on heavy bound paper" (3:553) — which documented the brutal suppression of the Warsaw Ghetto uprising and the razing of the ghetto. Other evidence told of the selections at the rail ramps at Birkenau, describing how the orderly process of destruction unraveled under the massive influx of Hungarian Jews in the summer of 1944. Documents and witnesses revealed that crystal pellets ordinarily used to kill lice were used in the gas chambers (6:225); that vans redesigned to gas their passengers failed to perform in inclement weather (3:560); and that a doctor named Mengele performed cruel experiments on twins (6:215). Witnesses described how those selected for immediate extermination at Birkenau passed to the gas chambers unregistered (6:215), how an orchestra of inmates had played such tunes as "The Tales of Hoffmann" and "The Merry Widow" during these selections (6:215), and how the rail ramps at Treblinka had been constructed to look like "a very good station" posted with schedules of trains departing to leading cities of Europe (8:326). Finally, the trial presented the first public census of the Holocaust. Relying on the Nazis' own data as well as on other population reports, the prosecution estimated the number of Jewish dead at 5.7 million (2:119) — rounding the figure off to the canonical 6.

Yet notwithstanding the abundant evidence of the final solution adduced at Nuremberg, the prosecution's effort at collective pedagogy was often less than successful. Some blunders are well known, such as Soviet prosecutor L. N. Smirnov's unfortunate assertion that "the excessive anti-Semitism of the Hitlerite criminals . . . assumed a perfectly zoological aspect" (8:294). Whatever else this opaque claim might have meant, it seemed to suggest that a measure of anti-Semitism was normal and that the Nazis were to be faulted only for their excessive acts. More egregious was French prosecutor François de Menthon's failure to mention the Jews in his opening statement. Reaffirming the original French belief that the trial should have been structured around crimes against humanity, Menthon offered in his opening address an ambitious understanding of 6(c) (fig. 3.3). Yet at the same time as he parsed crimes against humanity as crimes "against the human status" violative of "the whole of humanity" (5:407–08), Menthon managed somehow to omit the extermination of the Jews from his bracing oratory. Indeed, the only mention of Jews in his entire opening statement was the elliptical assertion that "racial discriminations were provoked against citizens of the occupied

Fig. 3.3. François de Menthon, the chief of the French prosecution, during his opening address to the IMT. In the address he managed only a single oblique reference to the Nazis' crimes against the Jews. Courtesy of National Archives.

countries who were catalogued as Jews, measures particularly hateful, damaging to their personal rights and to their human dignity" (5:412).

Such missteps, though troubling, can be dismissed as idiosyncratic — that is, they were not the inevitable or necessary result of attempting to represent and comprehend the extermination of the Jews in a juridical forum. Other miscues, by contrast, must be seen as structural, a direct consequence of the effort to digest history through an extraordinary effort of the law. The first of these structural problems arose from the conspiracy charge. Although, as noted, the tribunal ultimately concluded that the defendants could be condemned only for conspiring to wage aggressive war, the prosecution, following the lead of the indictment, had sought to prove that the defendants were also guilty of conspiring to commit crimes against humanity. Consequently the American prosecutors labored to show that the final solution was the result of a common plan hatched early in the Nazi regime.

The American team thus presented the extermination process as the result of planning that reached back into the years that preceded the so-called

Machtergreifung (the Nazis' seizure of power). In Walsh's words, "Now this ultimate objective, that is the elimination and extermination of the Jews, could not be accomplished without preliminary steps and measures. The German State must first be seized by the Nazi Party, the force of world opinion must be faced, and even the regimented German people must be indoctrinated with hatred against the Jews" (3:521). The statement unusually reverses the conventional logic of the politics of racism. In Walsh's formulation, anti-Semitism is not described as a tool for the consolidation of political power; rather, political power had to be consolidated in order to pursue a radical agenda of racial hatred. In other stages of the trial, the prosecution offered a more conventional understanding of the logic of anti-Semitism, and Walsh himself argued that in the Jew, the Nazis found a "'whipping boy' upon whose shoulders c[ould] be placed the blame for the world catastrophe to come" (3:527). Still, the vision of the final solution offered by the American prosecution was of a detailed plan incubating in the minds of leading Nazis long before they had captured the requisite state power to implement it. As Walsh parsed his own logic, "It is my purpose to elucidate the pattern, the successful and successive stages, the sequence of and concurrence of crimes committed, the pre-determined means to a pre-ordained end" (3:573).

Such extreme intentionalism is not necessarily to be dismissed. (By "intentionalism," I mean the idea that the final solution can be explained "in terms of Hitler's intentions derived from a coherent and consistent ideology and implemented through an all powerful totalitarian dictatorship.")[10] If historians like Hilberg have focused primarily on the obstacles hindering the implementation of the final solution, other leading scholars of the Holocaust have powerfully defended the intentionalist argument. For example, Lucy Davidowicz's study *The War Against the Jews: 1933–1945* sees the final solution as, in essence, the ultimate premeditated crime. Davidowicz's argument has, in turn, been sternly criticized, and the clash between intentionalists and functionalists (who claim that "the Final Solution was not a premeditated goal toward which Hitler and the Nazis consciously strived" but was "the unplanned product of an evolutionary process")[11] has emerged as one of the most contentious issues among scholars of the Holocaust.

Without committing to a specific position on this complicated question, one nevertheless must attend to the differences between the prosecution's stance and the historian's. For the Nuremberg prosecution's embrace of intentionalism was not in the first instance driven by a disinterested attempt to make sense of the historical record. Rather, the prosecution framed the historical record to agree with the legal terms of the case. In particular, the ill-fated claim of a conspiracy to commit crimes against humanity demanded a variety of intentionalism to make the argument work: for what else could a conspiracy mean in this context other than a plan of atrocity seeking occasion for its realization? Thus the picture of history supplied at Nuremberg must be seen through the case's legal filter.

The representation of the final solution was also shaped by Nuremberg's restrictive reading of 6(c). I have already observed that the court concluded that in order to be justiciable, crimes against humanity must have been committed in connection with the war of aggression. Here, again, the historical record was asked to submit to the legal strictures of the case. After promising in his opening statement to prove the Nazis' plan to "annihilate all Jewish people" (*IMT* 2:118), Jackson went on to explain, "Nor was [the policy of starvation and extermination] directed against individual Jews for personal bad citizenship or unpopularity. The avowed purpose was the destruction of the Jewish people as a whole, as an end in itself, as a measure of preparation for war, and as a discipline of conquered peoples" (2:119).

At this critical moment Jackson invoked, if not the term, then the logic of genocide. Yet his parsing of this logic was peculiar. The ghetto, he argued, "was the laboratory for testing repressive measures" (2:118), the Jews serving as exemplars of Nazi discipline to other citizenries under Nazi subjugation. Persecution, moreover, eliminated an obstacle to aggressive war, as "the purpose . . . of getting rid of the influence of . . . the Jews was to clear their obstruction to the precipitation of aggressive war" (2:127). Jackson returned to this position in his closing argument: "The same war purpose was dominant in the persecution of the Jews . . . the Nazis so regarded the Jews as foremost among the opposition to the police state with which they planned to put forward their plans of military aggression. . . . Accordingly, they were transported like cattle to concentration camps, where they were utilized as a source of forced labor for war purposes" (19:414).

As a matter of moral suasion, one must admire Jackson's struggle to find a way to sweep the prewar mistreatment of German Jews under the jurisdictional competence of the tribunal. Indeed, this strategy was all but baldly stated by Prosecutor Walsh in his effort to build on Jackson's approach: "The treatment of Jews within Germany was therefore as much of a plan for aggressive war as was the building of armaments and the conscription of manpower. It falls within the jurisdiction of this Tribunal as an integral part of the planning and preparation to wage a war of aggression" (3:520).[12]

The court, as mentioned above, rebuffed this effort in its final judgment, declaring that prewar atrocities were not crimes against humanity "within the meaning of the Charter" (1:254). But before this decision could be handed down, history had already been forced to accommodate itself to the restrictive understanding of 6(c).To return to Walsh's argument: "The anti-Jewish policy was part of this plan for unification because it was the conviction of the Nazis that the Jews would not contribute to Germany's military program, on the contrary would hamper it. The Jew therefore [had to] be eliminated. . . . The underlying purpose and objective to annihilate the Jewish race was one of the fundamental principles of the Nazi plan to prepare for and to wage aggressive war" (3:520–21). This reasoning is question begging on a number of scores. First, it seems to contradict the picture of the final solution offered under the conspiracy charge, which contained the radical proposition that the seizure of state power, the campaign of rearmament, and the war itself were simply stages in an elaborately premeditated plan to exterminate all Jews. Second, even on its own terms, this argument is unsound, for it goes without saying that the extermination of the Jews followed, as a temporal matter, the war of aggression and thus cannot be seen as a step in its preparation. Finally, the argument is question begging in that one must ask, What was the nature of the threat that the Jews posed to Nazi war plans?

To answer this question the prosecution quoted from Heinrich Himmler's infamous Posen speech before a meeting of ss major generals in October 1943: "We know how difficult we should have made it for ourselves if with the bombing raids, the burdens and deprivations of war, we still had Jews today in every town as secret saboteurs, agitators and trouble mongers" (3:520 [Himmler quoted in document 1919-PS]). Driven by the desire to link crimes against humanity with aggressive war, the prosecution was ironically prepared to accept the Nazis' characterization of the Jews as a potential military adversary, a fifth column lurking behind the lines, threatening acts of sabotage. Unfortunately, to explain the final solution in terms of military aims is inadvertently to anticipate the arguments of certain Holocaust revisionists who have argued that the Nazis reasonably viewed the Jews as military enemies in a time of war. (For example, the negationist booklet "Did Six Million Really Die? asserts that a statement made in 1939 [at the outbreak of the war] by Chaim Weizmann, president of the World Zionist Organization, that Jews would support England and fight for the democracies "constituted the Jews' declaration of war on Nazi Germany and transformed them into a threat to Germany's security.")[13] No simple misstatement of history, the vulnerabilities in the prosecution's picture of the final solution must again be seen as the direct result of the legal grid in which its understanding of extermination was framed.

If the attempt to make crimes against humanity an accessory of crimes against peace made for tortured history, the conflation of crimes against humanity with war crimes also left traces on the trial's representation of the final solution.[14] On one level, the conflation made for precisely the kind of misconstruing observed in the earlier discussion of *Nazi Concentration Camps*: the filmic witness neglected to distinguish the treatment of Jews in concentration camps from the treatment of prisoners of war or civilian political prisoners. This problem, in turn, resurfaced time and again throughout the trial. Echoing the film, the prosecution (particularly the American team) treated concentration camps and extermination camps as one and the same, a misstep that would not be corrected until the later stages of the trial when Smirnov specifically delineated the difference between concentration camps and "secret centers of extermination" such as Treblinka and Chelmno (8:322). Although this mistake could partially be attributed to prosecutorial ignorance, certainly the running together of legal categories both reflected and encouraged such misunderstandings.

Further evidence of such conflation may be seen in Thomas Dodd's assertion that "not only civilians of the occupied countries but also prisoners of war were subjected to the horrors and brutality of concentration camps" (3:504). Dodd's statement seems rhetorically to invert its priorities. One might have expected Dodd to say, "Not only were POWs brutally mistreated, but so were civilians," a statement that would have placed the force of its claim on the brutalization of noncombatants. Similarly, in Shawcross's closing argument, the British prosecutor declared, "What they [the Nazis] did to prisoners of war . . . [was] the clearest crime of all" (19:472). Shawcross's statement seems, on first blush, disappointing if not grotesque, insofar as he had just finished describing the final solution as "the greatest crime in history," a horror that left the "imagination and intellect shattered" (19:468). Yet in describing the mistreatment of POWs as the *clearest* crime, Shawcross was, of course, right. For as a matter of law, the mistreatment of POWs represented a classical example of precisely the kind of crime proscribed under customary and conventional international law. The statements of Dodd and Shawcross offered a recognition that war crimes constituted the master offense, which, with minor exceptions, included crimes against humanity within its ambit.

The idea that the crimes of the final solution could be treated as a subset of war crimes left its traces upon Nuremberg's representation of the Holocaust in a second, more subtle way. An unusual aspect of the trial was the virtual absence of the voices of the Nazis' principal victims. Although the prosecution imaginatively used documents and witnesses to prove the crimes of the final solution, the only Jews to appear before the court were a handful of witnesses called by the Russian prosecution: Abram Suzkever, a Jewish writer from Vilna; Severina Shmaglevskaya, a Polish survivor of Auschwitz; and Samuel Rajzman, a survivor of Treblinka.[15]

The importance of the testimony of these witnesses cannot be gainsaid. Not only was Suzkever able to offer horrific details about the liquidation of the Vilna ghetto, he also made vivid the constant moral and physical degradation that preceded the killing. (For example, Jews were required, when the local Nazi administrator visited the ghetto, "to fall down on the ground and bark like dogs" [8:305].) Rajzman presented the trial's most precise testimony about a pure extermination center, Treblinka. But the very power of their statements only underscores the curious fact that no other Jewish witnesses were called to the stand. Survivor testimony enjoyed pride of place at the Eichmann trial (see part 2); at Nuremberg, by contrast, testimony of the final solution was most importantly provided by non-Jews.

The question of how to present the voice of murdered Jewry before the court was one that had concerned the prosecution. Jackson, for example, had proposed calling Weizmann to offer a fifteen-thousand-word general statement about the final solution. The British, however, vetoed this idea out of a concern that testimony which aroused sympathy for Jewish causes might threaten the stability of British rule in Palestine.[16] Still, the prosecution's unwillingness to call Weizmann does not explain the absence of other Jewish voices at trial. Again, part of the answer clearly lies in the documentary approach, which, as we have seen, favored paper over people and preferred testimony by perpetrators. The use of non-Jewish witnesses, such as Vaillant-Couturier, was, then, an extension of an evidentiary logic which assumed that proof of extreme crimes became less credible and more impeachable as one moved from perpetrator to bystander to victim.[17] Thus, Severina Shmaglevskaya, who, like Vaillant-Couturier, described the horrors endured by Jewish children and pregnant Jewish women at Auschwitz, was brought before the IMT in a manner that obscured whether the witness was herself Jewish.[18]

Finally, the evidentiary strategy of using non-Jews at Auschwitz to testify about the treatment of Jews can be seen as echoing the larger jurisprudential complexion of the trial. For just as the crimes of the final solution could be contained within a legal category intended originally to protect POWs and other civilians, so the experiences of Jewish victims could be spoken for by political prisoners. The privileging of the testimony of, say, the French resister over the words of the Jewish survivor was fueled by the additional desire to cast the martyrdom of the French nation in terms of a story of heroic struggle and not helpless victimization.[19] Yet such motives merely reinforced the larger processes of displacement, conflation, and assimilation that one finds at work: Just as crimes against humanity were contained within war crimes, so the experiences of Holocaust survivors found restricted expression in the testimony of courtroom proxies.

This last observation, of course, cannot strictly be considered an instance of the trial distorting the historical record. Rather, it is an example of a more subtle form of misrepresentation—the kind that arises not from a misstatement of fact, but from a failure to find terms adequate to the task of doing justice to the gravity of an event. Thus even when the trial offered a reasonably reliable historical picture (such as the image of Auschwitz provided by Vaillant-Couturier), it marginalized the experiences of victims of traumatic history. Whether the law owes an obligation to survivors is, as we've seen, a contentious issue (one that I will examine in part 2); here it suffices to note that if an obligation to victims exists, the Nuremberg prosecution failed to honor it.

This point, in turn, brings to the fore a final set of insufficiencies in the picture of the final solution provided at Nuremberg. These problems, again, cannot be considered as distortions of the factual record per se; instead, they were instances of inappropriate juxtaposition, tortured analogy, and conceptual malapropism. Many of these mischaracterizations fit the model of misrepresentation described in the examination of *Nazi Concentration Camps*. Yet an entirely separate set of problems arose not because of the conflation of crimes against humanity with war crimes, but as a result of lingering ambiguities nestled within the very concept of crimes against humanity.

Indignity and Atavism

Like their predecessors at the Great Powers Conference in 1919, the parties to the London agreement never clarified what exactly they meant by "humanity." Whether the term stood for some standard of humaneness or for humankind as a whole was left crucially unresolved. The Americans and the British seemed to defend the former position, while the French embraced the latter. In his opening argument for the French, Menthon, as noted, offered a particularly capacious view of 6(c), reading it as proscribing crimes against the "human status" (this, of course, despite his failure to mention crimes against the Jews). At the beginning of his discussion Menthon argued "The body of Crimes against Humanity constitutes, in the last analysis, nothing less than the perpetration of . . . common law crimes such as theft, looting, ill treatment, enslavement, murders, and assassinations, crimes that are provided for and punishable under the penal laws of all civilized nations" (5:372).[20] Even as Menthon tried to tether crimes against humanity to common law municipal offenses, however, his vision ushered him toward larger philosophical reflections: "It [the human status] signifies all those faculties, the exercising and developing of which constitute the meaning of human life. Each of these faculties finds its corresponding expression in the order of man's existence in society. . . . This conception is defined in two complementary ideas: the dignity of the human being considered in each and every person individually, on the one hand; and, on the other hand, the permanence of the human being considered within the whole of humanity" (5:407–08).

Grandiloquent if not opaque, Menthon's argument sought to draw two distinct ideas of humanity together: first, a liberal vision of the dignitary rights of the individual; and second, the rights that attach to humankind as a whole. In the latter argument, crimes against humanity constitute a foundational assault on the ethical, spiritual, and metaphysical values that lie at the core of belonging to humankind. In this respect, Menthon's argument anticipated the scholar Harold Kaplan's sweeping formulation: "The crime against humanity is the crime against *all Being*."[21]

Unfortunately, the relation between the two parts of Menthon's argument, the dignitary norm and the metaphysical ideal, was never sufficiently elaborated, and both he and the other French prosecutors often retreated into the first, more conventional understanding of crimes against the human status. These dignitary rights included, in Menthon's words, "spiritual aspects": "a combination of possibilities to give out and to receive the expressions of thought, whether in assemblies or associations, in religious practice, in teachings given or received, by the many means which progress has put at the disposal for the dissemination of intellectual value: Books, press, radio, cinema" (5:407). This association of crimes against humanity with dignitary harms of a spiritual nature might have provided an arresting approach to the discussion of such offenses had the French prosecution not proceeded to treat 6(c) as essentially proscribing crimes against the distinctively French spirit. Instructive in this regard was Assistant Prosecutor Serge Fuster's indictment of German propaganda: "In France, for instance, the most illustrious names in history appeared on posters and were made to proclaim slogans against the enemies of Germany. Isolated sentences taken from the works of Clemenceau, Montesquieu, and many others who in this way were made to utter sentiments in favor of Nazism. . . . In this way, German propaganda, in attacking simultaneously the genius of a nation and the most intimate sentiments of its people, committed a crime against the spirit" (7:14–15).

Trivial as this argument may sound, the claim that strategic redactions of beloved French classics constituted crimes against the spirit was not an isolated misstep. In a similar vein, Edgar Faure, the French deputy prosecutor, posed the following question to Professor Van der Essen, a teacher of history at the University of Louvain, who was called as a witness to the Nazis' malicious destruction of Louvain's famous library:[22] "I would like to ask you a last question: I think I understood that you yourself were never arrested or particularly worried by the Germans. I would like to know if you consider that a free man, against whom the German administration or police have nothing in particular, could during the Nazi occupation, lead a life in accordance with the conception a free man has of his dignity?" (6:543). By way of response, Van der Essen observed, "Well, you see me here before you, I weigh 67 kilos, my height is 1 meter 67 centimeters. According to my colleagues in the Faculty of Medicine that is quite normal. Before the 10th of May 1940, before the airplanes of the Luftwaffe suddenly came without any declaration and spread death and desolation in Belgium, I weighed 82 kilos. This difference is contestably the result of the occupation" (6:543).

Having witnessed the walking skeletons of *Nazi Concentration Camps,* the tribunal must have been deeply dismayed by the claim that in the professor's weight loss (presumably from a condition of corpulence to a state of leanness) lay evidence of a crime against humanity. In fact, the ludicrousness of Van der Essen's testimony gave the defense one of its few victories on cross-examination. Thus the following exchange between the witness and Ludwig Babel, counsel for the ss:

HERR BABEL: Witness, you have said, if I understood you correctly, that you lost 15 kilograms weight.
VAN DER ESSEN: Yes, indeed.
HERR BABEL: What conclusion do you draw from that fact? I could not quite understand what you said.
VAN DER ESSEN: I simply meant to say that I lost these 15 kilos as a result of the mental suffering which we underwent during the occupation, and it was an answer to a question of M. Faure on whether I considered the occupation compatible with the dignity of a free man. I wanted to answer "no," giving the proof that as a result of the occupation we have suffered much anguish, and I think the weight loss is sufficient proof of this.
HERR BABEL: During the war, I also, without having been ill, lost 35 kilos. What conclusion could be drawn from that, in your opinion?
[Laughter.] [6:553]

Unfortunately, the French approach often produced precisely such ridiculous results. When the French finally corrected Menthon's startling failure to mention the Jews in his opening address and offered evidence of the final solution in the west, the material was sandwiched between a presentation of German propaganda film (presumably an offense against cinema and thus the human spirit) and a discussion of "the confiscation and plundering of works of art in France," technically a war crime according to the formal definition supplied in 6(b) (7:50). Compounding this indignity was prosecutor Faure's description of the final solution: "I shall not speak in detail of the great sufferings endured by persons qualified as Jews in France and in the other countries of western Europe. I should like simply to indicate here that it also caused great suffering to all the other inhabitants of these countries to witness the abominable treatment inflicted upon Jews. Every Frenchman felt a deep affliction at seeing the persecution of other Frenchmen" (7:25). Although, in fairness to Faure, the French prosecutor did offer a sophisticated analysis of the complex administrative subdivision of tasks responsible for the crimes against the Jews, one cannot help being disturbed by his conflation of the suffering of the Jews with the suffering of bystanders. Unfortunately, this again cannot be dismissed as an idiosyncratic rhetorical or imaginative lapse. The claim that reduced the crimes of the final solution to a dignitary offense against all Frenchmen simply echoed Menthon's analysis of crimes against humanity.

Problems within Nuremberg's understanding of crimes against humanity left traces upon the trial in still another way. Here one must bear in mind that despite the differences between the Anglo-American and the French understanding of the core concept of humanity, both views shared important ground. For whatever "humanity" meant, the Anglo-Americans and the French agreed that the principles contained within the concept derived from the customs and practices of civilized nations. This point is critical, as it helps make sense of a striking feature of the prosecution's rhetoric: the constant appeals to the concept of civilized practice. Indeed, the notion of civilization occupied the rhetorical center of Justice Jackson's famous opening address. In Jackson's account, civilization was presented as the principal victim and ultimate conqueror of Nazi pathology: "The wrongs which we seek to condemn and punish have been so calculated, so malignant, and so devastating, that civilization cannot tolerate their being ignored, because it cannot survive their being repeated" (2:99). Justifying a juridical response to Nazi crimes, Jackson insisted that "civilization can afford no compromise with the social forces which would gain renewed strength if we deal ambiguously or indecisively with [these] men" (2:99). Later, enumerating the chronology of Nazi outrages, Jackson asserted, "These are things which have turned the stomach of the world and set every civilized hand against Nazi Germany" (2:130).

Jackson used the idea of civilization as a rhetorical workhorse to distinguish the values and practices of the Allies from those of Nazi Germany. Yet he also used it as a legal term of art. In this respect, the concept of civilization was meant to serve as a bona fide source of international law, and appeals to it were offered to shore up one of the weakest aspects of the prosecution's case: the absence of unambiguous norms in conventional international law criminalizing, say, crimes against humanity. (And here recall Lansing's and Scott's vehement denial of the existence of any general principles of humanity shared by, and legally binding upon, all civilized nations.) To anchor its case, the prosecution could have openly and unapologetically appealed to natural law, the universal maxims of obligatory conduct binding upon reasoning beings. At times the prosecution seemed to move in this direction; Shawcross, for example, appealed to principles of "natural justice" in his summary argument (19:434). In general, however, the natural law argument went very much against the spirit of both the charter and the Nuremberg prosecution. Jackson in particular eschewed this approach, perhaps anticipating the disastrous appeals to natural law and specifically to "the Christian-Judeo absolutes of good and evil" made by Prosecutor Joseph Keenan in the war crimes trial before the International Military Tribunal in Tokyo that began six months after the Nuremberg proceeding.[23]

Alternatively, the prosecution could have attempted to secure the legal basis of its case by an appeal to principles of strict legal positivism. As the tribunal noted, "The making of the Charter was the exercise of the sovereign legislative power by the countries to which the German Reich unconditionally surrendered" (1:218). From a grimly positivist perspective, the legal basis of the charter was unimpeachable. Yet the positivist argument, by smacking of victors' justice, also promised to compromise the trial's ambition to serve both as a tool of justice and as an instrument of didactic legality.

The appeal to the customs and practices of civilization attempted to deliver an argument more consonant with the ideals of liberal legality. Even in the absence of a clearly determinable code of criminality it was possible, then, to locate binding rules of conduct within the very notion of civilized practice. By "binding," of course, the prosecution did not simply mean enforceable with a sanction. As Shawcross observed in his opening statement, many rules of international law would, in fact, fail under this stern Austinian definition (3:94). More to the point, such an understanding would not have served the prosecution's deeper juridical end. Bindingness, in this understanding, had to mean obligatory in a normative sense. The prosecution's argument can thus be understood as an effort to import a strong obligatory character into international law without appealing to natural law. By locating a deep normative core in the existing practices of civilized nations, the prosecution attempted delicately to steer a course between the Scylla of natural law and the Charybdis of strict legal positivism.[24]

Yet one important, if not inevitable, consequence of defining crimes against humanity as violations of civilized practice was that the prosecution came to characterize Nazi atrocities as *crimes of atavism,* horrific deeds committed in an orgy of primitive barbarism. As the Allies were paragons of civilization, the Nazis were consistently represented as atavistic. Menthon, in his opening address, openly wondered, "How can we explain how Germany, fertilized through the centuries of classic antiquity and Christianity, by the ideals of liberty, equality, and social justice, by the common heritage of western humanism to which she had brought such noble and precious contributions, could have come to this astonishing return to primitive barbarism?" (5:375). Unable to answer his own question, Menthon ultimately bemoaned Nazism as an uncontrolled outpouring of "all the instincts of barbarism, repressed by centuries of civilization, but always present in men's innermost nature, all the negations of the traditional values of humanity" (5:243).

The rhetoric of atavism was not limited to the speeches of prosecutors; it made itself manifest in the very documents and evidence brought before the court by the prosecution. Most remarkable in this regard was a piece of material evidence submitted by the American team during its presentation of life in the concentration camps. Dodd directed the court's attention to the unusual exhibit with words of apology: "We do not wish to dwell on this pathological phase of the Nazi culture; but we do feel compelled to offer one additional exhibit, which we offer as Exhibit Number USA-254" (3:516). Displayed on a table in the center of the crowded courtroom was, as Dodd explained, a human head "with the skull bone removed, shrunken, stuffed, and preserved" (3:516) (fig. 3.4).

Earlier that afternoon, the tribunal had endured a display of flayed human skin, covered with tattoos, allegedly preserved as an ornament for Ilse Koch, the wife of the Buchenwald commandant (3:514). Like the images in *Nazi Concentration Camps* (which had been screened two weeks earlier), the exhibits scandalized the court. The correspondent for the *Times* (of London) later described the "two gruesome relics from Buchenwald," focusing on the shrunken head: "At the time when Buchenwald was overrun many persons refused to believe the accounts of sadism practiced there. . . . But here in court was the proof—the preserved head of a hanged Pole, which, by removing the skull bones, had been reduced to the size of a fist."[25] Photos of the head (and to a lesser degree, the skin) became some of the best-known images associated with the trial. Especially astonishing is the photo in Whitney Harris's *Tyranny on Trial* of Dodd holding the shrunken head and gazing at it like Hamlet contemplating the skull of Yorick (fig. 3.5).

On one level, the shrunken head and the flayed skin, like *Nazi Concentration Camps,* did little to clarify the legal guilt of the defendants. One could

Fig. 3.4. Crimes of atavism: the shrunken head of Buchenwald against a map of
Nazi concentration camps, on display before the Nuremberg courtroom.
Courtesy of USHMM.

argue that the head and skin functioned largely as spectacle — at best, as
pieces of "stark reality" that penetrated the "air of remoteness that . . . hung
over the Nuremberg trial";[26] at worst, as grotesque artifacts offered more
to satisfy voyeuristic impulses than to elucidate questions of legal culpability.

Yet however minor its explicit evidentiary value, the shrunken head of
Buchenwald, like *Nazi Concentration Camps*, importantly served the didactic ends of the trial. The head performed a role, to borrow language from
Joseph Conrad's *Heart of Darkness*, "not ornamental but symbolic":[27] it
gave dramatic shape to the prosecutorial argument that conjured Nazi
atrocities as crimes of atavism. Taken together with Jackson's rhetoric of
civilization and Menthon's evocations of the primitive, the shrunken head
materialized a representation of Nazi crimes as born of a violent rebirth of
savage and primitive impulses.

This understanding of Nazi atrocity has been sternly interrogated in nu-

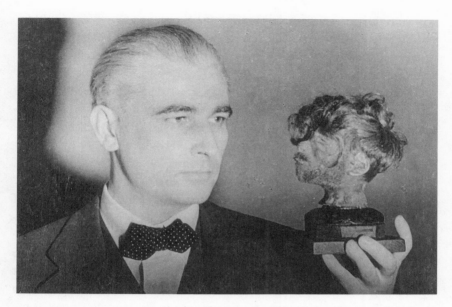

Fig. 3.5. U.S. Executive Counsel Thomas J. Dodd contemplates the shrunken head of Buchenwald. Courtesy of Sovfoto.

merous works on the Holocaust, perhaps most explicitly in Zygmunt Bauman's *Modernity and the Holocaust*. Bauman's study begins with a telling epigraph from Richard Rubenstein and John Roth's *Approaches to Auschwitz:* "Civilization now includes death camps and *Muselmänner* [literally, "Muslims," emaciated inmates selected for the gas chambers] among its material and spiritual products." The contrast between the prosecution's position at Nuremberg and the sensibility expressed in the epigraph could not be greater. Whereas the prosecution understood Nazi atrocities as acts *against* civilization, Rubenstein and Roth regard the Holocaust as an act *of* civilization. Carefully elaborating this latter understanding, Bauman challenges the understanding that would see the Holocaust as a "failure of civilization to contain the morbid natural predilections of whatever has been left of nature in man." Against this "malfunction" or "pathology" thesis, Bauman argues that "Holocaust-style phenomena must be recognized as legitimate outcomes of the civilizing tendency, and its constant potential." By "legitimate," Bauman does not, of course, mean to register approval. Rather, he challenges the belief in modern civilization as predominately a moral force, that is, as "a system of institutions that cooperate and complement each other in the imposition of normative order and the rule of law, which in turn safeguard conditions of social peace and individual security poorly defended in pre-civilized settings" — precisely the image of civilization presented by Jackson, Menthon, and the rest of the Nuremberg prosecution.[28]

Granted, the connection between Nazi atrocities and techniques of modernity was not entirely lost upon the prosecution. In his concluding argument, French prosecutor Charles Dubost vividly described the bureaucratized and industrialized nature of Nazi killing in a manner that anticipated the arguments that would play a critical role in the Eichmann trial. "The unique fact of this Trial, the fact that stands out above all others," Dubost declared, "is that of the methodical, systematic extermination of all those who occupied the living space coveted by Germany" (19:563). Indeed, Dubost's understanding of the bureaucratized nature of genocide specifically drew upon the visual evidence supplied in *Nazi Concentration Camps:* "Those who make the decision [to exterminate] do so without shuddering. It is possible that they have no accurate or concrete picture in their minds of the consequences of their orders. The stupefaction of some of the accused immediately after the showing of the film about the camps is understandable in light of this reflection" (19:564).

As noted in chapter 1, it was the prosecution's recognition of the inextricable link between unprecedented crimes and bureaucratic organizations that accounted for one of the most controversial aspects of the prosecution's case: the indictment of entire organizations such as the ss and Gestapo. The effort to criminalize these organizations was born, Jackson argued, of the recognition that "no system of jurisprudence has yet evolved any satisfactory technique for handling a great number of common charges against a great multitude of accused persons" (8:357). The organizational charge was meant, then, to make possible any number (potentially tens of thousands) of subsequent prosecutions based on evidence of a person's membership in a group declared criminal. Whether this effort was successful or even appropriate can be debated; ironically Hans Kelsen, the influential legal theorist and critic of Nuremberg, condemned this aspect of the trial as itself legally atavistic, "a regrettable regress to the backward technique of collective criminal responsibility."[29] Yet Jackson believed the charges against the organizations were critical to the law's response to Nazi criminality. "It would be a greater catastrophe to acquit these organizations," he argued with some hyperbole, "than it would be to acquit the entire twenty-two individual defendants in the box" (8:376).[30]

To recognize the bureaucratized and industrialized dimension of Nazi atrocity is not, however, necessarily to insist upon a connection between such atrocity and civilized practice. Barbarism of a primitive variety can, after all, exploit modern practices. This was the thrust of Jackson's assertion that "the terror of Torquemada pales before the Nazi inquisition" (19:397). The French position ultimately was similar to Jackson's, as it found summary in the following words: "The historian of the future . . . will know that the work of twenty centuries of civilization, which believed itself eternal, was almost destroyed by the return of ancient barbarism in a new guise, all the more brutal because more scientific" (19:530). At the same time that the prosecution recognized the technically and administratively advanced nature of Nazi atrocity, it insisted that these practices were not products of civilization. In defending the normative distinctiveness of occidental modernity, the prosecution merely conceded civilization's vulnerability to what Bauman has called "hiccups of barbarism."[31]

By viewing Nazi practice in these terms, the prosecution left intact the deeper jurisprudential vision that saw civilized practice as the fount of principles of international law and law as the bulwark of civilization. This is not to say that the Nuremberg prosecution intentionally conjured Nazi atrocity as atavistic to advance its legal agenda. Instead, it is to argue that the understanding and meaning of history at Nuremberg was shaped by the legal idiom through which Nazi atrocity was filtered and judged. If the legal basis of crimes against humanity had to be located in the practices of civilized nations, then it should come as no surprise that Nazi crime was comprehended and represented in terms of the "primitive barbarity of ancient Germany" (5:378).[32] Through the sober ministrations of the law, civilization could, then, recover from the worst "hiccups of barbarism."

Beyond 6(c): The Father Pointed to the Sky

Central aspects of the Nuremberg case—the charter's restricted view of 6(c), the attempt to use the conspiracy charge to reach prewar atrocities, and the prosecution's own uncertain parsing of the meaning and normative foundation of the concept of crimes against humanity—all compromised the trial's effort to do justice to the history of the Holocaust. At times, the legal lens through which evidence of atrocity was filtered resulted in substantial distortions of the historical record. More often, the legal structure fashioned at Nuremberg failed in a more complex fashion to represent and make sense of traumatic history. Ironically, these pedagogic shortcomings, as I have suggested, can be seen as a formal legal success, for Nuremberg recuperated the power of law to submit even the most radical crimes to neutral judgment.

Here the discussion could end were it not for the interesting fact that one can detect hints of an awareness within the prosecution itself that the proceeding had failed adequately to represent the crimes of the Holocaust. After all the missteps committed by the French team, the French delivered an impressive summary argument that notably described Nazi extermination as "the unique fact of this trial" (19:563). Lead Prosecutor August Champetier de Ribes, who began the summation before succeeding to Dubost, revived the use of Lemkin's neologism to describe Nazi extermination. At trial, the Americans had eschewed use of the term "genocide" (which, as noted, appeared in the indictment under war crimes), concerned as they were that any vocabulary that suggested the unprecedented would complicate issues of legal judgment. At the beginning of his summation, however, Champetier de Ribes forcefully conjured the specter of the unprecedented: "The scientific and systematic extermination of millions of human beings . . . is a crime so monstrous, so undreamed of in history throughout the Christian era up to the birth of Hitlerism, that the term 'genocide' has had to be coined to define it and an accumulation of documents and testimonies has been needed to make it credible" (19:531).[33]

Prosecutor Dubost echoed this position when he acknowledged the limits of applying the domestic analogy of murder to explain the Nazis' crimes: "To apply the same standard to them [the defendants] as that applied to hooligans or to murderers, would narrow the scope of the Trial and misrepresent the character of their crimes" (19:548). In making this argument, Dubost remarkably offered a critique of his own chief prosecutor, for it was Menthon who had described crimes against humanity as "common law crimes," indistinguishable, as a legal matter, from theft, looting, murder, and so on (5:372). If appropriate as a matter of law the domestic analogy, Dubost insisted, distorted the distinctive meaning of Nazi atrocity: "The crimes ordinarily tried by the courts of our countries show the criminal as opposed to the social order. These are individual deeds. Their range is limited and the consequences circumscribed. Their crimes never strike more than a very few victims, and there are no examples in the annals of our countries of murder methodically perpetrated by terror organizations whose victims number more than a few hundred people" (5:548). Nazi atrocity, by contrast, was a "State-Committed Crime" (5:564): "Genocide, murder, or any other crime becomes anonymous when it is committed by the State. Nobody bears the responsibility. Everybody shares it — those who by their presence maintain and support the administration, those who conceived the crime and those who ordained it, as well as he who issued the order. As for the executioner, he says to himself, 'Befehl ist Befehl.' 'An order is an order,' and carries out his hangman's task" (5:564).

Here Dubost presented an entirely different conception of crimes against humanity than that defended by Jackson and the tribunal. Sharply dissenting from the crabbed vision that located the international character of crimes against humanity in their connection to aggressive warfare, Dubost pinpointed the international element of these crimes in their connection to the actions of a state. Indeed, in Dubost's understanding, crimes against humanity *are* state-sponsored crimes: the connection to state practices constitutes an irreducible feature of such offenses.[34] If recent events in countries like Rwanda alert one to the perils of exclusively associating genocide with state practices, such an insight should not lead us to overlook the importance of Dubost's argument. For, remarkably, Dubost underscored the hollowness — incoherence even — of the restricted parsing of 6(c) that controlled Nuremberg. By restricting the reach of 6(c), the Nuremberg parties sought to remain mindful of classical principles of sovereignty. If, however, an irreducible feature of the Nazis' crimes against humanity was the connection to state practices, then it seems absurd to insulate such practices from legal scrutiny out of misplaced respect for sovereignty. Implicit, then, in Dubost's position is the suggestion that a respect for classical principles of legality led to a failure to shape an adequate answer to crimes that radically rejected assimilation into models based upon past practice.

This same spirit of doubt about the representational adequacy of the prosecution's case found expression in the closing argument of another leading protagonist for the prosecution. Hartley Shawcross, the British chief prosecutor, had delivered his concluding argument a couple of days before the French (fig. 3.6). Unlike the French, whose early disagreements with aspects of the case (such as the conspiracy charge) found voice in their summation, Shawcross remained faithful to Jackson's vision of the case to the end. He bravely soldiered on in the insistence that prewar crimes against the Jews and those committed against German Jews were justiciable

Fig. 3.6. "And the father pointed to the sky": Sir Hartley Shawcross, attorney general of Great Britain and lead prosecutor, during his summary argument before the IMT. Courtesy of USHMM.

only "because of [their] close association with crimes against the peace" (19:471).

Still, Shawcross's summation expressed a very different spirit from that of his opening statement. In his first address to the tribunal, Shawcross was called upon to introduce the British case dealing with crimes against the peace. Consequently, he tailored his words to deal with the evidence to be presented under this count. In his summation, Shawcross was free to roam more broadly, and he used this freedom to focus on crimes against humanity — specifically, the crimes of the final solution: "Both imagination and intellect, shattered by the horror of these things, recoil from putting the greatest crime in history into the cold formula described in the textbooks as a war crime. Yet it is important to remember that that is what these crimes were" (5:468).[35] As the dutiful jurist Shawcross linked crimes against humanity with war crimes, although he recognized the deeper misrepresentation contained within this conflation. In devoting his summation to the crimes of the Holocaust, Shawcross did not offer a more precise or complete factual account than that already given at the trial; neither did he abandon the prosecutorial design for rendering these crimes justiciable. Yet by focusing his speech upon the crimes of the Holocaust, he gave them an emotional weight missing in much of the rest of the prosecution's case. Taken together with the summary argument of the French, Shawcross's speech began to transform the Nuremberg trial, albeit tardily and incompletely, into a proceeding about the crimes against the Jews. It was as if the prosecution itself had finally absorbed the significance of its own terrible evidence and, in so doing, had come to recognize the insufficiencies of the legal case meant to contain it.

Indeed, not only did Shawcross place the crimes of the final solution at the rhetorical center of his speech, he also personalized the catastrophe. He ended his speech simply, by reading a lengthy excerpt from the affidavit of Hermann Gräbe. A German engineer heading a construction firm working in the Ukraine, Gräbe had been an eyewitness to *Aktionen* against the Jewish population. His affidavit was not unfamiliar to the court: early in the trial, the American prosecutor Robert Storey had read from Gräbe's description of killings in the Rovno ghetto (4:253). Shawcross, however, read from a part of the affidavit that described a mass execution that Gräbe had witnessed in Dubno. And whereas Storey had read material that illustrated the brutal technique of the perpetrators, Shawcross brought before the court the Jewish victims in their final moments of life:

> Without screaming or weeping these people undressed, stood around in family groups, kissed each other, said farewells, and waited for a sign from another ss man, who stood near the pit, also with a whip in hand. During the 15 minutes that I stood near I heard no complaint or plea for mercy. I watched a family of about eight persons. . . . An old woman with snow-white hair was holding the one-year-old child in her arms and singing to it and tickling it. The child was cooing with delight. The couple were looking on with tears in their eyes. The father was holding the hand of a boy about 10 years old and speaking to him softly; the boy was fighting his tears. The father pointed to the sky, stroked his head, and seemed to explain something to him. At that moment the ss man shouted something to his colleague. The latter counted off about 20 persons and instructed them to go behind the earth mound. Among them was the family I have mentioned. [19:508]

Despite the shattering power of the story, one could perhaps claim that by quoting it, Shawcross merely recapitulated the doubtful effort to reduce the

Holocaust to the model of municipal crime: extermination is telescoped into the cold-blooded killing of a single family. Such a reading, however, overlooks the nuance of Shawcross's appeal. For in asking the court to see the Holocaust through the figure of the father pointing to the sky, Shawcross did not conventionalize atrocity. Instead, he invited the court to see the victims in a manner almost entirely overlooked by the prosecution — as people.

Granted, Shawcross's story leaves one twice removed. It is the document, not the witness, that is present before the court; and the experience of the Jewish victims is related as seen through the eyes of the German bystander. Through these eyes, the victims appear dignified, though the absence of complaints and pleas for mercy would raise, for some, difficult questions concerning the behavior of the Jews in the face of their destruction, questions that played an important role in the Eichmann trial (see part 2). In the Nuremberg trial, these questions remained untouched by the tribunal — not simply because of their legal irrelevance, but because the Jews remained, on the whole, abstract victims. Even in Gräbe's statement, one cannot make out the words of the father to the boy. Though one can surmise their content, they remain unknown, unspoken before the court. Again, it will not be until the Eichmann trial that the victims will be permitted to be heard in court as fully embodied. Still, by quoting from the affidavit, Shawcross took an important step beyond the abstractions contained within Nuremberg's flawed conception of crimes against humanity. For the doomed family is not simply transformed into a symbol of martyred humanity. Instead, it is given a body and a voice, fears, and hopes. In this spirit Shawcross brings his summation to a close: "You will remember when you come to give your decision the story of Gräbe, but not in vengeance — in a determination that these things shall not occur again. 'The father' — do you remember? — 'pointed to the sky, and seemed to say something to his boy'" (19:529).

It is a remarkable ending. On one level the story of the boy and his father is linked to the imperative of rendering a just verdict. Yet by ending within a quotation, Shawcross permits the story to stand outside its legal frame. And though Shawcross presents the act of legal judgment as a potential safeguard against future atrocity, the thrust of his conclusion asks us to look not forward but back. The final imperative that Shawcross places before the court is the duty to remember.

Part Two
. . .
Eichmann

4

· · ·

Ada Lichtmann on the Stand

Q: Then you were put to death?
A: Yes.
—Attorney General of Israel Gideon Hausner, in
his examination of Chelmno survivor Mordechai
Zurawski, *The Trial of Adolf Eichmann*

"Brands Plucked from the Fire"

Nazi Concentration Camps, the Signal Corps documentary shown to dramatic effect at Nuremberg, was next screened in a trial of international significance on June 8, 1961. The place was the district court of Jerusalem; the trial was *Criminal Case 41/60: Attorney General v. Adolf Eichmann.*[1] It was to be the first and, in certain respects, only trial of international significance that explicitly focused on the crimes of the Holocaust. The importance of the trial in this regard was not lost upon the principal participants in the proceedings. In his opening address for the prosecution, the Israeli attorney general Gideon Hausner, declared, "The calamity of the Jewish People in this generation was the subject of consideration at a number of the trials conducted in the wake of Germany's defeat in World War II, . . . [b]ut in none of those trials was the tragedy of the Jewry as a whole the central concern."[2] The court echoed Hausner's words in the beginning of its judgment delivered nearly half a year later: "This is not the first time that the Holocaust has been discussed in court proceedings. It was dealt with extensively at the International Military Tribunal at Nuremberg during the trial of the Major War Criminals, and also at several of the trials that followed; but this time it has occupied the central place in the Court proceedings, and it is this fact which has distinguished this trial from those which preceded it" (*TAE* 5:2082). For the first time the Nazis' most spectacular crime occupied the direct attention of a court action of international significance. Indeed, this was inescapable, given the identity of the defendant who sat in the bulletproof glass booth in the Jerusalem courtroom. For, in Hausner's somewhat hyperbolic formulation, "there was only one man who had been concerned almost entirely with the Jews, whose business had been their destruction, whose place in the establishment of the iniquitous regime had been limited to them. That was Adolf Eichmann" (1:63).

An *Obersturmbannführer* (lieutenant-colonel) in the Gestapo from 1939 to 1945, Eichmann had served as the agency's leading expert on Jewish affairs and from 1942 to 1945 had directed section IV-B-4 of the RSHA, specifically responsible for "Evacuations and Jews."[3] Though not formally indicted at Nuremberg, Eichmann was, as noted earlier, frequently mentioned during the trial, most damagingly during the testimony of former SS *Hauptsturmführer* Dieter Wisliceny, who testified that Eichmann had organized "the planned extermination and destruction of the Jewish race" (*IMT* 4:356–57). Rudolf Höß, former commandant at Auschwitz, had further testified that all orders involving "mass executions through gassing" came "directly from Himmler through Eichmann" (*IMT* 11:420). Eichmann's special function within the machinery of the final solution was thus well established in the years after the war, and Israeli Prime Minister David Ben-Gurion's laconic announcement to the gathered parliamentarians of the Knesset on May 23, 1960, that Eichmann had been seized from his hiding in Buenos Aires and brought to Israel to stand trial had, predictably enough, caused a sensation. Befitting the drama, the district court had to convene in the Beit Ha'am (house of the people), a four-story community center and theater whose large municipal auditorium was hastily remodeled to serve as a courtroom that could accommodate seven hundred and fifty spectators (including four hundred members of the press) (figs. 4.1, 4.2).[4]

It was in this courtroom that *Nazi Concentration Camps* was screened (fig. 4.3). For security reasons, the courtroom had been cleared of the pub-

Fig. 4.1. "The trial is preeminently a theatrical form" (Sontag, *On Photography,*
118). The remodeling of Beit Ha'am, the municipal theater, to serve as the
courtroom. Courtesy of Yad Vashem.

lic, though official observers and members of the press were permitted to
remain.[5] As noted in part 1, in the fifteen years since its first screening in
a trial setting, the meaning of *Nazi Concentration Camps* had radically
changed. No longer a document about the Nazis' war crimes committed
against prisoners of war and civilians alike, the documentary now was seen
to provide visual proof of the crimes of the Holocaust. This transformation in the meaning of the visual evidence was underscored and also, in
part, affected by the fact that only excerpts of *Nazi Concentration Camps*
were screened at the Eichmann trial, spliced with other documentary
footage shown at Nuremberg (including the Soviet film, *The Atrocities
by the German Fascist Invaders in the USSR*). This assemblage of film was
shown without a soundtrack. As I have observed, it was the soundtrack, putatively a mere supplement to the film's visual register, that ultimately came
to exert control over the images of *Nazi Concentration Camps,* harmonizing
the documentary evidence with the prosecution's legal case before the IMT.

At the Eichmann trial, Attorney General Hausner took the place of the
soundtrack. His narration was laconic: "General Eisenhower visiting the

Fig. 4.2. The court in session: "The lights, so to speak, were not yet dimmed in
the auditorium. and the hall still hummed with the muffled whispering of an
expectant public" (Pearlman, *The Capture and Trial of Adolf Eichmann*, 97). The
spectators on the left are members of the press. Toward the center rear stands the
defendant in his glass booth. Seated obliquely in front of him are the members
of the defense and members of the prosecution. Above and to the right sit the
three members of the court. Courtesy of the Israeli Government Press Office.

camps, the surviving remnants of all kinds" (*TAE* 3:1285). But the shift of
meanings was unmistakable. The emaciated prisoners of war and "political
and religious enemies" of the regime encountered at the Nuremberg
screening had become, in Hausner's telling, "figures of *Muselmänner*" —
that is, the death camp inmates destined for the gas chamber because of
their broken physical and psychological state (3:1285).

Just as the meaning of *Nazi Concentration Camps* changed from Nuremberg to Jerusalem, so too did the role that the documentary played at the respective trials. At Nuremberg, *Nazi Concentration Camps* played a vital role
in the prosecution's argument — not as a piece of probative evidence, but as
a didactic vehicle. Shown early in the trial, the film was meant to jump-start
the proceedings by providing an unforgettable visual backdrop against
which the actions of the defendants in the dock could be framed.

By contrast, the excerpted and spliced version of *Nazi Concentration*

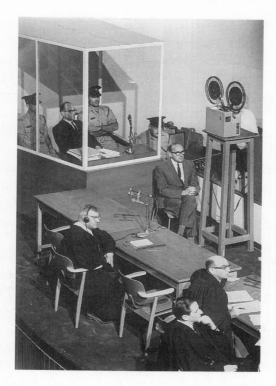

Fig. 4.3. The screening of *Nazi Concentration Camps* on June 8, 1961. "Eichmann never took his eyes from the film, never raised his hands to his face. The man who said he could not bear the sight of blood . . . was the very model of composure" (*New York Times,* June 9, 1961, 16). Seated to the left at the long table and wearing earphones is Robert Servatius, defense counsel. To the right, half-risen from his chair, is Attorney General Gideon Hausner.
Courtesy of the Israeli Government Press Office.

Camps was not shown until the seventieth session of the Eichmann trial, shortly before the Jerusalem proceeding entered its third month. Although the screening succeeded in disturbing the courtroom — Prosecutor Hausner expressed "regret that it was necessary to subject the Court to such a harrowing experience" (3:1285) — it did not rhetorically galvanize and frame the prosecution's case as it had at Nuremberg.

To find a moment of equivalent dramatic force, one must turn to an earlier point in the Eichmann trial, the morning of April 28, 1961, some ten days after Attorney General Hausner had begun his opening statement with the words, "When I stand before you here, Judges of Israel, to lead the prosecution of Adolf Eichmann, I am not standing alone. With me are six million accusers. But they cannot rise to their feet and point an accusing finger towards him who sits in the dock and cry: 'I accuse.' For their ashes are piled up on the hills of Auschwitz and the fields of Treblinka, and are strewn in the forests of Poland. The graves are scattered throughout the length and breadth of Europe. Their blood cries out, but their voice is not heard" (1:63). On the morning of the twentieth-eighth, then, the court heard the first murmurs of the voiceless dead. For on this day the prosecution called to the stand the first survivor witness, Ada Lichtmann, a woman of fifty originally from the Polish town of Wieliczka near Cracow, who offered testimony on the "small-scale terror in the occupied areas in Poland" (1:323).

Lichtmann's testimony was, in itself, unastonishing, especially when compared to some of the material recounted by the more than one hundred survivors who would take the stand in the weeks following her brief appearance before the court.[6] Moreover, her testimony took place in a largely empty courtroom, as the day had begun with a presentation of documentary evidence that, in the understated words of one reporter, "had failed to hold the public's interest."[7] Yet from the moment Lichtmann took her oath, the Eichmann trial assumed a radically different tenor. Until then, the proceeding, notwithstanding Hausner's stirring (and, as we shall see, controversial) opening address, had been bogged down, first with procedural motions brought by the defense and later by the tedious process of listening to lengthy excerpts of a recording of the accused's interrogation by members of a special bureau of the Israeli police. Legally relevant as these statements might have been, the disembodied words of the accused issuing from a tape recorder on the prosecution's table rendered the defendant and his crimes spectral.

Like its predecessors at Nuremberg, the Eichmann prosecution found itself, in the early going, struggling to reconcile the need to present a legally cogent case with the need to dramatize the spectacular nature of the crimes to be adjudged. Lichtmann's appearance on the stand promptly erased whatever distance might have separated the Israeli court from the history of the final solution. The first effect was linguistic as the official language of the trial was dropped in an effort to accommodate the witness:

PRESIDING JUDGE [*to witness*]: Do you speak Hebrew?

WITNESS LICHTMANN: Not too well, perhaps Yiddish would be better. . . .

ATTORNEY GENERAL: Does the Court wish me to put the questions in Yiddish?. . . .

PRESIDING JUDGE: Perhaps it should be right indeed to ask in Yiddish, for her to understand directly.

ATTORNEY GENERAL [*continues the examination of the witness in Yiddish*]: Where were you when the Second World War broke out? [*TAE* 1:323–24]

Suddenly, the language of the exterminated Jewish population of Europe filled the courtroom. As one observer commented, "You shivered on hearing the words of the language of the slaughtered and the burned."[8]

The acoustical impact of Lichtmann's testimony deserves particular attention, as the Eichmann trial was the first in Israeli history to be broadcast live on radio. In the words of another observer, "Everywhere people listened — in houses and offices, in cafés and stores and buses and factories. The stories of terror mixed in with the sounds of routine."[9] Speaking, then, in Yiddish, Lichtmann transported the court back to the first *Aktionen* that heralded the beginning of the final solution:

Q. Can you remember what they did there to religious Jews?
A. I was living in a house and in front of our window there was a hill. On that hill they drove together some twenty religious Jews, clad in the clothes of the religious, long caftans, with prayer shawls and prayer books in their hands. They ordered all of them to sing religious songs and to pray, to raise their hands to God, and then some German officers came up and poured kerosene or petroleum over them and set them on fire with prayer shawls, everything.
Q. This you saw yourself?
A. Myself, because this was before our window. We, the others, weren't allowed to leave our houses. We sat in our house and I saw everything. [*TAE* 1:326]

Though the court would hear more harrowing stories in the ensuing weeks, many of these testimonies would share a distinguishing feature of Lichtmann's words. The survivor, in her telling, is imagined as "We, the others" — the ones who somehow failed to be included among the exterminated. The survivor, in this respect, occupies a liminal position between the living and the dead: a freak who somehow escaped his or her fate. Moreover, by emphasizing that she needed only to gaze out the window of her home to behold mass murder, her words typify a larger phenomenon in which unimaginable atrocities came first to intrude upon, then to define, quotidian existence.

Yet her words alone fail to convey the manner of their utterance. At the same time that one listens to her words, one must heed her demeanor. (The visual element is also noteworthy as the trial marked an unprecedented intrusion of television technology into a legal setting: Eichmann's was the first trial ever broadcast live in other countries, although the trial was not shown in Israel because the country's communications infrastructure did not, at the time, include television.)[10] Lichtmann remained standing during the course of her testimony (as would many of the witnesses), and her voice remained firm throughout. Though she struggled to control her emotions, she did not weep (as numerous witnesses would); she did not stammer or wander, yet during her entire time on the stand her eyes remained concealed behind dark sunglasses (fig. 4.4). She appeared, then, to be blind (though she was not), an impression made all the more striking as the dramatic force of her testimony found focus in the words, "I saw everything." Her physical presence in the courtroom suggested a latter-day Tiresias, or rather a witness who has been blinded by what she has seen. No longer capable of sight, all that she can see is the vision of atrocity that has been permanently burnt upon an inner retina. Her clarity of vision comes from the simple fact that she has been consumed by the trauma of what she has seen.

On the most general level, Lichtmann's testimony exemplified the larger representational logic of the prosecution's case, one that dramatically departed from the precedent established at Nuremberg. As we have seen, the didactic paradigm of the Nuremberg trial was the documentary — conceived either as filmic, material, or written artifact. By contrast, the representational paradigm at the Eichmann trial was testimonial. Just as Nuremberg was not entirely bereft of eyewitness testimony, the Eichmann trial did not eschew the use of documentary evidence; indeed, the prosecution relied upon a full range of proof that included film, photographs, drawings, dioramas, letters, and diaries as well as a rather massive number of official documents. But the representational logics of the two trials differed dramatically. Whereas the witnesses at Nuremberg played a largely supplemental role to the evidence supplied by document, the opposite was the case in Jerusalem: documents were used to establish a tight criminal case against the accused, but it was the words of the survivors that provided the

Fig. 4.4. Ada Lichtmann on the stand, April 28, 1961. "I saw everything." Courtesy of the Israeli Government Press Office.

dramatic focus of the trial and that built a bridge from the accused to the "world of ashes."

This was by design. In his personal history of the trial, *Justice in Jerusalem,* Hausner explicitly defended the prosecution's decision to give pride of place to the testimony of the survivor witness. Although Nuremberg's didactic approach—"a few witnesses and films of concentration camps horrors, interspersed with piles of documents"—was in Hausner's words "efficient and simple," the strategy "failed to reach the hearts of men."[11] Not only would survivor testimony penetrate the "citadel of boredom"[12] that came to describe long stretches of the Nuremberg trial, it would also make tangible the "incomprehensible statistics," thereby doing "justice to the six million personal tragedies."[13] The survivors would supply the absent voice of the exterminated; as Primo Levi explained in *The*

Drowned and the Saved, because the stories of the dead are lost, survivors "must speak in their stead, by proxy."[14]

In parsing his own prosecutorial strategy, Hausner made clear that the proof of Eichmann's guilt and the imposition of a legal sanction, while of obvious importance, were not the "exclusive objects" of the trial. Indeed, if securing a conviction had been the only goal, "it was obviously enough to let the archives speak; a fraction of them would have sufficed to get Eichmann sentenced ten times over." But commenting on his own understanding of the trial, Hausner observed, "I knew we needed more than a conviction; we needed a living record of a gigantic human and national disaster." Like Nuremberg, the Eichmann trial was conceived explicitly in terms of its pedagogic value, a function that Hausner understood in more evocative and normative terms: the trial should not simply clarify the historical record—it should teach history lessons. On one level, it should instruct a younger generation of Israelis, who "had no real knowledge, and therefore no appreciation, of the way in which their own flesh and blood had perished"; as a second matter, it should educate the world at large, "which had so lightly and happily forgotten the horrors that occurred before its eyes, to such a degree that it even begrudged us the trial of the perpetrator."[15] The trial would, he believed, supply evidence of the court's very right to conduct the proceedings.

Justice, then, could not be done simply by condemning the accused. Rather, Hausner treated the Nazis' central crime as both the act of physical annihilation and the more profound attempt to erase memory itself—both of the cultural life of a people and of the crimes of the final solution. The act of creating an opportunity for the public sharing of the narratives of the survivors, the proxies of the dead, was itself a way of doing justice. Hausner's reflections on the strategy of the prosecution thus reveal a remarkable reversal of legal priority: instead of the testimony serving as a means of proving the state's case, Hausner asks one to imagine the trial itself as a means of offering public testimonials. No doubt Hausner would vigorously resist the force of this observation, arguing that the individual testimonies served to clarify the nature and meaning of the defendant's actions. Still, the juridical value of the testimony can be understood as largely a byproduct of a process prompted by a radical theory of the trial. The trial was a vehicle of the stories of survivors.

In terms of the trial's effect upon its observers, the success of Hausner's approach receives provocative confirmation from the many contemporaneous accounts and histories of the trial. In the case of Nuremberg, I observed the strikingly similar manner in which journalists, memoirists, and historians described the screening of *Nazi Concentration Camps,* viewing the film through the reflection of atrocity in the eyes of the defendants. Descriptions of the Eichmann trial, by contrast, reconstruct the testimony of the eyewitnesses through its effect not upon the accused, but upon the spectators at the trial. Indeed, many of the famous images associated with the trial—in addition to the obligatory shots of Eichmann in the glass booth—are photographs of courtroom spectators.[16] Reproduced in leading books about the trial, including Moshe Pearlman's *The Capture and Trial of Adolf Eichmann,* Lord Russell of Liverpool's *The Trial of Adolf Eichmann,* Tom Segev's *The Seventh Million* as well as Hausner's memoir, these photographs show spectators overcome with emotion: sobbing in anguish, staring in wide-eyed horror, collapsing altogether (fig. 4.5). These spectators, however, were not, on the whole, Israeli or foreign citizens learning for the first time the facts of the Holocaust. This, again, marks a critical difference from the Nuremberg trial. Nuremberg was concerned with pro-

Fig. 4.5. Spectators at the trial. "This audience . . . was filled with 'survivors,' with middle-aged and elderly people, immigrants from Europe, like myself, who knew by heart all there was to know" (Arendt, *Eichmann in Jerusalem,* 6).
Courtesy of the Israeli Government Press Office.

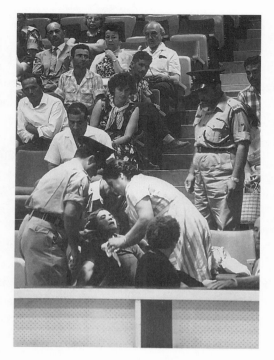

Fig. 4.5. (*continued*)

Fig. 4.5. (*continued*)

ducing knowledge of incredible crimes: the didactic paradigm was very much dictated by the need to offer undeniable evidence of crimes the very nature of which would invite popular skepticism.

The spectators at the Eichmann trial, on the other hand, were not shocked by the *fact* of the Holocaust. As Arendt observed in *Eichmann in Jerusalem,* "In this audience there were hardly any young people, and it did not consist of Israelis as distinguished from Jews. It was filled with 'survivors,' with middle-aged and elderly people, immigrants from Europe, like myself, who knew by heart all there was to know, and who were in no mood to learn any lessons and certainly did not need the trial to draw their own conclusions."[17] While Arendt's hard-boiled description can be faulted in two regards — first, she erroneously suggests that the testimony of the survivor witnesses was superfluous to the spectators; second, she ignores the fact that the trial had many spectators besides those crowding the courtroom — she alerts one to the critical fact that the value of such evidence could not be grasped simply in terms of the production of knowledge. Instead, the expressions of horror etched in the faces of spectators in photographs of the trial must be understood in terms of a more complex shock of recognition. In *The Seventh Million,* Segev understands the Eichmann trial principally as "national group therapy," a ritual of national catharsis in which a collective public space was made available in which to grieve for traumatic private memory.[18] Until the trial, Segev observes, the survivor experience was very much a suppressed fact of Israeli social and cultural life, one that conjured the despised history of the Jew as hapless victim and thus conflicted with the emerging national identity of the Israeli as a self-sufficient warrior. Survivors' memories, often enveloped in pain and shame, were secreted away, denied public or even private expression.

The faces of the spectators captured in the photographs of the trial express the horror and release one feels when one's deepest and most traumatic memories find public expression. A horrific and silenced past had intruded upon the present in the words and demeanor of the survivor witnesses. As Harry Mulisch observed, "As the witnesses spoke about events from their past, a past which will never become a 'past' but instead will always remain as close as the present day, if not closer, this 'present' became as real to those who listened."[19] Indeed, by privileging the testimony of the survivor, the Eichmann trial anticipated the documentary idiom of Claude Lanzmann's *Shoah,* arguably the finest film about the Holocaust, and one that notably abandons the representational logic of most documentaries by wholly eschewing the use of archival footage. By conjuring history through word and demeanor, *Shoah* stretched the available idiom of Holocaust representation in a manner pioneered at the Eichmann trial.[20]

If survivor testimony played a crucial role in a larger Israeli ritual of collective catharsis, how does one make sense of the juridical use of the survivor testimony? What role did it play in the determination of the legal guilt of the accused? Here one cannot escape critics of Hausner who questioned the ultimate relevance of much of the testimony of the survivor witnesses. Arendt, who, as we shall see, found little in the trial *not* to criticize, reserved special contempt for Hausner's use of these testimonies. Not only did Hausner present witnesses whose testimony upset the prosecution's "futile attempt" to proceed chronologically, he "went as far afield as to put witness after witness on the stand who testified to things that, while gruesome and true enough, had no or only the slightest connection with the deeds of the accused." Dismissively, Arendt accused the prosecution of creating a new legal entitlement: "The right of the witnesses to be irrelevant." Again one is reminded of Arendt's insistence that "the purpose of a trial is to render justice, and nothing else; even the noblest of ulterior purposes . . . can only detract from the law's main business: to weigh the charges brought against the accused, to render judgment, and to mete out due punishment."[21]

Here, however, it is necessary to examine Arendt's claim. Must one agree that the sole purpose of a trial should be to render justice narrowly conceived? As I stated in the introduction, although no one would deny that the rendering of justice is a necessary feature of the criminal process, the exclusivity of Arendt's formulation seems vulnerable to challenge. As one commentator on the Eichmann trial observed, "To criticize the holding of the Trial on the ground of these metalegal objects [that is, the pedagogic aims] is to suggest that the sole legitimate object of a criminal trial is the administration of criminal justice."[22] This, of course, is exactly what Arendt claims, though her argument is less one about legal form per se than about the invariable consequences that follow from introducing "even the noblest of ulterior purposes." Against those who would argue that the "wider purposes of the Eichmann Trial cannot as such constitute an abuse of legal form,"[23] Arendt insists that the introduction of these "wider purposes" will always, in effect, "detract from the law's main business."

If this claim is correct, Arendt's larger argument seems strong, as even the most passionate defenders of the trial would agree that the failure to determine the guilt of the accused through the use of legally probative evidence would constitute a serious violation of fundamental tenets of criminal justice. Indeed, it was the alleged failure of the prosecution scrupulously to respect these tenets that led Arendt to describe the Eichmann proceedings precisely as a "show trial" produced and choreographed by the "invisible stage manager of the proceedings," Prime Minister Ben-Gurion.[24] In calling the proceeding a show trial, Arendt was, as we have seen, stating the obvious, as Hausner himself explicitly framed the trial as a didactic exercise. Of course, by describing the trial in these terms, Arendt was aiming not to describe but to vilify. Yet even if one rejects, as I believe one must, Arendt's tendentious use of the term "show trial,"[25] one can still agree that there is a critical difference between condemning a man known to have facilitated a program of genocide and determining his guilt according to the dictates of the law. The former gesture truly must be considered extralegal, as it harks back to the British plan entertained toward the end of the Second World War of summarily executing leading Nazi functionaries without the pretense of fulfilling the requirements of legality. The latter gesture, of course, is the spirit of Nuremberg—the attempt to submit even the most extreme state-sponsored outrages to the sober logic of legal judgment. Once one has decided on the latter course, one must satisfy law's stern requirements. To permit even the most spectacular crimes to destroy legal form is to turn, *pace* Arendt, a trial into a grotesque show lacking the element of "irreducible risk" (that is, the specter of acquittal) that Otto Kirchheimer identified as an indispensable factor in all criminal proceedings.[26]

Arendt's jurisprudential claim presupposes, however, a particular theory of the law in general and of the trial as a specific legal form. This view is quintessentially formalist in nature. To borrow Hermann Kantorowicz's influential definition, this theory comprehends law, in its most general sense, as a "system of rules."[27] Perhaps an even more influential variation on this definition was supplied by H. L. A. Hart, who defined law not simply as rules, but as rules about rules;[28] and variations of this rules-based theory have long enjoyed a prominent position within liberal jurisprudence. Building on this tradition, Judith Shklar has described the "attitude that holds moral conduct to be a matter of rule following" as "legalism," a term meant to embrace a broad ideology of proceduralism. In Shklar's lexicon, "legalism" and "legalistic" are not meant pejoratively to conjure an arid ideology of formalism; rather, the terms are intended to designate a body of jurisprudential thought that has gained "complete expression . . . in the great legal systems of the European world." This rules-based vision of the law finds its purest expression, Shklar argues, in the criminal trial; indeed, it is the principle of legality in criminal law that she describes as legalism's "greatest contribution to a decent political order."[29] Arendt's vision of the trial clearly, then, is thoroughly legalistic in Shklar's sense: a proceeding whose only function is rendering justice — where justice is defined as the scrupulous observance of the rules that define legal form. It is this rules-based vision of the law that leads Arendt to dismiss as illegitimate and improper the attempt to use a trial for what she considers extralegal ends, even the "supposed higher aims of the Nuremberg Trials" — "the making of a record of the Hitler regime which would withstand the test of history."[30]

Though immensely influential, the rules-based theory of law has been widely challenged in terms of both its descriptive and normative adequacy. Decades ago, the legal realists argued that rules fail meaningfully to constrain and guide judges in the actual business of deciding cases, while more recently scholars associated with critical legal studies have argued that the dream of an entirely formal jurisprudence is at best delusory and at worst pernicious: an activity that directs attention away from a candid discussion of the values upon which a democratic polity should be predicated. More recently still, the rules-based theory of law has been challenged by a strand of legal theory often referred to as narrative jurisprudence.

Admittedly, many theorists of the rules-based vision of legality acknowledge law's power to generate and suppress narratives, and theorists of narrative jurisprudence do not necessarily dispute the centrality of rules to a definition of legality.[31] Still, for rules-based formalism, questions of narrative are extralegal, while narrative jurisprudence, by insisting that rules fail to exhaust the universe of what counts as law, insists on a more capacious understanding of the legal. Finding its most sophisticated elaboration in the writings of thinkers as diverse as Robert Cover and James Boyd White, this approach understands law as a vital cultural discourse through which social narratives are structured and suppressed and through which normative meaning is defined and contested. Not surprisingly, narrative jurisprudence has treated as its principal object of study the criminal trial, for in the words of one observer, "Of all of law's narrative arenas, the criminal prosecution most fully engages the public's narrative desires and the scholar's narrative speculations."[32] The trial, from this perspective, must be seen not simply as a procedural device whose legitimacy is governed by rules generated within the system of legality itself, but as a complex ritual which produces and suppresses narrative and clarifies and obscures history.[33]

Notwithstanding the legitimate reservations that some have expressed about the overuse and undertheorization of the term "narrative" in legal circles,[34] the ideas entertained under the rubric "narrative jurisprudence" are of critical importance to the present discussion inasmuch as they consider the meaning of survivor testimony from a very different perspective than that framed by rules-based formalism. The rules-based approach leads to an echo of Arendt when she asks what role survivor testimony played in clarifying the guilt of the accused. Against this familiar, though crucial, question, narrative jurisprudence supports a radically divergent line of inquiry: did the trial do justice to the testimony of the survivors? If the latter question does not sound like a legal question per se, it is the type of question that legal scholarship has begun increasingly directing toward trials, as, for example, scholars have weighed the appropriateness of permitting victim impact statements in the penalty phase of capital cases[35] and the efficacy of trying the former leaders of regimes accused of human rights abuses.[36] More critically from this book's perspective, it is a question that resonates with my deeper interest in asking not merely whether the law has succeeded in doing formal justice to the perpetrators of the Holocaust, but whether the law has succeeded in doing representational justice to the Holocaust qua event.

The questions raised by rules-based jurisprudence on the one hand and by narrative jurisprudence on the other cannot, however, be examined in isolation. To listen to the words of the survivor witnesses at the Eichmann trial and to consider how they were used and understood in court is to see how the clash between a rules-based vision of the law and a narrative-based notion — a clash I have located in the content of theory — was played out in the trial in a complex struggle between the court and the prosecution. Thus to ask whether the trial did justice to the words of the survivors is to embark on a study of how the trial enacted a drama between competing visions of the law itself.

The Court on Trial

Any act of judging, I would argue, implicitly involves a gesture of self-legitimation: at the same moment that judges sit in judgment on a person or a case, they, by the nature of their institutional role, will be called upon to engage in a performance that justifies their right to perform the judicial function.[37] In the overwhelming number of cases, these gestures proceed unself-consciously and take the form of simply following the forms and procedures required by ordered legality. In certain juridical institutions, however, particularly those occupying an anomalous position within a larger architecture of rules-based governance, the question of legitimation receives more explicit treatment. Here the U.S. Supreme Court is an excellent example. Occupying, to use Alexander Bickel's famous formulation, a "counter-majoritarian" position in a structure of government predicated on principles of majoritarianism, the Court's claim to offer authoritative and final readings of constitutional text has been subject to challenge.[38] As a consequence, the problematic of self-justification has been of central importance to the performance of the Court's judicial function. Many of the decisions handed down by the Supreme Court can be read as dual performances, pronouncing judgment in the case at hand while simultaneously attempting to justify the authority of the Court to do so. These gestures of self-legitimation, moreover, cannot be dismissed as mere rhetorical persiflage meant to anchor the Court's claims to authority. Rather, these complex gestures of self-justification and legitimation materially affect the content of the decisions rendered and, in so doing, shape the contours of constitutional doctrine.

In the case of spectacular and anomalous trials like Nuremberg and Eichmann, the problem of legitimation looms even larger. In both cases, it can be said that law itself stood in the dock. Justice Jackson, whose understanding of the judicial function was shaped by his tenure on the Supreme Court, reminded the tribunal that not only were the twenty-two defendants on trial, but so too was the very concept of ordered legality. The tribunal shared Jackson's concerns, and its attempt to secure its own claims to legitimacy affected the form and substance of its judgment. Indeed, as I argued in part I, the IMT's preoccupation with the charge of waging aggressive war, though controversial, can nevertheless be understood as its attempt to legitimate its authority by preserving the basic idiom of international law.

The issue of self-legitimation similarly preoccupied the Eichmann court. To borrow Arendt's vivid formulation, "The irregularities and abnormalities of the trial in Jerusalem were so many, so varied, and of such legal complexity that they overshadowed the central moral, political and even legal problems that the trial inevitably posed."[39] Many commentators have offered assessments of the seriousness of these central problems, and my goal is not to repeat or improve upon the work of these scholars.[40] For my purposes it suffices to note that the court itself acted in awareness of the trial's many abnormalities and attempted to preserve its claim to legitimate authority in face of them. I am less concerned, then, with rebutting or proving the specific charges leveled against the court than with examining how the court tried to legitimate the proceeding in light of its perception of the trial's unorthodoxy.

The first "abnormalities" that the court had to address were those immediately raised by the defense. On the very first day of the trial, April 11, 1961, the court — a specially convened three-judge panel that consisted of Presiding Judge Moshe Landau and Judges Benjamin Halevi and Yitzchak Raveh (fig. 4.6)[41] — had no sooner finished reading the fifteen-count indictment against Eichmann than the defense counsel, Robert Servatius, rose to challenge the proceeding.[42] A Cologne attorney, Servatius had defended Fritz Sauckel, the Reich plenipotentiary for labor, and the leadership corps of the Nazi party before the IMT. Now as Eichmann's counsel, Servatius declared,

Fig. 4.6. The tribunal. *From left to right:* Benjamin Halevi, Presiding Judge
Moshe Landau, and Yitzchak Raveh. Courtesy of the
Israeli Government Press Office.

Fig. 4.7. Defense Counsel Robert Servatius (standing with headphones),
Attorney General Gideon Hausner (to Servatius's right, standing), and
Eichmann (seated, in glass booth). Courtesy of the Israeli
Government Press Office.

"I request the permission of the Court to allow me to express an objection,
before the Accused answers the question whether he admits guilt or not"
(*TAE* 1:8). Even before Eichmann could rise to respond to the charges, Servatius managed to launch a barrage of objections to the trial (fig. 4.7). He
began by questioning the impartiality of the court. He did not challenge
the objectivity of any one member of the panel; rather, he claimed that because "the entire Jewish people were drawn into the holocaust of extermination," the specter of judicial prejudice would arise "from the very material of the proceedings" (1:8). Insofar as the state had "a political interest"
in the outcome, Servatius questioned the judges' capacity to "raise
themselves, without being influenced, above the material of the trial"(1:8).
Prime Minister Ben-Gurion had described Eichmann in the days before the
beginning of the trial as "the man who killed 6,000,000 Jews," and Moshe
Sneh, a member of the Knesset, had argued that the trial of Eichmann "is
not necessary for the defendant, whose name we need not soil our mouths
pronouncing too often."[43] Against these formidable political pressures,
Servatius questioned the capacity of the court to conduct a fair trial.

Servatius raised a second set of concerns that more fundamentally challenged the competence of the court. Because "the Accused was seized forcibly and kidnapped and brought before the Court" (1:8), the court could not claim legitimate jurisdiction over a defendant delivered to it through an illegal act. As a second matter, the Israeli statute under which Eichmann was charged, the so-called Nazis and Nazi Collaborators (Punishment) Law (5170/1950) was defective both because it was "enacted ex post facto" and because it contravened international law by distorting the territorial principle of jurisdiction (1:9). Indeed, the criminal acts enumerated in the prosecution's indictment had been committed neither on Israeli soil nor extraterritorially against Israeli citizens — at the time of the commission of the acts, the state of Israel did not even exist.

The Nazi and Nazi Collaborators (Punishment) Law was, admittedly, an odd legislative creation. Passed in 1950, two years after Israel's declaration of statehood, the law was never conceived as a tool to be used against leading Nazi fugitives. It was unlikely, most Israeli legislators agreed, that ex-Nazis would choose to seek anonymous refuge in Tel Aviv over, say, Buenos Aires. In an address before the Knesset, Minister of Justice Pinhas Rosen had urged passage of the bill not because it furnished needed legal ammunition for an anticipated courtroom battle against former Nazis; rather, he spoke in terms of the ritualistic discharging of a solemn obligation. "By enacting these laws we are fulfilling a duty, an elementary and natural duty, for it would be impossible for a legislative body, speaking the language of the rule of law, to pass over these crimes in silence" (quoted by Hausner in 1:31).

Insofar as the law intended to do anything besides serve as a legal marker, a statutory monument to the law's own violated sensibilities and impotence, it was meant principally to create a cause of action against Jews who were discovered to have collaborated with the Nazis. With the exceptions of the Eichmann and Demjanjuk trials, all of the twenty-five or so cases tried under the 1950 law have involved charges brought against Jewish collaborators, principally kapos — concentration camp inmates whom Nazi guards had assigned various supervisory and disciplinary tasks.[44] Some of these trials resulted in acquittals, and verdicts of guilt tended to issue in sentences whose severity was lessened on appeal (usually to two or three years of prison). Underscoring the political sensitivity of the issue, the Supreme Court commuted the punishment of the only Jewish defendant sentenced to death under the statute to ten years' imprisonment.[45]

Not only was the statute never envisioned as applying to a figure such as Eichmann, but its content was also deeply anomalous. While borrowing from both the Nuremberg conception of crimes against humanity and the definition of genocide used in the International Convention on the Prevention and Punishment of the Crime of Genocide of 1948,[46] the Israeli statute differed from these authorities in significant respects. On the one hand, the Israeli statute importantly eliminated the restrictions placed on crimes against humanity by the Nuremberg charter, making crimes committed between the years 1933–39 justiciable. On the other hand, the Israeli law created a more restrictive category of offense, crimes against the Jewish people.[47] Such a restriction was meant to offer legal cognizance of the fact that Nazi crimes had been directed not against humanity in general, but against the Jewish people in particular. And while the law also proscribed crimes against humanity, the spirit of the statute reversed the conventional understanding of these categories: crimes against the Jewish people were not to be considered a mere subset of crimes against humanity; rather, Judeocide defined an independent offense that marked the furthest and most horrific extremes of crimes against humanity. In the Eichmann trial, the fifteen-count indictment included crimes against humanity perpetrated against gypsies and Poles, but the gravamen of the charge remained the first four counts, all of which concerned crimes against the Jewish people. Most notable here was the first count, which charged the accused with causing "the deaths of millions of Jews" by implementing "the plan of the Nazis for the physical extermination of the Jews, a plan known by its title, 'The Final Solution of the Jewish Question'" (*TAE* 1:3).

In creating this anomalous cause of action, crimes against the Jewish people, the statute also raised ex post facto problems. Indeed, at the time the Nazi and Nazi Collaborators bill was submitted to the Knesset in 1950, Minister of Justice Rosen specifically distinguished it from another bill before the Knesset, one that dealt with genocide, by appealing to the concept of temporal efficacy: "That law [that is, for the prevention and punishment of genocide] applies to the future. . . . On the other hand, the law which is now being proposed applies to the past, to a certain period in history, which began with the rise to power of Hitler and ended with his destruction" (1:31).[48] For Servatius, however, it was the very specificity of the charging statute, its creation of a special offense for crimes against Jews, that signaled its defect. The Israeli state, he argued, lacked authority to speak on behalf of European Jews or, for that matter, of a people spread over the face of the globe.[49] By creating a special category of crimes against the Jewish people, he contended, the law attempted to confer upon Israeli courts a power that it was not authorized to grant. Therefore, Servatius concluded, no available principle of jurisdiction could confer competence upon the Israeli court.

Servatius's arguments echoed those of other legal authorities; indeed, in his reflections on the trial, Hausner ironically observed that never before had matters of jurisdiction, one of the more technical areas of the law, been so passionately examined and so vociferously debated in the world press than in the months before the start of the Eichmann trial. Telford Taylor expressed vocal concerns about the impartiality of the proceedings, arguing that a trial before an international tribunal would have avoided the suggestion of partisan justice. Taylor, in fact, went beyond Servatius's circumspect objections to attack the deeper jurisprudential vision implicit in the prosecution's principal charge, arguing that "to proscribe the murder of Jews as a 'crime against Jews' carries the implication that it is not a crime against non-Jews." Such a position, Taylor argued, harks back to "old Teutonic law, under which murder offended only the victim's kinsmen." Seemingly oblivious to the staggering insensitivity of associating Israeli justice with Teutonic tribalism, Taylor defended the abandoned principles of Nuremberg, based as they were on the proposition that "atrocities against Jews and non-Jews are equally crimes against world law."[50]

Thus Servatius's preliminary objections found support in a chorus of similar, if not more intense, criticisms issuing from a wide and disparate body of legal opinion.[51] By expostulating many of the reservations expressed by leading experts on international law, Servatius's objections immediately directed critical attention away from the accused and toward the court, which found itself at the very outset of the proceedings in the position of having to justify its authority and assimilate its extraordinary actions into a conventional framework of juridical function.

Given a chance to rebut these objections, the prosecution offered three lines of response (1:19).[52] To the ex post facto charge, Hausner responded that the Israeli law was the "outcome of a unique and special development in the history of law" (*TAE* 1:23). Echoing the rhetoric of Jackson at Nuremberg, Hausner conjured the image of a "legal vacuum" created by a series of unprecedented crimes against which it was "absolutely essential to formulate principles having retroactive application" (1:23). Without such principles, "the greatest sinner would have the greatest reward," as whoever "cast off every legal and moral restraint would have been rewarded by the fact that there was no law which he had infringed" (1:23). Moreover, *nullum crimen sine lege* cannot possibly be violated by a law retroactively criminalizing extermination — a course of conduct whose illegality must be manifest even in the absence of a statute specifying it as such. Quoting from the IMT's judgment, the prosecution reminded the court that as a maxim of fairness, *nullum crimen sine lege* must be weighed against competing values; in this case, it must be balanced against an "even more important principle: to do justice" (1:36–37).

In response to the extraterritoriality question, the prosecution offered two important responses. First, Hausner argued that Nazi criminals are to be considered as "enemies of the human race *hostes humani generis* and whoever lays his hands on them and arrests them is competent to judge them like pirates or slave traders" (1:44). By asking the court to imagine Eichmann as a kind of pirate on the high seas, Hausner sought to conjure a stateless pariah subject to the jurisdiction of the capturing authority. Along with this claim of universal jurisdiction, Hausner also attempted to argue in support of the specific jurisdiction of the Israeli court. While it was true that, technically speaking, Nazi crimes were not committed against Israeli citizens, Hausner asked the court to envision a more capacious concept of Israeli citizenship, one that predated the formal creation of the Jewish state. After all, he argued, the State of Israel had "existed as a political nucleus since 1917, and the historic connection between the Jewish People and this country has never been severed since the destruction of the Temple" (1:51). Thus at the time of the crimes, Israel existed as a "State on-the-way, not only here; it existed in all those countries overtaken by the Holocaust. And the Jews there waited for their State" (1:47). The argument is remarkable, conjuring as it does the embryonic state in which the exterminated Jews of Europe are imagined as absent would-be citizens: "If there is any country which feels the consequences of these crimes on its body and soul — it is the State of Israel first and foremost. In it there was the manpower, the faith and the inspiration of the Jewish State" (1:47). In a kind of juridical time warp, the trial is imagined as a gesture in which the present state projects itself into the recent past to vindicate the rights of those who would have become its citizens.

Hausner also constructed an unusual edifice of precedent to support the state's case. In addition to citing such obviously relevant authorities as the judgment of the IMT and leading cases of international law, the prosecution turned to the great works of Western jurisprudence. Quotations from William Blackstone were followed by the words of Hugo Grotius, the great seventeenth-century Dutch philosopher of natural and international law. Decisions of the King's Bench were cited along with detailed discussions of holdings by American federal courts. Maxims from the Pentateuch received mention alongside quotations from the Hague Conference of 1907. Part of this willingness to seek instruction from the courts of other nations no doubt had to do with the very newness of the Israeli judicial system, which had been formally established only twelve years before it was thrust into the position of adjudicating one of the great trials of the century.[53] Moreover, any case arising in international law will tend to draw on a wider, more diffuse body of precedent than would a conventional case arising under domestic law.

Still, the prosecution's attempt to generate a compelling jurisdictional argument remained provocatively anomalous. The principle of territoriality, the theory most commonly used to generate and support a jurisdictional claim, contains an implicit parochialism. Just as a court may claim jurisdiction over a case arising in a territory over which its legal potency is recognized, the same notion suggests that a court will be bound only by those cases adjudicated within this area. In this way, the concept of legal legitimacy is tied to a spirit of geographic exclusivity. It is the principle of exclusivity that explains the familiar though curious fact that an American court deciding, say, a right-to-die case will seek instruction not from a contemporary Canadian or German court addressing a similar issue, but from American cases, perhaps from the last century. A court's embrace of the temporally remote combined with its rejection of the geographically displaced is, then, evidence of juridical normalcy. By relying on far-flung precedents gathered from around the globe, the Eichmann prosecution sought to build a firmer and larger foundation for the court's jurisdictional competence. Yet in so doing, it succeeded only in calling attention to the curiously heterogeneous and thus unorthodox materials that made for this legal scaffold.

This observation does not impeach the legal adequacy of these efforts, but it does dramatize the specter of juridical illegitimacy against which the Eichmann court perceived itself to be laboring. And while this specter of illegitimacy was raised by Servatius at the outset of the trial, the deeper struggle that the court had to wage in order to preserve the integrity of the trial was fought not against Servatius and the defense, but against Hausner and the prosecution. For it was the narratives of the survivor witnesses that came to exercise the gravest threat to the court's control over the trial; and it was the court's response to this testimony that most powerfully revealed its strategies for recuperating its understanding of legitimate juridical function.

5
...
The Court v. the Prosecution: Policing
Survivor Testimony

Yet is not the right of the victim to have
his story told an absolute right?
— Harold Rosenberg, "The Trial
of Adolf Eichmann"

The Eichmann court responded to Servatius's objections laconically, reserving a more extended discussion of jurisdictional questions to the court's final decision. What little comment the court offered was directed not to issues of jurisdictional competence but to the impartiality of the judges. Acknowledging that "the memory of the Holocaust shocks every Jew to the depth of his being," the court insisted that "those charged with the task of judging are professional judges," fully capable of subduing and overcoming those feelings of revulsion naturally aroused by the facts of the Jewish catastrophe. "It will not be difficult for us," the judges confidently wrote, "to maintain the guarantees assured the Accused in any case conducted according to criminal law procedure, namely that every man is deemed to be innocent and that his case must be tried only on the basis of the evidence brought before the Court" (*TAE* 1:60). From the perspective of the bench, institutional constraints and the disciplining effects of procedural rules rendered even the most extraordinary trial juridically ordinary.

The court was given its first opportunity to test its powers to control the proceedings on May 1, 1961, shortly after Ada Lichtmann retired from the stand. The testimony of Leon Wells, formerly of the Polish town of Sto-janow and at the time of the trial a naturalized citizen of the United States, differed from Lichtmann's in important respects. While the court was never told very much about Lichtmann's background or life subsequent to her liberation, Hausner began his examination of Wells with a lengthy set of introductory questions that established the witness as a prominent me-chanical engineer, a respected figure widely published in his field. His writ-ings, moreover, were not limited to the area of mechanical engineering; Wells appeared before the court as the first in a series of author-witnesses who had written books about their Holocaust experience.[1] And if Licht-mann appeared as a kind of Tiresias, a witness blinded by what she has seen, Wells came before the court as Lazarus, a figure returned from the dead (fig. 5.1).

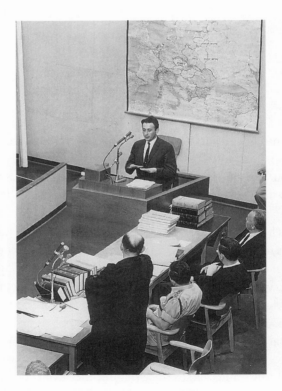

Fig. 5.1. Leon Wells on the stand. Courtesy of the
Israeli Government Press Office.

The story Wells told strains the conventions of narrative plausibility. As would befit a man of science, Wells spoke in relatively flat tones. His words, moreover, were largely absent of intensifiers and dramatic commentary. As one prominent observer of the trial noted, it was difficult to locate a single adverb or adjective in Wells's hours of testimony.[2] The terseness and flatness of his descriptions, however, only highlighted the extraordinariness of his story.

Wells began his testimony with a description of his exhausting labors in the working brigade in the Janówska concentration camp. As the camp became more crowded and the work more intolerable, a typhus epidemic spread among the inmates. Too sick to carry on, Wells was placed in a group of 182 men to be shot. They were marched to a field and given shovels to dig their own graves.[3] Delirious with fever and exhaustion, Wells began to hallucinate, an experience he vividly recalled: "My own dream at the moment was, as I was standing there, to get my own blood out, to have something to drink, because of my great thirst due to high fever in pneumonia and typhus. To drink my own blood — that was my vision, what I was looking forward to" (*TAE* 1:364). The image of sustaining oneself on one's own blood is nightmarish. Yet as Wells continued his testimony, it became clear that this horrific hallucination — the vision of killing oneself in order to survive — served as a premonition for the reality that Wells would live.

While awaiting his execution, the feverish Wells was commanded to return to the camp to carry back the body of a dead inmate whom the ss wanted to bury with Wells's group. While dragging the body back to the field, Wells managed to stumble away from his ss guard, who, Wells later learned, rather than admit that a sickly prisoner under his guard had escaped, simply listed Wells as among the 182 shot inmates. As Wells put it, "I was dead. . . . I knew that I am on the death list" (1:364).

A walking dead man, Wells made his way back to his family's house, where he "passed out and was unconscious for the next nineteen days" (1:364). Once he regained his strength, he left his family, fearful that news of his escape might endanger them. While wandering about, the dead man received news of the gradual liquidation of his entire family. After learning that his mother and four sisters had been sent to the Belzec extermination camp, the dead man attempted suicide ("I cut my veins on my arm"), only to be nursed back to health by a local doctor and one of his uncles. In Wells's telling, "Their idea was that none of us has the right to commit suicide because maybe you will be the last one . . . to tell what happened here"

(1:367). That many survivors of the final solution made it through the camps only to take their lives in the postwar years is well known. A significant number of the most brilliant writers of the Holocaust—Tadeusz Borowski, Jean Améry, Paul Celan, and Primo Levi—died by their own hand. Wells's testimony, by contrast, reminds us that many survivors attempted to take their own lives during the war, a circumstance mentioned by a number of the survivor witnesses called to testify. Yet Wells's testimony is exemplary also in terms of the link that is drawn between survival and narrative. Death, in this understanding, is seen as an unaffordable self-indulgence. Survival, by contrast, is viewed less as a goal than as an imperative, a means toward the end of telling. Again, one is made to think of the trial less as a forum for judging a specific defendant than as an occasion for narrative, a public event and solemn forum staged to satisfy the need of those who have survived to bear witness.

After recovering from his suicide attempt and learning of the extermination of the remaining members of his family, including the uncle who helped heal his self-inflicted wounds, Wells found himself rearrested and sent back to Janówska. There he was made a *Sonderkommando* (special commando) and was responsible for helping the Nazis remove all traces of the mass killings conducted by the Einsatzgruppen. As described by Wells in characteristically straightforward terms, the work of the Sonderkommandos required the inmates "to uncover all the graves where there were people who had been killed during the past three years, take out the bodies, pile them up in tiers and burn these bodies; grind the bodies, take out the valuables in the ashes such as gold teeth, rings and so on—separate them. After grinding the bones we used to throw the ashes up in the air so that they would disappear, replace the earth on the graves and plant seeds, so that nobody could recognize that there ever was a grave there" (1:370).

His precise, unadorned narration is filled with fascinating and grotesque details. The *Brandmeister* (master of the flames) was responsible for making sure that the pyramid of bodies did not extinguish the fire; and the *Zähler* (counter) made sure that all the bodies whom the Nazis had carefully recorded as buried in the mass grave were diligently unearthed. Given such work, the Sonderkommandos developed macabre rituals: as they would head off to work each day ("some days—eight, some days—ten hours; but normally it was an eight-hour day"), the Brandmeister would "march in front, he was clothed like a devil; he had a special uniform with a hook in his hand and we had to march after him and sing" (1:371). The Sonderkommandos were, Wells noted, relatively well treated by the overseeing *Schutzpolizei* (security police), though his laconic responses reveal the incoherence of these standards:

Q. . . . Did you get any food?
A. We got a lot of food.
Q. Where did you eat? Amongst the corpses?
A. On the corpses.
Q. On the corpses themselves?
A. Yes, on the corpses. [1:370]

The most remarkable moment in Wells's testimony involved his description of the day the Sonderkommandos were required to dig up the pit which, according to the official register, should have included the body of Leon Wells: "It was a year and month later when I uncovered . . . the grave where they looked for the 182nd body which had to be there" (1:371). The story of a man searching for his own missing body is so disorienting that the court itself struggled to make sense of what it had heard.

PRESIDING JUDGE: I didn't understand your last reply, Dr. Wells.
WITNESS WELLS: It was in July, at the end of 1943, I dug up the grave where I had to be buried the year ahead when I escaped among the 182 people.
PRESIDING JUDGE: I see. [1:371]

Because the Nazis had kept precise records of the location of each grave and the number of bodies each contained, and because the *Zähler* was required to make sure that all the numbers agreed, Wells and the rest of his unit were forced to spend two fruitless days searching for Wells's missing body.

Wells described how in the following months, the Sonderkommandos were enlisted in the task of burning the corpses of freshly massacred Jews. Each of these actions involved the execution of around two thousand Jews, usually shot "in groups of forty, thirty-five or fifty." These people were put to death in full view of the fires in which they would be cremated (1:373). Finally came the time for the Nazis to liquidate Janówska; some of the Sonderkommandos, including Wells, staged a successful escape. His testimony ended as laconically as it began:

Q. Now, my final question, Dr. Wells. Could you give the Court an approximate figure of the number of bodies burned by your brigade?
A. A few hundred thousand.

Q. Could you tell us how many were executed in front of those fires, approximately?

A. About 30,000 during the time that I was there. That was after the liquidation because there were no more Jews. [1:374]

It is a bland and terrible statement, "there were no more Jews," one that again confirms the spectral position of the survivor. Hausner seemed reluctant to permit Wells's testimony to end on such a bleak note, for suddenly he extended his examination, attempting to return the court and the spectators to the man first introduced on the stand:

Q. Now, my last question. I believe that when I was introducing you yesterday to the Court I forgot that you were given a scientific award this year. Is that correct?

A. I was given the International Award for the engineer who contributed most in the field of Cinematography and Optics for 1960; International Congress in Mar del Plata, Argentina. [1:374]

Here one notes the small irony that Wells was arriving in Argentina to receive an award roughly at the same time that Eichmann was being smuggled out of the country by Israeli special agents. More interesting, however, is the way Hausner's final question fails to provide the closure he seeks. Hausner often structured his examination toward the end of producing what Lawrence Langer has called "heroic memory" — memory that means to salvage "from the wreckage of mass murder . . . a tribute to the victory of the human spirit." Langer insightfully notes that such narratives of heroic memory often offer "a version of Holocaust reality more necessary than true";+ and by asking Wells to conclude his testimony with a description of the prestigious award recently bestowed upon him, Hausner attempted to close the harrowing narrative on a note of renewal and triumph. Yet the success of the effort is far from clear as one struggles to reconcile the accomplished scientist with the dead man who tried to kill himself; the laborer who ate atop a heap of corpses, and the digger who tilled the earth for his own missing grave. Along with respect for a man who managed to excel despite a horrific past, one is left wondering how such grotesquely disjointed life stories can be viably contained within the structure of single remembering mind.

It was these very dissonances that contributed to the power of Wells's testimony. His refusal to smooth over the jarring juxtapositions of past and present, the precision of his unadorned expression, the clarity with which he found terms for his impossible memory, and the incredible and harrowing details of the story itself—all made Wells an invaluable witness. Yet witness to what? Clearly, his testimony would be a crucial addition to any oral history of the Holocaust, and, not surprisingly, the interview with Wells conducted by the Fortunoff Holocaust Video project at Yale remains one of the most significant documents in this important archive. But how are we to understand the conventional juridical use of his testimony? Or more particularly, what role did it play in clarifying the guilt of the accused?

These questions were in fact posed to the court by Eichmann's defense counsel. At the beginning of the second session devoted to Wells's testimony, Servatius raised a troubling objection. While he acknowledged that Wells's evidence "has, perhaps, great significance from the point of view of its importance in a historical process," he argued, rather pointedly, that it "is not relevant to a judicial investigation, since it has no connection with the Accused's responsibility" (1:366). Servatius explicitly addressed the tension between general historical instruction and the legal determination of specific guilt. Insisting that "a courtroom is . . . probably the least appropriate place for the research of historical truth" (4:1371), Servatius tried to preempt the didactic drama by accepting the truth of the Holocaust, acknowledging that "the facts as described were unimpeachable" (5:2056). With few exceptions, he studiously avoided cross-examining survivor witnesses, out of "respect and reverence for their suffering" (5:2056). From the prosecution's perspective, then, Servatius's most subversive gesture was his effort not to question the history of the Holocaust, but to stipulate to it— that is, his attempt to streamline the entire trial by focusing all legal attention not on the crimes perpetrated, but on the accused's role in their commission. From such a perspective, the relevance of Wells's testimony would have been very questionable indeed. Although Wells demonstrated an uncanny ability to recall dates and names, one name that was never mentioned during the course of his testimony was that of the defendant. Wells had had, by all accounts, no contact with Eichmann—had never met him, had never seen him; there is no evidence that suggests Wells had ever even heard of the defendant until after the war.

The court, however, ruled against Servatius. Sound precedents argued against the defense: standard Anglo-American trial procedure, the model for Israeli criminal procedure, does not permit a defendant who has entered a plea of not guilty to stipulate to the facticity of the crime in order to limit the prosecution's case exclusively to those facts disputed by the accused.[5] (A defendant in a murder trial cannot, for example, stipulate to the homicide in order to prevent the prosecution from showing the jury or court graphic pictures of the murder scene and victim.) In the words of the Eichmann court, "The prosecution has firstly to prove that all these acts were committed and secondly—the responsibility of the Accused" (1:366). Thus the court concluded that "the evidence of the witness Wells is relevant to the subject of the trial" (1:366).

However sound the court's decision may have been from the perspective of criminal procedure, the controversy over Wells's testimony highlighted aspects of the prosecution's case that threatened the court's effort to normalize the proceedings and thereby recuperate its claims to juridical legitimacy. Some of these complexities owed their origin to the relation between the defendant and the Holocaust. As the former director of section IV-B-4 of the RSHA, Eichmann was, as I have observed, an ideal defendant for a trial focusing on the crimes of the Holocaust (fig. 5.2). Yet in contrast to the men tried before the IMT, Eichmann was never a high-ranking Nazi functionary.[6] As Eichmann himself would emphasize time and again while on the stand, he never advanced beyond the rank of lieutenant colonel, a respectable rank but far below the positions of authority that the Nuremberg defendants had occupied. Though dismissive of Eichmann's claims of relative impotence, Hausner acknowledged that Eichmann could not be regarded as the principal architect of the final solution, noting in his summation argument, "I have no doubt that it was not Eichmann who gave the first comprehensive order for the extermination of the Jews" (5:1988).

By the same token, however, Eichmann was hardly a low-ranking officer, an underling directly involved in the daily killing of Jews. As noted in part 1, the Allies held trials at Belsen, Dachau, and Buchenwald in which former guards and others responsible for the day-to-day misery of the concentration camps were made to answer for their crimes. Eichmann, by contrast, had never participated in the physical act of extermination. By his own admission—and here Eichmann supplied the court with information it otherwise would never have been able to obtain—he had served as an official witness to massacres, having been sent by the chief of the Gestapo, Heinrich Müller, to observe and report on the work of the Einsatzgruppen. He also visited several camps, including Auschwitz (which he visited on multiple occasions) and Treblinka, which he described as "the most terrible thing I have ever seen in the course of my life" (1:138). Concerning the activities of the Einsatzgruppen, Eichmann recalled watching an action that took place on the out-

Fig. 5.2. Eichmann in the glass booth. "This man did not seem a member of the vaunted *Herrenvolk* who had suppressed a continent and murdered millions of its people because they were considered vermin. Two members of the race of 'vermin' now sat behind him as guards. They sat stiffly to attention, each about half a head taller than the prisoner, imperturbable, their eyes unswervingly upon him, young, spare, and with chiseled features. A more striking contrast would have been difficult to imagine. It somehow made Eichmann look just a little more nondescript. . . . He was everyone's next-door neighbor . . . the clerk at the accountant's office" (Pearlman, *The Capture and Trial of Adolf Eichmann,* 89). Courtesy of the Israeli Government Press Office.

skirts of the Polish town of Lvov, the town in which Leon Wells had lived at the time of Germany's invasion of Russia and the site of the crimes captured in the brief film *Original German 8-millimeter Film of Atrocities Against the Jews* shown at Nuremberg. The ss marksmen fired into a pit, an act Eichmann vividly remembered: "I can still see a woman . . . with her arms behind her . . . and then her knees buckled and I made off. . . . Then I saw something else which was terrible: There was a pit, perhaps it was already closed. There welled up like a geyser blood . . . how should I say this . . . a jet of blood. I have never seen anything like it" (1:136).

The prosecution at times questioned the sincerity of Eichmann's claims of physical revulsion and attempted in the course of the trial to prove that he once had beaten a Jewish boy to death with his own hands. The evidence on this isolated charge, however, proved to be less than persuasive, and it was only when responding to this specific allegation that Eichmann demonstrated any vehemence on the stand. Indeed, one is left with little reason to doubt Eichmann's claim that "if today I see the gaping injury of an open cut on a person, I cannot look at it. . . . I am often told that I could never have been a doctor" (1:134). Notwithstanding the irony of a leading functionary within an organization of extermination admitting that a medical career would not have suited him, Eichmann's statement highlights his physical distance from the everyday business of killing. Indeed, the Israeli government sardonically commented on Eichmann's physical distance from acts of violence by releasing, on the day after the trial began, a provocative photograph of the manicured hands of the defendant with the caption, "His hands are clean" (fig. 5.3).

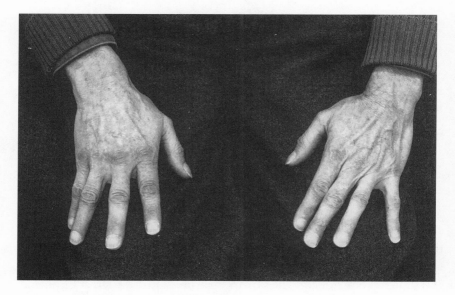

Fig. 5.3. The hands of the accused. The government released this picture on the eve of the trial with the sardonic caption, "His hands are clean." Courtesy of the Israeli Government Press Office.

As head of Section IV-B-4, Eichmann was principally responsible for organizing the identification, assembling, and transportation of Jews to the camps. Eichmann, of course, claimed — and made it his principal defense — that he "occupied a humble place in an inconspicuous corner of this conspiracy; that he fulfilled a technical function of secondary importance, in drawing up the timetables for moving the trains" (5:1975). The prosecution, by contrast, argued that Eichmann "occupied the very pivotal point in this huge slaughter-house" (5:1975). For "it was his word that put gas chambers into action; he lifted the telephone, and railroad cars left for the extermination centres" (1:62). Both parties agreed, however, that Eichmann's job was essentially bureaucratic, and while Arendt famously faults the prosecution for failing to appreciate the connection between a bureaucratic mentality and the logic of genocide, Hausner explicitly made this link in the first minutes of his opening statement, declaring, "In this trial, we shall . . . encounter a new kind of killer, the kind that exercises his bloody craft behind a desk" (1:62).

The fact that Eichmann was essentially a bureaucrat did not in and of itself present problems to the prosecution's case. As Hausner argued, "A transport official who arranges timetables for transports and trains, knowing that the journey is towards death — he, too, actively assists in the performance of the murder" (5:1996). Inasmuch as Eichmann had never denied that he was fully aware of the fate of the Jews whose deportations he efficiently arranged, the prosecution's case was solid. Moreover, despite Eichmann's attempt to rely on a legally questionable "superior orders" defense (5:2021),[7] the prosecution had ample evidence indicating that Eichmann had performed his bureaucratic duties not grudgingly under duress, but "with zeal, willingly, and with boundless passion" (5:2042). The prosecution, for example, had solid proof showing that Eichmann had personally contrived to make sure that a trainload of Hungarian Jews from the town of Kistarcsa was directed *back* to Auschwitz even after the train had been returned to its point of origin because of the Hungarian government's decision to suspend deportations. Equally telling was the evidence of Eichmann's reluctance to implement Himmler's famous *Stoppbefehl*, the cynical order ending the final solution as Germany faced certain military defeat. Demonstrating perhaps less a fanatical anti-Semitism than a pathological bureaucratic zeal, Eichmann contrived to continue to send Jews to their deaths even in the face of superior orders *to the contrary*. Yet despite the strength of the prosecution's case, Hausner refused to limit it to these matters. Although such a limitation would certainly have "simplified the legal argument," Hausner feared it would have "miss[ed] the point of the trial: the covering of the whole Jewish disaster" (1:298).

In this way, Hausner's didactic conception of the trial — as a tool of historical instruction and normative reconstruction — defined the very contours of the prosecution's charge sheet. In order to justify the broad fifteen-count indictment,[8] which basically imputed to Eichmann all the crimes associated with the final solution, Hausner relied on the conventional principle of complicity — "a necessary and a just rule of law, which imputes to every active participant in a crime all the natural consequences of the joint venture" (1:299). While such a broad approach was, as Hausner acknowledged, unnecessary from the point of view of trying to secure a conviction, it was invaluable in terms of the prosecution's interest in history and memory. For suddenly, the prosecution was not "fettered by details of dates, places and people affected" (1:298). Any and all evidence of Nazi genocide was now of legal relevance, including the testimony of persons like Wells who had never met, seen, or heard of the defendant. Servatius's objection to Wells's testimony was thus doomed, given the structure of the prosecution's case.

Although the court ruled against the defense, its decision betrayed its deeper anxieties about the prosecution's approach. After dismissing Servatius's objection, the court added, "We assume that the prosecution will take note of Defense Counsel's statement that he will not challenge one or the other fact in regard to the general background of events, and will accordingly limit the extent of its evidence"(1:366). This first, inconspicuous register of the court's concerns about the relevance of survivor testimony was followed quickly by a second. Early in the trial, Hausner had directed open-ended questions to the state's witnesses. While standard adversarial technique attempts to "formalize the conditions of telling" by presenting witness narratives in the form of highly tutored and tightly structured interrogatory exchanges, Hausner encouraged testimony to take a narrative form, permitting the witnesses to speak for minutes on end between brief questions.[9] This approach served his vision of the trial as an occasion for paying homage to the memory of the dead through the words of the survivors. Now, however, the court's desire to discipline the proceedings manifested itself in a direct challenge to the idea of the trial as an occasion for narrative. For no sooner had the court asked the prosecution to "limit the extent of its evidence" than it enunciated the following directive: "Mr.

Hausner . . . perhaps it would really be possible to accelerate somewhat the process of leading evidence by way of examining counsel guiding the witness by his questions more than has been done so far" (1:366). Hausner grudgingly acceded, with the words, "I have been avoiding leading questions all the time, but if the Court advises so, I shall do so" (1:366).

Hausner's attempt to comply with the court's decision had the immediate effect of transforming the tenor of Wells's testimony. The articulate free-flowing narrative vanished amid a barrage of questions that often served to disrupt, not streamline, the testimony:

> Q. You jumped the fence?
> A. Jumped over the fence and got inside.
> Q. You saw your brother Ya'akov?
> A. No, next day I was caught.
> Q. I know you were arrested and you escaped.
> A. I found my brother on the street. [1:368]

When Hausner faltered in his attempt to lead Wells, the court itself intervened. As Wells told the story of his escape, an involved tale that included the description of a ruse to catch two members of the camp's security force, the court interrupted, "All right, Dr. Wells, I am very sorry but we can't go into these details." Taking the court's advice to heart in a jarringly complete manner, Wells brought his story to an abrupt end with the words, "We cut the neck and choked these two people" (1:374).

The court's desire to curtail narrative, first evinced in its treatment of Wells, played an even more defining role in its treatment of subsequent witnesses. Again, this wariness of narrative was born not of an impatience with long-winded or unfocused witnesses, but of a deeper desire to defend a particular conception of legal form. On the very next day of the trial, during the testimony of Zvia Lubetkin-Zuckerman, the court once again struggled to maintain its juridical authority against the force of survivor narrative. As former leaders of the Warsaw ghetto revolt, Lubetkin-Zuckerman and her husband, Yitzhak Zuckerman, were Israeli national heroes, personifying the very traits that the fledgling state sought to foster among its citizens — the Jew as Zionist warrior heroically acting in self-defense. Lubetkin-Zuckerman's time on the stand, devoted to a detailed description of the Warsaw deportations and the ghetto revolt, again did little to clarify the guilt of the accused. As in Wells's testimony, Eichmann's name was never so much as mentioned during her lengthy examination. At best, Hausner could justify her testimony about the Warsaw ghetto by relying on the complicity theory, arguing that the revolt was relevant as it could be understood as a response to the large-scale deportations from the ghetto to the death camps. This, however, required even a further attenuation of the complicity theory, for although Eichmann had organized the deportation of Jews from Hungary and western Europe, his role in the liquidation of the Warsaw ghetto was less than clear.

Though only questionably probative, Lubetkin-Zuckerman's testimony nevertheless served Hausner's goal of constructing a narrative of heroic memory. Movingly her testimony helped explain why the Jews of the ghetto had waited so long to organize their self-defense. It made clear the immense obstacles they had had to overcome in order to do so, and described in valiant terms the struggle they had waged against impossible odds. When Hausner asked whether she had believed the first reports, received in late 1941, of mass killings of Jews, Lubetkin-Zuckerman's answer was thoughtful and nuanced: "It was hard to imagine that in fact an entire people would be exterminated. . . . The ordinary Jew didn't believe it, nor did the Jewish leadership. If you were to ask me why we believed it, was this because we were wiser? Were we greater heroes? I would not say so" (1:374).

Again the court intervened, yet in a manner that demonstrated its awareness of the delicacy of the matter:

PRESIDING JUDGE: Mr. Hausner, I think that we must after all make some progress, despite the difficulty involved.
ATTORNEY GENERAL: There is truly a great deal of difficulty.
PRESIDING JUDGE: I appreciate the point. [1:374]

To deal with the difficulty, the court made the same recommendation it did during Wells's testimony: "Mr. Hausner, you could make greater use of your liberty to guide the witness." Reluctantly, Hausner responded, "Yes, but I did not want to interrupt the flow of her statement" (1:408).

The identical problems reemerged two days later during the testimony of Abba Kovner. Like Wells, Kovner had published accounts of his wartime experiences, and, like Lubetkin-Zuckerman, he was something of a national hero, both as a former member of the Jewish resistance and as one of Israel's leading poets. When asked by Hausner to comment on why more Jews did not resist, Kovner replied, "We were in a glass cage — who would dare to ask: How is it that you did not rise up in a glass cage? An organization of this nature can be created only with people determined in their resolve, and people who are determined in their resolve are not usually to be found amongst those beyond despair, subjugated, and those tortured to the extreme" (1:461).

Kovner compellingly plays with the trope of the "glass cage," substituting the Jews of Europe for the defendant in Jerusalem. The thoughtfulness of his response notwithstanding, the court followed with an interruption: "Mr. Kovner, we have to make progress" — in which progress, again, was defined in the narrow terms of formal proof. Hausner, undeterred, continued to ask Kovner about the organization of the resistance, prompting the following exchange with the court:

PRESIDING JUDGE: I would ask you to be brief on this subject as well. You should always remember how we started yesterday morning.

ATTORNEY GENERAL: I am now coming to a very important subject, and I would crave the Court's patience. This, in fact, concerns the Accused.

PRESIDING JUDGE: I do not believe that you can complain of a lack of patience on the part of the Court.

ATTORNEY GENERAL: No, Your Honour. [1:461]

Hausner's desperate promise to link the testimony to the defendant was never, however, adequately fulfilled in his examination of Kovner, leading the court to issue a stern reprimand:

PRESIDING JUDGE: ... Mr. Hausner, we have heard shocking things here, in the language of a poet, but I maintain that in many parts of this evidence we have strayed far from the subject of this trial. There is no possibility at all of interrupting evidence such as this, while it is being rendered, out of respect for the witness and out of respect for the matter he is relating. It is your task . . . to eliminate everything that is not relevant to the trial, so as not to place the Court once again — and this is not the first time — in such a situation. I regret that I have to make these remarks, after the conclusion of evidence such as this.

ATTORNEY GENERAL: Your Honours, perhaps when my turn comes for a final summation of my arguments, it will become clear to the Court that these things are not of such a nature.

PRESIDING JUDGE: This was not the first time that I have mentioned this. The Court has a certain view of this trial according to the indictment, and we have stated this more than once — sometimes in a hint, sometimes more clearly, and the Prosecution must direct itself in accordance with what it hears from the Court.

ATTORNEY GENERAL: This we do, undoubtedly.

PRESIDING JUDGE: Yet, nevertheless, I do not see that these matters have penetrated to the extent that they should penetrate.

ATTORNEY GENERAL: Perhaps this is so, because Your Honours
are not yet aware of everything which we still intend to bring before you.

PRESIDING JUDGE: We heard your opening address which, it
seems to me, lays down the general lines of what you wish to place before
the Court. [1:466]

In this exchange lies the sharpest statement of the prosecution's and the
court's competing understandings of the trial. The court draws a distinction between the discourses of law and literature; whatever insights into
the nature of the Holocaust might find expression in "the language of a
poet," these have led the court to stray "far from the subject of this trial." In
particular, the court expresses its frustration at the awkward position in
which the prosecution's handling of the case had thrust it. By failing to police the parameters of the relevant, the prosecution had forced the court to
balance the legal integrity of the trial against the testimonial need of the
survivors. It was, for the court, a double bind, as legal integrity came at the
cost of insulting the memory of the dead and the experience of survivors,
while fully accommodating the narrative impulse would have distorted the
conventional legal form upon which the court believed its legitimacy
rested. Hausner, of course, did not attempt to justify his approach by pleading the case of didactic legality over rules-based formalism. Attempting
to work within the conventional idiom of criminal procedure, Hausner appealed to a deeper architecture of relevance, asking the court to imagine a
grand design of proof that would take shape gradually and whose full scope
and meaning could be divined only in retrospect.

As Hausner resumed the presentation of the state's case, the tensions between the prosecution and the court never again surfaced in such explicit
and dramatic terms. This is partially because Hausner succeeded in exercising greater control over his witnesses. The open-ended narrative style that
characterized the testimonies of Lubetkin-Zuckerman and Kovner turned
into the abbreviated question-and-answer of Hausner's concluding examination of Wells. These efforts, however, remained insufficient from the
court's perspective. But rather than openly clash with the prosecution, the
court adopted other strategies for disciplining the proceedings in face of an
irrepressible testimonial need. While attempting to be as sensitive to
survivors as possible, the court demonstrated its willingness to do what it

had described as impossible—"interrupting evidence such as this." As Mordechai Ansbacher, a survivor of Auschwitz and Dachau (and, at the time of the trial, an employee of Yad Vashem, the recently established Holocaust museum and research institute), told the story of his mother's death, the court broke in, "Mr. Ansbacher, you are trying to bring in too much, to compress too much. Please answer the questions." To the witness's plaintive explanation, "I merely wanted to describe the general background," the court responded, "Of course, one's heart is filled with many memories" (2:682).

At other times, the court demonstrated less sensitivity, as during the testimony of Raya Kagan, another Auschwitz survivor who had worked in the camp's registry. Kagan's testimony offered many revealing details about camp life. She described the ambivalent meaning of the inmates' tattoo, a mark that in the popular imagination stands as the most tangible bodily scar of the horrors of the "concentrationary universe." Because those arrivees immediately selected for extermination were never registered in any manner, Kagan testified that the inmates knew that "to be tattooed was a sign, a very small one, for continuing to live" (3:1280). As Auschwitz was also a destination for convicted criminals, Kagan pointed out the grotesque irony that Jewish convicts were more likely to survive than the normal Jews—the so-called *Transportjuden,* that is, the deported Jews who in large part were exterminated upon arrival at the camp. The Jewish convicts, by contrast, were sent to the camp by a separate department altogether and thus were not subjected to the selections that greeted the *Transportjuden.*

Though fascinating as a historical matter, the testimony's direct evidentiary relevance was again unclear. As Hausner attempted to bring Kagan's narrative to an end, the court insisted on a different form of closure:

Q. Did you remain in Auschwitz until the end?
A. Until 18 January.
Q. And then you were transferred—on a foot march or by train?
A. For four days and nights, we walked on foot. In Loslau, we were loaded on to open coal trucks. I merely wanted to add . . .
PRESIDING JUDGE: Would you please confine yourself to the questions that have been put to you. After all, there was an ocean of occurrences.
WITNESS KAGAN: I only wanted to add . . .
PRESIDING JUDGE: You did not want to add—that is to say, you wanted to, but we could not permit you to do so. [3:1279]

Here the court first tries to parse Kagan's testimonial desires — "you did not want to add" — but then corrects itself, insisting that the court's own rudeness is not a matter of choice but itself a compelled performance. The court sees itself as unable to grant her the permission to continue narrating; juridical authority is recuperated through a gesture of limitation.

The court's greatest impatience, however, was reserved for those witnesses who putatively performed the testimonial function more narrowly and traditionally conceived — that is, those who spoke directly about the activities of the accused. For example, Zvi Zimmerman, a former member of the Jewish underground and at the time of the trial a member of the Knesset, described his contact during the war with one of the "Righteous Gentiles," an Austrian named Busko who attempted to warn the Jews of the Nazis' plans. From Busko, Zimmerman learned that the person in charge of the special department devoted to the "total destruction of the Jews" was an "expert" who "had been in Palestine . . . and knew Hebrew and Yiddish" — rumors about Eichmann which, curiously enough, seem to have originated with Eichmann himself (3:1124). Regarding the name of this expert, Zimmerman was unable to give a clear answer: "I am almost sure that I heard it, but after a long time, it is difficult, nevertheless, to be certain when and where we heard the name for the first time" (3:1124). Emphasizing the power of this expert, Zimmerman referred to comments he heard from two members of the Gestapo suggesting that even the *Generalgouvernant* of Poland, Hans Frank, could not intervene in matters concerning the Jewish population. Zimmerman's testimony, in this regard, relied entirely on hearsay, and though the Eichmann trial was, like Nuremberg, governed by relaxed evidentiary norms, Presiding Judge Landau felt obligated to intervene: "Mr. Hausner, the value of this evidence is, shall we say, next to nothing. . . . This is, in fact, gossip about Frank and, as we may assume, about the Accused" (3:1124). Against the court's notion that the evidence supplied no more than "general rumor," Hausner attempted to demonstrate its relevance, leading to a brief but damaging exchange:

ATTORNEY GENERAL: I shall ask the witness right away, Your Honour. [*To witness*] Did you personally hear . . . [of the powers of Eichmann] . . . from Kunde and Heinrich [the two members of the Gestapo]?
WITNESS ZIMMERMAN: I heard it from them, when they were telling this to people with whom they were in contact, and I was present as an official.

PRESIDING JUDGE: Yes, this I understood. The question is: From whom did they hear it?

WITNESS ZIMMERMAN: This was a general rumour.

PRESIDING JUDGE: Well, there you are. [3:1124–35]

The embarrassing exchange typifies a separate problem characteristic of those testimonies meant specifically to clarify the actions of the accused. Although some witnesses, for example, Joel Brandt, a leader of the Hungarian Jewish community, were able to describe in detail discussions conducted with Eichmann,[10] most survivors were, not surprisingly, never close enough to positions of Nazi authority to be able to speak authoritatively about the activities of the accused. Others, such as camp inmates, who claimed to have seen or observed Eichmann often revealed the unreliability of their memories. When Ya'akov Friedman, a former prisoner at Majdanek, testified about a visit that Eichmann allegedly paid to the camp, defense counsel Servatius engaged in a rare cross-examination of a survivor witness (with the assistance of Judge Landau):

DR. SERVATIUS: . . . I understand from your remarks that Eichmann walked at the head of the group of officers?

WITNESS FRIEDMAN: Yes. He was surrounded by all these officers. There were about ten of them; he was in the middle, and he walked in front.

Q. What uniform was he wearing?

A. To the extent that my memory does not fail me, it was a black uniform — for all the ss men there wore black.

PRESIDING JUDGE: That is not enough. The question was: Do you remember his uniform? And not because all ss men wore black, and hence he also wore black. Do you remember the colour?

WITNESS FRIEDMAN: I don't remember the colour of the uniform so well — but I remember the face. . . . Generally speaking, it was the faces there that conveyed much, for in the case of each ss man we knew in advance whether he was bad or good.

PRESIDING JUDGE: Let us stay with this question of the colour of the uniform. I understood your evidence to be . . . that you knew that all ss officers wore black and, therefore, for this reason, you concluded that the man who, as you say, was Eichmann, also wore black?

WITNESS FRIEDMAN: Yes.

DR. SERVATIUS: I have no further questions to the witness. [3:1165]

The problems with Friedman's identification of Eichmann—in which the witness could not distinguish between authentic memory and understandings that have been read back upon the past—anticipate the kind of problems that would fundamentally undermine the prosecution's case in the Demjanjuk trial twenty-five years later (see chapter 7).[11] At the Eichmann trial, these vulnerabilities underscored the court's persistent ambivalence toward the juridical value of survivor testimony. When most reliable—that is, when limited to telling the astonishing stories of personal survival—such testimony was the least relevant. And when most relevant—detailing the activities of the accused—such testimony proved itself the least reliable.

Such direct interventions, however, placed the court precisely in the position it sought to avoid—patrolling the bounds of the legally relevant against the encroachments of difficult memory. At the conclusion of Zvi Zimmerman's testimony, Judge Landau issued an apology: "I should not like you to leave here with bad feelings. There was no intention to belittle your activities. . . . Whatever remarks I made . . . referred to the legal weight of certain statements in evidence. I hope this is clear to you as a jurist" (3:1127). From within the confines of his own institutional role, Landau appealed to Zimmerman as a fellow man of the law, asking the witness to understand that only the norms of the profession dictated the treatment that he had received.

At other times, the court adopted a more complex and less confrontational strategy for defending itself against exigent memory. Instructive is the court's treatment of the testimony of G. M. Gilbert (fig. 5.4). Gilbert, as noted in the discussion of Nuremberg, served as the United States Army's psychologist at the trial of the major war criminals; his contemporaneous personal journal, published in 1947 as *Nuremberg Diary*, recorded one of the most vivid descriptions of the defendants' responses to the screening of *Nazi Concentration Camps*. At the Eichmann trial, Gilbert was asked primarily to testify about the statements that the IMT defendants and witnesses had made about Eichmann. (Such hearsay was again admissible under the trial's relaxed rules of evidence.) Comments such as that attributed to Göring— "Wisliceny is a little *Schweinehund* who looks like a big one, because Eichmann isn't here" (3:1003)—tended to discredit Eichmann's claim to be no more than a middle-level bureaucrat lacking independent authority.

Toward the end of his testimony, Gilbert was invited by the prosecution to offer a larger, speculative "picture of the murderous personality of an SS

Fig. 5.4. Former Army psychologist G. M. Gilbert on the stand. The ss killer
"goes on with his ghastly work as though he were a machine made of electrical
wiring" (Gilbert, *Nuremberg Diary*, 36). Courtesy of the
Israeli Government Press Office.

officer" (3:1009). Gilbert had written on this topic in his book *The Psychology of Dictatorship* and shortly after the conclusion of the Eichmann trial, he would summarize his conclusions in an article that appeared in a special number of *Yad Vashem Studies*. The title of the article — "The Mentality of ss Murderous Robots" — is revealing, as it sharply differs from the image of Nazi atrocity rhetorically conjured at the trial of the major war criminals. As observed in part 1, such artifacts as the shrunken head of Buchenwald served at Nuremberg to materialize an understanding of atrocity as a crime of atavism, a return to a primitive state of savage lawlessness. By contrast, Gilbert imagines the ss killer as a "mechanical executioner," a "new inhuman personality" who "goes on with his ghastly work as though he were a machine made of electrical wiring and iron instead of a heart and mind."[12] In contrast to the image of the Nazi as a latter-day headhunter, Gilbert fashions him as a type of robot, an android created by the authoritarian state.

The theory of Eichmann as robot, however, was one that the court never permitted Gilbert to detail. For no sooner did the prosecution begin to explore these theories than the court asked, "What is the purpose of these questions, Mr. Hausner?" (3:1009). Hausner's response again revealed his capacious view of the trial: "The question is: How can it be that a man born of woman can perform these acts? . . . I know that I, and possibly many others, have been looking at this glass cage for the past six weeks and asking myself the question: How could this have happened from the point of view of the man himself?" (3:1009). The mention of the glass booth harks back to Kovner's testimony, only here Hausner conjures an entirely different image. Now the glass booth, a structure designed to protect the accused, has been transformed into a cage, a structure to confine and render available for scrutiny a dangerous creature (fig. 5.5). Because this creature was, according to Hausner, not like other humans, he asked the court to consider Gilbert as performing the conventional function of an expert witness—that is, supplying the court with distinctive technical knowledge "beyond the ken of laymen."[13] Gilbert could provide a "scientific explanation" for a phenomenon that defies conventional categories of knowing and thereby elucidate "a certain personality, the like of whom I doubt whether we shall ever have the opportunity of coming across again in our courts" (3:1010).

Without expressing disrespect toward Gilbert, the court voiced wariness about the line of questioning: "Is this a legal question which interests us here? It is a very interesting psychological question. But let us imagine that the facts have been established; we would be able to philosophize about the psychological aspect of the matter, in the same way as anyone could do. Professor Gilbert can do this much better than any of us. But is it relevant to the issues that we have to determine?" (3:1009). In refusing to admit Gilbert's theory of ss character, the court added an important new twist to its efforts to conventionalize the extraordinary trial. For Hausner, as we have seen, the magnitude of the crimes, their unprecedented nature, the scars on the survivors created the need to reimagine the legal form; the court, by contrast, reached the opposite conclusion. It was the very magnitude of the horrors that framed the futility of attempting to comprehend them fully. By noting that "we would be able to philosophize about the psychological aspect of the matter," the court gave word to a deeper skepticism about supposedly scientific answers to the impossible horrors of the Holocaust. The attempt to do so was an act of overreaching that, in the court's mind, would erode the legitimacy of the expert or institution making such pronouncements. To attempt fully to represent and explain the Holocaust is to exit the world of legitimate juridical function and to risk spectacular failure.

Fig. 5.5. The construction of the glass booth. In Hausner's attempt to convince the court of the relevance of Gilbert's theory of the robotic personality of the ss killer, the glass booth is transformed from a structure intended to protect the accused into a cage, a structure meant to confine and render available for scrutiny a dangerous and alien creature. Courtesy of the Israeli State Archives.

Such was the moral the court drew from perhaps the most famous incident associated with the trial — the collapse on the stand of the writer Yehiel Dinur. An Auschwitz survivor who had settled in Tel Aviv in the late forties, Dinur had published several well-known novels about the Holocaust, including *The House of Dolls,* which became something of an international best-seller. His name, however, was unknown even in Israel, as he published his works under the nom de plume "Katzetnik 135633" — that is, Concentration Camp Inmate #135633.[14] The gesture of using his Auschwitz number as his signature was not in itself unique; later in the trial, the prosecution submitted as evidence an album of nineteen watercolors of Auschwitz painted by a Polish Jew named Zofja Rozenstrauch, who, like Dinur, signed her works with her inmate number, "48035." Yet as Dinur told Hausner, "Katzetnik 135633" was no mere pseudonym: "It was not a pen name. I do not regard myself as a writer and a composer of literary material. This is a chronicle of the planet of Auschwitz." Just as Ada Lichtmann's sunglasses suggested a woman left blinded by what she had witnessed, Dinur's complete literary identification with his Auschwitz number reminds one that for many survivors the day of liberation remained forever belated and incomplete. Although he was called by the prosecution to testify about Auschwitz, Dinur acted as if he were not remembering per se; rather, he seemed to reenter a trauma that remained very much undigested and existentially present.[15] Indeed, his image of a "planet called Auschwitz" transposed the passage of time with displacement in space. The events did not take place at an earlier moment; rather, they occurred on another planet "according to different laws of nature" (3:1237). Survivors remain, then, aliens to life "here on earth." The survivor's fractured identity — at once Yehiel Dinur and Katzetnik — was thus unwittingly raised by the first innocent question directed to the witness by the court, "What is your full name?"

Dinur/Katzetnik began his testimony with a rambling recognition of his great responsibility as witness: "If I am able to stand before you today and relate the events within that planet, if I, a fall-out of the planet, am able to be here at this time, then I believe with perfect faith that this is due to the oath I swore to them there. They gave me this strength" (3:1237). But no sooner had Dinur described the oath to bear witness as "the armour with which I acquired the supernatural power" than the power failed him in spectacular fashion. Before Hausner could even properly begin his examination, the very inmates to whose memory Dinur/Katzetnik swore this oath began to crowd about him on the witness stand (fig. 5.6). The transcript, in its own schematic fashion, records the struggle:

WITNESS DINUR: . . . I see them, they are staring at me, I see them, I saw them standing in the queue . . .

Q. Perhaps you will allow me, Mr. Dinur, to put a number of questions to you, if you will agree?

A. [*tries to continue*] I remember . . .

PRESIDING JUDGE: Mr. Dinur, kindly listen to what the Attorney General has to say.

[*Witness Dinur rises from his place, descends from the witness stand, and collapses on the platform. The witness fainted.*]

PRESIDING JUDGE: I think we shall have to adjourn the session. I do not think that we can continue.

Fig. 5.6. "I see them, they are staring at me, I
see them": the collapse of Yehiel Dinur/
Katzetnik 135633 on the stand, June 7, 1961.
Courtesy of the Israeli Government
Press Office.

ATTORNEY GENERAL: I did not anticipate this.
PRESIDING JUDGE [*after some time*]: I do not think it is possible
to go on. We shall adjourn the session now. [3:1237]

Dinur never returned to the stand. Rushed from the courtroom by am-
bulance, he spent the next two weeks hospitalized. The *Jerusalem Report* reported that he had suffered a stroke, though others claimed that he experienced a nervous breakdown. Yet the spectacular testimonial failure — the
words "I remember" trailing off into silence — said, in many respects, more
than even the most articulate testimony could have. Ritually broadcast on
Israeli television on Yom Hashoah, the solemn holiday commemorating
the victims of the Holocaust, Dinur's courtroom collapse emerged as one
of the most recognizable moments of the Eichmann trial and came to sym-

bolize the unutterable horrors of the Holocaust. Indeed, this isolated moment from the proceeding serves as a noteworthy example of the power of trials not simply to shape collective memory but to serve as sites of memory, placeholders invested with the fraught and liminal traces of the past.

If Dinur's personal collapse has served as a symbol of the collective trauma of the Holocaust for the Israeli public, the Eichmann court found in Dinur a symbol of a very different kind.[16] In its final judgment, a characteristically restrained affair, the court delivered its verdict in language meant to anchor, once and for all, its claim to juridical authority. The judgment begins not with a discussion of the accused, but with an analysis of the court's own behavior during the trial: "The path of the Court was and remains clear. It cannot allow itself to be enticed into provinces which are outside its sphere. The judicial process has ways of its own, laid down by law, and these do not change, whatever the subject of the trial. Otherwise, the processes of law and court procedure are bound to be impaired . . . and the trial would . . . resemble a rudderless ship tossed about by the waves" (5:2082). The court did not articulate from whom this enticement issued, although by now it should be clear that it came principally from the prosecution. The consequences of succumbing to this enticement were, for the court, clear: "Not only is any pretension to overstep these limits forbidden to the court — it would certainly end in complete failure" (5:2082). And while the court did not explain what it meant by "complete failure," it obviously had a particular example in mind.

Toward the end of its judgment, the court reflected on the meaning of the Holocaust: "The sum total of the suffering of the millions . . . is certainly beyond human understanding, and who are we to try to give it adequate expression? This is a task for the great writers and poets" (5:2146). Here the court seems to say that imaginative literature enjoys a superior power to represent and comprehend the Holocaust than legal discourse, but its invocation of Dinur/Katzetnik's collapse qualifies this claim: "Perhaps it is symbolic that even the author, who himself went through the hell named Auschwitz, could not stand the ordeal in the witness box and collapsed" (5:2146). Suddenly, it is not the law alone that is unable to grapple with the deeper issues of meaning posed by the Holocaust. Even "the great writers and poets" fail in this task. Yet for the court, Dinur/Katzetnik's collapse was a symbol of more than the unspeakability of Nazi crimes. For the court, the collapse supplied a cautionary tale for all who attempt to reach beyond their powers of knowing and judging. Dinur/Katzetnik's collapse became, then, a trope of *juridical* failure: his experience offers the most vivid example of the "complete failure" which awaits those, such as judges, who attempt to overreach the limits of their discursive forms.

The court's move, in this regard, can only be described as remarkable, revealing as it does the deeply self-referential quality of legal judgment. The collapse of the writer, a moment of spectacular courtroom drama, is enlisted as evidence of the very proposition that the court labored during the trial to prove—that the testimony of survivor witnesses was of questionable value to begin with, and that a court must never distort its procedures for judging criminality even in the face of unprecedented atrocities. Because these witnesses "themselves could not find the words to describe their suffering in all its depth," their testimony remained if not entirely irrelevant, then of marginal value (5:2146).

It is no coincidence that immediately after its discussion of the collapse of Dinur/Katzetnik, the court returned one final time to consider the specific relevance of the survivor testimony at the trial. Here the court noted that the witnesses provided evidence on a "part of the indictment [that] is not in dispute in this case" (5:2146). This echoes words that appear at the beginning of the court's judgment: "Without a doubt, the testimony given at this trial by survivors of the Holocaust, who poured out their hearts as they stood in the witness box, will provide valuable material for research workers and historians but as far as this Court is concerned, they are to be regarded as by-products of the trial" (5:2083). Once again, the court's appeal to institutional role and regulative procedure defined a strategy of legitimation through limiting the scope of the trial. By checking the legal value of survivor testimony, the judges made good on the perceived juridical obligation, echoed by Arendt, that mandates that "everything which is foreign to the purpose of . . . clarify[ing] whether the charges . . . against the accused are true . . . must be entirely eliminated from the court procedure" (5:2082). Yet, as we shall see in the next chapter, the court's effort to confine the testimony of the survivor witnesses to the fringes of evidentiary relevance ultimately did not prevent the prosecution from pursuing its didactic ends.[17]

6

. . .

Didactic Legality and Heroic Memory

Oh son of death, we do not wish you death.
May you live longer than anyone ever lived.
May you live sleepless five million nights.
— Primo Levi, "For Adolf Eichmann"

The Eichmann court perceived its integrity to be most gravely challenged
not by the defense but by the prosecution. While the defense challenged
the court's impartiality and jurisdictional competence, the authority of the
court to control the proceeding on a day-to-day basis was left largely undis-
turbed by Servatius. The prosecution, however, by attempting to transform
the trial into a didactic spectacle, presented a more foundational challenge
to the court. In the previous chapter, I analyzed the court's complicated efforts to respond to this challenge, particularly in terms of its effort to exert
juridical control over the words of survivor witnesses and thereby preserve
and enhance its conception of juridical legitimacy.

In that struggle, the prosecution appeared as the great defender of narrative and memory against the court's rigid dedication to traditional trial
form. In this chapter, the picture becomes more complicated. For as we
shall see, the prosecution's goal was not simply to let the words of the survivors, in the parlance of *Nazi Concentration Camps,* "speak for themselves."
Like the court, the prosecution struggled to control the meaning of these

words and thereby enlist them to support its own peculiarly legal vision of the trial. If the court engaged in complex efforts to marginalize survivor testimony, the prosecution performed equally complex maneuvers designed to enlist the anguished words of the survivors into a larger narrative of the reconstruction of self and nation in which the trial itself was meant to form a crucial chapter.

As noted earlier, Hausner began his opening address with the words, "When I stand before you here, Judges of Israel . . . I am not standing alone. With me are six million accusers. . . . Their blood cries out, but their voice is not heard" (*TAE* 1:62) (fig. 6.1). His invocation of the "Judges of Israel" and the image of a martyred people anticipate the words that he would use months later at the end of his summary address before the court:

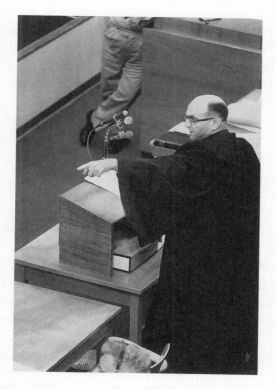

Fig. 6.1. "And lo, in the days of the return of Judah and Jerusalem, a trial is held here for the violence done to the sons of Judah" (*Trial of Adolf Eichmann* 5:2043). Attorney General Gideon Hausner assuming a characteristically accusatory pose. Courtesy of the Israeli Government Press Office.

"And lo, in the days of the return of Judah and Jerusalem, a trial is held here for the violence done to the sons of Judah and for their blood, the blood of innocents that was spilt, as foreseen by the prophet Joel. And again I ask you, Judges in Israel: Bring in a true and just verdict!" (5:2043).

The rhetoric is noteworthy for a number of reasons: First, the idiom of secular legality seems to be supplanted by the accents of Jewish law; second, the unprecedented catastrophe of the Holocaust seems to be recast as the fulfillment of a divine prophecy; third, the trial is seen as a celebration of legal self-sufficiency in which the power both to pass judgment and execute sentence is once again vested in a people left juridically and politically impotent since biblical times; and finally, the requirements of legal justice seem to be conceived in terms of a religiously inspired conception of vengeance.[1] This last point explains why Hausner's opening address and summary argument, despite its having many admirers, was subject to harsh criticism in certain legal circles. As Arendt points out, by conjuring the blood of innocents, "the prosecution gave substance to the chief argument against the trial, that it was established not in order to satisfy the demands of justice but to still the victims' desire for and, perhaps, right to vengeance."[2]

The court likewise believed that vengeance had no role in a legal forum and sternly rebuked those witnesses and spectators at the trial who made threatening or insulting statements to the accused and the defense. When the courtroom exploded in laughter after a witness's snide response to a question from Servatius, Presiding Judge Landau exclaimed, "We will have no demonstrations of feeling" (2:743), his very anger belying his command. And notwithstanding Hausner's occasional penchant for histrionics, the attorney general also refused to tolerate any disruptions that threatened to turn the proceeding into an exercise in collective vengeance. When a witness, asked if he still recognized the accused, responded, "Now he looks much better than he should look," Hausner interjected severely, "No, no, no, please, Mr. Gordon. No, no. I am asking you factual questions. Please answer them" (3:1130).

Hausner's position can be explained, then, by drawing a distinction between vengeance and retribution. Arendt herself drew such a distinction, noting that vengeance "acts in the form of re-acting against an original trespassing, . . . permitting the chain reaction contained in every action to take its unhindered course." By contrast, retribution, or what Arendt simply calls punishment, attempts "to put an end to something that without interference could go on endlessly."[3] The philosopher Jean Hampton has further elaborated the differences between vengeance and retribution, arguing that the "vengeful hater does not respect but aims to diminish the worth of the offender." The retributivist, on the other hand, "aims to defeat the wrong-doer in order to annul the evidence provided by the crime of [the wrong-doer's] relative superiority."[4]

Bearing in mind Arendt's and Hampton's positions, one can say that re-venge gains its passion from the absence of a legal remedy, while retribu-tion can be understood as the logic of punishment exacted by an authority confident in its monopoly of force. Thus the call to revenge represents a faute de mieux — want of a better alternative, as the absence of efficacious institutions of justice fuels the turn to urgent self-help.[5] Berel Lang notes that in a case brought against a Jewish collaborator, *Honigman v. The Legal Adviser to the Israeli Government* (1952), the Israeli Supreme Court had inter-preted the Nazis and Nazi Collaborators law of 1950 as designed "to 'seek revenge' on the enemies and haters of Israel."[6] This provocative conflation of legal punishment and revenge can perhaps be explained in light of the fact that, as we have seen, few believed the statute would ever be used against the principal perpetrators of the final solution: the spirit of revenge can thus be detected in a law cognizant of its own impotence. Hausner's powerful invocation "Judges of Israel," by contrast, does not rebel against institutions of ordered legality; on the contrary, Hausner's words are in-fused with the retributivist's pride of legal self-sufficiency, a spirit that im-plicitly rejects the logic of pure vengeance.

This point is strengthened by a closer consideration of Hausner's use of the words of the survivor witnesses. Earlier I suggested that Hausner at-tempted to use these words to construct a narrative of "heroic memory" — that is, memory that, in Langer's words, means "to salvage from the wreck-age of mass murder . . . a tribute to the victory of the human spirit." Langer argued that the logic of heroic memory often did violence to the experience of the survivor, as the insistence on the normative relevance of survival of-ten contradicted the radical melancholy of stories that "resist the organiz-ing impulse of moral theory."[7]

To understand how the prosecution attempted to turn survivor testi-monies into narratives of heroic memory, it is important to distinguish be-tween two different, though easily conflated, strategies used by the attorney general. In the first sense, the prosecution attempted to construct heroic memory by fashioning a history of the Holocaust in which the victims were seen not as helpless sheep or spineless collaborators, but as partisans and martyrs, fighters and heroes. The second sense in which the prosecution attempted to construct heroic memory involved its attempt to link the content of memory to the act of remembering *in a courtroom*. In this second regard, remembering, as a testimonial transaction performed in a court of law, was considered in itself a potent act, a gesture of resistance and normative reconstruction. The first technique of fortifying heroic memory attempted to shape a particular history of the Holocaust, while the second, more provocatively, strove to shape a history of the trial itself. In this way, the trial was seen as a necessary episode in the working through of the traumatic history of the Holocaust, providing correction and closure to individual and collective narratives of unredeemed horror. By using the testimony of the survivor witnesses in this dual fashion, the prosecution was able to expand the scope of the proceeding both to condemn the accused and to acquit his victims.

Erasing the Gray Zone

The roles that Jews played in the final solution has naturally been an extremely sensitive topic within Holocaust studies. The most nuanced and humane treatments of the subject, such as Levi's concept of the "gray zone" in *The Drowned and the Saved* and Bauman's interpretive discussion of the *Judenräte* (Jewish councils) in *Modernity and the Holocaust*,[8] discuss the opportunities for dignity and betrayal within a system of radically abrogated choice specifically designed to use victims as instruments of violence (either unwittingly, unavoidably, or sometimes willingly) upon each other. By contrast, Arendt's polemical claim that without the organizational assistance given by the various Jewish councils the aims of the final solution could never have been realized became the source of the most vehement attacks on *Eichmann in Jerusalem*. Indeed, the most controversial and vilified statement in her book was cast as an odd counterfactual: "The whole truth was that if the Jewish people had really been unorganized and leaderless, there would have been chaos and plenty of misery but the total number of victims would hardly have been between four and a half and six million people."[9] Arendt's blunt assertion, though lacking empathetic imagination, was, however, hardly novel: such an argument had already been the focus of intense legal and national attention in Israel. Before the Eichmann proceeding, the most important Holocaust litigation in the young state was the Kasztner trial of 1954, a civil suit involving a libel claim brought by Rezsö Kasztner, a former head of the Hungarian Jewish community and later a press spokesman for the Israeli Ministry of Commerce and Industry, against Malkiel Gruenwald, a marginal political fanatic who, in a newsletter printed and distributed at his own expense, accused Kasztner of "paving the way for the murder" of Hungarian Jewry.[10]

The Kasztner case posed a constellation of facts that tested a court's capacity sensitively to situate itself in an impossible history. How, for example, was one to make sense of the fact that Kasztner, as a prominent Jew, was able to negotiate a deal that permitted 1,685 Jews, among them a few dozen members of his family, to escape by a special train to Switzerland? Was this an example of a heroic effort to save a few in the face of otherwise certain destruction? or of a cowardly willingness to sacrifice the group to save one's kin and self? The trial dragged on for ten months, and another nine months passed before Judge Benjamin Halevi (later to be one of the three members of the Eichmann panel) issued his judgment: with the exception of one minor statement, Gruenwald's writings, Halevi concluded, had not been libelous. Following the sardonic English practice in such cases, Halevi awarded Kasztner the sum of one lira in damages. As a result of the verdict, Kasztner became a national pariah, a symbol of the Jew not simply as defenseless prey, but as venal accomplice in the destruction of his people. On appeal, however, the Israeli Supreme Court, by a vote of four to one, reversed the judgment of the trial court and reprimanded Halevi for having conflated Kasztner's moral conduct with the legal question of whether Gruenwald had proven that Kasztner had collaborated with the Nazis.[11] In accompanying dicta the Supreme Court went even further, acquitting Kasztner both legally and morally, observing that "there is collaboration that deserves praise and that, in any case, if it is not accompanied by malicious and evil intentions, it should not be condemned or seen as a moral failing."[12] Although the reversal, handed down in January 1958, may have helped rehabilitate Kasztner's reputation as a matter of collective memory, it failed to help him personally, for on March 3, 1957, he had fallen victim to the first political assassination in Israel since the creation of the state.

For my purposes the Kasztner trial is important for two reasons. First, it makes understandable the grave concerns that surrounded the announcement that Halevi was originally slated to serve as the sole trial judge in the Eichmann proceeding. Halevi's handling of the Kasztner trial had been so undisciplined that the chief justice of the Israeli Supreme Court complained that Halevi had acted as if there were no rules of judicial procedure. In his judgment, Halevi had characterized Kasztner's negotiations with Eichmann in Faustian terms, accusing the plaintiff of "selling his soul to the Devil."[13] This, at the very least, raised serious concerns about Halevi's objectivity, an issue that, as we've seen, was raised as a general challenge to the tribunal's competence. Indeed, the very statute mandating that persons tried under the 1950 law be judged by a three-person tribunal was amended specifically to obviate the possible embarrassment caused by permitting Halevi to preside by himself.[14]

As a second matter, the Kasztner affair revealed the extreme sensitivity of the topic of collaboration within the Jewish and Israeli community, a fact again made clear at the Eichmann trial. Of the numerous disturbances by spectators that marred the proceeding, a small but significant number were directed not at Eichmann, but at those Jewish witnesses who had served prominently in the Judenräte. Among these was Pinchas Freudiger, head of the orthodox community in Budapest in 1939–44, who had engaged in direct negotiations with Eichmann in the notoriously unsuccessful attempt to trade a million Jews for ten thousand trucks. Freudiger's testimony had to be temporarily adjourned because of multiple disturbances in the courtroom; one spectator shrieked at Freudiger in Hungarian, "You saved your own family and gave the rest of the Jews to the Nazis!" precipitating a volley of name calling.[15] Yet the Kasztner affair, too, revealed the tendency to examine the question of Jewish behavior in Manichean terms. It was often assumed that the survivor must have behaved venally in order to have lived. As in the medieval ordeal, one's innocence could be proved only by dying.

It is against this backdrop that one must understand the first sense in which Hausner attempted to create a narrative of heroic memory. Against the image of the helpless sheep on the one hand and the venal survivor on the other, Hausner used the trial to recast the terms of Holocaust history, forging a collective image of the victims and survivors as a people struggling valiantly to resist their physical, psychic, and religious destruction. In his opening address, Hausner claimed that the controversy regarding "the proper behaviour of a victim in his relations with the beast of prey" has "no place in the present trial," and "we shall leave it to the historian of the Holocaust" (*TAE* 1:71). Yet his own declarations notwithstanding, Hausner often labored not merely to condemn the accused but also to acquit his victims. It is, of course, not unusual for a prosecutor simultaneously to be involved in a process of defense; historically in American rape trials, the prosecution has often found itself forced to defend the victim. In the Eichmann trial, however, Hausner did not have to perform this act as a matter of prosecutorial necessity: Servatius, to his credit, never attempted to make the actions of the victims a matter of legal contention. Instead, Hausner's effort was directed against a collective understanding that existed outside the courtroom, and it was to the public at large, both nationally and internationally, that he directed his gestures of acquittal.

Emblematic was a question that Hausner posed to Moshe Beisky, a Tel Aviv magistrate (and future justice of the Israeli Supreme Court) originally from Cracow who survived internment at Plaszów: "15,000 people stood there—and opposite them hundreds of guards. Why didn't you attack then, why didn't you revolt?" (1:349). In the words of one journalist, Beisky "appeared staggered" by Hausner's "harsh question" and began "to talk in incomplete sentences, gesturing with both hands."[16] Yet it was a question that Hausner would pose again and again to witness after witness, and while Arendt condemns Hausner for humiliating the survivors, such obviously was not his end. Though at times histrionic, if not directly obnoxious, Hausner clearly was trying to accord the witnesses an opportunity to explain their (in)action to a skeptical nation and international community.[17] The devil's advocate, he hoped to provoke his witnesses to a more complete explanation of their behavior.

Hausner's effort to create a narrative of heroic memory also required offering the survivor witnesses numerous chances to describe their various gestures of resistance. As noted, heroes of the Jewish resistance like Pinchas Zuckerman, Zvia Lubetkin-Zuckerman, and Abba Kovner were called as witnesses. Still other witnesses were encouraged to describe less well-known acts of defiance and rebellion. Avraham Aviel, a survivor from Poland, described the "inner resistance" he felt to his mother's command that he chant the Sh'ma, the prayer signifying the readiness of a person to die for his faith, as they were marched to their execution; Aviel escaped and became active in the partisans (1:497). Joseph Reznik, at the time of the trial the owner of a modest store in Tel Aviv, described his daring escape from an SS extermination squad in simple but proud terms: "Our chains were inspected every day. One day, immediately after the inspection, we decided to break our chains. I do not want to brag. I broke the chains of eight men" (3:1161).

The survivors described not only their attempts to resist physical destruction, but also their myriad efforts to keep their religious and personal identities alive. Rivka Kuper, the widow of the leader of the Hebrew underground in Cracow, described lighting candles and singing Sabbath songs in the darkness of a Birkenau block (1:432). Liona Neumann, a survivor of the actions in Riga, told the court how she drew strength from studying Hebrew and Zionism with a group of young people in the evening (1:509). David Wdowinski, a survivor of the Jewish labor camp in Budzay'n, described how he baked *matzot* on the eve of Passover in 1944 in a camp oven (3:1236). These stories did more than simply contribute poignant examples of people struggling to maintain religious meaning in the face of catastrophe; more important, they suggested how a commitment to the Jewish religion and, more specifically, to the politics of Zionism supported acts of physical resistance. Aharon Hoter-Yishai, a former officer in the Jewish Brigade, the fighting unit sent to Europe by the British authorities in Palestine, recounted to the court how those who had survived the exterminations responded to the sight of a Jewish fighting force: "However miraculous these happenings might seem to me today, it was sufficient to take a sheet and paint a Shield of David on it with ink and, after attaching it to a broomstick, to give it to two to three hundred persons — each of whom looked like a skeleton — and then . . . they had the strength to congregate and to refuse" (3:1351).

On one level, these stories supported a particular understanding of the history of the Holocaust, one in which the religious commitment and indefatigable spirit of the Jewish people could not be vanquished even in the face of extermination. On another level, the narratives buttressed a specifically Israeli ideology of nationhood and Jewish identity. By emphasizing the role that Zionism and the Jewish Brigades played in helping Jews preserve hope and thereby both resist and survive, the prosecution was able to create a provocative post hoc picture of history, one in which the present is not born of the past, but in which the past is constituted by the terms of the present. This view of history is not without its implicit moral, as it suggests that those who were able to persevere psychically and physically were those who possessed, in embryonic form, precisely those characteristics that are seen by Hausner and his contemporaries as constituting the core of Israeli national identity. Survival is thus comprehended in a normative framework that affirms a present ideology of national self-determination. Indeed, the very pride in legal self-sufficiency that Hausner displayed in his appeals to the court became part of a deeper story of the link between political survival and legal potency.

At times, the trial itself contrived to support Hausner's logic. Early on, the proceedings were interrupted by the sirens observing Yom Hazikkaron, the day dedicated to the memory of those who had died in the Israeli war of independence.[18] The transcript captures the complex intrusions of past and present, as the interruption occurred precisely as the court was listening to the excerpt of Eichmann's interrogation in which the accused described his first contact with the technique of gassing:

E I C H M A N N: The captain of the Order Police . . . told me how he had made everything here hermetically sealed, . . . since an engine of a Russian submarine was going to operate here . . .
P R E S I D I N G   J U D G E: Please stop now. We shall have a two minutes' silence in memory of those who fell in our wars.
[*Silence*]
[*Continues reading the translation.*]
. . . and gases of this engine were going to be directed inside and the Jews would be poisoned. [1:134]

The memorializing logic of Yom Hazikkaron finds itself framed by Eichmann's words. The Holocaust, at this moment, is assimilated into the tortured history of the Jewish people at the same time that it is treated as the cataclysm that justifies the present military sacrifices of the Israeli state. Soldiers do battle so that the Jew will never again be mere victim, while the victims are recast as protean soldiers.

The image of the Holocaust victim as fallen soldier was conjured later in the trial during the testimony of Hulda Campagnano, an Italian survivor (and daughter of a famous professor of Semitic languages). Following Hausner's lead, Campagnano began by describing the fates of her brother and sister: "They were both for a certain time in Auschwitz, and they even managed to exchange some words in writing; he would send a note to her, and once she sent a note to him. Afterwards they were separated" (2:657). Campagnano never was able to learn what became of her brother. About her sister, however, she explained, "She was sent to Bergen-Belsen and finally to Theresienstadt, and there she was liberated. She reached this country in 1945. It is from her that I heard many of the details I have just told you. Later she was herself killed by Arabs in the convoy that went up to Mount Scopus in 1948" (2:657). On one level, Campagnano's story seems bitterly ironic, as the sister survived the death camps only to die at the hands of Arabs. It echoes, in this respect, other stories told by survivors at the trial. On the day before Campagnano's testimony, the court heard from Joseph Melkman, formerly a Dutch physician and from 1957 to 1960 the director of Yad Vashem. Melkman and his wife worked for a time in the children's home in Westerbork, the Dutch holding camp from which Jews were "dispatched . . . away to the East" (2:617). The home was for children who for all practical purposes were orphans—those whose parents had disappeared or had been deported. Melkman recalled a boy named van Dam, seized during a raid of his parents' place of hiding: "He was ten years old. He had been cooped up for a whole year in a narrow room, he was not allowed to talk in a normal voice. . . . He was not allowed to walk as a child would walk, lest the neighbors should hear him. When he came to Westerbork, he . . . began speaking in whispers. When we told him that there was no need to do so . . . he began running round the grounds of the children's home all the time, he could not stop himself, and he shouted very loudly" (2:616). The boy experienced the same fate as almost all the Westerbork orphans: "He was sent three days later to Auschwitz" (2:617).

Campagnano's and Melkman's stories seem, on the surface, to be of a kind. Indeed, Melkman's story perfectly fits Primo Levi's description of "moments of reprieve"—"bizarre, marginal moments . . . in which the compressed identity can reacquire for a moment its lineaments"[19]—as the boy's desperate, overzealous, altogether too brief celebration of his freedom is framed against his deportation to Auschwitz. And while Campagnano's story also brims with dark irony—the sister's liberation lasts no more than three years before her murder on Mt. Scopus—the story of her killing supports Hausner's larger effort to construct a heroic link between the history of the Holocaust and the reality of the Israeli state. For Campagnano's story forges an organic link between the past and present, one in which the very forces that were once bent on exterminating European Jewry now appear as the military enemies of the fledgling Israeli state. Campagnano's sister is recast, then, as a martyr for the young nation. Her death is not meaningless; on the contrary, she died having fulfilled her narrative imperative, as seen by the fact that her story lives on in her sister's testimony; moreover, her death stands as a poignant reminder that the struggle for a peaceful existence for the Jewish people is ongoing and can be accomplished only through the spirit of combat that made survival during the Holocaust possible. Again, the story supports the deeper claims of heroic memory. Just as Kuper's and Aviel's stories showed that survival during the Holocaust was not fortuitous—it was enabled by a determined allegiance to the Jewish faith and Zionist commitments—Campagnano's story, suggests that death was not meaningless: it was a sacrifice for the young state determined to offer security to all Jews.

The second sense in which the prosecution constructed heroic memory was by treating the act of narrative unburdening as normatively relevant and *legally potent*. As observed in the discussion of Leon Wells's testimony, the need to tell what happened gave camp inmates a powerful incentive for survival. In Wells's telling, personal survival was less relevant than the survival of the narrative: "The only idea was that one of us survives and tells the world what happened here" (1:374). Dov Freiberg, a survivor of Sobibòr, echoed Wells when he told the court, "We had to inform the world; somebody had to be sent outside, we had to try and escape" (3:1174). Similar as their words were, there is a small but crucial difference in the testimonial imperative of Wells and Freiberg. Wells understood the burden of testimony as a retrospective act of describing and recording a catastrophe that has happened. It is an effort to prevent the extinction of the memory of the horror. For Freiberg, however, the testimonial imperative is one of prospective warning. As a witness to an ongoing process of extermination, Freiberg believed it necessary to escape in order to tell others and thus organize effective resistance. Freiberg's need to bear witness was linked to a logic of resistance, whereas Wells contemplated a far bleaker situation in which resistance has been rendered futile and testimony serves to mark the traces of the exterminated.

In the prosecution's construction of heroic memory, Wells's and Freiberg's contrasting motives for bearing witness were complexly conflated. The prosecution understood the act of bearing witness as more than merely a memorializing performance, an agonizing ritual of tracing absence. Performed in a courtroom in a criminal trial, it *was* an act of resistance. Such an understanding again erased the fortuitous or accidental from the logic of survival. Because survival was a means of keeping a narrative of atrocity alive, the act of refusing to succumb was endowed with normative meaning. Second, the prosecution's vision of bearing witness as an act of post hoc resistance powerfully supported the trial as an exercise in didactic legality. Here, then, is an even more complex variation of the prosecution's challenge to the court's legalistic understanding of the trial. The trial, from the prosecution's perspective, was meant to be not only an occasion for the public sharing of difficult narratives, but also, more centrally, an event staged on behalf of survivors in order to fulfill an obligation to them. The trial was something owed to the survivors; it was the fulfillment of a teleology of survival. By turning testimony into legal evidence, the trial transformed the witness from Wells's ancient mariner, a stunned and isolated survivor, into Freiberg's potent resister. Meaning and normative coherence were thus stamped upon the act of surviving by transforming the narratives of horror into legal evidence. By using the narratives of survivors as legal proof, the prosecution turned them into juridically potent acts, challenging both the court's and Arendt's formal conceptions of legality. Even if shunted to the side by the court, bleak tales of the Holocaust became tools of legal justice.

Many of the prosecution's witnesses offered implicit support of this provocative logic. A number of witnesses testified that they had lived in anticipation of precisely the day when they would be called to tell their story in a court of law.[20] Adolf Berman, a former member of the Warsaw ghetto resistance, concluded his testimony by describing how he visited Treblinka shortly after his liberation by the Soviet army: "I saw a scene which I shall never forget: a tremendous expanse, extending over many kilometers, and on this area there were scattered skulls, bones, in tens of thousands, and very, very many shoes, amongst them tens of thousands of shoes of little children" (1:426). Berman proceeded, then, to remove one such pair of small shoes from his briefcase. In silence, he held them before the court (fig. 6.2). It was a stunning moment, in terms of the shoes' power to conjure the single missing child and of the power of a single object to stand for the slaughter of the innocents. Yet it was also Berman's position in the story that explains why the sight of the shoes emerged as one of the most moving moments of the trial. For one felt that Berman had been carrying the shoes around in his well-worn briefcase since the day he discovered them at the ruins of Treblinka. Only now had he finally been supplied an occasion for placing his terrible memento on display on a world stage. By permitting Berman to display his shoes in a manner that transformed this artifact of loss into evidence of criminality, the trial provided a degree of closure to the traumatic memories that Berman had been carrying around since the war's end.

Such was also the impression made by Martin Földi (fig. 6.3). A Hungarian lawyer, Földi described to the court the selection that took place immediately after he and his family arrived at Auschwitz:

> They said to us that the men should stand on the right side with children over the age of 14, and the women on the left with the young boys and

Fig. 6.2. Adolf Berman holds before the court a pair of children's shoes taken
from the "tens of thousands of shoes of children" left at Treblinka.
Courtesy of the Israeli Government Press Office.

girls. . . . I stood with my son who was only 12 years old. After we started
moving forward, I suddenly came up to a certain man. . . . He was dressed
in a uniform of the German army, elegant, and he asked me what my profession was. I knew that being a lawyer by profession would not be very
helpful and, therefore, told him that I was a former officer. He looked at
me and asked, "How old is the boy?" At that moment I could not lie, and
told him: 12 years old. And then he said: *"Wo ist die Mutti?"* (And where is
your mother?) I answered: "She went to the left." Then he said to my son:
"Run after your mother." . . . I wondered to myself, how would he be able
to find his mother there? After all, there were so many women and men,
but I caught sight of my wife. How did I recognize her? My little girl was
wearing some kind of a red coat. The red spot was a sign that my wife was
near there. The red spot was getting smaller and smaller. I walked to the
right and never saw them again. [3:968]

Fig. 6.3. "I could not lie." Martin Földi on the stand.
Courtesy of the Israeli Government Press Office.

It is, for many reasons, a difficult and poignant story. (Gabriel Bach, who examined Földi for the prosecution, was so affected by the testimony that he
momentarily was unable to continue his examination.) For one familiar with
popular-cultural representations of the Holocaust, the image of the re-
ceding red coat powerfully anticipates the device used to dramatic effect by
both the novelist Thomas Keneally and the filmmaker Steven Spielberg in
Schindler's List, in the scene in which Schindler tracks the fate of a single girl
dressed in a red coat during a ghetto action. Also provocative is the notion of
Földi's inability to lie to save his son. "At that moment I could not lie": we
are never told why he could not lie, though presumably at the time he had
absolutely no reason to believe that his veracity would have such tragic consequences. Yet he does not say this. He simply declares that he was disabled
from lying and is unable even to offer an entirely understandable postfactum

explanation for his fatal veracity. In this sense, Földi once again displayed before the court the very helpless fidelity to the truth that he had demonstrated before the Nazi officer. Yet the very quality that led him inadvertently to assist in his son's doom now appeared as the single greatest virtue for a witness testifying before a court. Importantly, then, the trial gave Földi more than the mere opportunity to describe the terrible consequences of his misplaced veracity. Instead, the trial rectified the normative imbalance of the "concentrationary universe," in which fidelity to the truth could prove catastrophic. By testifying at the trial, Földi was thus able to rehabilitate himself, as truthfulness is the most desirable and virtuous characteristic for a witness. By rewarding veracious testimony as probative of the guilt of the accused, the prosecution restored normative coherence to Földi's experience and conferred a degree of closure to his terrible narrative.

The testimonies of a number of witnesses, however, challenged and at times subverted the prosecution's effort to comprehend the act of bearing legal witness as an act that restores closure and normative coherence to a world disturbed by traumatic memory. At times this resistance manifested itself in the subtle ways that the survivor witnesses were unable to bring closure to their testimony. As noted, Hausner, at the insistence of the court, attempted to rein in the narrative impulse of the witnesses by structuring their testimony around a set of leading questions. Before the court's intervention, Hausner had attempted to encourage open-ended storytelling without the conventional structure of tutored interrogatories. Yet even this less formalized approach possessed an unmistakable structure.[21] Invariably, the attorney general began his examinations by asking the witness to state his or her name and his or her present circumstances; he then immediately shifted to the witness's wartime experiences, beginning with questions about the witness's activities before the coming of the Nazis. This line of questioning quickly turned to the story of atrocity and survival, exploring this material for the bulk of the examination, and then concluding with cursory questions about the witness's liberation. The general form of this examination structured survivor testimony as a tale of radical disruption framed by the bookends of the normal — that is, pre- and post-Holocaust existence. Balance, in this understanding, is incompletely restored, first through liberation at the war's end and now, more completely, at the trial that permits the survivor to satisfy the testimonial urge. Moreover, by situating the witness first in the present and then moving quickly back to his or her pre-Holocaust experience, these interrogatories insisted on the continuity of self through the episode of disruption. Although Hausner remained mindful of the enormous sufferings of the survivors, the narrative form through which this suffering was directed to speak had the consequence of conventionalizing it and, in so doing, containing its deeper, bleaker aspects.

The testimonies of a number of the survivor witnesses, however, resisted these efforts to conventionalize. The testimony of Ya'akov Biskowitz, a survivor of Sobibòr, does not stand out as an especially important moment in the trial, though it remains memorable in one respect. As a constable in the Israeli police, Biskowitz testified in uniform (fig. 6.4). The presence of a uniformed man on the stand created the initial impression that Biskowitz would testify about matters within his official function, such as the behav-

Fig. 6.4. "I should like to describe just one further incident": Police Constable Ya'akov Biskowitz on the stand. Courtesy of the Israeli Government Press Office.

ior of the accused during his time in custody. Instead, the uniform served to remind the spectators that the very officials responsible for overseeing the accused once numbered among his victims. Against the vision of the police as officials of the state, enjoying a monopoly on means of legitimate violence, spectators were asked to imagine the present officer as himself once a powerless, stateless inmate.

Biskowitz's story formally ended with the witness's description of linking up with Russian partisans. After a few clarifying questions from the court, Biskowitz was told that he could stand down. Yet the witness, dressed in the same khaki as the silent guards who kept watch on the man in the glass booth, was unable to bring himself to leave the stand. "There was another shocking case which I witnessed," Biskowitz suddenly declared, "and I should like to describe just this one further incident" (3:1188). The court responded, predictably enough, by declining the officer's invitation with an apology. Yet Biskowitz's need to circle back to the incomplete story of catastrophe, to resist the effort to conclude his testimony with a tale of liberation, became emblematic of a general pattern in which survivor narratives disturbed the coherent chronologies that the prosecution attempted to secure.

The line between past and present found itself blurred in the words of numerous survivors. Shim'on Srebrnik was one of only a handful of known survivors of the Chelmno extermination camp, whose victims numbered some 320,000 (fig. 6.5).[22] This fact alone renders him a statistical freak, and years after his appearance on the stand at the Eichmann trial, Srebrnik's story of survival would provide Lanzmann's *Shoah* with many of the documentary's most stunning moments. Indeed, for one familiar with the story told in Lanzmann's film of the agile boy who won "the jumping contests and speed races that the ss organized for their chained prisoners" and who serenaded his guards with his sweetly sung Polish folk songs, Srebrnik's testimony at the Eichmann trial is remarkable for its omissions. There is no melodious refrain of the simple tune that haunts both Lanzmann's film and the Polish residents of Chelmno who, decades later, can vividly recall the sound of his singing: "A little white house / lingers in my memory. Of that white house / each night I dream."[23] These gaps in the trial transcript remain telling, for the act of reading his testimony in light of what one learns about Srebrnik in *Shoah* reminds one that even in a trial that struggled toward a capacious understanding of the testimonial moment, the narratives presented to the court remained truncated and partial.

Fig. 6.5. Shim'on Srebrnik, the child-singer of Chelmno, testifying before
photographs of dioramas of Treblinka built by Ya'akov Wiernik.
Courtesy of the Israeli Government Press Office.

During his time on the stand at the Eichmann trial, Srebrnik limited his
testimony to a description of how he was a witness to his own execution.
Shot in the back of head, he survived because the bullet passed through his
mouth, knocking out his two front teeth. After asking Srebrnik to describe
his wounds, Hausner suddenly asked the witness about the fate of his
mother. Srebrnik described how while working in the extermination camp
sorting through the personal effects of the dead, he came across photographs of his mother. Whereupon Hausner asked, "Does this wound still
bother you occasionally?" (3:1201). Whether Hausner was referring to the
physical wound to his neck and mouth or to the psychic scar left by the
death of his mother remains unclear. And Srebrnik's answer—"I don't
sleep at night, I cannot sleep at night. I am constantly haunted" (3:1201) —
did not clarify the matter. Indeed, his response suggests that the physical
and psychic scars are inseparable. Neither have healed, and the wounds of
the past continue to disturb the present.

At times the slippage between past and present occurred inadvertently.
Gedalia Ben-Zvi, a survivor of Birkenau, described to the court her work
in the Canada kommando, the group of inmates responsible for sorting

through the vast storerooms crammed with the personal effects "plundered and taken from people who had been dispatched to the gas chambers" (3:1298). The storeroom, she explained, was called Canada because of its large size and abundance of goods; in Canada, one could find anything, "even lemons" (3:1298). Following the format used by the prosecution, her testimony ended with a story of liberation—a description of how, along with a man, she escaped from the ss and wandered about until the war's end. The story would be unremarkable, except for a detail that emerged about her co-escapee: "I happened to learn by chance today [that he] is at present in Canada" (3:1303). The unexpected mention of Canada led Hausner immediately to interject, "The real Canada?" (3:1303). It was an odd, even comic, question, yet we need but recall Dinur/Katzetnik's hallucinatory words, "I see them, they are staring at me . . ." to realize that Ben-Zvi's assurance, "Yes, the real Canada," was hardly gratuitous.

A number of witnesses also challenged the belief that the very act of survival can be comprehended in normative terms. Like Srebrnik, Michael Podchlewnik was one of the very few survivors of Chelmno, and, also like Srebrnik, Podchlewnik would appear in Lanzmann's *Shoah*. Podchlewnik, however, argued that he survived not as a result of his personal will, but in spite of it. As a member of a detail that had unloaded the bodies of his wife and two children from a mobile gassing van, Podchlewnik had lain down beside the members of his family and asked an ss man to kill him: "He hit me twice with a stick and dragged me away to continue working" (3:1192). Later, when he described his escape, Podchlewnik related how he tried to convince a fellow Jew to follow him, "but he said he still had family somewhere, he could not escape" (3:1192). In Podchlewnik's telling, normal human attachments, the binds of family, prove fatal to the project of survival. Against the prosecution's larger narrative, in which religious faith and political conviction were keys to physical survival, Podchlewnik's story suggests that the survivors were often those with nothing left to lose, persons who could persevere precisely because living was of no consequence, and for whom even the prospect of bearing witness at some speculative future moment offered little succor or incentive. As opposed to the prosecution's image of the survivor as hero—a warrior for the state of Israel years before the state's very founding, a fighter sustained by the quest for some possible future legal justice—Podchlewnik asks one to imagine the survivor as an untouchable, a lost soul left free to live *because* he or she has been severed from conventional human ties. The act of bearing witness does not restore meaning; on the contrary, Podchlewnik comprehends the act of testifying as simply a return to the abyss. When asked years later during the filming of *Shoah* whether he thought it was "good to talk about" the Holocaust, Podchlewnik responded (through his daughter's translation), "For me it's not good." When asked why, then, he was talking about it, his daughter replied, "Because you're insisting on it. He was sent books on Eichmann's trial. He was a witness, and he didn't even read them."[24]

The most provocative clash between the prosecution's normative understanding of survival and the words of a witness can be found in the testimony of Rivka Yoselewska. Like the testimony of Yehiel Dinur, the novelist who collapsed on the stand, Yoselewska's testimony gave the trial some of its greatest moments of melodrama. First her testimony had to be delayed, as Hausner shocked the courtroom by announcing that the witness had suffered a heart attack on the very morning she was to have taken the stand. Some days later, Yoselewska appeared before the court "with a gaunt and tragic face" (fig. 6.6).[25] A survivor of an *Aktion* on the outskirts of Pinsk in Russia, Yoselewska described how she witnessed the killing of her entire family — including her daughter, mother, father, grandmother, aunt, and cousins. Horrific in its own right was the tale Yoselewska told of her own "killing," a story echoed in such works as Anatoly Kuznetsov's *Babi Yar* and D. M. Thomas's *The White Hotel*. She described how immediately after her daughter (dressed in her Sabbath dress) was shot, she herself was shot and flung into the pit of corpses: "I felt nothing . . . I thought I was dead, but that I could feel something even though I was dead. . . . I felt I was suffocating, bodies had fallen on me. I felt I was drowning. But still I could not move and felt I was alive and tried to get up. I was choking, I heard shots, and again somebody falling down . . . I had no strength left. But I felt that somehow I was crawling upwards. As I climbed up, people grabbed me, hit me, dragged me downwards, but I pulled myself up with the last bit of strength" (1:517).

After managing to climb out of the pit, Yoselewska wandered about the mass grave, a spectral being seemingly invisible to those around her: "Germans came and helped round up the children. They left me alone. I just sat and looked" (1:517). Sometime later — it isn't clear when — Yoselewska dragged herself back to the grave which had since been covered with dirt: "Blood was spouting. Nowadays, when I pass a water fountain I can still see the blood spouting from the grave. The earth rose and heaved. I sat there on the grave and tried to dig my way in with my hands" (1:517–18).

Fig. 6.6. "Rivka Yoselewska symbolizes the entire Jewish people." The symbol on the stand, May 8, 1961. Courtesy of the Israeli Government Press Office.

The image of the blood spouting from the grave is astonishing, not least of all because it resembles the story that Eichmann himself had told when describing the killing operation he witnessed as a Gestapo observer. Here, then, a story whose details suggest the figurative prose of a biblical allegory forges a remarkable link between the accused and a survivor. Also striking is the image of the survivor as an undead — a person condemned to live, unable, despite her efforts to claw her way back into the grave, to receive the comfort and the companionship of the corpses. For three days Yoselewska remained sprawled naked on the grave while Polish peasants on their way to and from their fields threw stones at her (1:518). After wandering around for several weeks, Yoselewska was taken in by a peasant who gave her food; later she joined a group of Jews in the forest, and there she lived until the arrival of the Soviets. Absent from her story is any notion of resistance and any idea that her personal survival can be ascribed to anything other than the most inscrutable and, from her perspective, cruel logic. Equally absent is any sense that she was sustained by the prospect of offering testimony or that the act of now bearing witness was one that restores any normative or existential order to her life. Indeed, she seems to comprehend her survival as the punishment for an unnamed sin.

The prosecution's response to this narrative followed the pattern already observed. The prosecution brought Yoselewska's testimony to a close with a single concluding question: "And now you are married and you have two children?" (1:518). Here one must acknowledge how difficult it is to imagine a woman who once tried to claw her way into a mass grave now as a mother and wife; yet, the question and her simple response, "Yes," were meant to return the witness to the present and bring closure to her story on a note of affirmation.

In its concluding argument before the court, the prosecution returned to Yoselewska's testimony, transforming the witness into a symbol. We have already seen how the court, in its final judgment, turned Dinur's collapse into a cautionary tale of legal failure, a trope for the spectacular debacle that awaits those who transgress discursive and institutional limits; now in its own summary argument, the prosecution also treated the witness as a symbol, only this time discovering a very different moral. For Hausner, then,

> Rivka Yoselewska embodies in her person all that was perpetrated, all that happened to the Jewish people. She was shot. She was already amongst the dead in the funeral pit. Everything drew her downwards, to death. Wounded and wretched, with unbelievable strength she arose out of the grave. Her physical wounds healed, but her heart was torn asunder and broken forever. She found asylum in our country, established her home here and built her life anew. She overcame the evil design. They wanted to kill her, but she lives — they wanted to blot out her memory, but she has brought forth new children. The dry bones have been given sinews, flesh has grown upon them and they have taken on skin; they have been infused with the spirit of life. Rivka Yoselewska symbolizes the entire Jewish People. [5:2004]

Evocative if not melodramatic, the statement encapsulates the prosecution's understanding of the case. The stunned and disoriented survivor is transformed into both a hero and a symbol; the cruel and inscrutable logic of survival is translated into a morality play about the tenacity of the will; a tale of the desolation of meaning is turned into a story of personal and collective rebirth; and the ruins of memory become the vibrant source of a new generation to keep the narrative alive.

But by turning the survivor into a trope of the rebirth of the Jewish people in the state of Israel, the prosecution portrayed the Eichmann trial as something more than a tool for adjudging the guilt of the accused or even for memorializing the dead and honoring the experience of the survivors. By identifying the survivor's struggle with the state's fight for self-determination, Hausner ultimately turned the *trial itself* into an expression of the very powers of will and memory that made individual survival possible.

This understanding was more complex than the court's. For the prosecution, the survivor was imagined as a symbol of the rebirth of the Jewish people, and the trial as an example of the newfound efficacy of a reborn nation. Together they served, in the minds of the prosecution, as instances of the reconstruction of a people organized around a new national identity. The unburdening of memory, the sharing of narrative, were means of doing justice, at the same time that doing justice served to preserve the memory of the catastrophe. Memory and justice, then, were ingredients in the normative reconstruction of a people once slated for extermination. The experience of juridical potency and the power to give tortured memory the force of legal evidence were not merely examples of what the state could do for survivors. They were part of the ongoing project of "infusing the spirit of life" into a damaged people.

Banality and Legality

In the last pages of *Eichmann in Jerusalem*, Arendt arrogates unto herself the voice of juridical authority, supplying the missing terms of the decision that she believes should have been written by the Jerusalem court. Whatever one may think of this imagined act of judicial usurpation, it highlights Arendt's belief that the trial was, in the final analysis, a legal failure. Although in general she gives the court higher grades than the prosecution, she argues that both failed to grasp the distinctive meaning of the Holocaust as a matter of law — a failure she traces back to the charging statute.[26] By framing the crimes of the accused as committed against the Jewish people, the court treated these crimes "as not much more than the most horrible pogrom in Jewish history."[27] In so doing, she claims, it failed to provide the law with the proper idiom to digest a crime whose complexly enfolded bureaucratization demanded a reimagined connection between the criminal mind and criminal act.[28] Such an idiom was at hand, she argues: the concept of crimes against humanity, pioneered at Nuremberg, could have been used to confer legal recognition on the fact that genocide offends against "mankind in its entirety" and cannot be comprehended by the ordinary legal category of murder.[29] By failing to try Eichmann for crimes against humanity, the trial missed, in her view, an opportunity to build on the one distinctive achievement of the IMT and undercut its relevance as a precedent for the evolving body of international law.[30]

Here one cannot help noting the unintended irony of her critique. For as we have seen, the Nuremberg trial never used crimes against humanity as the boldly innovative legal instrument envisioned by Arendt. Indeed, the Israelis' creation of a separate offense, the crimes against the Jewish people, can be seen as born of the failure of crimes against humanity adequately to name and comprehend the crimes of the Holocaust. Of course, the failure of the Nuremberg trial to articulate a robust concept of crimes against humanity does not in and of itself discredit Arendt's point, which remains aspirational: the Eichmann trial, she contends, missed a critical chance to improve upon the imperfect legal instrument fashioned at Nuremberg.

While there is merit to this position, I still believe Arendt was wrong to characterize the failures of the Eichmann trial as legal. As Arendt herself had to acknowledge, the skeptics who feared a show trial in the Stalinist sense were on the whole silenced by the court's vigilant policing of trial procedure (unorthodox as it may have been). Finally, to judge the success of a trial exclusively in terms of the juridical precedent it delivers to future courts is to entertain precisely the classically formalist vision of the criminal law challenged by the prosecution. Evaluated from the prosecution's legal perspective, the Eichmann trial did serve as a precedent in a distinctive way: it galvanized legal, political, and cultural interest in the Holocaust in much of Europe and above all in Germany, clearing the path to the important Auschwitz trial staged in Frankfurt in 1963–65.[31] Within Israel, the process of testimonial unburdening occasioned by the trial led to a dramatic increase in the number of survivors who subsequently came forth to record their stories at Yad Vashem. The Eichmann trial demands, then, to be viewed as a legal success insofar as it transformed understandings of what the law can and should do in the wake of traumatic history.

A more provocative challenge to the trial issued not from Arendt, but from her *Doktorvater*, the philosopher Karl Jaspers, who argued for the staging of what he called a "moral trial." In a letter written to Arendt in December 1960, several months before the start of the trial, Jaspers wrote, "Just as the actions like Eichmann's—you said it beautifully—stand outside the pale of what is comprehensible in human and moral terms, so the legal basis of this trial is dubious. Something other than law is at stake here — and to address it in legal terms is a mistake."[32]

In certain respects, Jasper's critique of the Eichmann proceeding simply repeated attacks that Arendt, to her credit, dismissed. He decried the kidnapping that brought Eichmann from Buenos Aires to Jerusalem as illegal and questioned the jurisdictional competence of the Jerusalem court on the grounds that "Israel didn't even exist when the murders were committed."[33] But on a more interesting level, Jasper's idea that "something other than law is at issue here" extended the insight of Arendt that I examined in part I — namely, that Nazi crimes stretch and overtax conventional jurisprudential understandings.

Instead of focusing on the question of responsibility, Jasper argues that courts should be centrally concerned with digesting the past in a manner that does justice to the historical record. He recognizes, of course, that the law can play a useful role in advancing this goal. The law's immense powers of discovery and fact-finding can be deployed to uncover historical truth, while a quasi-juridical setting, with the calling of witnesses and the submission of physical evidence, would provide the kind of highly visible forum best suited to advance the goal of exigent pedagogy. Jaspers himself expands upon this vision, imagining a tribunal that anticipates the truth commissions later to be used in South America and South Africa: "Now I have this foolishly simplistic idea: It would be wonderful to do without the trial altogether and make it instead into a process of examination and clarification. The goal would be the best possible objectification of the historical facts. The end result would not be the judges' sentence, but certainty about the facts, to the extent that certainty can be attained."[34]

Jaspers's proposal asks one to consider whether the interests of didactic pedagogy would be better served by a trial, however capaciously conceived, or by a forum relieved of the need to satisfy the core concerns of legality. In embracing the latter, Jaspers overlooks the notion that the very attention directed at a legal proceeding might be born of the drama produced when stories receive resolution in judgment and when narratives find emphatic closure in juridically sanctioned violence (fig. 6.7). For a trial without judgment is like a race without a finish — it lacks the sine qua non of dramatic closure that frames and adds meaning to the shared narratives. As a strategic matter, then, it is questionable whether the end of exigent pedagogy can be advanced by a forum stripped of the essential characteristics of the trial as a legal form.[35] Absent the disciplining drama of judg-

Fig. 6.7. The drama of legal judgment: the trial as televised spectacle.
Courtesy of the Israeli Government Press Office.

ment, such an exercise has the attractions of the meandering lecture or the interminable story.

Indeed, it was this insight that animated the prosecution's powerful arguments for the death penalty. In the penalty phase of the proceeding, Hausner acknowledged, "It is not always possible to apply a punishment which fits the enormity of the crime" but still asked the court to "remember the faces and the reactions of those survivors who testified here, when the suffering and the anguish buried in their hearts re-emerged, when the conjuring up of the images of those who have gone struck down a man in a dead faint" (5:2214, 2213). Distinctive in the prosecution's approach (and in distinction to Jasper's "simplistic idea") was the notion that the imposition of the law's most severe sanction was a means of providing a sense of an ending to traumatic memory. Against Servatius's argument that the pedagogic "purpose of the trial is achieved with the guilty verdict," and therefore the court could afford to "show mercy," Hausner framed the necessity of the death penalty both in terms of legal potency and narrative closure (5:2216). The law could not serve as the great tool of normative restoration, capable of reinserting meaning into a universe evacuated of existential and ethical significance, in the absence of the death penalty.

The court sentenced Eichmann to death but, predictably enough, offered a justification very different from the prosecution's. At the same time that the court recognized that the crimes of the Holocaust were of "unparalleled horror and scope," it framed the necessity of the death penalty in terms of a conventional logic of punishment and deterrence (5:2218). The logic was suspect on its own terms — how would the imposition of the death penalty deter others from committing crimes which, by the court's own description, were without parallel in human history? — yet, the court's sober insistence on deciding upon the proper sanction by relying on conventional legal theories of punishment must by now strike one as wholly consonant with its general effort to normalize the extraordinary trial.

The Gray Zone Revisited

Against the tedium and missteps of Nuremberg, a trial that understood the Holocaust as essentially an accessory crime, the Eichmann trial furnished a complete and exceptionally moving digest of the Nazis' campaign to exterminate European Jewry. Like Nuremberg, the trial uncovered documents and material that have been the source of important scholarly study. Yet in stark contrast to Nuremberg — and largely as a result of the prosecution's tenacious rebellion against the court's formalism — the trial was able to "reach the hearts of men."[36]

This is not to suggest that the court's defense of formalism was misplaced; on the contrary, it was only because of the struggle between the court and the prosecution that the trial could succeed both as law formally conceived and as a didactic event. Indeed, both the court and the prosecution struggled to conduct the trial in a manner that would recuperate the legitimacy of both the proceeding in particular and the law in general. The court's and prosecution's notion of legitimacy, however, differed importantly, and nowhere was this disparity more visible than in the clash that erupted over the relevance and meaning of the testimony of survivors of the Holocaust. The court, as we have seen, sought to shield itself from the challenge of traumatic history by vigorously defending legal form.

The prosecution, by contrast, saw the trial not simply as a means for adjudging the man in the glass booth, but as a complex drama meant to demonstrate the law's power to support a project of normative reconstruction. By comprehending the act of survival as legally relevant and by hearing the words of the survivors as personal petitions for legal justice, the trial was treated as the fulfillment of a teleology of bearing witness.

Although the struggle between the court and the prosecution threatened to undermine the trial, in fact the delicately maintained equilibrium between the two permitted the trial to realize its diverse goals. As a triumph of didactic legality, the Eichmann trial importantly served to create the Holocaust in the popular imagination, transforming the destruction of the European Jews into *the* emblematic event of the twentieth century.

These successes came not without a cost. In *The Drowned and the Saved*, Primo Levi described the "gray zone" as the area of morally ambiguous and compromised behavior that many survivors inhabited. As Levi argued, it would be absurd to claim that the space between victims and persecutors was empty; on the contrary, "it is studded with obscene and pathetic figures (sometimes they possess both qualities simultaneously) whom it is indispensable to know if we want to know the human species." Levi specifically bemoans a "Manichaean tendency which shuns half-tints and complexities" by emulating "Christ's gesture on Judgment Day: here the righteous, over there the reprobates." In certain respects, the prosecution was responsible for precisely the kind of "hagiographic and rhetorical stylization"[37] that is the focus of Levi's critique. For the gray zone was notably absent from the prosecution's case, which presented the victims as having the innocence of children or the bravery of soldiers.

The corollary of the prosecution's hagiography of the victims was its demonization of the accused. This is the force behind Arendt's claim that the court's failure to comprehend the unprecedented found its complement in the prosecution's gross misrepresentation of the character of the accused. By casting the accused as a "Satanic personality" (5:2028) a murderer "with diabolical wickedness" (5:2212), the prosecution, she argues, failed to perceive the deeper, more sinister lesson of the Holocaust: that acts of radical evil could be planned and administered by petty bureaucrats who were "neither perverted nor sadistic," but "were, and still are, terribly and terrifyingly normal."[38] This, of course, is Arendt's famous thesis concerning the banality of evil, and in her eagerness to make distinctive her theory concerning the relation between genocide and the bureaucratic mind she overlooks those statements by Hausner that seem to anticipate her argument.[39] As noted earlier, Hausner declared in his opening argument before the court, "In this trial, we shall . . . encounter a new kind of killer, the kind that exercises his bloody craft behind a desk" (1:62). Hausner drew, then, a clear connection between bureaucracy and genocide: "We have had to wait till the twentieth century to witness with our own eyes a new kind of murderer: not the result of the momentary ebullition of passion or the darkening of the soul, but of a calculated decision and painstaking planning; not through the evil design of an individual, but through a mighty criminal conspiracy involving thousands" (1:62).

Yet Arendt is not incorrect in her observation that while the prosecution introduced this new kind of criminal, it continued to cast the accused as a savage sociopath whose abominations made the crimes of "Genghis Khan, Attila, or Ivan the Terrible . . . pale into insignificance" (1:62). During his lengthy cross-examination of Eichmann, Hausner labored to portray the accused as "not only a murderer stained with the blood of millions, but also a disgusting liar" (5:1988). In particular, he refused to accept the accused's repeated claims that he had not been aware of the manifest illegality of his actions. Hausner, for example, could hardly conceal his contempt when Eichmann, asked to reflect on the question of his own guilt, responded, "From the legal point of view, as a recipient of orders, I had no choice but to carry out the orders I received" (4:1575) (fig. 6.8). This response echoed Eichmann's earlier answer to a question posed by Servatius during the counsel's direct examination of his client: "I believe that the basis of all organized states is order and obedience. . . . In order to increase security, the leadership of the state must make use of compelling means, namely the oath. . . . Where the leadership is good, the subordinate is lucky; where it is bad, he is unlucky. I was unlucky, because the head of state at the time issued the order to exterminate the Jews" (4:1568).

As grotesque as it was for Eichmann to comprehend the final solution in terms of his personal bad luck, what irritated the prosecution above all else was his conflation of compulsion and obligation. He had no choice but to be blindly obedient (or as he himself put it, *kadavergehorsam,* obedient like a cadaver), not because the failure to do so would have been harshly punished, but because he had sworn an oath to do so.[40] The oath at once compelled and obligated. To have betrayed the oath would have been to break the law in both a positive and normative sense. That Arendt accepts Eichmann's tortured logic as truthful is itself a bit incredible (the accused

Fig. 6.8. Eichmann poring over organizational charts. "I [was] transferred from
Prague or Vienna to Berlin to Department IV. Until then, I belonged to the
Senior Commander of the Security Police and the Security Service in Prague,
and before that to the Inspectors of the Security Police, but as a member of the
Security Service, from Department II, which was later designated Department
VII" (*Trial of Adolf Eichmann* 4:1555). Courtesy of the
Israeli Government Press Office.

demonstrated himself to be a resourceful liar on a number of occasions,
and one is reminded of the discomfiting fact that Arendt attended only ten
weeks of the four-month trial, leaving Jerusalem just *before* Eichmann began his three weeks on the stand [fig. 6.9]);[41] still, her argument remains
important as it suggests that the prosecution and the court had to cast Eichmann as a liar. For Eichmann's statements, she argues, threatened to undermine the concept of *mens rea* upon which the criminal law remains largely
predicated — the idea that all serious criminals have moral knowledge of the
illegality of their acts and thus that "intent to do wrong is necessary for the
commission of a crime."[42] If one accepts Eichmann's claims — as Arendt

Fig. 6.9. Hannah Arendt in Jerusalem. Arendt attended ten weeks of the four-month trial. Courtesy of the Israeli Government Press Office.

does — that he helped organize acts of genocide out of a spirit of *law-abidingness,* then it is far from clear how one can condemn Eichmann under conventional theories of "the criminal mind."

The prosecution and to a lesser degree the court responded to this challenge in a manner consonant with the standard idiom of criminal law: either by insisting that Eichmann was lying and knew of the deeper illegality of his actions, or by claiming that only a moral monster could fail to perceive the manifest illegality of such actions. Both responses, Arendt argues, failed to confront the grave challenge posed to the criminal law by this "new type of criminal" — the normal man who commits atrocious acts.[43] Whether one accepts in full Arendt's banality thesis or her credulous belief in the truthfulness of Eichmann's testimony is beyond the point; importantly it reminds us that the representation of the accused found in the state's case must be understood as part of an attempt to preserve the law's idiom of wrongdoing. Thus at the same time that Hausner powerfully reimagined the domain of the legal in his use of survivor testimony, he embraced a conventional understanding of mens rea in his portrait of the accused.

In any trial, the prosecution will attempt to define as sharply as possible the radically distinct normative universes inhabited by victims and perpetrators. This would especially hold in a case in which the victims — by virtue of their alleged passivity — were seen by many as instruments in their own destruction, and in which the atrocities under consideration seemed to resist assimilation into any conventional models of criminal wrongdoing. Finally, in a trial constructed to serve pedagogic and commemorative ends, it is to be expected that the prosecution will attempt to define the lessons to be learned and the memories to be honored in a simplified fashion.

Levi has observed that simplification is "useful as long as it is recognized as such and not confused for reality."[44] Whether the prosecution's simplified portrait of Eichmann led to such confusion remains open to debate. What is clear, however, is that the prosecution did not use the law simply to pursue extralegal ends. Instead, by interrogating the standard conception of law, the Eichmann prosecution pushed the trial and a reluctant court to become a powerful forum for understanding and commemorating traumatic history.

Part Three

· · ·

Zundel

7

Retrials and Precursors: Klaus Barbie and John Demjanjuk

Memory has imprescriptible rights.
— *Le Monde*

It might seem odd to include the Ernst Zundel trial, a prosecution of a Holocaust denier, in the pantheon of exemplary Holocaust trials. If one were looking for more recent trials that galvanized the attention and passions of the Nuremberg and Eichmann prosecutions, one would more naturally turn to the trial of Klaus Barbie for crimes against humanity in Lyon in 1987 or the trial of John (Ivan) Demjanjuk, allegedly Ivan the Terrible of Treblinka, which began in Jerusalem in the same year.[1] Yet important as they were, both the Barbie and Demjanjuk proceedings can be best understood as moments of juridical transition, as trials that served as restagings and precursors: the Barbie trial echoed Nuremberg while the Demjanjuk case disastrously recapitulated the Eichmann trial.

Like Nuremberg and Eichmann, the Barbie and Demjanjuk trials were staged to serve the ends of both justice and didactic legality. The French government described the Barbie prosecution as "a pedagogic trial,"[2] which, in the words of Prime Minister Pierre Mauroy, would "enable French justice to do its work, and second, . . . honor the memory of that time of grieving and struggle by which France preserved her honor."[3] Minister of Communication Georges Filioud proposed broadcasting the trial live on French television, something without precedent in the annals of French broadcasting. Although Filioud's proposal ultimately was rejected, cameras were present in the Lyon courtroom — not to show the trial live on television but to record it for posterity, as the Parliament passed a law permitting the filming of important trials for historical purposes.[4]

Similarly, the Demjanjuk trial was seen as a tool of collective memory. Like the Eichmann trial, the Demjanjuk proceeding was staged in a public space hastily converted into a courtroom (fig. 7.1). Jerusalem's convention center, the Benyanei Haooma — the hall of the people — housed the trial, accommodating more than three hundred spectators. In 1961, Israelis listened to the Eichmann trial on radio; a quarter of a century later, they could watch the Demjanjuk trial live on television, the first trial to be so broadcast in Israel's history.

Moreover, the trial was intended to serve many of the same pedagogic ends as the Eichmann trial. "The Holocaust," declared Prosecutor Yonah Blatman in the state's summation, "seems to have been forgotten from the collective memory. . . . Here in Israel . . . people tend to push out of one's

Fig. 7.1. The courtroom as stage in the Demjanjuk trial.
Courtesy of the Israeli Government Press Office.

consciousness whatever is not to be found in the day-to-day reality. Moreover, this is fed by a phenomenon that is to be condemned outright, the denial of the Holocaust."[5] A quarter century after the Eichmann trial, the Demjanjuk trial would introduce a new generation of Israelis to the traumatic history and memories of their elders. And if the Eichmann trial aimed to teach an indifferent world about the horrors of the final solution, the Demjanjuk trial was justified as a repudiation of the hateful arguments of Holocaust deniers.[6] Finally, like its famous predecessor, the Demjanjuk trial also meant to commemorate and memorialize the experience of the victims of the Holocaust. In an extraordinary gesture, the trial court that condemned Demjanjuk to death entitled a section of its judgment, "A Monument": "We shall erect in our judgment, according to the totality of the evidence before us, a monument to their [the victims'] souls, to the holy congregations that were lost and are no more, to those who were annihilated and did not receive the privilege of a Jewish burial because hardly a trace remained of them, to those who were burned on the pyre and whose skeletons became ashes and dust, used to fertilize the fields of Poland, which they made fertile when alive, and on which they found their horrible death."[7] The aims of commemoration could not have been made more explicit, as the court's secular judgment assumed the tones of a religiously inspired eulogy.

Barbie

As the first trial in French history involving crimes against humanity, the Barbie case turned on the meaning and scope of the category of radical criminality pioneered at Nuremberg. In Alain Finkielkraut's memorable formulation, Barbie was a "poor man's Eichmann," a German officer (this despite his French-sounding name) who served as head of the Information Section of the Gestapo in Lyon from 1942 until 1944. By the war's end, Barbie's work in Lyon had gained the thirty-two-year-old officer recognition from the Nazis and the Allies alike: he was promoted to captain (*Hauptsturmführer*) by the Nazis, and his name was placed on a United Nations' list of war criminals by the Allies. He was able to elude capture, in no small measure because he went to work for the U.S. Army's Counter-Intelligence Corps in Germany. In 1951, using the assumed name of Klaus Altmann, Barbie fled to Bolivia, where he spent the next three decades managing businesses and unapologetically touting Nazi and other militaristic causes. He was tracked down by Beate Klarsfeld, the indefatigable French hunter of Nazis, and although Bolivia originally refused France's petition of extradition, the so-called Butcher of Lyon finally arrived on French soil in 1982 to stand trial for crimes against humanity.

This was not Barbie's first trial. Twice during his years of hiding Barbie had been tried in absentia and sentenced to death. In 1952 a permanent military tribunal in Lyon convicted him of war crimes, and in 1954 he was again convicted of separate war crimes committed in a different region of France.[8] These convictions named a large number of crimes — including assassination, arson, and pillage — though Barbie remained most reviled in the national consciousness as the alleged torturer and killer of Jean Moulin, the hero of the French resistance.

In neither trial in absentia, however, was Barbie prosecuted for crimes against humanity. The reason was simple. At the time, such an incrimination did not exist in French law. Postwar French trials for war-related crimes fell into one of two categories. Frenchmen were tried as collaborators under laws of treason, and non-Frenchmen, such as Barbie, were tried as war criminals. It was not until the mid-1960s that crimes against humanity gained an independent status in French law, largely in response to rising international concerns that statutes of limitations might shield Nazi criminals from prosecution.

The charter of the IMT had unfortunately neglected to mention what statute of limitations, if any, should apply to the crimes tried at Nuremberg.[9] This oversight, of minor importance at the time of the prosecution of the major war criminals, began to emerge as a concern in the early 1960s, as prescriptive periods for the prosecutions of certain Nazi atrocities neared. West Germany, for example, had adopted a special provision against genocide in its criminal code in 1954, but German courts controversially concluded that ex-Nazis could not be tried under this law because of constitutional bars against ex post facto prosecutions.[10] As a consequence, Nazi atrocities had to be tried in the Federal Republic as conventional crimes like murder and manslaughter. In part I, I examined the difficulties associated with using domestic analogies to explain crimes against humanity; these difficulties were exacerbated in the case of postwar German prosecutions, as the crimes of the Holocaust had to be pigeonholed to fit legal categories designed to deal with discrete acts of killing. The first great trial in Germany of perpetrators of the final solution, the trial of the Auschwitz guards[11] in Frankfurt that began in 1963, offered a bracing case in point.[12]

Because the gravest offense for which the defendants could be tried was murder, the prosecution often had to torture history to show that the behavior of the defendants satisfied the elements of the offense. The murder statute, enacted in the German Penal Code of 1871, did not so much define the act of killing as the character of the killer: "A murderer is a person who kills another person from thirst of blood (*Mordlust*), satisfaction of his sexual desires, avarice or other base motives in a malicious or brutal manner."[13] Because of its emphasis on malice and brutality, the statute forced prosecutors to prove that the Auschwitz defendants had engaged in supererogatory acts of cruelty and sadism, extreme behavior that contravened the code and rules even of the ss.[14] Because only those killings that overstepped the ordinary brutality of the concentrationary universe could be considered murder, the charging statute had the curious effect of turning ss rules into codes of normal, lawful conduct. Such a mangling of history was not lost upon the trial's observers: echoing, though now with greater plausibility, her criticism of the Eichmann trial, Arendt faulted the flawed effort to comprehend genocide through ill-suited legal categories: "What the old penal code had utterly failed to take into account was nothing less than the everyday reality of Nazi Germany in general and of Auschwitz in particular."[15]

Troubling as these matters were, graver still were the problems posed by ordinary statutes of limitations. The only imprescriptible crime (that is, one not controlled by a statute of limitations) in the Federal Republic was genocide, but, as noted, Nazis could not be charged with this crime. Every other crime in Germany was controlled by a statute of limitations. The prescriptive period for murder, the most serious crime, was twenty years. The statute of limitations for manslaughter was fifteen years, and for intentional bodily harm, ten years. This meant that after May 8, 1965, at the latest, no German court could have tried any ex-Nazi for any crimes associated with acts of mass extermination. Needless to say, many persons within the German and international legal community were not pleased with this arrangement, and the German government dealt with the problem in a painfully stopgap fashion that only heightened concerns.[16] First the government used the circumstances of Germany's occupation to recalculate the starting date for the statute of limitations for murder, arbitrarily shifting the date from Germany's capitulation to January 1, 1950. This made possible prosecutions for Nazi-era murders until New Year's Day, 1970. As this date neared, the Bundestag hastily changed the prescriptive period for murder from twenty to thirty years: now Nazis could be prosecuted until January 1,

1980. In 1979, faced with yet another crisis of prosecutorial deadlines, the Bundestag by a narrow majority succeeded in eliminating the statute of limitations on murder altogether.[17]

The German struggle with statutes of limitations raised for many in the international legal community larger issues about the kinds of prescriptive periods that should attach to radical crimes. Legal commentators found the Germans' hand-wringing terribly misplaced, as many of the strongest arguments in support of statutes of limitations manifestly did not apply in the case of the crimes of the Holocaust. Less a fundamental maxim of justice, conventional limitations on the prosecution of crimes can be better understood as acknowledging the temporal vulnerabilities of proof: "With the passage of time, evidence disintegrates, testimony by witnesses becomes more difficult or even impossible, the traces of the offense are lost, other means of proof disappear," and as a consequence the possibility of a successful and fair prosecution dims.[18]

In the case of the crimes of the Holocaust, many of these concerns were misplaced. The German experience itself revealed that troves of valuable and unimpeachable documents were, for the first time, being discovered by German researchers and prosecutors just as the prescriptive period threatened to expire. Moreover, the Eichmann trial had made clear that if prosecutors had anything to fear, it was not that witnesses would prove forgetful, but that they would be overwhelmed by the experience of reentering the trauma. Finally, the very radical nature of the atrocities of the final solution made offensive any temporal limitation upon the power to prosecute. Marie Claude Vaillant-Couturier, the former witness at Nuremberg and member of the National Assembly (see chapter 3), powerfully argued that such crimes could not be pardoned or forgotten. Karl Jaspers, who, as noted, had questioned the wisdom of the Eichmann trial, now strenuously insisted that Nazi crimes had to be imprescriptible.[19] In the words of another commentator, these were crimes on which "le temps n'a oas de prise" (time has no hold).[20]

Such an understanding ultimately found itself inscribed into the very content of international law. On November 26, 1968, the General Assembly of the United Nations adopted the Convention on the Non-Applicability of Statutes of Limitations to War Crimes and Crimes against Humanity.[21] Prompted largely by the German struggles over prescriptive periods, the convention was, in the words of one prominent scholar, "perhaps the most tangible result of the Nuremberg Principles": "If nothing else its message reveals the world community's refusal to condone morally these acts only because the statute of limitations has lapsed without the apprehension and trial of the perpetrators. Indeed, justice cannot hang on the ability of those who evade it."[22]

Before the adoption of this convention, France had passed a similar, though not identical, domestic law. In 1964, as an appalled nation watched the statute of limitations in Germany near expiration, the French parliament incorporated crimes against humanity into the nation's penal code and made such crimes imprescriptible. Unfortunately, the law failed to define crimes against humanity precisely: it merely referred to the definitions that had been supplied by the United Nations and the charter of the IMT.[23] And in contrast to the convention adopted by the United Nations in 1968, the French law extended only to crimes against humanity and not to war crimes, an arrangement prompted less by a nuanced recognition of the differences between these offenses than by a desire to insulate French conduct in Algeria from future prosecution.

After 1964, crimes against humanity enjoyed, then, a nominal basis in French domestic law. Still, it was not until the mid-1970s that French court decisions resolved whether the 1964 law even authorized trials of former Nazis and collaborators.[24] In these decisions, the courts decided that any such trials were not barred by rules against ex post facto prosecutions. Moreover, the French accepted the position argued by the Israelis in the Eichmann trial, that prosecutions of crimes against humanity could be based on universal jurisdiction. Such crimes could be prosecuted whenever and wherever they took place.

Yet it was not until Barbie's trial in 1987 that a person in France finally stood trial for crimes against humanity.[25] Even then, Barbie's prosecution raised a host of difficulties. Because the ten-year statute of limitations for war crimes had already run and because the death sentence from his first two convictions had also prescribed after twenty years,[26] Barbie could be tried only for crimes essentially different from those for which he had already twice been condemned to death. The legal case against Barbie thus raised afresh the fraught question addressed at Nuremberg: How did crimes against humanity differ from war crimes?

As I concluded in part 1, the Nuremberg trial provided a less than satisfactory answer to this question: crimes against humanity were essentially enfolded into war crimes, treated either as a subcategory of war crimes or as an interstitial offense covering a small range of conduct not formally covered by conventional laws of war. The Barbie trial, in a stunning inversion, did just the opposite: war crimes were enfolded into crimes against humanity, which now, in the interpretation of French courts, became a master category embracing a wide variety of wartime transgressions.

To see how the Barbie trial effected its own remarkable inversion of the Nuremberg understanding, one must follow the odyssey of Barbie's indictment through the French courts. The original indictment prepared in 1982 charged Barbie with a host of offenses putatively not litigated in his earlier convictions. These included arrest, torture, and deportation of members of the resistance as well as his order to arrest and deport the so-called children of Izieu, forty-three French Jewish children sent to be gassed at Auschwitz in 1944. As French criminal procedure permits in certain circumstances an appeal before trial, Barbie's lawyer, Jacques Vergès, immediately challenged the legality of the indictment, arguing in effect that these charges were barred by prior adjudications or, alternatively, constituted war crimes that had prescribed.[27]

On October 4, 1985, the first court of appellate review, the Indicting Chamber of the Court of Appeals of Lyon, delivered a mixed judgment on these matters. The court upheld several of the counts against Barbie, yet dismissed others. In reaching this decision, the court revisited the issue left unresolved by the 1964 law, namely, what exactly crimes against humanity meant in the French penal code. Because the law relied on the charter of the IMT, the court used the language of 6(c) to engage in a count-by-count examination of the indictment. Satisfied that persecutions against "innocent Jews" constituted an "imprescriptible crime against humanity for which Barbie must answer," the court upheld the charge concerning the deportation of the children of Izieu.[28] By contrast, the court concluded that charges concerning the mistreatment of members of the resistance had to be dismissed. "These acts," the court declared, "even if atrocious and committed in contempt of the human person and the laws of war, can only constitute war crimes which have already prescribed."[29]

Certainly this decision, which aroused universal indignation in French political circles, made for certain absurdities of classification. How, for example, would the court deal with the mistreatment of a Jewish member of the resistance? Would that constitute an imprescriptible crime against humanity or a prescribed war crime? The case of Marcel Gompel presented the court with precisely this question, as Gompel, a Jew and a member of the resistance, had allegedly been tortured to death by Barbie. Here the court reasoned that because it was unclear whether Gompel had been killed because of his resistance activities or "in his capacity as Jew," the law would give Barbie the benefit of the doubt and strike the charge from the indictment.[30]

The Gompel example highlighted the problems with the appellate decision. In the words of one commentator, the court found itself in the position of "having to morbidly sift out those whose deportation was a lapsed crime from those whose deportation was still punishable."[31] As a jurisprudential matter, the decision was faulted for overlooking the fact that, as one French legal expert put it, under the charter of the IMT, the same act could unmistakably constitute both a war crime and a crime against humanity. Ultimately, however, the court's decision aroused fury in France not because it required painful acts of legal categorization, but because it promised to remove Barbie's crimes against the resistance from the purview of the trial court. In a trial staged, in part, to commemorate the sacrifices of the heroes of the nation, the trial court would lack the authority "to even mention the acts that earned him his name [viz., the Butcher of Lyons] and his place in the national memory."[32]

Yet the very deficiencies in the court's reasoning also described its strengths. Four decades after the trial of the major war criminals, a European court finally had acknowledged that the extermination of the Jews constituted the paradigmatic case of crimes against humanity, imprescriptible offenses of a qualitatively more serious nature than crimes against members of a political resistance. Unfortunately this juridical recognition of the distinctive aspect of crimes against humanity was short-lived. On December 20, 1985, the Cour de Cassation, the French high court of appeals, reversed the decision of the first appellate court. The Cour de Cassation reinstated the Nuremberg insight that certain offenses may constitute both war crimes and crimes against humanity, but in so doing, the French court offered a provocative and ostensibly novel interpretation of 6(c): "What constitutes imprescriptible crimes against humanity, within the sense of article 6(c) . . . even though they could also be characterized as war crimes according to article 6(b) of the same text — [are] the inhumane acts and persecutions which, in the name of a State practicing a hegemonic political ideology, have been committed in a systematic fashion, not only against persons because they belong to a racial or religious group, but also against the adversaries of this [State] policy, whatever the form of their opposition."[33]

Thus according to the court, crimes against humanity are defined by a special intent that distinguishes them from war crimes. Attacks on individuals that intend to destroy the group to which such persons belong — in the language of the court, crimes that aim to "victimize a group by victimizing the individual" — constitute crimes against humanity.[34] Cogent enough, the court went on to conclude that crimes against humanity are not limited to inhumane acts and persecutions directed at a racial or religious group, but "also against the adversaries of this [State] policy [that is, of inhumane persecution], whatever the form of their opposition." While arguably consistent with the terms of 6(c), the court's reasoning nonetheless seemed dramatically to broaden the ambit of crimes against humanity.[35] Acts against members of a resistance operation, even one engaged in organized acts of military opposition, could now constitute imprescriptible crimes against humanity.

Having ambitiously, perhaps bizarrely, broadened the scope of crimes against humanity, the Cour de Cassation also strangely restricted their application. Only those inhumane acts and persecutions perpetrated on behalf of a "State practicing a hegemonic political ideology," the court insisted, constitute crimes against humanity. At the very least, this holding raised the question, What is a hegemonic political ideology and what does it mean to practice it? Beyond confusing, the holding appeared outrageous, as it implied, seemingly by definition, that democratic states cannot commit crimes against humanity. If a democratic state such as, say, France, engaged in inhumane acts of racial persecution, these acts would not constitute crimes against humanity because France does not, presumably, practice a "hegemonic political ideology."[36]

Not surprisingly, the court's reasoning was widely attacked in legal circles. As one commentator bluntly observed, "It was without foundation in the text of Article 6(c)."[37] Yet however creatively the Cour de Cassation might have interpreted the charter of the IMT, its holding again echoed positions taken by the French prosecution at Nuremberg. The Americans at Nuremberg argued that crimes against humanity were international crimes because of their connection to the Nazis' war of aggression. Dubost, the French deputy prosecutor, quietly dissented, arguing that the international component of crimes against humanity was satisfied not by the connection to aggressive war, but because the agent of such crimes was a state. Forty years later, the Cour de Cassation affirmed Dubost's position, severing crimes against humanity from acts of war and tying them to state practices.[38] Anomalous, then, was not the view that the juridical essence of crimes against humanity lay in their state sponsorship, but that such crimes could be committed only by states practicing a "hegemonic state ideology." Not only was such a proposition without basis in 6(c), it aroused added controversy because it seemed strategically crafted to advance narrow political goals.

On the one hand, the capacious view of crimes against humanity restored the intended grand scope of the Barbie trial: the nation could now receive evidence of atrocities committed against members of the resistance. Indeed, as a result of the court's decision, Barbie was recharged with the deportation of three hundred non-Jewish members of the resistance and with the killing of Gompel.[39] On the other hand, by linking crimes against humanity with the actions of a state practicing a hegemonic political ideology, the court essentially rendered French conduct in Algeria, already shielded from prosecution by the run of the statute of limitations for war crimes, immune from fresh court actions. Thus at the same time that the court expanded the domain of crimes against humanity, it exempted the French nation from any possible complicity in such crimes.

Though controversial, the court's holding was not entirely born of expediency. In certain respects, the judgment made excellent formal legal sense. It freed crimes against humanity from its restrictive Nuremberg yoke, and even the question-begging language of "hegemonic political ideology" was not indefensible. For the decision attempted to prevent the open politicization of crimes against humanity—preempting the tendentious use of the incrimination to challenge every unpopular act by any government. In so doing, the court inscribed into doctrine the distinction, articulated in philosophical circles by Jaspers among others, between states that on occasion commit crimes and the *Verbrecherstaat*—a state that is criminal by its very nature and to its very core.[40]

Still, the court's decision meant that the deportations of the Jews and of the members of the resistance were legally equivalent acts.[41] Predictably enough, this made for rancorous relations between the various plaintiff groups. As the president of Lyon's Jewish community asserted, "We're confusing two different types of crimes. Jews weren't opponents. They didn't fight." Simone Veil, an Auschwitz survivor and later president of the European Parliament, insisted that the conflation of these experiences would "trivialize the Holocaust." By contrast, the attorney for the resistance groups protested that "Nazi ideology was an attack on all humanity."[42]

More provocatively, this conflation reversed the record of Nuremberg.

There, the voice of Jewish victims was largely absent. The French prosecution was especially interested in presenting tales of atrocity through the testimony of political prisoners, casting the suffering of the nation not in terms of the bleak logic of helpless victimization, but rather as the consequence of patriotic, heroic acts of armed resistance. At the Barbie trial, the story was inverted, as now the resisters claimed to be of a kind with the defenseless victims. At Nuremberg, the Jew was treated as a kind of lesser political prisoner, a victim of a novel species of war crime; at the Barbie trial, the resistance member was treated as an innocent martyr, a kind of Jew, slaughtered for his membership in a reviled group. Finally, at Nuremberg, the final solution became a kind of war crime, an offense born of the poisonous business of aggressive war, while at the Barbie trial, war crimes were turned into a form of extermination, an extension of the logic of the Holocaust. The inversion was not without its ironies. As Finkielkraut observed, "There was . . . something paradoxical in the spectacle of Resistance groups demanding an extension of crimes against humanity and asserting their right today to a status they had rejected in the past."[43] Veil echoed this sentiment as she rhetorically asked, "We the victims have never been asked to be considered as heroes, so why do the heroes now want, at all costs and at the risk of mixing everything up, to be treated as victims?"[44]

Freed from Nuremberg's restrictive jurisdictional moor, crimes against humanity now were rendered overinclusive: all atrocity was enfolded within its bloated domain.

Demjanjuk

The Demjanjuk trial was also a drama of repetition, a complex renegotiation of the issues of representation and proof raised at the Eichmann trial. Indeed, the Demjanjuk trial powerfully recalls Karl Marx's famous dictum that world historical facts always occur twice: "the first time as tragedy, the second as farce."[45] Put more sympathetically, the Demjanjuk trial was a tragic farce, a cautionary tale about the dangers of relying on the legal process to honor the pathos of memory.

The testimony of survivors, as noted, occupied the didactic and commemorative heart of the Eichmann trial, though its evidentiary relevance, conventionally conceived, was subject to stern challenge. At the Demjanjuk trial, there could be no similar challenges to the relevance of survivor testimony. Inasmuch as the trial was not about motive and deed but about identity and identification, the prosecution's case was essentially based on the testimony offered by survivors who claimed to have seen and known the defendant. At issue was not the relevance of testimony but the reliability of memory.

Born in the Ukraine in 1920, Demjanjuk had emigrated to the United States in 1952. He settled in Cleveland, where he worked as a machinist in a Ford Motor plant, raised a family, and was known as an affable neighbor — "the kind of guy who would stop to help you fix a flat on the road."[46] In the late seventies, prosecutors working for the Immigration and Naturalization Service(INS) began investigating Demjanjuk as a suspected war criminal.[47] The INS was not interested in trying suspected Nazis living in the United States as war criminals or as perpetrators of crimes against humanity — to this day, crimes against humanity have not been incorporated into the federal law of the United States. Instead, the INS sought to deport resident aliens or naturalized citizens (such as Demjanjuk), not as war criminals, but as persons who lied on their emigration forms and thus never should have been permitted to enter the country in the first place.[48]

The INS first learned of Demjanjuk through the activities of Michael Hanusiak, a member of a Soviet organization established to promote cultural exchange between the Ukraine and the United States. Hanusiak supplied the service with a list of possible former Ukrainian Nazi collaborators residing in the United States.[49] Having ostensibly reliable evidence suggesting that Demjanjuk had served as an SS guard at Sobibòr, one of the three "pure" extermination facilities constructed by the Nazis (along with Treblinka and Belzec) to implement Operation Reinhard, the INS asked the Special Unit of the Israeli Police for the Investigation of Nazi Crimes (known at the time of the Eichmann trial simply as Bureau 06) to assist in its investigation. As the majority of the tiny group of Sobibòr survivors lived in Israel, the INS hoped that these individuals would be able to identify and supply information about the former guard. The investigation was aided by the fact that the American investigators had a copy of a photo I.D. of Demjanjuk from his service in the Trawniki camp, an SS facility used to train Ukrainian and ethnic German POWs to serve as death camp guards.[50]

Yet an odd thing happened at the identification parades conducted by the Israelis. The survivors of Sobibòr failed to pick out Demjanjuk's photo from an album of pictures of suspects. But a number of Treblinka survivors, enlisted to assist the investigation of a second suspect pictured in the photospread,[51] blanched at the photo of Demjanjuk. This, they declared, was the operator of the Treblinka gas chamber, a guard whose unusual cruelty and viciousness had earned him the sobriquet Ivan Grozny, Ivan the Terrible. As early as the Eichmann trial, the Treblinka survivor Eliahu Rosenberg had testified about the excesses of a sadistic Ukrainian guard named Ivan, who, along with a colleague, had used a bayonet to shove Jews into the gas chamber and then had "introduced the gas."[52]

At first, the Israeli investigators doubted these identifications. The Trawniki card, after all, identified Demjanjuk as a Sobibòr guard. Gradually, however, as the number of Treblinka survivors who identified Demjanjuk as Ivan the Terrible grew to ten, Israeli investigators became convinced of the accuracy of these statements. After extensive negotiations with American authorities, the Israelis agreed to request the extradition of Demjanjuk. His American citizenship revoked and the extradition petition accepted, Demjanjuk found himself, on February 27, 1986, on an El Al 747 bound for Ben-Gurion Airport near Tel-Aviv.

Demjanjuk would be the first perpetrator since Eichmann tried under the Nazis and Nazi Collaborators Law of 1950. In this and many other respects the Demjanjuk trial came to echo the Eichmann proceeding. The Israelis briefly considered jailing Demjanjuk in the very cell of the Ayalon prison that Eichmann had occupied. Courtroom security officers debated placing Demjanjuk in the glass booth that Eichmann had once sat in and that now was on permanent display at the Holocaust Museum of the Lohamei Ha-Getta'ot, the Kibbutz of the Ghetto Fighters on the outskirts of Haifa. Like the Eichmann trial, the Demjanjuk proceeding threatened to turn arid questions of jurisdiction into high legal drama. Demjanjuk's attorneys specifically argued that the Israelis were not authorized to try their client under the Nazis and Nazi Collaborators Law because the extradition agreement named murder as the crime for which Demjanjuk would stand trial. To try Demjanjuk under the 1950 law both would impermissibly change the terms of the extradition and would imply that "murder" and "crimes against the Jewish people" were equivalent terms. Ironically, Demjanjuk's attorneys came to press for the very categorical clarity missing at the Barbie trial. "We would diminish the Holocaust," the defendant's counsel stated, "were we to view the acts of the Nazis and their collaborators as 'ordinary' acts of murder."[53]

In the clearest parallel to Eichmann, the Demjanjuk trial turned into a drama of collective unburdening, a public rehashing of both the history of the Holocaust and the horrific tales of the survivors. The photos of the Treblinka model built by Ya'akov Wiernik and displayed at the Eichmann trial again hung from a courtroom wall, framing the witness box. Eliahu Rosenberg, who had told the Eichmann court how the Germans would announce, after the gas chambers had done their work, "Alles schläft" (all asleep), was again called to the stand. The witness Yossef Cherney came close to repeating the spectacular collapse of Dinur/Katzetnik at the Eichmann trial, stammering, "I am now in Treblinka" before succumbing to uncontrollable sobs.[54]

Still, the trial often seemed less a reenactment than a caricature of its famous predecessor. Eichmann's defense — namely, that the dutiful *Obersturmbannführer* had acted out of a spirit of cadaver-like obedience — had lent itself to broad speculation: about the relation between bureaucracy and genocide, about the nature and limits of obedience, about the very human capacity for evil. By contrast, Demjanjuk's defense — simply and categorically, that the Israelis had gotten the wrong guy and that the accused had never served as a guard and in fact had himself been a POW in a German camp — frustrated the trial's ambitious design.

These frustrations were exacerbated by the character and demeanor of the accused. Eichmann, with his bank teller's appearance, had cut a thin, chilly figure, prone to blinking nervously and twisting his mouth into a grimace; Demjanjuk, by contrast, was an avuncular fellow who liked to josh with his guards during lulls in the proceeding (fig. 7.2). On the stand, Eichmann demonstrated an excellent if selective memory, at times revealing details unknown even to Israeli investigators, at times stonewalling tenaciously. His command of administrative detail remained outstanding, and his intelligence, if invisible to Arendt and often expressed through a Teutonically opaque bureaucratese, was redoubtable. Demjanjuk, quite the opposite, was plainly a man of limited intelligence. On the stand he made a terrible impression, not because traces of his alleged former cruelty became visible, but because his testimony sounded like a pathetic tatter of lies. The vapidity of his story, the huge and seemingly incredible gaps in his memory, and the glaring contradictions in his alibi so astonished the court that the presiding judge interrupted Demjanjuk's testimony to remind the defendant of the importance of an alibi in a criminal trial. (In an earlier statement, for example, Demjanjuk had claimed to have forgotten the name of the very POW camp in which he allegedly spent eighteen months at hard labor and even struggled to remember just what work he had done there, first claiming he had built huts and then claiming he had cut peat.) Indeed, in a

Fig. 7.2. The accused and his guards. Courtesy of the
Israeli Government Press Office.

statement that sounded more like an inadvertent confession than a statement of exculpation, Demjanjuk himself attempted to express the differences between Eichmann and himself: "Why are you making such a fuss of
my matter, like with Eichmann? Eichmann was big, while Ivan is little, and
what's more it isn't he, as there is a mistake in identification."[55]

The tactics and conduct of the defense lawyers also turned the Demjanjuk trial into a caricature of the Eichmann proceeding. Compared to the
dignified, if not entirely resourceful, defense of Servatius and his assistant
Dieter Wechtenbruch at the Eichmann trial, Demjanjuk's team of lawyers
put on an inept and frequently offensive show. Mark O'Connor, an American attorney who served as the chief counsel in the early stages of the trial,
had virtually no trial experience and often left the court numb with his rambling, disorganized presentations. His cross-examinations of the survivor
witnesses appalled the court. Whereas Servatius had delicately avoided confronting survivors, only directly challenging those witnesses who, for example, claimed to have seen Eichmann in person, O'Connor attempted to
challenge the accuracy of survivors' identifications of his client by attacking
the larger reliability and precision of their memories of the camp. As a consequence, Pinchas Epstein found himself aggressively interrogated about

the shape of the buildings at Treblinka, while Eliahu Rosenberg was grilled about the precise color of the flames that issued from the Treblinka crematoria (fig. 7.3).[56] O'Connor's missteps were so egregious that he was finally dismissed from the defense, which thereafter was directed by Yoram Sheftel, a flamboyant Israeli attorney cut from the mold of William Kunstler.

Though a far more resourceful and energetic counsel than O'Connor, Sheftel, too, hampered the defense with a number of dreadful miscues. The expert witnesses he called to prove that the Trawniki photo I.D. that identified Demjanjuk as a Sobibòr guard was a KGB forgery were shredded by the prosecution on cross-examination. One expert for the defense, exposed on the stand as having lied about her credentials, tried to kill herself in her hotel room after the conclusion of her testimony. Sheftel also perfected the art of insulting the court. On numerous occasions he referred to the proceeding as a show trial, by which the counsel meant not to recall the

Fig. 7.3. Mark O'Connor's appalling cross-examination of Eliahu Rosenberg. Hanging from the wall are photographs of Ya'akov Wiernik's models of Treblinka, used at the Eichmann trial. On the right sit the members of the prosecution, Michael Shaked, Michael Horovitz, and Yonah Blatman *(left to right),* registering their impression of O'Connor's courtroom skill. Courtesy of the Israeli Government Press Office.

obvious pedagogic purposes of the prosecution, but to invoke the memory of Stalinist miscarriages of justice. Sheftel's Canadian co-counsel went so far as to compare Demjanjuk to Alfred Dreyfus, oblivious to the insensitivities contained within the accusation.[57]

These claims enraged the spectators at the trial, who, in the penalty phase of the trial, broke out in chants of "Death to the defense attorneys!"[58] Sheftel's tactics also enraged the court, which struggled, often in vain, to maintain the juridical dignity that had characterized the Eichmann trial. The three-judge panel, presided over by Dov Levin, a sitting member of the Israeli Supreme Court,[59] frequently lost patience with Sheftel, who, in his spirited and polemical memoir of the trial, describes with relish his various techniques for baiting the presiding judge. (In his book, Sheftel tauntingly refers to Levin as Dovele, an affectionate diminutive of Levin's first name.) Sheftel went so far as to file a motion demanding that the judges disqualify themselves because of obvious hostility and bias toward the defense, a motion that only intensified the court's irritation. In their final judgment, the judges insisted on their absence of bias, though in terms that begged the question: "We are convinced . . . that we shall be able to eradicate from our consciousness all those unfounded and absurd claims voiced . . . by one or another of Counsel for the Defense."[60]

Indeed, the court often seemed swept up in the legal spectacle over which it presided. I have already mentioned that the court referred to its judgment as a "monument . . . to the holy congregations that were lost." Sheftel reports that the judges used a clipping service to gather daily press reports of the trial that they would then read in the privacy of their chambers — an act that arguably violated the rule of *sub judice,* the principle that matters under judicial consideration should not be subject to public discussion. The court, moreover, seemed preoccupied with the Barbie trial, which began shortly after the Demjanjuk proceeding but ended ten months earlier. Unable to contain his impatience with the defense's tactics of delay and disruption, Levin exploded, "We will soon be legendary for our patience — in the rest of the world such trials take two months."[61] On another occasion, Levin lamented, "Soon we will be the laughingstock of the world. Klaus Barbie's trial . . . ended long ago, but we continue to tread water with no end in sight."[62]

But the court's greatest misstep was in its treatment and evaluation of the testimony of the survivor witnesses. Early in the trial, the court had to address the issue of the scope of this testimony. Following the strategy of

Eichmann's defense, Demjanjuk's team attempted to streamline the trial by stipulating to the facts of the Holocaust. After all, Demjanjuk did not deny that exterminations had taken place; he simply denied that he had played any role in the killing process. In both trials these efforts to narrow the focus failed, and in the case of the Eichmann proceeding it is easy to understand why. Given Eichmann's central position within the administration of genocide, one could reasonably argue that the accused was implicated in virtually all aspects of the final solution. In this regard, Eichmann was a helpful medium through which the prosecution could pursue its didactic agenda.

Ivan the Terrible, by contrast, was but a single, if unusually cruel, death camp guard. Presumably one could have considered the charges against Demjanjuk without revisiting the larger history of the final solution. Yet the court refused to do this, for two reasons. First, in contrast to the Eichmann court, the Demjanjuk tribunal seemed to believe that the pedagogic purpose of the trial itself justified a sweeping prosecutorial excursion into the history of the final solution. At the beginning of its published opinion, the court included among the questions that lay at the heart of the trial, not simply the specific question of identification, but also queries that were astonishing in their breath and generality: "Is it possible that one of the nations of this world, which has produced people of the spirit, and of morality, giants of culture and science, should set before itself, as a target and supreme objective, 'to destroy, to kill, and to cause to perish, all Jews, both young and old, little children and women (like the plot of Haman the Agagite — Esther 3:13)?'"[63] The court, in sharp contrast to the Eichmann tribunal, unapologetically embraced its tutelary role. "We are charged with the duty to determine," the court declaimed, "through due process of law, historical truths in regard to the events that befell our world in one of the darkest periods in the history of all nations."[64]

Second, and more portentously, the court held that the larger story of the final solution had to be rehashed because it was not possible to judge the reliability of the identifications of Demjanjuk by the eyewitnesses "without also forming . . . an opinion as to the reliability and the quality of their memory . . . regarding all the other events which they . . . experience."[65] O'Connor appalled the courtroom by challenging the memory of survivors concerning matters that had nothing to do with the identification of Ivan; ironically, O'Connor's strategy was simply the obverse of the court's. The court would measure the reliability of eyewitness identifications against the general accuracy and clarity of their memories of the camp.

In adopting this approach, the court sought to "consider the possibility of treacherous memory, of true and sincere error in identification."[66] Yet even here the court posed its basic query in terms that made the question entirely rhetorical: "We must ask: is it at all possible to forget? Can people who were in the vale of slaughter and experienced its horrors, who lived in an atmosphere of oppression, terror, fear, and persecution within the narrow confines of the extermination camp; people who saw, day after day, the killing, the humiliation, the brutality, the abuse by the German oppressors and their Ukrainian vassals in the Treblinka camp, forget all this?"[67]

To answer this question, the court turned to the testimony of the survivors, meticulously reconstructing the world of Treblinka from their anguished words. After devoting fifty pages to a testimonial recreation of the death camp, the court concluded with the following lapidary pronouncement: "*We reply to the inquirer and say:* No, it is not possible to forget the scenes of horror, the atmosphere of terror, all that took place in the extermination camp. It is impossible to forget Ivan the Terrible and his atrocities."[68] With this declaration, the court gave word to a fatal (mis)understanding of survivor testimony, measuring the clarity of memory by the intensity of trauma.

When the court turned its attention to the actual identifications supplied by the witnesses, its evaluations were framed by this understanding. It accepted at face value the tortured hyperbole of Pinchas Epstein's declaration, "I see Ivan every single night. . . . I dream about him every night. . . . He is etched in me, in my memory, every night. I cannot free myself of this."[69] The court discounted the evidence suggesting that the initial identification parades conducted by the Special Unit of the Israeli Police had fallen far short of satisfying normal police practice. For example, Demjanjuk's photo was larger than the others in the album, and none of the other photos showed men with similar physical features. The court dismissed the relevance of the testimony of defense witness Willem Wagenaar, an experimental psychologist from the University of Leyden and a leading expert on memory problems, because Wagenaar's studies of treacherous memory all focused on the difficulty of recalling discrete moments of trauma.[70] Such studies, the court reasoned, could not offer insight into the Demjanjuk case, which involved not an isolated episode but a pattern of horror that had been experienced daily for months on end.[71] "There is no room whatever for comparing the trauma experienced by the survivors of Treblinka," the court concluded, "with the traumatic experience undergone by a person who was a victim of harsh violence, rape, or similar crimes. . . . The traumatic shock suffered by the victims of Treblinka is a thousand times greater in its intensity and influence."[72] Finally, the court dismissed the importance of an affidavit of a former Sobibòr guard, submitted after the summations of the parties, stating in great detail that he had known Demjanjuk as an "experienced and efficient" guard at that camp, not at Treblinka.[73] The idea that there had been "two Wachmans from Trawniki, one in Treblinka and one in Sobibòr, both Ukrainians named Ivan . . . and both with protruding ears, both the same age and becoming bald in the same way" was, the court simply noted, "far-fetched."[74]

In a sense, one cannot fault this reasoning. The chance that the case involved a doppelgänger must have seemed remote. Though several of the survivors who had originally identified Demjanjuk had died by the time of the trial, those who did take the stand offered passionate and detailed testimony. Finally, the very weaknesses of the defense's case — its failure to impeach the authenticity of the Trawniki card, its utter inability to construct a plausible alibi, and its steadfast denial, in the face of overwhelming evidence to the contrary, that Demjanjuk had served in any way as a camp guard — supported the court's conclusions.[75] Yet beyond the strengths of the prosecution's case, the court's mode of reasoning all but obligated it to accept not simply the sincerity but the accuracy of the survivors' identifications. For by evaluating the identifications in light of the "total testimony," the court had assumed a position in which it could not question the accuracy of these identifications without implicitly casting doubt upon the larger reliability of survivor narratives.

And so the court convicted Demjanjuk and sentenced him to death. The process of appeal, mandatory in such cases, dragged on for years, first as a result of a number of calamities that befell the defense, later as a consequence of several fact-finding missions to the states of the crumbling Soviet empire to examine recently unearthed or released evidence.[76] These missions met with some success, and a slow but steady stream of information began to emerge from the collapsing Soviet Union suggesting precisely what the trial court had dismissed as far-fetched: that, in fact, there had been two Ukrainian Ivans, one at Sobibòr and one at Treblinka, who bore a small but not entirely negligible resemblance to one another. According to this material, Ivan the Terrible had been one Ivan Marchenko, a guard who, as the German war effort collapsed, had last been seen serving with Yugoslavian partisans.[77] Photographs of Marchenko showed a man with an astonishingly brutal face, yet one with Demjanjuk's protruding ears, round cheeks, and high hairline. While none of this information entirely exculpated Demjanjuk — on the contrary, it only strengthened the conviction that he had served at Sobibòr — it did cast doubt on whether Israeli justice was about to execute the right man as Ivan the Terrible. Worse, it suggested that much of this information had been available to the U.S. Justice Department's Office of Special Investigations at the time of the Jerusalem trial, but had not, for whatever reasons, been passed on to the Israelis.[78]

In a brave yet entirely necessary step, the Israeli Supreme Court, in July 1993, overturned Demjanjuk's conviction. An elaborate piece of juridical damage control, the Court's judgment attempted both delicately to overturn an apparently mistaken verdict and to defend the integrity of the system that had produced the erroneous decision. Except in a divine system of perfect procedural justice, courts inevitably will make mistakes, and isolated blunders usually do little to undermine the legitimacy of the court or the larger legal system of which it is a part. Yet when such misjudgments occur in trials staged as didactic spectacles, rituals of justice designed to place the institutions of criminal justice in the fore of the public's mind, then errors seem more consequential — less the chance mistake than a kind of structural breakdown that follows from overburdening the system with pressures that many observers would consider extralegal. And these concerns would loom especially large in a trial in which the lead defense attorney had never stopped complaining that the interests of commemoration and pedagogy were overwhelming the requirements of legal justice.

The Supreme Court's judgment was devoted, then, to making the case that the trial court's mistake — if, in fact, it had erred — was a chance misfire and not a systemic failure. Levin and his colleagues had not derogated their judicial function; instead, they had suffered a legal misfortune: their verdict had been undermined by facts about which they could not have possibly known. The Supreme Court offered a painstaking, point-by-point defense of the methods and procedures of the district court. The Court's opinion is long, in excess of four hundred pages; yet only twelve pages are devoted, almost by way of afterword, to explaining the acquittal. The judgment begins with the issue of jurisdiction, carefully arguing that under the "principle of specialty" the terms of Demjanjuk's extradition (for murder) clearly permitted the Israelis to try him for crimes against the Jewish people and humanity. The judgment then spends more than two hundred pages reviewing and validating the entire identification process. Even when it weighs the new evidence naming Marchenko as Ivan the Terrible, the Court labors to argue that this material does not show that the district court was wrong; the fresh material simply introduces an element of reasonable doubt that mandates reversal.

Yet at the same time that the Supreme Court elaborately defended the lower tribunal, its decision found word in a rhetoric that could not be further from the prose of the district court. In contrast to the district court's tone of poetic anguish, the Supreme Court delivered its opinion in sober, even arid terms. The Court's review of the "substantive foundations and basic typology" of the principle of specialty, a legal rule controlling matters of extradition, and its discussion of the meaning of reasonable doubt, are staggeringly dry affairs — not simply to a lay reader, but even to a scholar accustomed to the muted drama of, say, a bankruptcy opinion of a U.S. federal court. Indeed, much of the Court's decision reads less like a legal judgment than like an excursus into analytic philosophy, in which the slightest distinctions invite an orgy of ostensibly pointless hairsplitting. Yet the excess of analysis was hardly pointless. By translating a spectacle of didactic legality into the technical parlance of legal formalism, the Court sought to avert a juridical catastrophe. The Court's concluding words powerfully evoked memories of the Eichmann court: "The matter is closed — but not complete. The complete truth is not the prerogative of the human judge."[79] By adopting the Eichmann court's rhetoric of humility, the Israeli Supreme Court struggled to turn the Demjanjuk affair into yet another tale of legal insularity. It sought to recuperate the law's legitimacy through a gesture of conventional self-limitation.

The Bridge to Zundel: Relativizing History and Volatilizing Memory

At the same time that the Barbie and Demjanjuk trials complexly reenacted Nuremberg and Eichmann, they established a conceptual bridge to the Zundel trial. Both the Barbie and Demjanjuk trials were intended, in part, as public responses to the spread of Holocaust denial. Elie Wiesel, who testified at the Lyon trial, said it was necessary to open "this secret and painful door to our common memory" to answer the arguments of deniers and thereby "stop the killer from killing again."[80] At the Demjanjuk trial, the prosecution explicitly defended the proceeding as a response to "those who wish to rewrite history."[81]

On a more profound level, the Barbie trial forged a conceptual link to the Zundel trial by relativizing the history of the Holocaust. This it did in two ways. First, as we have seen, the Cour de Cassation conflated, on a categorical level, crimes against humanity and war crimes. This decision, in the words of one prominent observer, "undeniably undermined the principle of the uniqueness of the Final Solution and genocide of the Jews."[82] Second, and more crucially, the decision of the French court offered Barbie's lead counsel, Jacques Vergès, an opportunity to make bold revisionist claims at the trial. A charismatic and mercurial figure who had fought with the Algerian resistance, befriended the young Pol Pot, and trained Palestinian terrorists, Vergès launched what he called a "defense of rupture." This strategy was designed to unmask hypocrisy; often Vergès seemed less interested in proving Barbie innocent of the charges — indeed, his client was sentenced to life imprisonment and died in 1991 — than in using the trial to reveal the pervasive complicity of ordinary Frenchmen in the crimes attributed to the aging German. Before the trial began, he threatened to prove that Jean Moulin, the martyred hero of the resistance, had been betrayed by fellow members of the underground. When the Cour de Cassation concluded that even under its capacious parsing, Moulin's murder did not constitute a crime against humanity and thus could not be one of the crimes charged to Barbie, Vergès took a different tack, arguing that Barbie's actions were of a kind with French behavior in Algeria. In this respect, Vergès's strategy of rupture was ironically served, rather than frustrated, by the decision of the French high court.[83] Because the court had parsed crimes against humanity to include certain acts against political opponents, Vergès could argue that Barbie was being held accountable for actions which, in other contexts (such as the Algerian), had been deemed immune from prosecution. Though Judge André Cerdini restricted the testimony of witnesses called to show the symmetry between Barbie's actions and those of the French military in Algeria, even this restriction did not entirely frustrate Vergès's efforts, as the *tu quoque* argument was meant largely to embarrass the French legal system for its apparent use of a judicial double standard.

Vergès's revisionism, of course, must not be confused with the kind of blatant Holocaust negationism I take up in the next two chapters. Indeed, Vergès did not deny Nazi crimes; rather, he did just the opposite: he globalized them. In his telling, there was nothing extraordinary or unique about Nazi offenses; they were of a kind with the normal excesses of war. And just as there was nothing unique about Nazi crimes, there was nothing unique about Nazism itself. Challenging the Cour de Cassation's conclusion that only ideologically hegemonic states could commit crimes against humanity, Vergès boldly declared, "The word Nazi doesn't exist."[84] Adding a neo-Marxist edge to this critique, Vergès insisted that crimes against humanity were no more than the rhetorical window dressing Europeans used to describe crimes committed against fellow Europeans, as against those perpetrated against the colonized Other.

And so everyone became a Nazi: the French in Algeria, the Americans in Vietnam. Vergès's co-counsel, Nabil Bouaita, railed against the "Nazification of the Jewish-Israeli people" that had led to "Palestinian genocide."[85] Echoing arguments made by Vergès, Bouaita described the Israeli invasion of Lebanon in 1982 as a holocaust, a claim that prompted Michel Zaoui, an attorney for the Jewish victims, to shout out, "This is extremely grave and intolerable."[86] In his summation before the court, Zaoui struggled to give words to his outrage. "Your condemnation of Barbie," he argued to the judges and lay jurors, "will serve as a rampart against such rumors, based on lies and inexactitude. . . . we must preserve the memory of what took place for this memory can serve to prevent evil."[87] In Zaoui's formulation, however, the lies to be rebutted were not those of the Holocaust denier, to which Wiesel had earlier referred during his time on the stand. Instead, the evil to be prevented was the spread of the very lies produced by the trial *itself*. In his final appearance before the court, the attorney for the Jewish victims found himself pleading for a guilty verdict in order to prevent history from being abused by the very legal process meant to protect it.

The Demjanjuk trial, by contrast, did not relativize history — it volatilized memory. It meant, of course, to do just the opposite: to demonstrate that the living memory of survivors continues to constitute the ultimate bulwark against the spread of negationist lies. Prosecutor Michael Shaked began his opening argument with the poignant observation, "This may be one of the last trials where it is possible to bring to the stand witnesses who can say 'we were there'. . . . The subject sooner or later will have to step down from the witness stand and become a part of history." The trial itself offered a number of links to the phenomenon of Holocaust denial that underscored Shaked's concern. Demjanjuk's defense, particularly in the early stages, was closely linked to and partially subsidized by Jerome Brentar, a Cleveland travel agent who testified as a character witness for Zundel in his Toronto trial and who maintained ties to denial groups. The Demjanjuk family's staggering ignorance about the Holocaust and strange views about Jews — Sheftel reports that Demjanjuk's wife long labored under the belief that Eichmann was Jewish[88] — provided a model of the mindset receptive to revisionist claims. By putting survivors on the stand, perhaps for the last time, the prosecution sought to fight ignorance and answer the specious claims of deniers.

Unfortunately, the strategy backfired terribly. By revealing the foibles of such memory — its vulnerability to suggestion and misidentification — the trial unintentionally invited negationists to attack the larger truths contained in survivor narratives. Such was the fatal logic of the trial court, which insisted on linking the accuracy of the identifications with the veracity of memories of the camp. Though one may rightfully insist that the harrowing descriptions of Treblinka were not impeached by the misidentifications, it was the court that disastrously maintained that the accuracy of the identifications and the truthfulness of the survivor narratives had to be treated as a whole.

This problem was not lost upon the Supreme Court. At the outset of its judgment, the Court stressed that "the district court's verdict is not only a legal document, but also an historical and educational document of great significance."[89] Indeed, the Court labors to assure us that by sweeping aside the verdict of the lower tribunal, it has not wholly discredited the trial court's published opinion, itself a four-hundred-page document handsomely published in an English edition by the Israeli Bar Association. On the contrary, the Court proclaims that the acquittal leaves intact the district court's holding as a historical and educational document of "great significance."

This time, however, the Court's attempt at damage control fails to convince. Although the acquittal offered the ultimate refutation of Sheftel's claim that the entire proceeding was a Stalinist sham, it also made clear the risks of pursuing the interests of collective tutelage and commemoration in trials. This point applies with singular strength in the Demjanjuk trial, in which memory was directly deployed as the weapon of indictment, the instrument for preparing the gallows. The prosecution itself understood the calamitous consequence that an acquittal would have on the pedagogic purpose of the trial. Quoted in a leading Israeli newspaper, a senior member of the prosecution expressed his concerns about the appeal: "The most important thing now is at least to prove that Demjanjuk was part of the Nazi extermination machine. . . . otherwise . . . we will be making a great contribution to the new world-wide movement of those who deny the Holocaust took place."[90] It is an astonishing statement, a bold insistence that Demjanjuk must be condemned (presumably for having served as a guard at Sobibòr, a crime for which, even if guilty, the accused had never been charged or tried), lest the acquittal send the wrong signals to gleeful deniers.

In a sense, the Supreme Court did not err in describing the lower tribunal's opinion as a document of great educational value. But instead of serving as one of the great history texts of the Holocaust, as does the published transcript of the Eichmann proceedings, the judgment of the Demjanjuk trial court teaches lessons of an entirely different sort. A cautionary tale, the opinion of the lower court stands as a reminder of the perils of relying on the legal process as a means of safeguarding and memorializing traumatic history. A trial staged to demonstrate the strong ties between history and memory served only to volatilize these bonds. In so doing, the Demjanjuk affair inadvertently ushered the world toward the day when the truths of the Holocaust no longer find protection in the living memory of survivors.

8

. . .

"Did Six Million Really Die?":
Holocaust Denial and the Law

For every man and every event, there comes a
moment, an hour . . . a stroke of midnight sounds
on a certain village clock when the
real event passes over into history.
— Charles Péguy

The great perpetrator trials were largely spared the need to deal with the issue of Holocaust denial. At Nuremberg, Ernst Kaltenbrunner may have brazenly disavowed any personal knowledge of the extermination camps, but neither he nor his colleagues in the dock disputed the authenticity of the prosecution's documents. Similarly, Servatius tried to upset the prosecution's case at the Eichmann trial not by denying the Holocaust, but by stipulating to it. By acknowledging the broad history of the final solution, Servatius hoped to focus attention narrowly upon the conduct and responsibilities of his client. And although the Demjanjuk defense team may have challenged aspects of survivor memory, it left untouched the larger history of the Holocaust.

Altogether different, then, were the trials of Ernst Zundel in Toronto, Canada, in 1985 and again in 1988. Born in Germany in 1939, Zundel had immigrated to Canada in 1958, settling in suburban Toronto. There he established himself as a photo retoucher for mass circulation magazines; his work twice received awards from the Art Directors' Club of Toronto.[1] His success at photo retouching vaguely echoed his passion for falsifying history. An ardent neo-Nazi, Zundel founded Samisdat (*sic*) Publications, a publishing house devoted to printing and distributing racist, anti-Semitic, and Holocaust denial literature.[2] One of Samisdat's more popular publications was a thirty-page pamphlet called "Did Six Million Really Die?" Originally published in England in 1974, the pamphlet was written by one Richard E. Harwood, purportedly "a writer and specialist in political and diplomatic aspects of the Second World War . . . at present . . . with the University of London."[3] In fact, Harwood was the nom de plume of a number of fascist writers; in this case, "Did Six Million Really Die?" issued from the pen of Richard Verrall, a member of the British fascist organization the National Front.

"Did Six Million Really Die?" was hardly a pioneering work of denial literature. A relatively concise summary of many leading negationist claims, the pamphlet advanced two principal arguments. First, it contended that the "story that no less [*sic*] than Six Million Jews were exterminated" is nothing more than "the most colossal piece of fiction and the most successful of deceptions." Second, the pamphlet claimed that the Holocaust was "the most profitable atrocity allegation of all time," a figment of the Zionist imagination crafted to extort money from Germany and sympathy from the world for Jewish causes.[4]

Zundel added "Did Six Million Really Die?" to Samisdat's list (which included such notable titles as *Samisdat's Battle Tips* and *The Hitler We Love and Why*) in the late seventies and mailed out, by his own estimation, thousands of copies. Disturbed by this proliferation of neo-Nazi literature, a number of Canadian Jewish groups, including the Canadian Holocaust Remembrance Association, petitioned the Crown prosecutor to indict Zundel. In 1970, the Canadian criminal code was amended to include a hate crimes provision against persons "who, by communicating statements, other than in private conversation, willfully promote hatred against any identifiable group."[5] The Crown attorney for Ontario, however, balked at indicting Zundel under this law — arguably for good reason. Despite its offensive content, "Did Six Million Really Die?" carefully avoided the inflammatory rhetoric of undisguised hate speech. The pamphlet begins with an odious claim, cast, however, in seemingly neutral terms: "Rightly or wrongly, the Germany of Adolf Hitler considered the Jews to be a disloyal and avaricious element within the national community," and concludes with the acknowledgment that "doubtless, several thousand Jewish persons did die in the course of the Second World War."[6] Given the pamphlet's veneer of objectivity, it might have been difficult to convict Zundel for willfully promoting hatred.

Instead, the Crown decided to try Zundel under section 177 of the Canadian criminal code.[7] Section 177 set forth that "everyone who willfully publishes a statement, tale or news that he knows is false and that causes or is likely to cause injury or mischief to a public interest is guilty of an indictable offense and is liable to imprisonment for two years."[8] Admittedly, the charging statute left undefined the meaning of such critical terms as "mischief" and "a public interest." This vagueness no doubt explained why the statute had supported but four known prosecutions, of which only one, a case tried in 1907, led to a conviction. Still, the "false statements" statute seemed to offer a potentially adequate legal tool for prosecuting the publisher of "Did Six Million Really Die?" And so in January 1985, Zundel found himself standing trial in a Toronto court for having committed the crime of publicly denying the Holocaust.

Policing the Past

The notion that denying the Holocaust constitutes a crime may sound strange if not troubling to American ears. Yet in using the coercive power of the state to sanction a denier of the Holocaust, the Canadian court both followed and anticipated the response to denial followed by many Western democracies. After more than a decade of experimenting with laws proscribing Holocaust denial, Germany in 1994 amended its criminal code to include the denial and trivialization of National Socialist genocide specifically as a form of racial incitement. Likewise, an Austrian statute passed in 1992 makes it a crime if a person "denies, grossly trivializes, approves or seeks to justify the national socialist genocide or other national socialist crimes against humanity."[9] France passed a law in 1990 (known as the Gayssot law after the Communist legislator Jean-Claude Gayssot, who drafted the law) making it a crime for anyone to contest "the existence of one or several crimes against humanity as defined in Article 6 of the Statute of the International Military Tribunal."[10] Similar legislation has been passed by Belgium, Switzerland, and Israel.

Certainly these laws make for certain ironies. If we recall the discussion of the French prosecution at Nuremberg, one could tendentiously argue that the Gayssot law would hardly even touch Holocaust denial, as the extermination of the Jews barely constituted, judging by the evidence submitted by the French team, one of the "several crimes against humanity as defined in Article 6 of the Statute of the International Military Tribunal." Similarly bearing in mind the language of the German and Austrian statutes, one could argue that by treating the final solution as an accessory of crimes against peace and as a subset of war crimes, Nuremberg itself grossly trivialized the crimes of the Holocaust. These facetious observations notwithstanding, the deeper point remains that numerous nations have sought to turn Holocaust denial into a criminal offense.

In the United States, such an effort would almost certainly founder on the First Amendment.[11] Succinctly expressing the free speech argument, Alan Dershowitz has insisted, "I don't want the government to tell me that it [the Holocaust] occurred because I don't want any government ever to tell me that it didn't occur."[12] Yet despite the seemingly insurmountable constitutional bars to criminalizing Holocaust denial in this country, Holocaust denial has led to domestic civil litigation. In 1985 Mel Mermelstein, an Auschwitz survivor, sued the Institute for Historical Review, a California "think tank" dedicated to Holocaust "revisionism," for its failure to honor a pledge to pay fifty thousand dollars to anyone who could prove that gassings took place at Auschwitz. Claiming injury as a result of both breach of contract and the intentional infliction of emotional distress, Mermelstein accepted a pretrial settlement in which the institute agreed to pay the promised original sum and an additional forty thousand dollars in damages. Although the precedential implications of the case are less than clear as a result of the pretrial settlement, the Mermelstein litigation suggests that the First Amendment might not bar civil suits claiming that Holocaust denial constitutes tortious conduct.[13]

Lurking beneath the doctrinal issue, however, is the more interesting question: Why seek a legal remedy to Holocaust denial? The most obvious answer seems to be the one that prompted Mermelstein to bring his suit. As Elie Wiesel has argued, Holocaust denial defames the dead and insults survivors. In this respect, the trial of Holocaust deniers can be seen as conceptually linked to the trials of perpetrators, as the logic of the final solution contemplated not only the extermination of Jewry but the erasure of any memory of the killings. Holocaust denial preys, then, upon the disbelief that, as I noted in chapter 1, greeted news of the camps. Legal responses to Holocaust denial thus seek to contain one of the most odious features of such speech: the way it twists the very extraordinariness of the atrocities into prima facie evidence of their impossibility.

Moreover, if the First Amendment counsels that the best response to odious speech is more speech, such an approach plays into the hands of Holocaust revisionism. As Deborah Lipstadt argued in *Denying the Holocaust,* to debate Holocaust deniers is already to accede to the force of their logic — it is to admit that the topic is one about which reasonable persons can have reasonable disagreements.[14] There is, of course, a difference between refusing to debate and turning to the law to silence those eager to do so; in this regard, I believe it is necessary to understand legal responses to Holocaust denial as born of an additional desire to safeguard this past from what Geoffrey Hartman has termed an "encroaching anti-memory," in which the past is trivialized and banalized through a "culture industry that can simulate anything and everything."[15] Proscribing Holocaust denial is meant to remove the topic from the spectacle of talk show contention and the circulation of ambient media noise. Here one recalls Lipstadt's story of the talk show host who reminded his viewers, as his show cut to a commercial, to stay tuned so they could learn whether the Holocaust was a "myth or . . . truth."[16] The move toward sanctioning Holocaust denial asks the law to perform a sacralizing function, to shield a realm of sacred facts from the profane banality of media culture. As the world anticipates a time when the Holocaust will no longer be sustained in the living memory of survivors, the law is asked to protect the past.

Compelling as these reasons might be, they do not exactly explain the logic of *criminalizing* Holocaust denial. To permit survivors and families of survivors to bring civil suits against deniers remains fundamentally different from treating denial as a criminal offense. Although one might well understand why certain groups, such as the children of survivors, would support statutes proscribing denials of the Holocaust, one must ask why the state would consider denial a threat to public order and why it would provide the facticity of the Holocaust a degree of legal insulation not given other facts. That the Holocaust would require such legal protection may seem remarkable, for despite the Nazis' best efforts to hide their atrocities, it is difficult to imagine an event of recent history for which the factual record is more complete. Indeed, the Holocaust now stands as one of the most thoroughly documented events in human history. Why does the law need to secure the Holocaust in responsible memory, when it does not protect the fact that the earth revolves around the sun or that Napoleon's armies fought at Waterloo?

One answer is that Holocaust denial is an especially invidious form of hate speech. Though often cast in the pseudoscholarly terms of "Did Six Million Really Die?" the literature of Holocaust denial presents classic anti-Semitic stereotypes of Jews as conspiratorial, money-hungry internationalists shamelessly attempting to extract advantage from the history of their own alleged victimization. Criminalization of Holocaust denial can thus be seen as part of a larger effort to fight hate speech with the power of the criminal law, an effort that remains more controversial in the United States than in many other Western democracies.

Another answer focuses on the very magnitude of the rupture that the Holocaust caused to liberal and Enlightenment sensibilities. In this regard, to deny the Holocaust is not simply to offend a single group or the historical record; it is to insult the very notions of meaning upon which the liberal concept of public discourse is predicated. By making a mockery of conventions of truth testing and good faith conversation, Holocaust denial violates the most basic norms that inform the concept of public discourse. Stipulating to the facticity of the Holocaust thus serves as a litmus test of one's willingness to participate in the thinnest version of the discursive community. As such, Holocaust denial threatens less a specific group than the discursive basis of the liberal state.

The Fraught Case of Germany

This explanation of the complex logic of Holocaust denial laws finds provocative support in the country that remains most traumatized by the final solution — the Federal Republic of Germany.[17] As I mentioned earlier, the German parliament passed a law in 1994 making Holocaust denial a form of racial incitement. This law was merely the latest in a number of German statutory and juridical responses to the problem of Holocaust negationism. In the seventies, German law treated Holocaust denial as a form of insult (*Beleidigung*). The offense of insult, codified in section 185 of the German penal code, functioned as a hybrid of civil and criminal law, relying upon the insulted individual — the person who had putatively suffered the legal harm — to petition the state to initiate criminal proceedings against the alleged insulter. This arrangement, however, had raised the question of who, within the meaning of the statute, could claim to be insulted by denials of the Holocaust.

As the legal scholar Eric Stein has shown, the answers that German courts had supplied were problematic at best.[18] A case in 1979, for example, posed the question of whether a German citizen with one Jewish grandfather could petition the state to prosecute a man who had publicly posted a leaflet attacking the Holocaust as a Zionist swindle.[19] The Bundesgerichtshof (the federal court of justice) concluded that the man could bring an insult claim because, though not a "full Jew," he would have been classified as a second-degree *Mischling* (mixed breed) according to the notorious Nuremberg laws of 1935 and thus subject to considerable discrimination.[20] Extending this mode of analysis, an appellate court in 1985 acquitted a defendant because the petitioner was, according to the Nuremberg laws, neither a Jew nor a Mischling and therefore could not claim to be offended by the words of a Holocaust denier.[21] The unseemliness of relying on the standards and definitions supplied by the laws that paved the way to the Holocaust to decide who may legally claim to be insulted by Holocaust denials was not lost upon legal observers. As a result, and in light of a disturbing rise in neo-Nazi activities, the Bundestag amended the law of insult in 1985.

The 1985 law, known as the *Auschwitzlüge,* or "Auschwitz-lie," law, continued to treat Holocaust denial as an insult. The amended law, however, abolished the requirement of the private petitioner, authorizing the state to initiate criminal prosecution ex officio "if the [publicly] insulted person was persecuted as a member of a group under the National Socialist or another violent and arbitrary regime." Ignoring for the moment the meaning of "another violent and arbitrary regime," one can see that by placing the state in the position of the complainant, the statute seemed to recognize that Holocaust denial insults not only Jews as "a group singled out by fate" but also the German state itself and its historical record.[22] Indeed, the Bundesgerichtshof implicitly recognized this in its decision of 1979, which relied, however unfortunately, on Nuremberg law definitions to decide what defined "an insultable group" (eine beleidigungsfähige Gruppe):

Alone the historical fact that people were robbed of their individuality by being sorted according to the genealogical criteria of the Nuremberg laws (with the goal of extermination), creates a special personal relationship between Jews residing in the Federal Republic and their fellow citizens. . . . It belongs to their self-understanding to be identified as members of a group of persons singled out by fate. . . . The recognition of this self-understanding constitutes for each of them a guarantee against the repetition of such discrimination and a basic condition for their life in the Federal Republic.[23]

Here the court recognized that Holocaust denial, by repudiating the history that undergirds the collective identity of German Jews, challenges the very foundations of their secure existence within a country that once strove to exterminate them. This argument is crucial, for the larger legitimacy of a liberal state is itself called into question when it ceases to be able to offer a citizen group the basic guarantee of a secure existence within a democratic community. Proscribing Holocaust denial is thus a means of protecting not simply the sensitivities of German Jews but the very legitimacy of the German state responsible for their secure existence.

Unfortunately, the 1985 law was itself not unproblematic. As noted, the amended law empowered the state to prosecute also on behalf of insulted victims of "another violent and arbitrary regime."[24] This language was included in the statute at the insistence of the conservative Christian Democrats, the senior party of the ruling coalition, and, though oddly inexact, it was "unequivocally meant to refer to German refugees driven west in 1945" as a result of Soviet-sponsored expulsions.[25] In its final form, then, the law came to proscribe two distinct negationist statements: those that deny the Nazi death camps and those that deny the forced expulsion of "ethnic" Germans from the former German provinces of Poland at the war's conclusion. As such, the law implicitly equated the destruction of European Jewry with the forced migration of Silesian and East Prussian Germans. That one would be hard-pressed to find in Germany any groups dedicated to challenging the "myth" of the Silesian expulsions only underscores the inanity of the law. The legal instrument originally meant to protect the survivors from insults to the historical record itself became a source of fresh insults.

The 1994 law rectified this problem by focusing statutory attention exclusively upon Holocaust denial. Instead of considering denial a form of insult under section 185, the law enabled the prosecution of Holocaust deniers under section 130, the statute against racial incitement (*Volksverhetzung*), which was amended to make possible the punishment of persons who "express approval of, deny, or trivialize genocide perpetrated under the regime of National Socialism."[26] Not only did this law increase the severity of sanctions facing negationists — insult carries a maximum sentence of one year, while incitement carries a possible penalty of five years — it also now made possible conviction for mere denial of the Holocaust, absent the additional claim that the Jews themselves had fashioned the myth of their extermination to extort money from Germany (which had previously been required under the law).[27]

Although the emendation of the law of incitement has not escaped criticism in Germany on free speech grounds,[28] it powerfully supports the view that efforts to criminalize denial cannot be understood simply as attempts to protect the sensitivities and dignity of the Jewish minority. By directing the focus of the law away from group libel — that is, the charge that Jews fabricated the Holocaust for strategic reasons — and toward the disputation of a historical moment, the new law underscores the state's complex interest in proscribing denial. Indeed, by criminalizing denial, the German state has confirmed the sacral status of the Holocaust — as the foundational cataclysmic violence out of which the Federal Republic was born. Both Max Weber and Walter Benjamin detailed the complex ways in which states buttress their claims to legitimacy through acts of forgetting — rituals of erasure that obscure any connection to the state's foundational moment, inevitably a time of violent, lawless instantiation.[29] In his study of the politics of memory in Vichy France, the historian Henry Rousso articulated the idea concisely: "At the social level, memory is the structuring of forgetfulness."[30] German law, by contrast, demands that no one deny the state's monstrous past. In this manner, the German Federal Republic attempts to redeem its claims of legitimacy through acts of coerced remembering, in which the history of past crimes remains ever present and in which the law serves as the muscle of memory.

Of course, the very reliance upon the law to police responsible memory serves not only to connect the present German state to its past incarnation but also to sever such ties. Here the state's candor in admitting past transgressions appears as a legitimating virtue, and the law that proscribes denial of the historical record also serves to create a gulf that separates the present state from its reprobate precursor. And so Germany has adopted a posture of obsessive mindfulness of the past.

The German example thus supports the understanding that laws proscribing Holocaust denial offer symbolic protection to the norms of public discourse. Holocaust denial, in the German context, challenges not simply these liberal norms, but the very integrity of a state whose legitimacy depends upon its confessional embrace of the past. Holocaust denial, in this regard, poses a threat to both the Jews left in Germany and to the state attempting to make good on its effort at liberal redemption.

"Did Six Million Really Die?"

Clearly Holocaust denial does not raise the same fraught specter for the Canadian state. Canada has not, for example, fashioned a statute similar to those passed in Germany and France specifically proscribing Holocaust denial. As noted, the absence of such a statute meant that Zundel had to be prosecuted under an obscure article of the Canadian legal code. Even then, it was only after the Canadian Holocaust Remembrance Association initiated litigation by bringing a private charge against Zundel under section 177 that the Crown decided to intervene and assume the burden of prosecution.[31]

In addition to requiring the state to demonstrate that Zundel's publications harmed a definable public interest, section 177 required the state to assume three additional evidentiary burdens. First, the state had to prove that Zundel had, in fact, published "Did Six Million Really Die?" Second, it had to demonstrate that the statements contained in the pamphlet were false. Finally, it had to prove that Zundel published these false statements with full knowledge of their falsity.

Of these elements, the first was the easiest to prove. At his arrest, Zundel had freely admitted to the police that he was the publisher of "Did Six Million Really Die?" (At trial, the attempt by Douglas Christie, Zundel's counsel, to suppress these statements as inadmissible was seen largely as a token gesture, and the court dismissed the motion after brief deliberation.) The third element, by contrast, seemed the trickiest to prove. As a false but honestly held belief was insufficient to sustain a conviction, the prosecution faced the difficult task of convincing the jury that Zundel was a committed falsifier of history and not a sincere though misguided eccentric. To meet its burden, the Crown tried to piggyback the third element onto the second — that is, it sought to extrapolate from the fact that Zundel was well versed in mainstream Holocaust scholarship that he must have published "Did Six Million Really Die?" with full knowledge of its falsity.

This, however, raised the question of how the Crown would go about proving the falsity of the pamphlet's claims. Ultimately, the prosecution adopted a two-pronged strategy, at once evidentiary and judicial. The evidentiary strategy called for the submission of three kinds of proof. Following the Nuremberg example, the prosecution retrieved *Nazi Concentration Camps* from the National Archives, screening it on the final day of the Crown's case. Forty years after its first complex use as legal evidence, the film was now considered such a transparent representation of the Holocaust that the Crown prosecutor, Peter Griffiths, dramatically ended his presentation with a gesture to the film and the statement, "That's the case for the prosecution, Your Honour."[32]

The prosecution also relied on survivor testimony. Following the Eichmann approach, the Crown called four Holocaust survivors to the stand, three of whom had been interned at Auschwitz. The most important of these was Rudolf Vrba, who, along with Alfred Wetzler, had famously escaped from Auschwitz and fled to Slovakia in April 1944. Vrba and Wetzler's description of the camp was communicated that June to Allen Dulles, head of the U.S. Office of Strategic Services, and was documented in a famous report of the War Refugee Board. Now a professor of pharmacology at the University of British Columbia and a recognized expert on neurochemistry, Vrba was considered an extremely attractive witness, one who could advance both the narrow legal aims of the prosecution as well as the larger didactic purposes of the trial. Indeed, a number of Jewish groups supported the decision to prosecute precisely because they believed that Zundel had to be tried before, to paraphrase Norbert Frei, the survivors had "disappeared from the scene." A prosecution of a denier, it was feared, would lack dramatic substance and legal force without the viva voce of survivors to make the horror of history real and concrete to a jury.

Finally, the central pillar of the prosecution's case rested on historical treatises. The testimony supplied by the Crown's key expert witness, Raul Hilberg, doyen of Holocaust scholars and the author of *The Destruction of the European Jews,* lacked the graphic power of *Nazi Concentration Camps* and the emotional appeal of the testimony of survivors. Still, Hilberg's testimony served as the Zundel trial's central didactic paradigm. At the Eichmann trial, Salo Baron, the eminent professor of Jewish history at Columbia, had testified as an expert about the distinctively "biological" aspects of Nazi anti-Semitism (*TAE* 1:181). The Holocaust itself, however, had to be presented not through the discourse of history but through the voice of memory. Although Hilberg's pathbreaking work appeared in the same year as the Jerusalem trial (and, to Hilberg's distress, importantly influenced Arendt), arguably the trial paved the way for the comprehension of the book, and not vice versa. A quarter of a century later, by contrast, the Holocaust had been rendered largely, if not always adequately, intelligible as an object of historical inquiry. Thus in a trial staged to punish willful distortions of the historical record, it only made sense for the prosecution's paradigm of proof to be anchored in the dispassionate discourse of the professional historian.

At the same time that the Crown developed this evidentiary approach, it pursued a second, seemingly related strategy: it petitioned the court to take judicial notice of the Holocaust. Largely a device of courtroom economy, judicial notice permits a judge to stipulate to the truth of "what is considered by reasonable men of that time and place to be indisputable either by resort to common knowledge or to sources of indisputable accuracy" (*TEZ-1985*, 2079). Crown Prosecutor Griffiths asked the court to take judicial notice of the fact that "millions of Jews were annihilated from 1933–45 because of deliberate policies of Nazi Germany" and that "the means of annihilation included mass shootings, starvation, privation and gassing" (*TEZ-1985*, 2073). In making this petition, Griffiths was following the example of other Holocaust denial litigations. German courts, for example, had declared the Holocaust to be *offenkündig* (public knowledge), thus sparing prosecutors the need to lead evidence of the final solution.

In the Zundel trial, however, the court refused to take judicial notice of the Holocaust. Some legal observers have argued that the refusal was a result of Griffiths's mistimed petition.[33] The Crown did not formally request judicial notice until the conclusion of its case — Hilberg and the survivors had already testified, and all that remained to complete the prosecution's submissions was the screening of *Nazi Concentration Camps*. Because "the fields of judicial notice and expert testimony are on the whole mutually exclusive" (*TEZ-1985*, 2079), and insofar as topics granted notice are "not subject to attack by evidence," acceding to the Crown's petition arguably would have insulated evidence supplied by its witnesses. Although the presiding judge, the Honorable Hugh Locke, conceded in a curious, though apparently well-meaning statement that "it would appear to me, on what I have read and heard, that there exists wide and highly regarded opinion that the Holocaust did occur," the judge decided it would not be "judicially prudent . . . to grant the Crown's motion" (*TEZ-1985*, 2188). Doing so, he feared, would relieve the Crown of the burden of proving guilt and create a perception of unfairness in the proceedings. Whether Locke's reasoning was altogether sound remains open to debate.[34] In any case, Locke dismissed the Crown's request, and, as we shall see, an appellate court concluded that he was well within his powers of judicial discretion to do so.

The refusal to take judicial notice seriously upset the didactic ends of the trial. At the very least, it seemed troubling that a court would refuse to stipulate to the facticity of the Holocaust in a trial meant to demonstrate that certain statements are so beyond the pale of legitimate dispute as to justify the imposition of a criminal sanction. More important, the decision had the consequence of shifting the focus of the trial away from the sincerity of Zundel's beliefs and to the truthfulness of the Holocaust. Suddenly the Holocaust itself was on trial, as history had to be judged not by the standards of scholarly inquiry but in accordance with legal conventions of proof and evidence.

This played into the hands of Zundel's lawyer, Douglas Christie. Without a doubt, Christie emerged as the dominant figure of the trial. Whereas at the Nuremberg and Eichmann trials, the prosecutors — in particular Jackson and Hausner, respectively — played the leading roles in the legal drama, at the Zundel trial, as at the Barbie and Demjanjuk trials, the dramatic focus shifted to the defense. Described in one popular account as "counsel of the damned," Christie had established his name as an attorney for neo-Nazi and white supremacist causes.[35] A zealous advocate, Christie has been attacked for embracing the same politics as his clients, and his conduct during the Zundel trial earned him a sharp rebuke from the disciplinary committee of the Law Society of Upper Canada. Despite his reputation as a showman and demagogue, Christie's mastery of Holocaust scholarship — both mainstream and otherwise — caught the Crown off guard.

As a strictly strategic matter, Christie did not launch a particularly sound defense. As noted, the matter of Zundel's mindset represented the most vulnerable link in the Crown's case, and Christie presumably could have mounted an effective defense by focusing on the sincerity of his client's beliefs. Instead, Christie chose to overdetermine the defense — he tried to prove that Zundel's beliefs were both honest *and* true. Likening the Holocaust to the "Belgian baby stories after the First World War," Christie sought to demonstrate that the "gas chambers were a myth" and that his client was a latter-day Galileo, a visionary persecuted for his intrepid rejection of a dogmatic orthodoxy (*TEZ-1985*, 2341, 2399).[36] The strategy was risky if not foolhardy, as it asked jurors to accept the negationists' position. As a result, many commentators credit Christie with winning the Crown's case.

Yet if Christie's strategy backfired as a narrowly tactical matter — and it remains less than clear whether Zundel even cared about being acquitted — it certainly succeeded in hijacking the didactic ends of the trial. Staged to protect and promote the interests of responsible memory, the trial turned into a grotesque spectacle, an offensive and often bizarre drama that displayed the perils of relying on legal dramaturgy as a means of buttressing the integrity of history.

9

Historians and Hearsay: The Denial
Trials of Ernst Zundel

It [is] true that historians aren't judges and
historians aren't eyewitnesses.
— Robert Paxton, *New York Times*,
January 31, 1998, A17.

The Crown's case in the first Zundel trial, then, was supported by three evidentiary pillars: the film *Nazi Concentration Camps,* the eyewitness testimony of survivors, and the expert testimony of the historian. Christie aggressively attacked all three. He found a potent weapon in the concept of
hearsay, the principle of proof, central to Anglo-American legal systems,
that bars a court from accepting as true the testimony reported to a witness
by a third party unavailable to the court. These evidentiary concerns, as we
have seen, did not vex the Nuremberg and Eichmann trials, as both proceedings were governed by streamlined procedure that specifically counte-
nanced the submission of evidence and testimony that otherwise would
have failed as hearsay.[1]

The Zundel trial, however, was a procedurally ordinary case tried before
a jury. Although the subject matter and atmosphere of the proceeding were
unusual, the trial itself was legally conventional, conducted in accordance
with standard norms of Canadian criminal procedure. Consequently,
Christie was able to use the hearsay rule strategically to exploit the disso-

nance created by the attempt to do justice to extraordinary history through ordinary legal means. Indeed, Christie used the bar against hearsay as more than a technical legal tool; it emerged as the controlling trope of Zundel's defense, deployed to volatilize memory and relativize history in a manner far more radical than would be the case in either the Barbie or Demjanjuk trials.

Christie lodged his most convincing hearsay objection against the screening of *Nazi Concentration Camps*. The soundtrack, he argued, was problematic, as the unnamed narrators were unavailable for cross-examination. He correctly pointed out that the affidavits that introduce the film are not read by the affiants but by unidentified narrators. He was also correct in observing that the version of the film screened at trial was not even identical to the film shown at Nuremberg (the original contained a number of splicing errors that were corrected in later copies of the film produced by the National Archives). He pointed out what apparently had escaped the notice of Prosecutor Griffiths, namely, that "very little reference is made there to Jews at all in the film" (*TEZ-1985*, 2344). The heaps of corpses shown in *Nazi Concentration Camps*, he contended, could just as easily have been victims of a typhus epidemic — which the defense readily acknowledged had ravaged the camps toward the war's end — as victims of a campaign of systematic extermination. The voice-over describing the working of the gas chamber in Dachau, he asserted, was unreliable, as historians of the final solution are not of one mind about whether the Dachau facility was ever made operational.[2] Christie thus insisted that the film itself be barred. Although Judge Locke ultimately permitted the film to be screened, Christie questioned the wisdom of this holding with the rhetorical question, "How do you cross-examine a film?"

Christie launched a similar attack on the survivors. In *The Drowned and the Saved*, Levi observed, "We, the survivors, are not the true witnesses."[3] Those who experienced the Holocaust in its purest and most distilled form were, Levi suggested, the dead. In his cross-examination of survivors, Christie took this insight to its most literal and odious extreme. Emblematic was his attack on the testimony of the Auschwitz escapee Rudolf Vrba. During Prosecutor Griffiths's examination-in-chief, Vrba had already run afoul of the hearsay rule on a number of occasions. In the Eichmann trial, many survivors, for example, Leon Wells, were permitted to present their testimony in the form of a loose narrative. By contrast, Vrba found his story constantly interrupted by Christie, Judge Locke, and finally even Griffiths, who labored to remind the witness to tell the court only what he saw and did and not what others had told him. These restrictions drastically truncated the sweep and compass of his narrative, at times rendering it all but unintelligible. Hearsay objections, for example, mangled Vrba's story of how inmates forced to assist in the unloading of trains were strictly forbidden from talking to new arrivees:

> THE WITNESS: . . . So one woman [a new arrivee] walked up to the officer and she said — we were dressed in prisoner's garb — and she said to him, "one of the gangsters has told me that I and my children will be gassed."
>
> MR CHRISTIE: Your Honour, excuse me. You know, I realize the gentleman wants to give us a full explanation and all, but it's obvious that we aren't in a position to hear this conversation, and I think it's clear it's hearsay. . . .
>
> THE COURT: . . . I think that what you [Griffiths] should do is ask the witness what, if anything, he saw as a result of the conversation he overheard.
>
> MR GRIFFITHS: Thank you, Your Honour . . . Dr. Vrba, what, if anything, did you see happen as a result of the conversation you may have overheard between this woman and the S.S. officer?
>
> A: The S.S. officer mollified her. He says, "Madam" —
>
> Q: Don't tell us what he said. Just what you saw happen.
>
> A: Yes . . . The woman took the S.S. officer to the prisoner and showed which said it.
>
> Q: And what happened to that man?
>
> A: . . . The prisoner was taken to the wagons and shot. [*TEZ-1985*, 1279]

Although the story is disturbing in its truncated form, the hearsay objection transforms the narrative into a tale about the strictness of camp regulations. Lost from the story is, in effect, the heart of the matter — namely, the fact that the woman and her children were to be gassed.

In his cross-examination, Christie contended that Vrba's testimony as a whole was no more than an elaborate edifice of hearsay. Christie began his cross with the purposefully disorienting question, "Will you say it's true that you have told stories about Auschwitz?" (1387). One could understand the question as asking the witness whether he had testified about Auschwitz on previous occasions or whether he had ever invented stories about Auschwitz. Christie obviously intended the ambiguity. Vrba, whose report to the War Refugee Board was submitted at Nuremberg, whose affi-

davit was used at the Eichmann trial, and who had testified in person at the
Auschwitz trial in Frankfurt, had also written a memoir, *I Cannot Forgive*,
in 1963. Though Christie did not challenge the witness's prior testimony,
he pounced on the memoir. Referring to the book, Christie asked, "Did
you say things that you say you saw . . . that you did not actually see?"
(1392). By way of response, Vrba likened his memoir to an "artistic picture"; like "every art piece in literature," Vrba explained, the book relied
not only on the author's "own eyewitness abilities, but also on the experience of others" (1392). Unsatisfied with Vrba's response, Christie continued to hammer away:

> C H R I S T I E: Did you put in the book statements that you said you saw
> which you did not see?
> A: I am not aware of that.
> Q: So do I take it from your answer that when you say you saw something
> in the book, you actually did see it?
> A: I will discuss with you the book on the literary afternoon at your dis-
> posal. At the moment I am not prepared to discuss the book unless the
> book has been read by the jury. [1392]

This reply earned Vrba a sharp rebuke from the court. "Dr. Vrba, I'm going
to say this once and only once," Judge Locke declared. "You are here as a
compellable witness. . . . You are not to give orders as to what this jury will
do and what you will do or not do. You will answer counsel's questions unless I tell you not to. Do you understand?" (1393).

Emboldened, Christie proceeded to read aloud a page from *I Cannot
Forgive* describing one of Himmler's visits to Auschwitz: "Himmler and
Höß got out and chatted for a while to the senior officers present. Himmler
listened intently as they explained the [gassing] procedure to him in detail.
He ambled over to the sealed door [of the gas chamber], glanced casually
through the small, thick observation window at the squirming bodies inside, then returned to fire some more questions at his underlings" (1405).
To Christie's incredulous question, "Are you telling this Court you actually
saw Heinrich Himmler peeping through the doors of the gas chamber?"
Vrba had to acknowledge, "I have put together a story which I've heard
many times from various people who were present and related it to me"
(1409). For Christie, this did not settle the matter:

> Q: Well, in your book you indicate that you saw, and you don't indicate
> that you heard from other people the story that you related.

A: In this particular case the story is related.

Q: And you say that these things happened as you described, even though you acknowledged they were on the basis of hearsay; right?

A: Yes. [1410]

Having wrestled this initial concession from the witness, Christie launched a broadside against Vrba's claim to have watched an ss officer deposit Zyklon B into an opening on the roof of the gas chamber. After a barrage of questions about the height and angle of the roof, Christie asked Vrba how he knew it was a gas chamber:

Q: I suggest to you that what you are talking about is the roof of the mortuary, and the mortuary was underground.

A: Have you been there?

Q: No, I haven't, sir. Have you?

A: No, but I've heard that it was a gas chamber from those who worked there. [1433–34]

Having again shown Vrba's statements to be based on hearsay, Christie continued to challenge Vrba's authenticity as an eyewitness. In the famous report of the War Refugee Board issued in 1944, Vrba had claimed that 1.765 million Jews had been gassed during his internment at Auschwitz. Vrba arrived at this calculation, he reported, through a process of memory and calculation. For months he tallied the number of trucks dispatched to the gas chambers while also estimating the number of persons on each vehicle. In this way, the witness arrived at a figure that he believed to be accurate within a 10 percent margin of error. Christie challenged Vrba's powers as an observer and methodology as a counter:

Q: You say 1.75 —

A: 1.765 [million] according to my count.

Q: Of people gassed while you were there.

A: Yes.

. . . .

Q: How do you explain the fact that experts like Dr Raul Hilberg dispute that figure and say it is closer to one million, or in Reitlinger's case, 800,000 at Birkenau?

A: It is not for me to explain the scholarships of Reitlinger and Hilberg . . . they are bound by historical discipline, whereas my figure is based on eyewitness account.

Q: You claim that you, then, were an eyewitness to the gassing of 1,765,000 people, right?

A: Right. [1454]

At first blush, Christie's attack on Vrba's accuracy as an eyewitness seems oddly self-defeating, insofar as Hilberg and Vrba, despite the discrepancies in their calculations, agree that at least one million Jews were gassed at Birkenau. Yet Christie tried to turn the numbers game to his advantage, arguing that the numerical difference between the eyewitness and Hilberg was actually greater than that between Hilberg and the negationists, who allowed for between 100,000 and 300,000 Jewish dead. The smaller figure, of course, supported the negationists' claims that most of the Jews in the camps had died of disease; how, for example, could Vrba be sure that the corpses he had seen were victims of gassing and not of typhus? Had he ever seen an autopsy report indicating gas as the cause of death? When Vrba decried the absurdity of the question, Christie simply stated that this was additional proof that Vrba's eyewitness account was, in fact, based on unsubstantiated inference. Indeed, Vrba's refusal to acknowledge the possibility of serious error in his calculations only supported Christie's effort to turn the eyewitness into an outsider and a hysteric — an impressionable dupe whose testimony was built on unstable memory informed by insupportable surmise.

Earlier, Christie had used a similar strategy to attack Hilberg. During his examination by the prosecution, Hilberg had described his scholarly method as empirical, based on the close examination of such documents as railroad schedules. On cross, Christie vehemently attacked the reliability and integrity of this methodology:

Q: In regard to Bergen-Belsen, have you ever visited that camp? . . .

A: No.

Q: In regard to Buchenwald, have you visited that camp?

A: No.

Q: In regard to Dachau, have you visited that —

A: No, I have not visited — I can tell you, to save your questions, I have visited only two camps.

Q: What were they?

A: Auschwitz and Treblinka.

Q: Now, Auschwitz is compiled of two and perhaps three camps. Is that right?

A: Yes. There are three parts to it.

. . . .

Q: . . . So you have been to Auschwitz 1, 2, and 3?
A: 1 and 2, not three.
Q: So you have been to Auschwitz and Birkenau?
A: That's correct.
Q: How many times?
A: One time.
Q: Once. And you also went to Treblinka.
A: That's correct.
Q: And how many times there?
A: Once.
Q: And when did you go there?
A: 1979.
Q: After you wrote your first book [*The Destruction of the European Jews,* published in 1961].
A: Yes.
Q: So you wrote a book about a place before you went there. [770–72]

Summarizing this exchange, Christie concluded that "as far as researching the scene of Auschwitz, Treblinka, Sobibòr, Chelmno, Stutthof, you didn't do any firsthand, on-site research whatsoever until after you wrote your book" (871). Dismissing Hilberg's characterization of his work as empirical, Christie quipped, "The examination of documents may be scholasticism, but it certainly isn't empiricism, sir" (967). Against the methodology of the historian, Christie pitted a model of the empirical method imported directly from the natural sciences. This permitted him, again, to attack evidence of the gas chambers:

Q: . . . Name one [scientific] report of such a kind that showed the existence of gas chambers anywhere in Nazi-occupied territory.
A: I still don't quite understand the import of your question. Are you referring to German, or a post-war —
Q: I don't care who — German, post-war, Allied, Soviet — any source at all. Name one that —
A: To prove what?
Q: To conclude that they have physically seen a gas chamber. One scientific report.
A: I am really at a loss. I am seldom at such a loss, but —
Q: I put it to you, you are at a loss because there isn't one. [968–69]

Contending that the historian, as opposed to the scientist, was no more than a dutiful compiler of hearsay, Christie argued that Hilberg's method was based on certain axioms — the existence of the death camps, for instance — whose truth the historian had never bothered to call into question. This was doubly problematic, Christie insisted, inasmuch as the sources upon which Hilberg had relied were of doubtful reliability. Christie claimed, for example, that Hilberg had cited the statements of Kurt Gerstein, the chief hygienic officer of the ss, on numerous occasions in *The Destruction of the European Jews*. The Eichmann court in its final judgment quoted sparingly from survivor testimony but offered lengthy excerpts of Gerstein's statements prepared before the ss officer's apparent suicide in a French prison in 1945. Gerstein's statements had also been submitted to the IMT and were used in subsequent Nuremberg trials, especially the Pohl case, conducted by the Americans. In his documentary biography of Gerstein, published in 1969, Saul Friedlander had described him as a "tragic figure," one who had "labored untiringly to keep the Germans and the world informed" of atrocities against the Jews.[4]

Christie, by contrast, painted Gerstein as a delusional, unbalanced figure. The ss officer's written reports, prepared while he was in French custody, were filled with extravagant, impossible claims. In one document, for example, Gerstein estimated the number of exterminated at twenty-five million, and Hilberg himself acknowledged, "I am not a judge of sanity, but I would be careful about what he [Gerstein] said" (905). Christie averred that by selectively quoting from Gerstein — that is, by using his more plausible assertions while redacting out his more incredible claims — Hilberg had used precisely the same selective method for which he condemned the authors of "Did Six Million Really Die?" More important, he had, in effect, relied upon unreliable hearsay.

The same was true, Christie charged, of Hilberg's use of Höß's testimony at Nuremberg. Höß, the former Auschwitz commandant, had riveted the Nuremberg courtroom with his chilling descriptions of the extermination process. Now Christie declared it all unreliable. Quoting from the Nuremberg psychologist G. M. Gilbert's own assessment of Höß as a psychotic "suffering from what is known as schizoid apathy," Christie insisted that Höß's statements, which likewise contained some exaggerated numbers and other inaccuracies, had to be discarded. Moreover, Christie claimed that Hilberg had overlooked or ignored evidence that Höß's statement at Nuremberg had been elicited through coercion (though he characteristically failed to substantiate this), not to mention the fact that all evidence gathered by all the Nuremberg tribunals was intrinsically suspect. Even Nuremberg's critics agree that the trial succeeded as an invaluable tool of fact finding; Hilberg's work, along with a number of other seminal studies of Nazism, could never have been written without Nuremberg's extensive documentary trove. Christie, however, used the attacks on the legal adequacy of the trial to impeach the veracity of its documentary record. The relaxed rules of procedure that governed the trial, and the prosecution's heavy reliance on affidavits, merely confirmed that Nuremberg's evidentiary edifice was built on hearsay. Moreover, evidence of the final solution uncovered at Nuremberg had to be taken with a grain of salt insofar as the entire trial was an irregular exercise in victors' justice. Harlan Fiske Stone's infamous characterization of the IMT proceeding as a "high-grade lynching party" showed, Christie held, that many prominent legal authorities believed that the Nazis' most serious crime was losing the war.

Hilberg labored bravely to correct Christie's misappropriation of Stone. He pointed out that criticism of Nuremberg had focused primarily on the fairness of trying heads of state for having waged an aggressive war and had little to do with the justice of holding persons accountable for crimes against humanity. Unfortunately, Hilberg's involved explanation inevitably presupposed an understanding of the Nuremberg charter, and in particular, of the differences between 6(a), crimes against peace, and 6(c), crimes against humanity. As a result of their nuance and complexity, Hilberg's explanations did little to deter Christie from persisting in his view that the chief justice of the United States Supreme Court had condemned Nuremberg in terms essentially the same as those found in "Did Six Million Really Die?"

In casting the words of survivors and the works of historians as likewise based on unreliable hearsay, Christie came to echo the very arguments found in "Did Six Million Really Die?" The pamphlet, for example, also warranted that "no living authentic eyewitness of these 'gas chambers' has ever been produced and validated," dismissing Gerstein's statements as "fantastic exaggerations." And it launched the same attack on the procedural and substantive fairness of the IMT, stating that "the Rules of Evidence, developed by British jurisprudence over the centuries in order to arrive at the truth of a charge with as much certainty as possible, were entirely disregarded at Nuremberg."[5]

The crucial point, however, is not that Christie sounded like a negationist (though certainly he labored to defend not simply the sincerity but the truth of his client's convictions). More significant, Christie's advocacy highlighted the complex ways in which negationist arguments appropriate the rhetorical conventions of attorneys practiced in the art of adversarial litigation. I have already noted that "Did Six Million Really Die?" presents at first blush a superficially balanced argument, and many negationist articles like those published by the Institute for Historical Review, with their cumbersome footnotes and extensive bibliographies, ape the rhetorical conventions of standard scholarship. But in questioning the adequacy of the evidence of extermination, documents such as "Did Six Million Really Die?" resemble less mainstream academic work than the argumentative strategies of a counsel in a trial setting.[6]

Clearly there is something fundamentally problematic in modeling a mode of supposedly scholarly inquiry on adversarial jurisprudence. As the legal scholar Marvin Frankel has observed, "We know that others searching after facts — in history, geography, medicine, whatever — do not emulate our adversary system."[7] Criminal justice, in both Anglo-American and Continental contexts, has long been dedicated to such values as protecting the dignity and autonomy of the accused, which may actually disable the pursuit of truth in a particular case. (The "exclusionary rule," for example, suppresses the use of highly relevant evidence if illegally obtained.) By casting the trial as a truth-seeking device, Holocaust negationists are able to justify their strategic appropriation of the rhetorical conventions of counsels arguing in an adversarial context. As a result, they behave as if the most tendentious and partisan hyperbole serves as a proper contribution to public debate and historical instruction.[8] Thus it should come as no surprise that Christie's arguments sounded so much like those in the pamphlet. For "Did Six Million Really Die?" was itself based on a disturbing mimicry of legal discourse and conventions of proof.

The End of History

Christie's effort to unmask the testimony of the survivor and the historian as hearsay fueled, in turn, a more radical attack on the meaning of history and memory. Insofar as historical inquiry is mediated, and the historian's treatment of his sources is prefigured by his understanding of events, Christie claimed that all history is inescapably interpretive, and the past is consequently enveloped in an impenetrable hermeneutic haze.

In his cross of Hilberg, Christie labored to emphasize the numerous areas of disagreement among mainstream historians of the Holocaust. First, there was the question of the number of victims. About Auschwitz alone, one can find wild discrepancies in the estimations of the dead. The Polish-Soviet Investigation Commission estimated 4 million dead; Höß had put the figure at 2.5 million; Vrba had counted 1,765,000 victims; Hilberg himself had arrived at the figure of roughly 1 million (*TEZ-1985*, 1135). Then there was the question of the means of killing. *Nazi Concentration Camps* had purportedly shown victims of Dachau's "lethal gas chamber," but now there was doubt whether it had ever been made operational. Hilberg stated that gassings took place at Mauthausen, but Yehuda Bauer, another prominent authority on the Holocaust, had written that no gassings had taken place there (1009). At Nuremberg, the Soviet prosecutors submitted as evidence a bar of soap allegedly made from human fat, but later this claim was found to be spurious.

Finally, there was the question of intent—that is, the degree to which historians understood the Holocaust as, to use the relevant legal term, a premeditated crime. To the frustration of many, no historian has yet discovered a written order issuing from Hitler commanding the extermination of Europe's Jews.[9] Indeed, it remains unclear whether Hitler issued even a specific oral command ordering the implementation of the final solution. In *The Destruction of the European Jews* and again on the stand, Hilberg advanced his belief that Hitler had issued such an oral command sometime before April 1941. But lingering uncertainty about the specifics of this order left Hilberg vulnerable to Christie's ridicule. "So you say there is an order," Christie declared, "to exterminate the Jews from Adolf Hitler that was oral, the content of which you don't know, and apparently nobody knows" (*TEZ-1985*, 833). When Hilberg insisted that Alfred Jodl, who as the former chief of operations of Hitler's military staff had been condemned at Nuremberg and executed, had reported receiving such an order, the problem of hearsay resurfaced. "So really . . . " Christie declaimed, "we have from you an interpretation of what Jodl is supposed to have said Adolf Hitler was supposed to have said" (835). Frustrated by Christie's twisting of his words, Hilberg exclaimed, "This is the problem of teaching complex history in such a small setting" (840), inadvertently calling into question the very purpose of the trial.

Christie used the uncertainty about the existence of a Hitler order to challenge Hilberg's interpretation of all documents. In his fascinating reading of the subversive hermeneutics of Robert Faurisson, a leading denier who served as a witness for the defense in both Zundel trials, Pierre Vidal-Naquet identified a number of principles of argument and interpretation that guide negationist rhetoric. In addition to questioning the adequacy and reliability of evidence, negationists interpret in a tactically contradictory fashion, such that any Nazi document written in coded language is read literally, whereas any document written plainly is underinterpreted or overinterpreted.[10] Thus, such terms as *Umsiedlung* and *Sonderbehandlung* are read, respectively, literally as "resettlement" and "special treatment," not as code words for annihilation; *das Lager der Vernichtung,* words that appear in the diary of an ss doctor at Auschwitz, are read as referring not to a "camp of extermination" but to a camp visited by a typhus epidemic.[11]

Although Vidal-Naquet asserts that these interpretive strategies are born of, or at least are exploitative of, the renegade hermeneutics of poststructuralist critics (and here Faurisson's career as a scholar of French literature may be apposite), Christie's performance at the Zundel trial again reminds us that the arguments of revisionists are suggestive less of Paul de Man than of Johnnie Cochran. Instructive is Christie's attack on Hilberg's interpretation of the Stroop Report, a lavishly published ss document submitted at Nuremberg and devoted to describing the suppression of the Warsaw ghetto uprising and the liquidation of the ghetto. According to Hilberg, the report described how the ghetto's remaining Jews were, with the exception of a few skilled laborers, "to be annihilated." Christie responded with incredulity:

Q: Annihilated.
A: Yes.
Q: The words you read from the report were "relocated" — right?
A: That's correct. Yes, that is the correct —
Q: Now, that doesn't . . . indicate an intention to annihilate, to me. Does it to you?
A: Yes. That is the difference between us, you see, because I have read thousands of German documents and you haven't.
Q: Sure. And you have the view that to relocate, in the German language, is to annihilate.
A: No. No.
Q: No?
A: It means to relocate in certain contexts.
Q: And you alone know the context?

A: I am not alone in knowing the context. I have mentioned colleagues and fellow workers who know the context also.

Q: Those who share your view of "annihilate" . . . and interpret "relocate" to mean "liquidate." Right? [*TEZ-1985*, 796–97]

The point of these attacks was not simply to discredit Hilberg as a scholar. Although Christie devoted a substantial part of the defense to proving the truth of his client's belief, his focus on the interpretive disputes within Holocaust studies was meant to support a more radical and, in a sense, contradictory claim. For while Hilberg acknowledged that "there is such a thing as a gap in knowledge of history" (837), Christie held that there are only gaps — that there is no such thing as positive historical knowledge. His concluding colloquy with Hilberg about the Hitler order encapsulated Christie's larger understanding of history:

Q: So it's an article of faith based upon your opinion?

A: No, it is not an article of faith at all. It is a conclusion. One can come down one way on it, or the other.

Q: Because there is no evidence to prove one side or the other, right? [850]

According to Christie, the absence of indisputable evidence concerning the existence of a Hitler order could be generalized to the Holocaust itself. Anchored in hearsay, unquestioned axioms, opaque documents, and unreliable memory, all historical claims about the Holocaust are characterized, Christie contended, by an irreducible uncertainty that turns all disagreement into an irresolvable interpretive dispute. Given the absence of "scientific validation," Hilberg's history became, in Christie's formulation, "a theory" — enjoying the same epistemological status as the negationists' thesis (872). Such an argument did not simply relativize history, as Vergès would later do in his defense of Klaus Barbie; instead, it advanced the far more radical thesis that all history is irreducibly indeterminate.

Ironically, Christie was unintentionally aided in his attempt to deprive history of its rootedness in fact by the court. With some reluctance, Judge Locke agreed to permit the defense to respond to Hilberg's expert testimony by calling Faurisson as an expert. Although Faurisson added few new arguments and was difficult to understand in his heavily accented English, his certification as an expert by the court was not lost upon the negationists, who later publicized the judicial recognition that implicitly had been conferred upon one of their ilk. Indeed, in his certification hearing, Faurisson behaved very much like a legitimate scholar, expressing the greatest admiration for Hilberg's work, while, of course, emphasizing that "we are not of the same opinion" (2375). Hilberg himself, he noted, had once publicly stated that Faurisson's work had raised questions that caused Holocaust researchers to clarify and sharpen their positions (2395). Thus in certifying Faurisson as an expert, the court implicitly accepted Faurisson's division of Holocaust scholars into "exterminationists" like Hilberg and "revisionists" like himself—suggesting that each defined an entirely plausible parsing of the historical record.

Christie's treatment of memory echoed his attack on history. We have already seen how Christie tried to show that even the testimony of survivors was riddled with hearsay. Along with this strategy, Christie pursued a second approach, one designed to unmask the pitfalls and politics of memory. Tenacious and often simply rude, Christie subjected the four survivor witnesses to a tedious and humiliating exploration of the microdetails of remembrance. Vrba recalled seeing bodies burned in an open-air pit; Christie wanted to know exactly how deep the pit was. Vrba remembered seeing an ss officer clamber on top of the roof of a gas chamber; Christie wanted to know precisely the height and angle of the roof. Dennis Urstein, another Auschwitz survivor, recalled seeing flames belch from the smokestacks of the crematoria; Christie wanted to know the precise height of the flames.

As noted in chapter 8, Demjanjuk's first lawyer, Mark O'Connor, subjected survivors to similarly obnoxious questions. Although O'Connor's examinations appalled even other members of the defense and contributed to his removal from the team, arguably they were of some possible relevance, as inaccuracies in survivors' recollections of the physical aspects of the camp might have cast doubts upon the precision of their identifications of Demjanjuk. Christie's strategy, however, supported a far more extreme and dubious logic. Insofar as Vrba first claimed that the pit for burning bodies was six meters deep and later four, such discrepancies were again used by Christie to suggest the indeterminacy of historical fact. The minute slippages of memory recapitulated, in Christie's rhetorical universe, the larger discrepancies between the arithmetic of atrocity defended by the exterminationists on the one hand and the revisionists on the other. Just as Vrba could not know for sure how deep the pit was, no one can say for sure how many Jews died: there are just reasonable disagreements among reasonable people.

Finally, Christie cast aspersions on the reasonableness and integrity of the survivors. Not only were their memories built on hearsay and warped by the passage of time, their stories were invented out of whole cloth to serve strategic ends. Thus Christie asked whether Urstein had benefited from restitution claims brought against the German government—planting the suggestion that Urstein had invented the story of his family's extermination for his financial gain. In his cross of Vrba, Christie baldly stated that Vrba was a liar who, fabricated his stories out of a hatred for Nazism (1443). Following the standard negationist position, Christie conceded that the Nazis had treated Jews harshly. Indeed, in a bizarre inversion of logic, Christie implied that the very skills that permitted Vrba to survive and escape from Auschwitz made him less than credible as a court witness. After all, Vrba's real name was Walter Rosenberg, and Vrba only began using the assumed name after he had escaped to Slovakia. In an outrageous twist, Christie turned Vrba's tale of survival against his own testimony, arguing that "one of the methods to survive in the camp was to learn how to lie very effectively" (1563). In the Eichmann trial, the memory of survivors was considered the most precious source of unspeakable truth. In the Demjanjuk trial, memory was volatilized, shown to be vulnerable on the level of the most minute identifications. At the Zundel trial, memory was ridiculed, the survivor transformed into an amnesiac at best, an outright liar at worst. In a stunning inversion of the evidentiary logic of the Eichmann trial, Christie was able to conclude his cross-examination of Vrba with the dismissive question, "Am I to take it, then, that you are the proof? Is that it?" (1592).

Zundel Redux

On the most obvious juridical level, Christie's strategies failed: at the end of the seven-and-a-half-week trial, Zundel was convicted.[12] He was sentenced to prison for fifteen months and probation for three years, a condition of which prohibited him from publishing on any subject related to the Holocaust during this time. There seems little doubt that Christie's harassing cross-examinations of Hilberg, Vrba, and the other survivors alienated a number of jury members. Moreover, Christie's decision to permit his client to take the stand turned into a mistake. Zundel began his testimony on an affable note, describing his respectable career as a photo retoucher and businessman and telling how, until the early sixties, he too had believed in the Holocaust; on cross-examination, however, Griffiths succeeded in painting Zundel as a hate-filled zealot. Crucially, Griffiths was able to impeach Zundel's credibility by reading excerpts from a publication that the defendant had cowritten, *The Hitler We Love and Why*. Using the pseudonym Christhof Friedrich, Zundel, together with another ultrarightist, had written a 120-page tribute to the Nazi leader. Hitler's spirit "soars beyond the shores of the White Man's home in Europe," the booklet stirringly concluded. "Wherever we are, he is with us. WE LOVE YOU, ADOLPH HITLER!"[13] *The Hitler We Love and Why* not only thoroughly undermined the claim that the defendant was a sincere skeptic searching in a disinterested fashion for historical truth (the very existence of which Christie denied), but also suggested his motive for denying the Holocaust. Insofar as extermination might seem excessive even to die-hard anti-Semites and racists, the crimes of the Holocaust continue to represent the greatest obstacle to the rehabilitation of Hitler's image and, in turn, the politics he espoused. In decrying the Holocaust as a phantasm of the Zionist imagination, Holocaust deniers engage in a form of anti-Semitic speech that simultaneously seeks to rehabilitate a political vision that would legitimate and endorse still bolder displays of anti-Semitism. Thus Christie's misstep permitted the prosecution to show the intelligent, seemingly personable defendant to be a fervent, short-tempered neo-Nazi.

But to conclude that Zundel's conviction reveals the errors of Christie's defense is to embrace the narrow conception of legality that this book and the trials it has studied has challenged. For like the great perpetrator trials, the Zundel trial was staged as a drama of didactic legality, and its success or failure must be evaluated, at least in part, in terms of its ability to advance these pedagogic ends. In this regard, Christie succeeded in desecrating the courtroom as a space in which to defend the claims of history and honor the memory of survivors. In the Eichmann trial, such treatment of the survivor witnesses was unthinkable, not because it would have spelled legal suicide—Servatius must have known all along that his client's case was hopeless—but because the courtroom served as a sacral commemorative space. In the Demjanjuk trial, offending the survivors, though now thinkable, was still considered legally transgressive.

In the Zundel trial, however, offending the survivors was perhaps a risky courtroom strategy, but it hardly appeared legally impermissible. On the contrary, it was made possible, even encouraged, by the very terms of adversarial jurisprudence. Accused by Christie of mendacity, Rudolf Vrba indignantly declared, "To consider a person who fought Nazis a liar is a misuse of a free Court in Canada"—but, of course, Vrba was wrong. Truthful witnesses are called liars everyday in courtrooms all over the English-speaking world, and the Zundel trial simply demonstrated that one's status as a survivor of the most horrific crime in history did not insulate one from the indignities suffered by the typical courtroom witness. Indeed, as we have seen, Judge Locke found it necessary on a number of occasions even to remind Vrba of his obligation to answer all the questions posed by Christie and not to substitute his own sense of propriety for the judge's. The courtroom also failed to offer any succor. At the Eichmann and Demjanjuk trials, the spectators came prepared to draw the proper lessons from the legal drama; at the Zundel trial, by contrast, the gallery was filled with a sizable contingent of supporters of the defendant. So partisan was the gallery that Dennis Urstein was choked with outrage as he concluded his horrific description of corpses in a gas chamber: "I see somebody smirk at me and I can smirk right back at the audience" (*TEZ-1985*, 1797).

Thanks to Christie's tactics, the trial inadvertently supplied the negationist cause with a tremendous amount of attention — in Zundel's own assessment, "with a million dollars of free publicity."[14] Whether this actually contributed to a swelling of the ranks of deniers is unclear; in a comprehensive study of the public's reception of the trial, Gabriel Weimann and Conrad Winn concluded that, if anything, the trial led to a marginal increase in the public's sympathy for Jews.[15] Yet at the same time, the pollsters detected a substantial rise in the public's *perception* that the trial had contributed to the increased popularity of the deniers' position. This perception, even if not supported by numbers, is itself significant, for it reveals a widespread belief that the legal process failed — that it served to advance the very cause it was enlisted to combat.

This perception was further fueled by the press coverage of the trial. Although the case attracted little attention in the United States, it was nothing short of a media sensation in Canada, where many observers found the quality of reportage distinctly disturbing. Mimicking Christie's own tendentious rhetoric, a front-page headline in the *Globe and Mail,* one of Canada's largest circulation dailies, proclaimed, "Lawyer Challenges Crematoria Theory."[16] A lead article in the *Globe and Mail* that covered Faurisson's testimony bore the headline "No gas chambers in Nazi Germany, Expert Witness Testifies."[17] On one level, one can explain these headlines in terms of the media's insatiable appetite for sensationalism. The same impulse that leads a talk show producer to invite viewers to watch a debate about whether the Holocaust happened might lead an editor to run a catchy headline. To this extent, relying on the criminal law to insulate an inviolate historical fact from profane infotainment industries seems peculiarly self-defeating. On the other hand, it is possible to explain the newspaper's coverage as born of an effort to report from the same position of neutrality from which the law judges. From this perspective, the press can be faulted not for having betrayed the legal system, but for having emulated it.

Christie's hijacking of the trial thus exemplifies how the formal evidentiary agnosticism of adversarial jurisprudence may have the ironic effect of contributing to the erosion of the very boundary between truth and fiction that the criminal law is asked to police. This point only gains support in the decision of the Ontario Court of Appeals handed down on January 23, 1987, almost two years after Zundel's original conviction.

The five-person appellate tribunal unanimously reversed Zundel's conviction, though it did not accept all of Christie's arguments on appeal. The appellate court rejected, for example, Christie's argument that section 177 of the Canadian Criminal Code, the false public news statute, was unconstitutional because it violated the fundamental right to free expression guaranteed by the Canadian Charter of Rights and Freedoms. Concluding that "the words 'injury or mischief to a public interest' are not vague or overly broad in their context," the court rebuffed the constitutional challenge to section 177. Moreover, not all the defects that the appellate court found in the trial are directly of importance for my purposes here. For example, the court identified miscues in the impaneling of and in the instructions to the jury.[18] Thus the decision to overturn the verdict, though perhaps regrettable from the standpoint of the fight against anti-Semitism, seemed in parts legally unremarkable — the result of procedural defects that were not implicated in the pedagogic drama of the trial.

The appellate court, however, made a number of other rulings that more directly addressed the didactic aspects of the trial and raised afresh matters of history and hearsay. First, dismissing arguments made by the Crown, the court concluded that Locke had not abused his judicial discretion in refusing to take notice of the Holocaust: "If the trial judge had taken judicial notice of the existence of the Holocaust, he would have been required to so declare to the jury and to direct them to find that the Holocaust existed, which would have been gravely prejudicial to the defense in so far as it would influence the drawing of the inference concerning the appellant's knowledge of the falsity of the pamphlet" (31 CCC, 152).

Though reasonable, the court's conclusion remains ironical, as it suggests that a judicial acknowledgment of the Holocaust as historical fact would have put the defense at a disadvantage. But certainly that is the point in a trial of a denier: the indisputable facts of history *do* present an annoyance and obstacle to the die-hard negationist. More important, the court's reasoning suggests that Locke's refusal was something more than an idiosyncratic exercise in legal judgment, as it had been called by a number of critics of Locke's notice ruling. In holding that the taking of notice "would have been gravely prejudicial to the defense," the appellate court not only supported Locke's act as a matter of discretion, but came close to declaring that the bench's decision was mandated. The trial of the denier properly refused to accept the Holocaust as a historical and legal fact.

Also discomfiting was the court's discussion of Hilberg's testimony. On appeal, Christie had argued that Hilberg's testimony had been improperly admitted at trial in violation of the hearsay rule. In the most detailed section of its opinion, the appellate court conceded that Hilberg's testimony was technically hearsay. This did not settle the matter, as the court pointed out that the hearsay rule provides an exception for "accepted historical treatises" about "events of general history" (31 CCC, 143). The court, however, found few precedents that actually applied this exception, for the available case law indicated that "if the event is of such general interest as to render an accepted historical treatise admissible, the fact is of such notoriety as to permit the court to take judicial notice of it" (144).

Ignoring this irony, the court turned instead to a larger body of case law holding that exceptions to the hearsay rule "are based upon (a) necessity, and (b) the circumstantial trustworthiness of the evidence to which the exception applies" (145). The court concluded that the criterion of necessity had been satisfied in this case, inasmuch as it was highly unlikely that "living witnesses could be obtained" (144) to offer testimony on matters covered by Hilberg: "The events sought to be proved by Dr. Hilberg's opinion occurred more than forty years ago, and while there are survivors of the Nazi concentration camps, some of whom were called as witnesses, it is unlikely that living witnesses responsible for formulating the policy of the Nazi government or carrying out the policies in relation to the events alleged, could be obtained" (144).

Here the court recognized that necessity mandated the turn to Hilberg: although survivors such as Vrba had been able to offer eyewitness accounts about conditions in specific camps, presumably the survivors could not have offered firsthand testimony about what happened at, for example, the Wannsee conference. Hilberg's work also satisfied the second criterion of trustworthiness, as it was based upon "material to which . . . any careful and competent historian would resort" (148). Notwithstanding the technical bar, the prosecution could legitimately turn to expert hearsay testimony in order to present evidence of the planning and organization behind the final solution.

Though supportive of the Crown, the court's reasoning gives pause. For the notion that historical studies can be admitted only as *hearsay exceptions* again echoed Christie's arguments at trial. Not surprisingly, negationists found the court's characterization of Hilberg's testimony as permissible hearsay a validation of their attacks on the historian's methodology. However twisted this appropriation may have been, Christie's arguments found direct confirmation in the court's discussion of *Nazi Concentration Camps.* On appeal, Christie had again insisted that the film should have been barred as hearsay. At trial, Locke had admitted the film under yet another hearsay exception, permitting the admission of "statements made by public officers in the discharge of their official duty and recorded in public documents" (166). Although the appellate court did not directly discuss the admissibility of the images captured in *Nazi Concentration Camps,* it concluded that the film's narration did not constitute a "public document." In chapter 2, I discussed how at Nuremberg the narration came to exercise control over images of atrocity, and in so doing harmonized the visual record with the prosecution's idiom of indictment. Properly the court now observed that "the narrative is more than a statement of fact as to what the film shows" (167). Because "the narrator is unknown; the author of the narrative is unknown; and the source of the information is frequently not revealed," the film — at least with its soundtrack — had to be barred (167). Suddenly *Nazi Concentration Camps* was recognized as a deeply ambiguous document, one whose horrific and by now famous images could not be said "to speak for themselves." Thus the erroneous admission of the Signal Corps documentary, along with the other procedural defects in the first trial, led the court to throw out the conviction.

Zundel's second trial lasted from mid-January until early May 1988. Though it featured many of the same characters, including Christie, Faurisson, and many of the other witnesses who had originally testified on behalf of the accused, the second trial differed from the first in a number of crucial respects. First, *Nazi Concentration Camps* was not shown. Although the Crown, now led by Prosecutor John Pearson, originally planned to screen the documentary without the narration, the presiding judge, Ronald

Thomas, held that showing the film without its soundtrack could be even more prejudicial to the accused.[19] Second, the prosecution chose to present its case without calling any survivors to the stand. Indeed, as Christie emphasized on several occasions, the only survivor to testify at the second trial was a former Birkenau inmate (an eccentric woman named Maria van Herwaarden) called by the defense. The Crown's decision to proceed without survivors was remarkable insofar as the demeanor and words of those who had experienced the concentrationary universe firsthand were considered, before the first trial, as the living embodiment of the truth of the Holocaust. Yet Christie had been so successful in his campaign of humiliation and harassment that few survivors were prepared to subject themselves to such an ordeal a second time. And so the second trial proceeded in the absence of the very persons on whose behalf the litigation was, in important respects, staged.

Because the trial unfolded without the voice of memory, all the more pressure was placed on the words of history. But Hilberg, like the survivor witnesses, refused to testify in the second trial, as he, too, was reluctant to subject himself to the ordeal of Christie's badgering for a second time. In his stead, the prosecution called upon another eminent Holocaust historian, Christopher Browning, to parry Christie's attacks. The Crown, however, was not the only party to alter its tactics. Zundel's disastrous appearance on the stand in the first trial fueled Christie's decision to keep his client safely behind the defense's table at the second trial. Also, stung by Griffiths's characterization of the defense's witnesses as a bunch of "crazies and misfits" (*TEZ-1985,* 4655), Christie sought to strengthen his client's case by relying on the testimony of David Irving, a controversial British historian whose early scholarship on Nazism had been rigorous but whose more recent work has flirted with the negationist fringe.[20]

Finally, the second trial differed from the first insofar as Judge Thomas agreed, before the prosecution began its case, to take judicial notice of Nazi genocide. Although the appellate decision strongly upheld Judge Locke's decision to refuse notice, implicitly it suggested that taking notice was also within a judge's discretion — provided that such notice did not overly prejudice the defense. Dismissing Christie's objections, the judge directed the jury to accept that "the mass murder and extermination of Jews in Europe by the Nazi regime during the Second World War is so notorious as not to be the subject of dispute among reasonable persons" (*TEZ-1988,* 35). Crucial as this gesture was, Thomas did not "take judicial notice of the facts alleged in the appellant's pamphlet."[21] Thus Thomas's notice ruling was general enough to permit the defense to challenge whether the final solution had been ordered by Hitler, whether the Nazis had used gas chambers, and how many had actually died. Moreover, because the decision left the question of the accused's personal beliefs untouched, the defense was again free to lead evidence by negationists. As Christie said in his summation, the judge's instructions did not necessarily contradict his client's thesis: "His Honour will tell you what he says is reasonable for reasonable men to contest. But it won't include the six million, it won't include the gas chambers and it won't include an official plan. That's basically what this book is all about" (*TEZ-1988,* 9900). And so one can appreciate the Crown's morbid observation that Thomas had taken no more than "bare bones" notice of the Holocaust.[22]

Once under way, the trial retrod much of the terrain covered in the first prosecution. Christie again called to the stand a veritable Who's Who of Holocaust negationists. Although supposedly called to shed light on Zundel's beliefs, these witnesses once again seemed intent on demonstrating the accuracy and veracity of "Did Six Million Really Die?" Relying on his witnesses, Christie claimed once more that no physical evidence supported the existence of gas chambers — on the contrary, all available scientific evidence, he maintained, challenged the gas chamber "theory." Again Christie played his word game, disputing accepted parsings of such words as *Sonderbehandlung* and *Umsiedlung.* He played his numbers game, emphasizing the large discrepancies in the estimations of the numbers of victims. He repeated his attack on the Nuremberg trial and on subsequent trials of perpetrators. He continued to challenge the reliability of the statements made by Gerstein and Höß, reregistering his belief that a combination of mental imbalance and physical coercion had brought these men to make their extravagant claims. He introduced fresh evidence challenging the statements of Hermann Gräbe, whose precise description of a killing action by an *Einsatzgruppe* had served as the bookend of Shawcross's stirring peroration at Nuremberg (see chapter 3).[23] He again ridiculed the stories of such survivor witnesses as Rudolf Vrba — although this time Vrba was not present to serve as a foil for Christie's barbs. And Christie continued to echo the negationists' obsession with legal process, insisting that those survivor witnesses who had testified in earlier proceedings, such as the Eichmann trial, had never been "validated" — which in the negationists' lexicon meant subject to cross-examination (*TEZ-1988,* 3917). (Servatius's failure to cross-examine these witnesses did not, Christie asserted, indicate that Eichmann's counsel had believed their stories. On the contrary, as Faurisson handily explained Servatius's inaction, "Exactly as in the witchcraft trial, when the people were accused of meeting the devil, they wouldn't say, Your Honour, the best proof that I have not met the devil is that the devil does not exist, it would have been the end. No. The tactic was to say, oh yes, the devil was there on top of the hill. Myself I was down, and [with] Auschwitz it's exactly the same thing") (*TEZ-1988*, 8237).[24]

Still, the second trial assumed a different tenor. Crown Prosecutor Pearson had clearly benefited from having closely studied the transcript of the first trial. Able to anticipate Christie's tactics, Pearson was substantially better versed in the history and historiography of the Holocaust than was his counterpart at the first trial. This permitted Pearson to cross-examine the defense's witnesses far more effectively. Faurisson, for example, was often reduced to rambling, unintelligible explanations of his own numerous run-ins with the French legal system. The prosecution also benefited from Thomas's judicial notice ruling, "bare bones" as it might have been. While Griffiths had led evidence demonstrating that the Holocaust had, in fact, happened, Pearson eschewed that approach, focusing instead on the contradictions, inconsistencies, and falsehoods contained in "Did Six Million Really Die?" Early in the Crown's case, Pearson also read the entire text of *The Hitler We Love and Why* into the record, thus painting the accused from the outset as a neo-Nazi with a motive to lie about the Holocaust. In addition, he entered all of Hilberg's testimony from the first trial into the record and thus was able to draw upon this body of evidence without having to subject Hilberg to Christie's indignities a second time.[25]

The absence of survivor witnesses (with the exception of the defense's eccentric Maria van Herwaarden) and the inadmissibility of *Nazi Concentration Camps* also significantly altered the spirit of the trial. Now the paradigm of proof was entirely historical. Given Hilberg's reluctance to appear again, the Crown found the voice of history in the person of Browning, now renowned as the author of *Ordinary Men: Reserve Police Battalion 101 and the Final Solution in Poland*, a meticulous study of the actions and motives of a battalion of reservists responsible for the killing and deportation of more than eighty thousand Jews.

Browning proved to be, in a number of ways, a better witness than Hilberg. Trained as a political scientist, Hilberg was vulnerable to Christie's charge that he was no better equipped to write history than were many of the negationists whose credentials Hilberg had questioned. Browning's professional training, by contrast, was in history. Hilberg was Jewish and, as such, invited Christie's insinuation that all testimony provided by Jews was partisan and tainted. Browning was a non-Jew, and his strapping athletic frame created a distinctly Teutonic impression. (This, of course, did not stop Christie from beginning his cross-examination with the accusation that Browning was a "propagandist for Israel") (*TEZ-1988*, 3290). As circumspect as Hilberg, Browning managed to avoid long, convoluted responses, and did not let Christie get under his skin, as Hilberg had. On the whole unflappable, Browning used sarcasm effectively and even pulled off a number of devastating responses to Christie's questions. When asked by Christie, "Are you aware of how difficult it is to burn a human body?" Browning sardonically answered, "I have not burned one myself, personally" (3474). When Christie suggested that rumors of the Holocaust were purposively spread by the Allies to create a justification for continuing the war, Browning responded with incredulity, "Occupation of Poland, occupation of France, of Netherlands, of Belgium, of Norway, of Denmark. No reason to continue the war? Invasion of Yugoslavia, conquest of Greece. No reason to continue the war, sir?" (3375). And when Christie suggested that Browning was being handsomely remunerated for his work as an expert witness, Browning dryly commented, "For this particular episode, I am being paid . . . more like a lawyer than a professor" (3800).

Christie, however, was not entirely mastered by the historian. Given the complete ascendancy of historical testimony as the prosecution's paradigm of proof, Christie attacked the methodology and epistemology of history in more concentrated terms than in the first trial. At times his strategy emphasized the relatively modest point that the pamphlet was composed largely of statements of opinion and therefore not subject to the application of section 177. More generally, however, Christie distilled and strengthened the position he had defended in the first trial — that all history is ineluctably opinion and interpretation. In so doing, he turned the trial into a bizarre seminar on historiography, its methods and epistemology.

The odd classroom quality of the trial was nowhere more apparent than in Christie's cross of Browning on whether Hitler had ever specifically ordered the final solution. Shortly after Zundel's first trial, Hilberg had issued a revised second edition of *The Destruction of the European Jews*. The second edition altered the first in a number of respects, and none was more central than Hilberg's new handling of the refractory question of the Hitler order. In the original work, Hilberg had suggested that an oral command had been made, probably on two separate occasions; in revisiting the question, Hilberg argued that Hitler had probably made his wishes known not through an order per se but through a series of decisions and responses to queries from subordinates in the state and ss bureaucracy.

Browning was well aware of the change in Hilberg's position. In the *Simon Wiesenthal Annual no. 3,* Browning had published "The Revised Hilberg," a review essay closely comparing the first and second editions. In the essay, Browning had written, "In the new edition, all references in the text to a Hitler decision or order for the Final Solution have been systematically excised."[26] Christie jumped all over this language: "You used the word 'systematically excised'. What does this mean in ordinary English?" (*TEZ-1988,* 3299). Unsatisfied by Browning's answer that it simply meant "reworded," Christie pointedly asked, "Would you agree that Hilberg made, from his first to his new edition, a significant change in interpretation concerning the decision-making process and role of Adolf Hitler?" Here Browning conceded, "Yes, he did make a significant change" (3358).

In wresting this concession, which made the courtroom sound all the more like a history seminar, Christie hoped to make three substantive points. First, he aimed to discredit Hilberg's testimony from the first trial that had been entered into the record of the second. The second edition of Hilberg's magnum opus had come out scant months after his appearance at the first trial. When Hilberg had testified that he continued to believe in a Hitler order, he must have been misrepresenting his present thinking, Christie insisted, as the second edition was already at press. Thus Christie opined that Hilberg had refused to testify at the second trial not because he was fatigued by the lawyer's tactics, but to avoid having to explain his absence of candor during his first time on the stand.

Second, Christie argued that Hilberg's present position was itself untenable. Quoting Hilberg's new language — namely, that the final solution unfolded as an "incredible meeting of minds, a consensus, mind-reading by a far-flung bureaucracy" — Christie insisted, echoing Faurisson, that such a position was not history but "metaphysics" (8159). To assume that a complex bureaucratic organization could, without clear directions or budget, orchestrate as complex a logistical feat as the final solution was, Christie argued, preposterous.

Third, Christie toiled to use Hilberg's change in thinking as evidence that all historical writing is necessarily in a constant state of reinterpretation and revision. At one point, he asked Browning, "Do you accept the proposition that some of the historians are becoming revisionists" — a question that framed a deliberate ambiguity. On the one hand, Christie wanted to know whether historians like the functionalists were presently revising the received understanding of Nazism, and on this score Browning acknowledged that "all historians, I hope, are constantly engaged in revision" (3358). At the same time, of course, Christie wanted to know whether formerly mainstream historians (such as Irving) were gradually coming around to the negationists' position. Here Christie attempted to reason by bold, if not outlandish, analogy: Just as some historians (read: Hilberg) had revised their thinking on Hitler's order, perhaps other historians were now revising their view on such matters as the existence of gas chambers and whether Jews had ever been singled out for extermination.

To support this argument, Christie offered the example of the fractious debate between the functionalists and the intentionalists. In the three years since Zundel's trial, historiography on the Holocaust had become increasingly divided between those like Lucy Davidowicz and Saul Friedlander, who continued to emphasize the role that Hitler, anti-Semitism, and central planning played in the Holocaust; and those like Martin Broszat and Hans Mommsen, who focused on the role played by competing bureaucracies and low-level officials in paving the "twisted road to Auschwitz."[27] Extending his troubled analogy, Christie insisted that the debate between the intentionalists and the functionalists was no different in kind from the colloquy between the exterminationists and the revisionists. Thus the following exchange between Christie and Browning:

B R O W N I N G: Indeed, Martin Broszat and Hans Mommsen have argued that there wasn't a Hitler decision, that it was a matter of local initiatives that kind of snowballed into a major extermination program. . . .
Q: And would you refer to Mommsen and Broszat as reasonable men?
A: I would refer to them as reasonable men.
Q: So you would not allow reasonable men to differ on whether there was any actual gassings or not? You wouldn't allow reasonable men to doubt that? [*TEZ-1988*, 3398]

When Browning responded, "If . . . an argument . . . simply denies the evidence that I have seen, then I . . . wonder very gravely whether it is a serious or honest argument," Christie simply returned to his attack on the meaning of evidence (3399). Disparaging Browning and Hilberg as "paper historians" who had never physically examined sites of extermination, Christie launched his most sweeping attack on the notion of historical facts. Time and again Christie challenged Browning to "concede that what you . . . stated as a fact in history, . . . remains your opinion" (3672). He quoted from Browning himself: "History is probably the most inexact of all social sciences" (3794). When Browning insisted on defending the distinction between facts, interpretations of great certitude, and opinions, Christie turned to E. H. Carr's *What is History?* once a widely read introduction to historiography. As if in a seminar or before a debate society, Christie read aloud the words of the eminent Oxbridge historian:

> CHRISTIE: . . . Let me read on a wee bit. "When you read a work of history always listen out for the buzzing. If you can detect none, . . . either you are tone deaf or your historian is a dull dog"; right?
> BROWNING: That's what it reads.
> Q: "The facts are really not at all like fish on the fishmonger's slab." Correct?
> A: That's what it reads.
> Q: "They are like fish swimming about in a vast and sometimes inaccessible ocean and what the historian captures will depend partly on chance, but mainly on what part of the ocean he chooses to fish in and what tackle he chooses to use. . . . By and large, the historian will get the kind of facts he wants." Is that correct?
>
> . . . .
>
> A: That has been read correctly. [3808–10]

Ultimately, the Crown felt obligated to join the seminar, as Prosecutor Pearson began his own brief redirect examination of Browning by immediately asking the witness to read aloud a passage from *What is History?* ignored by Christie: "The duty of the historian to respect his facts is not exhausted by the obligation to see that his facts are accurate. He must seek to bring into the picture all known and knowable facts relevant, in one sense or another, to the theme in which he is engaged to the interpretation proposed" (3988). In light of this quotation, Pearson asked,

> Q: . . . Does E. H. Carr draw a distinction between fact and interpretation?
> A: Yes.
> Q: And what does he say they have to do with facts?
> A: That you must respect the facts.
> Q: Thank you. [3989]

In his summation, Pearson returned to "Mr. Christie's . . . startling submission . . . that all history is opinion," presenting the Crown not simply as the defender of the Holocaust but as the defender of a world of epistemological stability and coherence (10258).

As a result of Christie's defense of skepticism, the jury was thrust in a peculiar position. Indeed, in his instructions to the jury, Judge Thomas stated that the distinction between facts and opinions as it applied to the pamphlet was itself a question of fact for the jury to decide. The jury seemed understandably reluctant to accept Christie's radical indeterminacy thesis, perhaps because it oddly deconstructed the very coherence of the jury's institutional function as a fact-finding body. In any case, Zundel was again convicted. Reluctant to make him a martyr to rightist causes, Judge Thomas nevertheless sentenced him to nine months in prison.

Zundel's legal odyssey, however, was not over. In 1992, the Canadian Supreme Court declared unconstitutional section 177 (which had been recodified as section 181). A vigorous dissent noted that "the appellant seeks to draw complex epistemological theory to the defense of what is . . . at worst pure charlatanism" (75 CCC, 449, 494). Unfortunately, the majority seemed to accept the broad outlines of Christie's epistemology. Writing for the majority, Justice McLachlin expressed grave doubts about "whether the defendant was accorded procedural justice." The very concept of "false news" created by section 181 he deemed problematic, as "the question of the falsity of a statement is often a matter of debate, particularly where historical facts are at issue" (449, 494). McLachlin noted that "historians have written extensively on the difficulty of ascertaining what actually occurred in the past," citing, no doubt to the delight of Douglas Christie, the "famous treatise" of E. H. Carr (503). Moreover, the majority was not satisfied with Judge Thomas's decision to submit the question of whether the pamphlet stated facts to the jury for decision; because Thomas had already taken judicial notice of extermination, he had "effectively settled the issue" for the jury (504). Using language that might have been scripted by Christie, McLachlin feared that Zundel's "verdict flowed inevitably" from the pamphlet's "divergence from the accepted history of the Holocaust" (505). Thus he concluded that "this was not a criminal trial in the usual sense" (505).

Ultimately, however, the problem was not Judge Thomas — it was section 181. Reviving the argument that Christie had unsuccessfully tried to launch in the first trial, the Court now held that section 181 violated the constitutional right to free expression. Specifically, the Court found the statute defective in two regards. First, it was based on the untenable assumption that "we can identify the essence of a communication and determine that it is false with sufficient accuracy" (509). Though conceding that this may have been easy in the instant case, the Court questioned the institutional competence of juries and judges to distinguish among truth, falsity, and interpretation "where complex social and historical facts are involved" (510). Second, the statute assumed that "deliberate lies can never have a value." Echoing John Stuart Mill's canonical argument in *On Liberty,* the Court insisted that even a publication as crude as Zundel's may have value and "illustrates the difficulty of determining its meaning," as the text may stand for the idea that "the public should not be quick to adopt 'accepted' versions of history, truth, etc" (510).

Having established that the law imposed a limitation on a constitutional right, the Court examined the statute to see if its benefits justified its cost to free expression. Here the Court concluded that the concept of "public interest" was far too broad and ill-defined to support the statute's intrusion upon expressive freedoms. In a remarkable rhetorical inversion, the Court went so far as to decry the challenged statute as itself Hitlerian in its control of speech. By making possible conviction "for virtually any statement which does not accord with currently accepted 'truths,'" the law could be used, the Court warned, in a manner akin to the suppressive measures of "totalitarian states like the Nazi regime in Germany" (519). As a consequence of this overbreadth, the Court struck down section 181 as unconstitutional. Zundel was a free man. Now copies of "Did Six Million Really Die?" available on the Internet bear the legend, "The concepts expressed in this document are protected by the basic human right of freedom of speech."

Beyond Zundel

The decision of the Canadian Supreme Court was at once remarkable and entirely predictable. Stunning were the Court's agreement with the substance of Christie's deconstruction of the concept of historical facts and its characterization of Zundel's pamphlet as a "divergence from the accepted history of the Holocaust." Yet predictable, and perhaps laudable, was its decision striking down section 181. For the wisdom of the statute naturally had to be considered beyond the narrow confines of the Zundel case, as the Court had to consider not only the justice done to Zundel but the prospective justice awaiting future defendants. Thus the decision was less concerned with the truth of the Holocaust than with the legitimacy of the law.

Yet the very reasons that justify the decision as a constitutional matter should sound a warning about using criminal law to respond to Holocaust denial. Understandably preoccupied with how its decision would serve as precedent, the Court treated the Holocaust as just another historical event about which unpopular claims can be made. Whether the challenged law could reliably serve to protect the history of the Holocaust from distortion did not trouble the majority. Instead, the Court was concerned only with the statute's threat to the law's responsibility to do justice to the accused. Here the Court reached the understandable conclusion that the state's interest in defending the Holocaust failed to justify its encroachment upon a fundamental right. The choice between protecting the Holocaust and safeguarding expressive freedoms was, for the Court, an easy one.

Perhaps, then, the striking down of section 181 simply means that it is more efficacious to try the likes of Ernst Zundel with more precise legal instruments — laws with the specificity of, say, the German, French, or Austrian laws proscribing Holocaust denial. Perhaps Zundel should have been tried under Canada's hate crime law, a statute that has passed constitutional challenge. Attractive as such a diagnosis might sound, it does not solve the deeper problems with the two Zundel trials.

For the problems with the trials cannot be ascribed simply to the constitutional defects of section 181. As we have seen, the problem with using the law to proscribe Holocaust denial is not just that one runs the risk of chilling protected speech; it is that the criminal law often fails to do justice to the history it has been enlisted to protect. As the two Zundel trials make clear, when the law intervenes to protect the Holocaust from the arguments of deniers, the law's evidentiary constraints and its concerns with its own legitimacy may demand that it approach the past from a position of formal agnosticism — a peculiarly weak position from which to defend the integrity of the historical record. Indeed, the law's tendency to view the past agnostically may unwittingly lead to the erosion of the very distinction between historical fact and falsehood that the law has been asked to support.

Thus the failings of the Zundel trials, while provocative, were not idiosyncratic. Even in a legal system that might permit the taking of a more robust judicial notice of the Holocaust, problems similar to those that confronted the Zundel courts are likely. In light of the structural similarities between the discourses of deniers and of legal advocates, negationists will strategically formulate their claims to explore and exploit the gray zone of any judicial notice. And insofar as deniers often seem more interested in forcing a legal confrontation than in prevailing in court, one should be all the more wary of using the criminal law as a response to their odious, but not unresourceful, arguments.

This observation is not meant to suggest that civil remedies remain the more efficacious tool for silencing Holocaust denial. As already noted, the impulse to silence denial is born less of a desire to compensate survivors than to prepare for a day when the Holocaust has passed from memory into history. It aims less to protect the dignitary concerns of a specific group or to enforce codes of civil speech than to define the frontier beyond which public discourse ceases.

This raises a final issue, one that returns to my point of departure. If the law can often serve as a useful tool of historical instruction in the wake of traumatic history, as I believe it did, problems notwithstanding, at the Nuremberg and Eichmann trials, how can a conclusion that questions the wisdom of relying upon legal means to safeguard the facticity of the Holocaust be understood? Part of the answer, I believe, has already been suggested: when the state attempts to silence Holocaust deniers by criminalizing their statements, it pursues a path that obligates it to defend certain norms whose claim upon the law trumps the claim of historical truth. This becomes particularly problematic, as we have seen, when the law is confronted with hateful lies that have been structured specifically to exploit its obligation to pursue justice at the expense of truth. Moreover, in traveling from Nuremberg to Jerusalem to Toronto, I have observed the crucial difference between using the law to clarify or elucidate the historical record and relying upon the law to police a history that has already been adequately clarified. The former seeks to use the power of the state as a tool of discovery, the latter seeks to dictate the terms of responsible memory through an act of legal will.

Dictating the terms of memory through an act of legal will is destined to fail not because the state is corrupt and any truth supported with a legal sanction is tainted. Rather, trials of deniers will fail to do justice to the memory of the Holocaust because the law ultimately will remain less interested in safeguarding history than in preserving the conditions of its own complex normativity and discursive neutrality. This does not mean that efforts to proscribe the Holocaust necessarily disturb this neutrality. Yet, ironically, it does suggest that in attempting to maintain the terms of its neutrality, the law's effort to silence the hateful voice of Holocaust deniers may create a new obligation to listen.

IO

· · ·

The Legal Imagination
and Traumatic History

In his parable "The Witness," Jorge Luis Borges writes, "There was a day in time when the last eyes to see Christ were closed forever."[1] Fifty years after the liberation of the death camps, Borges's words find a grim echo. In the not too distant future, the last eyes to have seen Auschwitz—from the in-side—will close forever. Their closing will not, however, bring to an end the law's engagement with the extermination of European Jewry. More than half a century after the first juridical effort to condemn these crimes, the law still struggles with their legacy.

Thus far, these struggles have represented impressive acts of legal will and intelligence. Each of the trials I have examined offered a distinct study of how prosecutors and courts labored to construct paradigms of proof adequate to the task of presenting unspeakable evidence in proceedings staged to serve both strictly juridical and broadly pedagogical ends. All the trials provided foundational procedural guarantees (such as a right to cross-examine witnesses), although the Nuremberg, Eichmann, and Demjanjuk trials were controlled by relaxed rules of procedure that permitted the sub-mission of a wider range of evidence than normally available in a court con-trolled by Anglo-American rules. These unorthodox rules, I have argued, did not upset the overall fairness of the proceedings, yet permitted Nurem-berg to adopt a didactic paradigm organized around documentary proof: it brought before the IMT everything from astonishing films like *Nazi Concen-tration Camps* to such morbid material artifacts as the shrunken head of

Buchenwald. Less spectacularly, it inundated the court with thousands upon thousands of written documents, many captured from the Nazis. While at times tedious, the trial by document aimed to make astonishing horrors real upon a world stage.

The didactic paradigm at the Eichmann trial, by contrast, was testimonial. Here the pedagogic imperative differed from that of Nuremberg, for the Israeli prosecution strove not simply to prove the facts of the crime and create an unshakable historical record, but to link this evidence to the personal tragedies and sufferings of Holocaust victims. In so doing, it hoped to counter the remoteness produced by a recitation of the Holocaust's numbing arithmetic of death and also to explain to an Israeli and international audience the behavior of the seemingly passive victims. By presenting a picture of traumatic history through the filter of anguished memory, the survivor testimonial became the focus of the trial: a means of making the spectators witnesses of the witnesses and, consequently, of defining the terms of responsible memory.

The Zundel trials, by contrast, were controlled by standard evidentiary norms, and here the didactic paradigm was historical — the testimony of the professional historian. This prosecutorial strategy sought to refute the hateful arguments of Holocaust negationists through the expert testimony of the historian, whose authoritative account would be less susceptible to challenges of authenticity than documents and less vulnerable to challenges of accuracy than the memory of survivors. Taken together, these proceedings describe a shift from displaying atrocity in its documentary materialization to reconjuring traumatic history through the voice of anguished memory, to providing a digest of the Holocaust in the sober terms of historical discourse. In so doing, the trials capture the evolution in the law's response to the representational problems posed by the Holocaust.

Equally impressive have been the efforts to master problems of judgment. The legal imagination's struggle to condemn unprecedented crimes has led to the articulation and definition of two novel concepts of criminality in international law: genocide and crimes against humanity. Coined by Raphaël Lemkin in 1943, "genocide" was not, in the first instance, envisioned as a legal category, though it supplied the basis for the definition of the crime formally incorporated into international law in 1948 and served as one of the models for the Israeli charging statute in the Eichmann case. The crime against humanity created one of the principal legal channels through which evidence of the Holocaust entered the Nuremberg courtroom. Fif-

teen years later, a modified (and controversial) version of this crime constituted, along with genocide, the legal foundation for the Israeli state's case
against Adolf Eichmann. A quarter century later, the incrimination made
possible the prosecution of Klaus Barbie.

As we have seen, in none of these trials was the crime against humanity
an altogether satisfactory legal tool for grasping the Nazi campaign to exterminate the Jews of Europe. Yet notwithstanding its conceptual limitations, the crime continues to represent an extraordinary legal innovation
exempt from conventional spatiotemporal limitations on a state's authority to prosecute. Exploding conventional jurisdictional barriers, the crime
against humanity authorizes the exercise of universal jurisdiction (in which,
for example, a Canadian court could try a German national for crimes committed against Polish Jews). Second, the imprescriptibility of crimes
against humanity insists that the extreme horror of these acts makes unnecessary and even offensive any temporal limitation upon the authority to
prosecute. Although the exercise of universal jurisdiction for imprescriptible crimes may raise a host of thorny diplomatic and political problems — as the Augusto Pinochet affair made clear — the recognition of
crimes against humanity in courts around the world reminds one that the
atrocities of the Holocaust have left their indelible imprint upon the content of international criminal law.

Finally, in part 3, I identified a third, more recent doctrinal innovation
that extends the law's idiom of judgment to reach the crimes of the Holocaust: statutes now common among a number of Western democracies
specifically proscribing Holocaust denial. In their unusual willingness to
use legal force to proscribe orchestrated efforts to erase history and mock
memory, these statutes again dramatize the doctrinal legacy of the crimes of
the Holocaust.

These three doctrinal innovations — the articulation in international law
of the crime of genocide and the crime against humanity and the passage of
statutes proscribing Holocaust denial — represent significant, imaginative
solutions to the problems of judgment posed by the crimes of the Holocaust. Indeed, the concepts of genocide and crimes against humanity have
demonstrated their importance not simply as terms of legal art, but perhaps
more importantly as terms of cultural meaning. Here, then, one finds the
law contributing to historical and cultural understanding, forging the
terms and concepts that have helped fill the conceptual vacuum created by
the Holocaust.

Yet in spite of the efforts of jurists to do justice to the Holocaust, the Nuremberg, Eichmann, and Zundel trials have left an uncertain legacy. In the case of the Nuremberg trial, the crimes of the final solution were often crucially misrepresented by the novel legal category through which they were juridically comprehended. The Eichmann trial, by contrast, painted a far more detailed portrait of the Holocaust and witnessed a more complex struggle over the terms of collective memory. Although the court often struggled to silence the words and memories of the survivor-witnesses and although the prosecution at times manipulated these same memories to advance its didactic agenda, the trial was an extraordinary success, creating a site of remembrance and commemoration that served to confer iconic significance upon the Holocaust. Finally, in the Zundel case, the effort to clarify history and to enforce the terms of responsible memory backfired in an even more dramatic fashion than in the Barbie and Demjanjuk trials, as the court became hostage to its own evidentiary and epistemological constraints.

What larger forces account for this uncertain legacy? At the heart of these trials, I have argued, lay competing conceptions of the law itself. On one hand, the trials sought to reintroduce sober, rule-bound authority into a terrain of lawlessness by bringing perpetrators of atrocity to justice. On the other hand, the trials sought to serve the interests of history and memory. They sought to clarify the historical record, define the terms of responsible memory, and make visible the efficacy of the rule of law. In so doing, the trials redefined conventional understandings of legal form, challenging courts to engage in delicate acts of balancing and boldly reimagining the domain of permissible legal purpose.

At times, as in the Eichmann trial, these acts succeeded. At other times, they failed. Yet the failures were themselves instructive, as they followed a pattern. Because the courts in these extraordinary proceedings took seriously their obligation to a formal conception of legality, this vigilance brought them to sacrifice didactic legality in the interests of conventional justice.[2] Indeed, it was the very intensity of the efforts to legitimize anomalous proceedings that often compromised each trial's power to represent and judge traumatic history. And so it was not the pursuit of didactic history that ultimately eroded the legal integrity of the proceeding conventionally conceived; rather, it was the strenuous efforts to secure formal legal integrity that often led to a failure fully to do justice to traumatic history. Moreover, the Barbie, Demjanjuk, and Zundel trials revealed an additional, though predictable, peril associated with exercises in didactic legality: how a resourceful defense counsel can hijack a criminal proceeding to advance pedagogic ends diametrically opposed to those imagined by the state and pursued by the prosecution.

Should, then, the criminal trial be shunned as a tool for responding to traumatic history? My criticisms notwithstanding, I believe the Eichmann trial and aspects of Nuremberg possessed greatness — as dramatic and necessary acts of legal and social will — that fully justified their historic undertaking. In the wake of traumatic history the decision to prosecute may not be a choice at all: it may be an imperative born of the scars left on an outraged collective consciousness.[3] If there is a policy implication to these reflections, it issues from my study of the Zundel trial: the grave problems posed by this case suggest that the legal community should be wary of relying on criminal law as a tool for responding to the arguments of Holocaust deniers — not simply because such efforts might erode rights of free speech, but because they may lead to an erosion of the very boundary between truth and falsehood that the law has been asked to police.

Forensic teams fan out over the rugged countryside of Kosovo, searching for traces of atrocities. The human remains they uncover are not, however, simply the latest relic of centuries of ethnic hatred and political violence. As a consequence of the legal legacy of the Holocaust, these remains are the evidence of *international crimes*. But while the experts sift through the evidence and the prosecutors prepare the indictments, let them bear in mind the law's first attempts to master the problems posed by mass killing. For they remind the world of the extraordinary power of the law to submit unprecedented atrocity to its institutional will and of the limits of the law to speak adequately on behalf of humanity's most traumatic histories.

Appendix: Nuremberg Counts, Verdicts, and Sentences

Defendant	Count 1	Count 2	Count 3	Count 4	Sentence
Hermann Goering	G	G	G	G	Hanging
Rudolf Hess	G	G	I	I	Life
Joachim von Ribbentrop	G	G	G	G	Hanging
Wilhelm Keitel	G	G	G	G	Hanging
Ernst Kaltenbrunner	I	—*	G	G	Hanging
Alfred Rosenberg	G	G	G	G	Hanging
Hans Frank	I	—	G	G	Hanging
Wilhelm Frick	I	G	G	G	Hanging
Julius Streicher	I	—	—	G	Hanging
Walther Funk	I	G	G	G	Life
Hjalmar Schacht	I	I	—	—	Acquitted
Karl Doenitz	I	G	G	—	10 Years
Erich Raeder	G	G	G	—	Life
Baldur von Schirach	I	—	—	G	20 Years
Fritz Sauckel	I	I	G	G	Hanging
Alfred Jodl	G	G	G	G	Hanging
Martin Bormann	I	—	G	G	Hanging
Franz von Papen	I	I	—	—	Acquitted
Arthur Seyss-Inquart	I	G	G	G	Hanging
Albert Speer	I	I	G	G	20 Years
Constantin von Neurath	G	G	G	G	15 Years
Hans Fritzsche	I	—	I	I	Acquitted

*A dash indicates that the defendant was not charged.

Notes

Introduction

1. Hannah Arendt, *Eichmann in Jerusalem: A Report on the Banality of Evil* (New York: Viking, 1963), 233.

2. An early critique of this position is presented in Judith Shklar, *Legalism: Law, Morals, and Political Trials* (Cambridge: Harvard University Press, 1964), a work that implicitly challenges Arendt's insistence that a trial should never serve an extralegal end. Using the Nuremberg trial as a case study inter alia, Shklar questions the prevailing legal orthodoxy that associates legal integrity with the systematic exclusion of all extralegal ends from the criminal trial. Though, as as I point out in part 1, Shklar counts herself among the critics of the Nuremberg trial, her argument, in contrast to Arendt's, does not rely on any notion of the sanctity and purity of the legal process; on the contrary, she dismisses such a jurisprudential vision as limited, offering in its stead an image of the law in which the ends of justice and pedagogy can be entirely compatible.

3. Ian Buruma, *The Wages of Guilt: Memories of War in Germany and Japan* (New York: Farrar, Straus & Giroux, 1994), 142.

4. All trials must, to a degree, resolve contested history, for one of the functions of the legal process is to clarify, in the public's mind, whether, why, and how the accused committed the acts he or she is accused of. While the conventions of proof that guide historian and judge differ importantly (see, for example, Carlo Ginzburg, "Just One Witness," in Saul Friedlander, ed., *Probing the Limits of Representation* [Cambridge: Harvard University Press, 1993], and Carlo Ginzburg, *The Judge and the Historian* [London: Verso, 1999]), these disparities do not pre-

vent the law from playing a valuable role in clarifying the historical record. Yet even if virtually all trials are burdened with the implicit task of clarifying contested history, it remains important to distinguish such proceedings from trials staged for the explicit purpose of providing history lessons.

5. Quoted in Buruma, *The Wages of Guilt,* 144–45. Kempner was referring to both the trial of the major war criminals and the subsequent trials of Nazi criminals before American courts.

6. *Trial of the Major War Criminals Before the International Military Tribunal, Nuremberg, 14 November 1945–1 October 1946,* 42 vols. (Nuremberg: International Military Tribunal, 1947), 3:92 [hereafter cited (often parenthetically in the text) as *IMT* followed by volume and page number].

7. Quoted in Tom Segev, *The Seventh Million: The Israelis and the Holocaust,* trans. Haim Watzman (New York: Hill and Wang, 1993), 348.

8. The term "responsible memory" may seem oxymoronic, erasing the distinction between history and memory; still, it reminds one that trials involving Holocaust denial are likewise concerned with something more than merely protecting the facticity of the historical record. For an influential discussion of the distinction between history and memory, see Pierre Nora, "Between Memory and History: *Les Lieux de Mémoire,*" *Representations* 26 (Spring 1989): 7–25.

9. Such a view finds expression in Hellmut Becker's blunt condemnation of the Nuremberg trial before the International Military Tribunal: "Few things have done more to hinder true historical self-knowledge in Germany than the war crimes trials." Quoted in Buruma, *Wages of Guilt,* 143.

10. Richard L. Rubenstein, *After Auschwitz: Radical Theology and Contemporary Judaism* (Indianapolis: Bobbs-Merrill, 1966).

11. Buruma, *The Wages of Guilt,* 152–53.

12. Michael Marrus, "History and the Holocaust in the Courtroom," in Gary Smith and Florent Brayard, eds., *Vom Prozeß zur Geschichte: Die juristische und historische Aufarbeitung der Shoa in Frankreich und Deutschland* (Berlin: 2001), MS 28–29.

13. For the most part, these problems have not been explored within the world of legal scholarship. The important exceptions here are Mark Osiel, *Mass Atrocity, Collective Memory and the Law* (New Brunswick: Transaction Press, 1997); Carlos S. Nino, *Radical Evil on Trial* (New Haven: Yale University Press, 1996), Martha Minow, *Between Vengeance and Forgiveness: Facing History after Genocide and Mass Violence* (Boston: Beacon Press, 1998), Ruth Teitel, *Transitional Justice* (New York: Oxford University Press, 2000), and Gerry Simpson, "Didactic and Dissident Histories in War Crimes Trials," *Albany Law Review* 60 (1990). Other important recent studies of legal responses to the Holocaust, such as Alain Finkielkraut's *Remembering in Vain: The Klaus Barbie Trial and Crimes Against Humanity,* trans. Roxanne Lapidus (New York: Columbia University Press, 1992); Henri Rousso,

The Vichy Syndrome: History and Memory in France Since 1944, trans. Arthur Gold-hammer (Cambridge: Harvard University Press, 1991); and Michael Marrus, "History and the Holocaust in the Courtroom," have issued from scholars outside the law.

14. As I observe in the following chapters, Nazi genocide represented a challenge to several critical tenets of the rule of law: first, that the sovereignty of the state is the inviolate basis of a rule-based order; second, that criminality can be comprehended and condemned in terms of violations of ordered legality; third, that principles of ordered legality preclude a sovereign from sitting in criminal judgment upon another; and fourth, that the imposition of a justly adjudicated legal sanction constitutes the proper corrective to criminal excess.

15. The literature on trauma is the current focus of intense scholarly attention; indeed, much of the contemporary scholarly fascination with the concept can be understood as part of an effort to locate conceptual terms adequate to the task of making sense of the Holocaust experience. While my study remains indebted to a psychoanalytic understanding of that term, my book is not, in contrast to numerous recent studies of the Holocaust, anchored in a Freudian model. See, for example, Dominick LaCapra, *History and Memory After Auschwitz* (Ithaca: Cornell University Press, 1998) and *Representing the Holocaust: History, Theory, Trauma* (Ithaca: Cornell University Press, 1994); Shoshana Felman and Dori Laub, *Testimony: Crises of Witnessing in Literature, Psychoanalysis, and History* (New York: Routledge, 1992); and Saul Friedlander in *Memory, History, and the Extermination of the Jews of Europe* (Bloomington: University of Indiana Press, 1993). As James Young has observed, to speak of *collective* trauma is to invoke the concept of trauma as a trope, and it is in this sense that I use the term. See James Young, *The Texture of Memory: Holocaust Memorials and Meaning* (New Haven: Yale University Press, 1994), xi.

16. Despite the widespread and largely accurate perception that the vast majority of participants in the Holocaust were never brought to justice, the crimes of the Holocaust did trigger a substantial mobilization of legal resources culminating in countless trials in many nations. Michael Marrus has identified six distinct kinds of trials that have been concerned—to a greater or lesser degree—with the crimes and history of the Holocaust. These include (1) the international trial (of which the Nuremberg proceeding remains the only example); (2) the trials held by the Allies in their respective zones of jurisdiction in the wake of the trial of the major war criminals (e.g., the subsequent trials in Nuremberg conducted by the Americans before their own military tribunals); (3) trials of Nazi criminals conducted by successor regimes in countries across Europe (e.g., the Polish trial of Höss; the Norwegian trial of Quisling, the collaborationist leader; and the French trials of Barbie, Touvier, and Papon); (4) the trials "of Jews by other Jews" (such as the Kasztner libel suit discussed in part 2); (5) third-party proceedings,

that is, "actions taken against alleged war criminals identified in countries that were not directly involved in Nazi-sponsored wartime actions against the Jews" (these include everything from denaturalization proceedings brought in the United States by the Office of Special Investigations to, most spectacularly, the Eichmann and Demjanjuk trials in Israel); and finally (6) trials involving the prosecution of Holocaust deniers (e.g., the Zundel case in Canada). Marrus, "History and the Holocaust in the Courtroom," 4–17. As Marrus's enumeration makes clear, there has been no want of litigation involving the Holocaust. Indeed, if one considers simply the trials included in Marrus's third category—that is, trials by successor regimes in previously occupied countries—more than 5,500 court proceedings were staged in Poland alone. Ibid., 7. Obviously not all of these trials of former Nazis and Nazi collaborators directly or even tangentially involved the Holocaust, yet clearly a substantial number did. Indeed, a full reckoning would recognize that even Marrus's detailed typology is underinclusive, for it excludes all civil litigations (principally in German courts) involving the payment of restitution and compensatory damages (the so-called *Wiedergutmachunggeld*) for individual and group harms resulting from Nazi atrocities.

17. For an argument supporting the idea of a continuing moral and legal imperative to bring Nazi criminals to justice, see Alan S. Rosenbaum, *Prosecuting Nazi War Criminals* (Boulder: Westview Press, 1993).

Chapter 1. Film as Witness

1. Michael Marrus, *The Nuremberg War Crimes Trial, 1945–46: A Documentary History* (Boston: Bedford Books, 1997), 242.

2. Robert G. Storey, "Foreword" to Whitney R. Harris, *Tyranny on Trial* (Dallas: Southern Methodist University Press, 1954), vii.

3. Rebecca West, *A Train of Powder* (New York: Viking Press, 1955), 3.

4. Ibid., 11.

5. Ibid., 5.

6. Bradley Smith, *Reaching Judgment at Nuremberg* (New York: Basic Books, 1977), 103.

7. These figures are supplied in the *Report of Robert H. Jackson, United States Representative to the International Conference on Military Trials, London, 1945* (Washington, D.C.: Department of State Division of Publications, 1949), 433 [hereafter *Jackson Report*].

8. But as Chief of Counsel Robert Jackson soberly noted, the figure of 60,000 is confusing, as "there is considerable and unknown amount of duplication as a visitor was required to have a separate permit for each session attended." *Jackson Report*, 433.

9. Ibid., 434.

10. Marrus, *Nuremberg War Crimes Trial,* 21. It should be noted that the declaration does not commit specifically to trying these figures.

11. West, *A Train of Powder,* 5.

12. As noted, altogether twenty-one defendants were tried before the IMT. The twenty-second defendant, Martin Bormann, was tried in absentia. Robert Ley, who would have stood with the other defendants, committed suicide in custody shortly before the beginning of the trial. The Allies considered trying Gustav Krupp von Bohlen und Halbach, but owing to his mental and physical condition he was never brought to trial. A full list of the defendants, along with crimes charged and the court's verdict, appears in the appendix.

13. Not all the defendants stood accused of committing all four of the crimes enumerated in the indictment. For a complete list of the various charges against the individual defendants, see the appendix.

14. *Jackson Report,* 434.

15. Smith, *Reaching Judgment at Nuremberg,* 102.

16. Janet Flanner, *Uncollected Writings: 1932–1975* (New York: Harcourt, Brace, Jovanovich, 1979), 104.

17. Smith, *Reaching Judgment at Nuremberg,* 102.

18. Ibid., 103.

19. Francis B. Sayre, "Criminal Conspiracy," *Harvard Law Review* 35 (1922): 427.

20. The concept of a "common plan" was meant to relax the prosecution's commitment to a strict notion of conspiracy, a point emphasized by Jackson in his summary statement before the IMT: "The Charter forestalls resort to such parochial and narrow concepts of conspiracy taken from local law by using the additional and nontechnical term, 'common plan.'" *IMT* 19:419.

21. Smith, *Reaching Judgment at Nuremberg,* 85.

22. Telford Taylor, *The Anatomy of the Nuremberg Trials: A Personal Memoir* (New York: Knopf, 1992), 146–49. See also Telford Taylor, "The Use of Captured German and Related Records in the Nürnberg Trial," in *Captured German and Related Records: A National Archives Conference,* ed. Robert Wolfe (Athens, Ohio: Ohio University Press, 1974), 92–100.

23. James F. Willis, *Prologue to Nuremberg* (Westport: Greenwood Press, 1982), 228.

24. Taylor, *Anatomy of the Nuremberg Trials,* 149.

25. Willis, *Prologue to Nuremberg,* 12.

26. See "Annex I to the Report of the Commission" ("Summary of Examples of Offences committed by the Authorities or Forces of the Central Empires and their Allies against the Laws and Customs of War and the Laws of Humanity"), in *Violations of the Laws and Customs of War: Reports of Majority and Dissenting American and Japanese Members of the Commission of Responsibilities, Conference of Paris, 1919* (Oxford: Clarendon Press, 1919) [hereafter *Conference of Paris*].

27. See Taylor, *Anatomy of the Nuremberg Trials* (discussing reports of conduct of German troops in Belgium); see also Willis, *Prologue to Nuremberg*, 12–13.

28. Article 228 of the Versailles Treaty required the German government to hand over its own citizens for war crimes trials to be conducted before tribunals of the victors. An initial Allied list of individuals to be surrendered named 854 persons, including many leading military and political figures. The storm of indignation unleashed in Germany led to a compromise between the Allies and the Germans: the Germans would try those accused of war crimes before the German Supreme Court in Leipzig. The Leipzig trials concluded in acquittals or short sentences, before being formally abandoned. See Taylor, *Anatomy of the Nuremberg Trials*, 16–18; see also, Willis, *Prologue to Nuremberg*, 126–47.

29. Primo Levi, *The Drowned and the Saved*, trans. Raymond Rosenthal (New York: Summit Books, 1988), 11–12.

30. Robert H. Jackson, *The Nürnberg Case* (New York: Alfred A. Knopf, 1947), 10.

31. John Mendelsohn, "Trial by Document: The Problem of Due Process for War Criminals at Nuernberg," *Prologue* 7 (1975): 228. This latter concern might have been misplaced — the Nuremberg defense attorneys, unaccustomed to Anglo-American trial procedure, proved themselves on the whole to be remarkably inept in the art of cross-examination. Often cited in this regard is the inept cross-examination by Hanns Marx, attorney for Julius Streicher and counsel for the ss, of the Auschwitz survivor Marie Claude Vaillant-Couturier. See *IMT* 6:228–30.

32. *Jackson Report*, 6.

33. Ibid., 433.

34. Smith, *Reaching Judgment at Nuremberg*, 84.

35. Flanner, *Uncollected Writings*, 100.

36. Ibid., 117.

37. Quoted in Walter Lacquer, *The Terrible Secret: Suppression of the Truth About Hitler's Final Solution* (Boston: Little, Brown, 1980), 2.

38. *Reporting World War II*, Part Two: *American Journalism 1944–46* (New York: Library of America, 1995), 685.

39. Robert H. Abzug, *Inside the Vicious Heart: Americans and the Liberation of Nazi Concentration Camps* (New York: Oxford University Press, 1985), 128.

40. Letter from Gen. Dwight D. Eisenhower to Gen. George C. Marshall (April 15, 1945), repr. in *The Papers of Dwight David Eisenhower: The War Years*, Alfred D. Chandler, ed. (Baltimore: Johns Hopkins University Press, 1970), 2616.

41. *Jackson Report*, 10–11, 9–10.

42. Taylor, *Anatomy of the Nuremberg Trials*, xi.

43. See Erik Barnouw, *Documentary: A History of the Non-Fiction Film*, 2d ed. (New York: Oxford University Press, 1993), 173–75. See generally Ilan Avisar, *Screening the Holocaust: Cinema's Images of the Unimaginable* (Bloomington: In-

diana University Press, 1988), discussing representation of the Holocaust in different film genres; and Barbie Zelizer, *Remembering to Forget: Holocaust Memory through the Camera's Eye* (Chicago: University of Chicago Press, 1998).

44. Pierre R. Paradis, "The Celluloid Witness," *U. Colorado Law Review* 37 (1965): 235. In a famous early case, a "moving picture of plaintiff's performance in a vaudeville entertainment" had been introduced as evidence of the plaintiff's condition before a debilitating accident. *Gibson v. Gunn,* 202 N.Y.S. 19, 20 (App. Div. 1923) (per curiam), *aff'd on reh'g,* 202 N.Y.S. 927 (App. Div. 1924). The appellate court held that the film showing plaintiff's "eccentric dancing" and "comic songs" "tended to make a farce of the trial," as evidenced by the "excessive verdict returned by the jury." Ibid.

45. Such a view saw in documentary film a transparent window upon the "real" and anticipated the arguments of those who have championed film as the medium best suited to mastering the crisis of representation posed by the Holocaust's inexpressible horror. Anton Kaes, for example, has argued that "what Lyotard demands of the historian of Auschwitz, namely to lend an ear 'to what is not presentable under the rules of knowledge', may well be the real domain of the filmmaker; it may in fact, be expressible only in such a syncretistic medium as film." Kaes, of course, is not speaking here of conventional documentary, but of film that can "transcend the 'rules of knowledge.'" Anton Kaes, "Holocaust and the End of History: Postmodern Historiography in Cinema," in Friedlander, ed., *Probing the Limits of Representation,* 208.

46. It would not be entirely accurate to claim that the screening of *Nazi Concentration Camps* marked the first time that evidence of the final solution had been presented in *any* courtroom. The British trial of Josef Kramer and Forty-Four Others, the so-called Belsen Trial, began on September 17, 1945, two months before the Nuremberg proceeding. And while evidence of the extermination of the Jews was imperfectly presented (Belsen was not a death camp), the Belsen trial can be seen as an earlier instance of juridical contact with the Holocaust.

47. Though this short sequence was the only description of the film's presentation in the actual trial transcript, a transcript of the film's narration was included in the volume titled "Documents and Other Material in Evidence," which was appended to the trial transcript. See *IMT* 30:462–72.

48. "Atrocity Films in Court Upset Nazis' Aplomb," *New York Herald Tribune,* Nov. 30, 1945, 11; see also, "Nazis on Trial See Horror Camp Film," *Washington Post,* Nov. 30, 1945, 2.

49. Raymond Daniell, "War-Crimes Court Sees Horror Film," *New York Times,* Nov. 30, 1945, 6.

50. Gilbert, *Nuremberg Diary,* 45–46.

51. Airey Neave, *On Trial at Nuremberg* (Boston: Little, Brown, 1979), 247.

52. Taylor, *Anatomy of the Nuremberg Trials,* 187.

53. As we shall see toward the end of chap. 3, this is the parsing offered by the French prosecutor Charles Dubost in his summary argument before the court.

54. Taylor, *Anatomy of the Nuremberg Trials,* 187.

55. Flanner, *Uncollected Writings,* 100.

56. Michael T. Isenberg, *War on Film: The American Cinema and World War I, 1914–1941* (Rutherford: Fairleigh Dickinson University Press, 1981), 74.

57. George H. Roeder, Jr., *The Censored War: American Visual Experience During World War Two* (New Haven: Yale University Press, 1993), 17.

58. See Paul Fussell's outstanding *The Great War and Modern Memory* (New York: Oxford University Press, 1975).

59. A pictorial album of Brady's photography is provided in James D. Horan, *Mathew Brady: Historian with a Camera* (New York: Crown, 1955). Barthes, for example, drew attention to "that rather terrible thing which is there in every photograph: the return of the dead." Michael Renov, "Toward a Poetics of Documentary," in *Theorizing Documentary,* ed. Michael Renov (New York: Routledge: 1993), 12, 25 (citing Roland Barthes, *Camera Lucida: Reflections on Photography,* 9). But the relationship between photography and death that Barthes named is very different from what I have in mind. If Barthes intended to identify the eerie temporality of photography, the image's resistance to the decay of that which it represents, war photography discovers a disturbing harmony between the dead subject and the still image. (For a remarkable study of the aesthetics of the photographed murder victim, see Luc Sante, *Evidence* (New York: Farrar, Straus & Giroux, 1992). Film, by contrast, provides the documentation not of death's stillness, but of the instant of its violent intrusion.

60. See Max Hastings, *Victory in Europe* (Boston: Little, Brown, 1985), 10.

61. See, generally, Donald Richie, *George Stevens: An American Romantic* (New York: Garland, 1985).

62. Yet as George Roeder has demonstrated, the censoring and suppression within the United States of horrific battlefield images from the American theater in World War II intensified and complicated the response to footage of German atrocities. Pictures of horrors from culturally remote areas — such as those committed by the Japanese upon the Chinese — were, by contrast, more widely circulated. Roeder, *The Censored War,* 125–27.

63. Susan Sontag, *On Photography* (New York: Farrar, Straus & Giroux, 1977), 20. Yet once this limit has been reached, Sontag notes how quickly the individual becomes immune to any effect the photographs might originally have had: "Once one has seen such images, one has started down the road of seeing more and more. . . . The shock of photographed atrocities wears off with repeated viewings." Ibid.

64. For a discussion of the prosecution's use of documentary evidence, see John Mendelsohn, *Trial by Document: The Use of Seized Records in the United States*

Proceedings at Nürnberg (New York: Garland, 1988), 15–18, 95–109; also, Mendelsohn, "Trial by Document," *Prologue* 7 (1975): 227, 227–34. Finally, *Nazi Concentration Camps* was not the only film screened at Nuremberg. The prosecution showed sections of films made by the Nazis themselves, including footage from Leni Riefenstahl's *Triumph of the Will*, see *IMT* 3:400–02; as well as films documenting atrocities in the east, see ibid., 7:601; and a pogrom in a Jewish ghetto, see ibid., 3:536. These films, however, were not placed at the rhetorical center of the prosecution's case as *Nazi Concentration Camps* was.

65. See Paradis, "The Celluloid Witness," 235–47.

66. Ibid., 250 (citing *UAW v. Russell*, 88 So. 2d 175 (Ala. 1956), *aff'd*, 356 U.S. 634 (1958)); see also *Beattie v. Traynor*, 49 A.2d 200, 204 (Vt. 1946) ("A photograph . . . is merely a witness's pictured expression of the data observed by him . . . and its admission when properly verified, rests on the relevancy of the fact pictured.").

67. "The mere picture . . . cannot be received except as a non-verbal expression to the *testimony of some witness* competent to speak to the facts represented." John H. Wigmore, *Wigmore on Evidence* § 790 (James H. Chadbourn ed., rev. ed. 1970), 218–19.

68. Paradis, "The Celluloid Witness," 257–60.

69. See, e.g., *United States v. 88 Cases, More or Less, Containing Bireley's Orange Beverage*, 187 F.2d 967, 975 (3d Cir.), *cert. denied*, 342 U.S. 861 (1951) (holding that the trial court erred in admitting into evidence pictures of guinea pigs dying in agony from vitamin C deficiency after being put on diet of orange drink).

70. Charter of the International Military Tribunal, sec. V, art. 19, reprinted in *IMT* 1:15.

71. In fact, the documentary used two narrators, who alternate in narrating the footage from the camps.

72. See *George Stevens: A Filmmaker's Journey* (Castle Hill Productions, 1984). Stevens's color footage can be seen at the U.S. Holocaust Memorial Museum.

73. Zoë Heller, "The Real Thing," *The Independent* (London), May 23, 1993, 24. By contrast, Alain Resnais relied upon the juxtaposition between documentary footage in black and white and contemporary footage in color for much of the unsettling force of his film *Night and Fog* (1955).

74. See, e.g., Bill Nichols, *Representing Reality: Issues and Concepts in Documentary* (Bloomington: Indiana University Press, 1991), 7; see also, Sontag, *On Photography*, 7: "There is an aggression implicit in every use of the camera."

75. See William Guynn, *A Cinema of Nonfiction* (Rutherford: Fairleigh Dickinson University Press, 1990).

76. For an examination of how efforts to critique the pornographic recapitulate its representational logic, see Susan Stewart, *Crimes of Writing: Problems in the Containment of Representation* (New York: Oxford University Press, 1991), 235–72.

77. The documentary erroneously attributes this footage, which includes shots

of Germans filing past a table displaying flayed human skin and shrunken heads prepared by the Nazis, to the liberation of Arnstadt. In fact, the footage is from Buchenwald, a fact corrected in the published transcript of the documentary. See ibid., 30:469.

78. In a remarkable column in *The Nation,* James Agee condemned the showing of clips of atrocity films in the United States precisely because such films "pin the guilt for these atrocities on the whole German people." James Agee, "Films," *The Nation,* May 19, 1945, 579. Dismissing the films as mere "propaganda," Agee pointed out, "I have not felt it necessary to see the films themselves." Ibid. He further claimed that the showing of such pictures makes Americans worse "in some respects, than the Nazis," for such screenings have the effect of spreading blame over the entire German citizenry. Ibid.

79. Kramer was later executed by the British after his conviction in the so-called Belsen trial. See *The Trial of Josef Kramer and Forty-Four Others (The Belsen Trial),* ed. Raymond Phillips (London: Hodge, 1949).

Chapter 2. The Idiom of Judgment

1. See Smith, *Road to Nuremberg,* 45.

2. See István Deák, "Misjudgment at Nuremberg," *New York Review of Books,* Oct. 7, 1993, 48 and n. 8 (reviewing Taylor, *Anatomy of the Nuremberg Trials*).

3. *Hannah Arendt-Karl Jaspers Correspondence 1926–1969,* ed. Lotte Kohler and Hans Saner, trans. Robert Kimber and Rita Kimber (New York: Harcourt Brace & Jovanovich, 1992), 54 (footnote omitted).

4. Hannah Arendt, *The Human Condition* (Chicago: University of Chicago Press, 1958), 241.

5. See Dennis E. Curtis and Judith Resnik, "Images of Justice," 96 *Yale L.J.* 1727 (1987), 1731.

6. *Jackson Report,* 11.

7. "Aide-Mémoire from the United Kingdom, April 23, 1945," repr. in *Jackson Report,* 19.

8. Quoted in Bradley F. Smith, *The American Road to Nuremberg* (Stanford: Hoover Institution Press, 1982), 199.

9. "Memorandum to President Roosevelt from the Secretaries of State and War and the Attorney General, January 22, 1945," repr. in *Jackson Report,* 6.

10. Smith, *Road to Nuremberg,* 251.

11. The gradual rallying of support in both American circles and abroad for Bernays's juridical solution is well documented. See Smith, *Road to Nuremberg.* For an interesting discussion of the role played by the United Nations War Crimes Commission, see Arieh Kochavi, *Prelude to Nuremberg: Allied War Crimes Policy and the Question of Punishment* (Chapel Hill: University of North Carolina

Press, 1998). Also of interest are Taylor, *Anatomy of the Nuremberg Trials,* 35–42; Fogelson, "The Nuremberg Legacy," 861–67; and Whitney R. Harris, *Tyranny on Trial* (Dallas: Southern Methodist University Press, 1954).

12. The issue of prejudgment had, in fact, created considerable controversy at the conference. General I. T. Nikitchenko, the Soviet representative, had argued, "We are dealing with the chief war criminals who have already been convicted and whose conviction has been already announced by the Moscow and Crimea declarations" (*Jackson Report,* 104–05). Jackson vehemently disagreed. Expressing a "philosophical difference," Jackson insisted "If we are going to have a trial, then it must be a real trial." Though he acknowledged that there "could be but one decision in the case," he insisted that "the reason is the evidence and not the statements made by heads of state" (ibid., 115).

13. See "Charter of the International Military Tribunal," article 7: "The official position of defendants, whether as Heads of State or responsible officials in Government departments, shall not be considered as freeing them of responsibility or mitigating punishment." *IMT* 1:12.

14. See *Jackson Report* and Smith, *Road to Nuremberg.* The formal indictment later issued by the Allied prosecutors ostensibly scrapped this compromise, as "The Common Plan or Conspiracy" appeared in this document as a separate offense; indeed, it is listed as the first count of the four count indictment. The final judgment of the Tribunal, however, completed this legal see-saw, largely reinstating the Charter's more restrictive, if deeply ambiguous, understanding of the conspiracy charge.

15. Bernays quoted in Smith, *Road to Nuremberg,* 51.

16. *Jackson Report,* 6.

17. See Jacob Robinson, "The International Military Tribunal and the Holocaust: Some Legal Reflections," *Israel Law Review* 7 (1972): 3; and H. Lauterpacht, "The Law of Nations and the Punishment of War Crimes," *British Yearbook of International Law* 21 (1944): 58–95.

18. Shklar, *Legalism,* 158.

19. M. Cherif Bassiouni, *Crimes Against Humanity in International Law* (Dordrecht: Martinus Nijhoff, 1992), 166, 167.

20. *Conference of Paris,* 21.

21. Ibid. As the Allies negotiated the terms of the charter of the IMT, the French were most concerned by the precedent created by the commission of 1919. André Gros, an expert on international law, bluntly summarized the French position at the London Conference in the summer of 1945: "We do not consider as a criminal violation the launching of a war of aggression" (*Jackson Report,* 295). Specifically, Gros worried that Germans would use the report of the 1919 commission to attack the legal foundation of the Nuremberg trial. Jackson and his compatriots tried to answer the concerns of the French by arguing that, as a result of conven-

tion (such as the Kellog-Briand Treaty of 1928) and customary practice, the status of aggressive war in international law had changed since the end of World War I. Although the Americans were not prepared to state when precisely aggressive warfare became an illegal act, they were prepared to defend the notion, as Jackson flimsily put it at trial, that "sometime prior to 1939 [it became] illegal and criminal for Germany or any other nation to redress grievances or seek expansion by resort to aggressive war" (*IMT* 19:399). Of course, declaring aggressive warfare illegal is altogether different from calling it criminal, as the former suggests sanctions imposed on a state while the latter supports punishments exacted upon persons. The question of criminal responsibility also proved vexing at the conference. Again, the French provided the dissenting voice, arguing that it "may be a crime to launch a war of aggression on the part of the state that does so, but that does not imply the commission of criminal acts by individual people who have launched a war" (*Jackson Report,* 297); still, the American argument provided a plausible rebuttal to the discomfiting precedent created by the Great Powers' commission.

22. *Conference of Paris,* 24.

23. Ibid., 20. The language of "shock the conscience" should be equally familiar to the student of international law and American constitutional law. In his summation at Nuremberg, Shawcross spoke of conduct that "outrages the conscience of mankind," words that would be imported into American constitutional law in cases such as *Rochin v. California* in 1952. In *Rochin* and its progeny, the "shock the conscience" standard was meant to define the outer limits of state power; under this theory, acts such as forcibly pumping the stomach of a criminal suspect, though not proscribed by a specific article of the Constitution, shock the conscience, failing to pass constitutional muster. The authors of the Commission's Report (1919), however, invert this standard formulation for rhetorical effect: here the conscience is shocked not by the outrages of the German military, but by the suggestion that international law provides no redress for such acts. It is not the transgressive behavior of the state that shocks but the hint that the law remains impotent to deal with state-sponsored outrages.

24. Ibid., 64, 72.

25. As we shall see in part 2, Jacob Robinson faults Arendt for treating the notion of "humanity" contained in 6(c) as referring to humanity as a whole.

26. Ibid., 65, 65–66. Apparently Lansing in particular was wary of creating any precedent for curtailing the right of a sovereign to defend its safety and interests in any manner that it chose. See Willis, *Prologue to Nuremberg,* 41.

27. 7 Cranch 116, 137.

28. Schwelb, "Crimes Against Humanity," 178.

29. Ibid., 179.

30. As we have observed, Lansing and Scott parsed the phrase "crimes against humanity" as referring to some (in their minds, ill-defined) standard of "humane-

ness." This parsing seems supported in 6(c) which, after enumerating such crimes as murder and extermination," describes "other inhumane acts." Implicitly, however, the normative sensibility contained in 6(c) seems to contain an entirely different notion of "humanity." On this view, 6(c) condemns extermination not because it is inhumane, but because such a radical crime offends and threatens humankind as a whole. This, in fact, seems to be the parsing of 6(c) provided by the French prosecutor François de Menthon at trial, who described crimes against humanity as crimes "against the human status" violative of "the whole of humanity" (*IMT* 5:407, 408). Thus, just as murder is a state crime because it is seen as threatening the physical and normative well-being of a domestic social order, extermination must be seen as an international crime because it offers an analogous, but more radical, threat to the international order.

31. *IMT,* 1:11.

32. Ibid., 1:254. As a doctrinal matter, this conclusion is important because it helps explain how the IMT was able to argue that "murder, extermination," etc., constituted *international* crimes. In his opening statement for the British prosecution, Shawcross tried to defend the legal pedigree of crimes against humanity by simple analogy: "If murder, rapine, and robbery are indictable under the ordinary municipal laws of our countries, shall those who differ from the common criminal only by the extent and systematic nature of their offenses escape accusation?" (ibid., 3:92). Logical as Shawcross's reasoning may have been, it nevertheless begged the question. For, as Bassiouni reminds us, "The demonstration that a given crime, for example murder, exists in all legal systems, does not make murder an international crime" (Bassiouni, *Crimes Against Humanity,* 287). What is required, Bassiouni argues, "is the existence of an 'international element' that takes such a national common crime out of the exclusive sphere of national criminal jurisdiction and moves it to that of international criminal law" (ibid.). In the case of the extermination of the Jews and other Nazi atrocities, one might have argued that the "international element" was satisfied insofar as such acts were so radically incompatible with the notion of rule-governed existence that they threatened humankind as a whole. As promising as such an approach might have been, the IMT took an entirely different position, arguing that the international element of crimes against humanity was satisfied by their connection to aggressive war, an international offense. See Guyora Binder, "Representing Nazism: Advocacy and Identity in the Trial of Klaus Barbie," 63 *Yale Law Journal* 1321 (1989): 1331–39.

33. Schwelb, "Crimes Against Humanity," 198.

34. *Jackson Report,* 333.

35. Robert K. Woetzel, *The Nuremberg Trials in International Law* (New York: Frederick A. Praeger, 1960), 184.

36. Some legal scholars have attempted to answer the victors' trial charge by pointing out that all criminal trials are, in a sense, victors' trials — as the presence

of any defendant in a courtroom already speaks of the victory of the state's powers of detection and discipline over the accused. More specifically, Herbert Wechsler, who served as a legal adviser to Judge Biddle, pointed out that such crimes as treason rely upon a logic not dissimilar from that employed by the tribunal. See Herbert Wechsler, "The Issues of the Nuremberg Trial," in *Principles, Politics, and Fundamental Law* (Cambridge: Harvard University Press, 1961), 138, 144–45. A rejoinder and fresh elaboration of the victors' trial critique is offered by Deák, "Misjudgment at Nuremberg," 51–52.

37. Stone quoted in Jeffrey D. Hockett, "Justice Robert H. Jackson, the Supreme Court, and Nuremberg Trial," *Supreme Court Review* 8 (1990): 258.

38. *Jackson Report*, 331, 333, 335.

39. See Shklar, *Legalism;* and David Luban, *Legal Modernism* (Ann Arbor: University of Michigan Press, 1994).

40. Schwelb, "Crimes Against Humanity," 207.

41. Elegant reasoning, perhaps, but still not altogether persuasive, for as one critic has noted, "To the extent that the law of Nuremberg . . . was made not at Nuremberg . . . but in London, it is not a case of judicial legislation analogous to the role of judges in the development of common law." Richard H. Minear, *Victor's Justice: The Tokyo War Crimes Trial* (Princeton: Princeton University Press, 1971), 61.

42. This was the criticism advanced by Anatole Goldstein in "Crimes Against Humanity: Some Jewish Aspects," *Jewish Yearbook of International Law* (1948), 225.

43. This, however, is not to suggest that concerns about legitimacy alone led Jackson to favor a trial centering on the aggressive war charge. In addition, it seems that Jackson, along with other leading Americans, firmly believed that the aggressive war was the Nazis' most serious crime. See Smith, *Road to Nuremberg.*

44. See Roger S. Clark's valuable discussion of the Semicolon Protocol in "Crimes Against Humanity at Nuremberg," in *The Nuremberg Trial and International Law*, ed. George Ginsburgs and V. N. Kudriavtsev (Dordrecht: Martinus Nijhoff, 1990), 190–92.

45. "Protocol to Agreement and Charter, October 6, 1945," in *Jackson Report*, 429.

46. Clark, "Crimes Against Humanity," 191–92.

47. It isn't clear why Jackson neglected to draft an independent conspiracy charge into the charter. Taylor argues that for Jackson "the conspiracy charge had always been important primarily in aid of proving individual guilt for waging aggressive war, and its role as a device for criminalizing prewar atrocities may not have been in the forefront of his mind." Taylor, *Anatomy of the Nuremberg Trials* 76. It should, however, be noted that Bernays's design might itself have been based upon a fundamental misapprehension of the magnitude of prewar atroci-

ties compared to wartime crimes. Apparently as late as 1949, Bernays made the astonishing assertion that the bulk of atrocities against the Jews had been committed "before the war." Smith, *Reaching Judgment at Nuremberg*, 26.

48. Sontag, *On Photography*, 108 (quoting film *A Letter to Jane* [1972]).

49. Guynn, *A Cinema of Nonfiction*, 155 (quoting Roland Barthes, "Upon Leaving the Movie Theater," in *Apparatus: Cinematographic Apparatus: Selected Writings*, ed. Theresa Hak Kyung Cha, trans. Bertrand Augst and Susan White [1981], 2).

50. Sontag, *On Photography*, 111 (quoting Robert Frank).

51. The identity of the writer of the text of the film remains unknown. As I point out in part 3, this anonymity importantly compromised the evidentiary value of the film at the Zundel trial. The staff of the Special Coverage Unit of the U.S. Army Signal Corps (SPECOU) included the writers Irwin Shaw, William Saroyan, and the future screenwriter Ivan Moffat. These writers were largely responsible for composing the captions and narration for the black and white film shot by the unit as it crossed western Europe, though it remains unclear who specifically wrote the text of *Nazi Concentration Camps*. See Hastings, *Victory in Europe*, 8.

52. See, e.g., Lucy Davidowicz, *The War Against the Jews, 1933–1945* (New York: Holt, Rinehart, and Winston, 1975), 15–19; Steven T. Katz, "The 'Unique' Intentionality of the Holocaust," in *Post-Holocaust Dialogues: Critical Studies in Modern Jewish Thought*, ed. Steven T. Katz (New York: New York University Press, 1983), 287, 290, 310. For a useful recent attempt to define the uniqueness of the Holocaust in terms of the practices of its perpetrators, see Avishai Margalit and Gabriel Motzkin, "The Uniqueness of the Holocaust," *Philosophy and Public Affairs* 25, no. 1 (1996): 65–83.

53. For a revisionist account of the Holocaust arguing against the thesis of uniqueness, see Ernst Nolte, *Der europäische Bürgerkrieg, 1917–1945* (Berlin: Propylaen, 1987), 503 (noting parallels between German National Socialism and Russian Communism, especially with regard to deportation of ethnic minorities). For a discussion of the controversy within German academic circles about the causes and nature of the Holocaust (the so-called *Historikersstreit*), see Charles S. Maier, *The Unmasterable Past: History, Holocaust, and German National Identity* (Cambridge: Harvard University Press, 1988).

54. See Jacob Robinson, "The International Military Tribunal and the Holocaust: Some Legal Reflections," *Israel Law Review* 7 (1972): 1, 8–12.

55. Ascherson, "The Film Britain Hid from Germany," *The Observer* (London), Sept. 8, 1985, 7.

56. At the time of its liberation, approximately forty thousand Jews were interned at Belsen — roughly two-thirds of its final population. See Jon Bridgman, *The End of the Holocaust: The Liberation of the Camps* (Portland: Areopagitica, 1990), 34; see also Martin Gilbert, *Atlas of the Holocaust* (New York: Pergamon

Press, 1988), 206–26 (documenting death marches toward the end of the war leading up to Allied liberation of Belsen and other camps).

57. See Bridgman, *The End of the Holocaust.*

58. Ibid., 14.

59. Ascherson, "The Film Britain Hid from Germany," 7. Publications commemorating the fiftieth anniversary of the end of the war continued to associate Buchenwald and Belsen with centers of genocide. See, e.g., Tom Infield, "Witness," *Philadelphia Inquirer Magazine,* Apr. 9, 1995, 12, 15 ("This is how America learned of the Holocaust. It was only when U.S. troops began stumbling onto concentration camps as they overran the heart of Germany in April 1945 that America came to realize the absolute evil of the Nazi regime").

60. *The Trial of Adolf Eichmann: Record of Proceedings in the District Court of Jerusalem* (1993) 3:1283–85 .

61. *Judgment at Nuremberg* (Metro-Goldwyn-Mayer, 1961).

62. *United States v. Josef Altstoetter et al.* (also known as the Justice case), in *Trials of War Criminals Before the Nuernberg Military Tribunals Under Control Council Law No. 10, October 1946–April 1949,* vol. 3 (Nuremberg: Nuremberg Military Tribunals, 1949–53). The trial was one of the twelve subsequent Nuremberg trials conducted by American military courts.

63. R.S.C., ch. C-34 §177 (Supp. 1970) (Can.).

64. As a related matter, it seems ironic that Eisenhower's famous words should be inscribed upon the entrance to the U.S. Holocaust Memorial Museum, as it is far from clear that by speaking of things that "beggar description" Eisenhower meant the mass extermination of Europe's Jews.

65. Primo Levi, *The Reawakening,* trans. Stuart Woolf (Boston: Little, Brown, 1965), 54.

Chapter 3. The Father Pointed to the Sky

1. Raphaël Lemkin, *Axis Rule In Occupied Europe* (Washington, D.C.: Carnegie Endowment for International Peace, 1944), 79. According to Lemkin, the objectives of a genocidal plan "would be the disintegration of the political and social institutions of the culture, language, national feelings, and the economical existence of national groups, and the destruction of personal security, liberty, health, dignity, and even lives of the individuals belonging to such groups" (ibid). Although his new concept was not, in the first instance, envisioned as a legal category, it supplied the basis for the definition of genocide incorporated into international law in 1948. According to the Convention on the Prevention and Punishment of the Crime of Genocide, genocide "means any of the following acts committed with intent to destroy, in whole or in part, a national, ethnic, racial, or religious group as such: a. Killing members of the group; b. Causing serious bod-

ily or mental harm to members of the group; c. Deliberately inflicting on the group conditions of life calculated to bring about its physical destruction in whole or in part; d. Imposing measures intended to prevent births within the group; e. Forcibly transferring children of the group to another group." U.N. GAOR Res. 260 A (III), December 9, 1948; 78 U.N.T.S. 277.

2. The indictment's description of genocide includes the extermination of "Jews, Poles, and Gypsies and others." *IMT* 1:44.

3. At times, the presentation of evidence of the final solution also suffered from the documentary approach, as the court on several occasions expressed concern that the prosecution's case was becoming numbingly cumulative. In the law of evidence, the concept of cumulative refers to evidence that goes to establishing what has already been more than well enough established by other proof. The court, for example, expressed weariness about certain details concerning the deportation of Greek Jews to Auschwitz: "Does it matter [that they had to furnish their subsistence] if they were 'brought to the final solution' which I suppose means death?" (*IMT* 4:366). Yet in important respects, the full horror of the final solution lay precisely in small, perhaps cumulative, details, such as the fact that people slated for deportation basically had to subsidize their own extermination.

4. As Judith Levin of Yad Vashem has pointed out, apparently these scenes were, in a manner of speaking, staged, as the documented re-creations of what conditions in the camp had been like and of the moment of liberation.

5. "Films Back Charge of German Crimes," *New York Times*, 20 February 1946, 6.

6. Robert E. Conot, *Justice at Nuremberg* (New York: Harper & Row, 1983), 371.

7. Taylor, *Anatomy of the Nuremberg Trials*, 248.

8. In the 1950s, Vaillant-Couturier disputed the existence of Soviet Gulags. See Marrus, "History and the Holocaust in the Courtroom." In this controversy, Vaillant-Couturier was pitted against David Rousset, a former Communist militant and Buchenwald survivor (whose memoir, *L'univers concentrationnaire*, became an early classic of concentration camp literature) who was among the first French intellectuals to decry the Soviet Gulag. Later she played an important role in the passage of the statute incorporating crimes against humanity into the French penal code. In 1987, she also testified at the Barbie trial.

9. Despite the shocking and articulate details provided by this witness, Michael Marrus reports that Judge Birkett found the testimony of Vaillant-Couturier cumulative, bemoaning in his diary that "from the point of view of this trial it is a complete waste of valuable time. The case has been proved over and over again." This comment underscores the tension between the juridical and didactic concerns of the trial. Quoted in Michael R. Marrus, "The Holocaust at Nuremberg." *Yad Vashem Studies* 26, ed. David Silberklang (Jerusalem: Yad Vashem, 1998), 20.

10. Browning, *Fateful Moments,* 8–9.

11. Ibid., 10.

12. Jewish groups concerned with the punishment of prewar atrocities supported this approach, as "the Jewish Organizations called particular attention to the fact that the persecution of the Jews had been embarked upon with a view to the future war." Anatole Goldstein, "Crimes Against Humanity: Some Jewish Aspects," *Jewish Yearbook of International Law* (1948): 212.

13. Deborah Lipstadt, *Denying the Holocaust: The Growing Assault on Truth and Memory* (New York: Free Press, 1993), 110.

14. Shklar, *Legalism,* 147.

15. Defendant Julius Streicher, a fanatical anti-Semite, insisted, however, that three of the tribunal's judges were Jews, claiming, "I can recognize blood. Three of them get uncomfortable when I look at them. I can tell. I've been studying the race for twenty years. The body structure shows the character." Gilbert, *Nuremberg Diary,* 41.

16. As Michael Marrus has demonstrated, Weizmann himself was ambivalent about testifying. He was dissatisfied with the statement that had been prepared for him ("entirely insufficient . . . an essay which would have been written by almost anybody") and wary about subjecting himself to cross-examination "without being adequately prepared." Weizmann, quoted in Marrus, "History and the Holocaust at Nuremberg," 8–9.

17. Again, it should be noted that this approach was also embraced by some Jewish strategists concerned with the issues of dispassionate proof. See Marrus, *The Nuremberg War Crimes Trial 1945–46,* 192.

18. Smirnov called Shmaglevskaya to the stand with the introduction, "I would now request the Tribunal's permission to summon as witness a Polish woman . . . to have her testify regarding . . . the attitude of the German fascists toward the children in the concentration camps." *IMT* 8:317.

19. In chapter 7, I contrast this with the image of the French resister presented in the Barbie trial.

20. The fact that an offense states a crime in municipal law does not, as Bassiouni reminds us, make it an international crime. As we recall, the international character of crimes against humanity ultimately was supplied by their link to aggressive warfare, an international offense.

21. Harold Kaplan, *Conscience and Memory* (Chicago: University of Chicago Press, 1994), 17.

22. The library at Louvain was razed by German soldiers of the 9th Reserve Corps in 1919. Meticulously reconstructed with great international support, the library was again destroyed on May 17, 1940, by advancing German soldiers.

23. See Shklar's excellent critique of Keenan's position in *Legalism.* Within the trial itself, Keenan's argument was sternly criticized by Justice Radhabinod Pal of

India, who, in a dissenting opinion, reminded the tribunal that "for many the term 'natural law' still has about it a rich, deep odor of the witches' caldron" and in particular argued that "when the conduct of the nations is taken into account the law will perhaps be found to be THAT ONLY A LOST WAR IS A CRIME." *International Military Tribunal for the Far East: Dissentient Judgment of Justice Pal* (Calcutta: Sanyal & Co., 1953), 69, 59. See also Woetzel, *The Nuremberg Trials in International Law,* 226–32; and Minear, *Victors' Justice.* More important, Justice Pal attacked the implicit conservatism of Keenan's (and Jackson's) argument, which by proscribing aggressive war would freeze the international status quo. This status quo, Pal argued, was itself defined by aggressive military conquest by the very powers now arguing the illegality of aggressive warfare: "Certainly, dominated nations of the present *status quo* cannot be made to submit to eternal domination only in the name of peace. . . . War and other methods of SELF-HELP can be effectively excluded only when this problem is solved, and it is only then that we can think of introducing criminal responsibility for efforts at adjustment by means other than peaceful." *International Military Tribunal for the Far East: Dissentient Judgment of Justice Pal,* 114. Pal thus concludes with a sweeping attack on Keenan's jurisprudential vision, insisting that the very rhetoric of legality that once rationalized acts of colonial conquest by the West is now being used to prevent others from tampering with the international status quo.

24. That legal positivism has long struggled to offer a satisfactory account of the obligatory character of law is familiar to any student of jurisprudence. See, for example, Hart's famous critique of John Austin in H. L. A. Hart, *The Concept of Law* (Oxford: Oxford University Press, 1961). Hart's attempt to reformulate the positivist position to account for law's normativity has, in turn, been challenged, famously by Ronald Dworkin, *Taking Rights Seriously* (Cambridge: Harvard University Press, 1978).

25. *Times* (London), 14 December 1945, 4.

26. *Times* (London), 30 November 1945, 4.

27. Joseph Conrad, *Youth and Two Other Stories* (New York: Doubleday, 1922), 130.

28. Richard Rubenstein and John Roth, *Approaches to Auschwitz,* quoted in Zygmunt Bauman, *Modernity and the Holocaust* (Ithaca: Cornell University Press, 1992), 1, 13, 28.

29. Hans Kelsen, "Will the Judgment in the Nuremberg Trial Constitute a Precedent in International Law?" *International Law Quarterly* 1, no. 2 (1947): 153–71, 167.

30. As noted, there were actually twenty-one defendants in the box, as Martin Bormann was tried in absentia.

31. Bauman, *Modernity and the Holocaust,* 13.

32. From Menthon's opening address.

33. Admittedly, the association of civilization with Christian practice was, in the context of a discussion of the Holocaust, unfortunate, suggesting that, like the Nazis, the Jews also have excepted themselves from civilization.

34. This argument anticipated the influential position argued in Peter Drost, *The Crime of State: Penal Protection for Fundamental Freedoms of Persons and Peoples,* 2 vols. (Leyden: A. W. Sythoff, 1959). The insistence on the connection between crimes against humanity and state practices also deeply complicated the legal and historical profile of the Barbie case (see chap. 7).

35. Admittedly, his vision of these crimes was not free of ambiguity. Thus Shawcross declared, "The war crimes were in their very enormity crimes against humanity. The crimes against humanity were not seldom war crimes, larger still" (*IMT* 5:470). Though a bit opaque, this formulation subtly attempted to make crimes against humanity something other than an interstitial or accessory offense. In important respects his argument anticipated, then, the summary of the French. While his appeal to the concept of "sheer enormity" might have fallen short of the French idea of state sponsorship, his argument at least attempted to locate the distinctive feature of crimes against humanity that distinguished these crimes from war crimes.

Chapter 4. Ada Lichtmann on the Stand

1. The prosecution team consisted of Attorney General Gideon Hausner; Yaacov Baror, a deputy state attorney; Gabriel Bach, who had served as the Ministry of Justice's adviser to Police Bureau 06 (the special section of the Israeli police created to interrogate Eichmann and help prepare the state's case); and Jacob Robinson, an authority on international law who had served as a special consultant to Justice Jackson at Nuremberg and who now served as an adviser to the prosecution. In addition, Zvi Terlo, a deputy state attorney, served as an aid to Hausner but rarely appeared in court. Like all the principals in the trial, the members of the prosecutorial team spoke fluent German: Hausner was born in Lvov, Galicia; Bach grew up in Halberstadt, outside Berlin; and Baror was born in Frankfurt.

2. *The Trial of Adolf Eichmann: Record of the Proceedings in the District Court of Jerusalem,* 6 vols. (Jerusalem: Ministry of Justice, State of Israel, 1992–95), 1:63 [hereafter cited (often parenthetically in the text) as *TAE* followed by volume and page number].

3. Raul Hilberg, *The Destruction of European Jews* (New York: Harper & Row, 1961), 185.

4. The theatre-turned-courtroom supplied an architectural trope for the dramatic nature of the trial that found expression in many of the contemporaneous accounts of the trial. Exemplary is Moshe Pearlman's description of the first day of the trial: "The lights, so to speak, were not yet dimmed in the auditorium, the

play had not yet begun, the curtain was still down, and the hall still hummed with the muffled whispering of an expectant public." *The Capture and Trial of Adolf Eichmann* (New York: Simon and Schuster, 1963), 97.

5. "Eichmann Is Unmoved in Court as Judges Pale at Death Films," *New York Times,* June 9, 1961, 16.

6. Bureau 06 was also responsible for interviewing prospective witnesses. Fearing the vulnerability of survivor testimony, Bureau 06 recommended that the number of witnesses be kept to a minimum. Hausner disagreed and with the assistance of Victoria Ostrovski-Cohen and Chief Inspector Michael Goldmann of the police (himself a survivor who as a boy had survived eighty lashes from an ss officer during his internment at Auschwitz) attempted to identify a much larger pool of prospective witnesses. They were guided in this effort by the extensive collection of survivor statements deposited at the department for oral testimony at Yad Vashem, Israel's national memorial and research institute for the Holocaust. See Gideon Hausner, *Justice in Jerusalem* (New York: Harper & Row, 1966), 292–96.

7. "Eichmann Court Told of Jews Burned Alive," *Times* (London), April 29, 1961, 7.

8. Natan Alterman, quoted in Segev, *The Seventh Million,* 350.

9. Segev, *The Seventh Million,* 350.

10. See Jeffrey Shandler, *While America Watches: Televising the Holocaust* (New York: Oxford University Press, 1999), 90. The televising was overseen by the American company Capital Cities, which used new soundless equipment. Three cameras were installed in fixed positions behind grilles in special openings in the walls of the auditorium; later, a fourth was added. See Pearlman, *The Capture and Trial of Adolf Eichmann,* 90–91.

11. Hausner, *Justice in Jerusalem,* 291.

12. West, *Train of Powder,* 3.

13. Hausner, *Justice in Jerusalem,* 292.

14. Primo Levi, *The Drowned and the Saved,* 84.

15. Hausner, *Justice in Jerusalem,* 291, 292.

16. Spectators queued up hours in advance to gain entrance to the trial; only twenty seats were reserved for the Israeli public. "Eichmann on Trial," *Newsweek,* April 17 1961, 42.

17. Arendt, *Eichmann in Jerusalem,* 6.

18. Segev, *The Seventh Million,* 351.

19. Harry Mulisch, *Strafsache 40/61* (Cologne: M. Dumont Schauberg, 1963).

20. Commenting on his own work, Lanzmann has said, "*Shoah* is certainly not a historical film. . . . The purpose of *Shoah* is not to transmit knowledge, in spite of the fact that there is knowledge in the film. . . . I would say that the film is an *incarnation,* a *resurrection,* and that the whole process of the film is a philosophical

one." Lanzmann quoted by Shoshana Felman, "The Return of the Voice: Claude Lanzmann's *Shoah*," in *Testimony: Crises of Witnessing in Literature, Psychoanalysis, and History*, ed. Shoshana Felman and Dori Laub (New York: Routledge, 1992), 213–14.

21. Arendt, *Eichmann in Jerusalem*, 204, 15, 205, 233. For a useful discussion of Arendt's critique of the prosecution's use of survivor testimony, see Leora Y. Bilsky, "When Actor and Spectator Meet in the Courtroom: Reflections on Hannah Arendt's Concept of Judgment," *History and Memory* 8, no. 2 (1996): 137–73.

22. Georg Schwarzenberger, "The Eichmann Judgment: An Essay in Censorial Jurisprudence," *Current Legal Problems* 15 (1962): 250.

23. Ibid.

24. Arendt, *Eichmann in Jerusalem*, 2–3.

25. Clearly the charge is grossly overstated, conjuring, as it must, the show trials staged in Stalin's Soviet Union. As Shklar has argued, the concept of criminal justice demands "a law and also an act made criminal by law"; in the case of a show trial, "most often the act is missing since prosecution aims at preventing future dangers, either criminal acts will be falsely charged, or legally innocent acts will be misinterpreted so as to seem criminal. . . . Evidence presented by perjured witnesses may be used, which will result in purposive miscarriage of legal justice" (Shklar, *Legalism*, 152). Given Shklar's definition of the show trial, it would be perverse to describe the Eichmann proceedings as such—it would be difficult to claim that the court, by relying on irrelevant testimony, twisted legally innocent acts into evidence of criminal wrongdoing.

26. Kirchheimer, quoted in Arendt, *Eichmann in Jerusalem*, 244.

27. Hermann Kantorowicz, *The Definition of Law* (Cambridge: Cambridge University Press, 1958), see 11–20.

28. Hart, *The Concept of Law*, see 89–96.

29. Shklar, *Legalism*, 1, 146.

30. Arendt, *Eichmann in Jerusalem*, 232; Robert G. Storey, executive trial counsel at Nuremberg, quoted in ibid.

31. In many ways, the clash between the rules-based theory of law and narrative jurisprudence can be seen as a struggle waged within liberal jurisprudence. In this regard, narrative jurisprudence can be seen as one in a number of important recent efforts to revive liberal theory by freeing in from the yoke of formalist and analytic conceptions.

32. Paul Gewirtz, "Narrative and Rhetoric in Law," in *Law's Stories: Narrative and Rhetoric in the Law*, ed. Peter Brooks and Paul Gewirtz (New Haven: Yale University Press, 1996), 2–3.

33. For a particularly rich—and critical—discussion of the uses of criminal trials as sources of historical instruction and narrative construction, see Osiel, *Mass Atrocity, Collective Memory, and the Law*. See also the essays in *Law's Stories*, ed.

Brooks and Gewirtz, and *Law Stories,* ed. Gary Bellow and Martha Minow (Ann Arbor: University of Michigan Press, 1996).

34. See, for example, Robert Weisberg's "Proclaiming Trials as Narratives: Premises and Pretenses," in *Law's Stories,* ed. Brooks and Gewirtz, 61–83.

35. See Austin Sarat, *When the State Kills* (Princeton: Princeton University Press, 2001).

36. See Osiel, *Mass Atrocity, Collective Memory, and the Law.*

37. See, for example, Lawrence Douglas, "Constitutional Discourse and Its Discontents," in *The Rhetoric of Law,* ed. Austin Sarat and Thomas Kearns (Ann Arbor: University of Michigan Press, 1994), and Robert Ferguson, "The Judicial Opinion as Literary Genre," *Yale Journal of Law and the Humanities* 2, no. 1 (1990): 201–19.

38. Alexander Bickel, *The Least Dangerous Branch: The Supreme Court at the Bar of Politics* (New Haven: Yale University Press, 1986).

39. Arendt, *Eichmann in Jerusalem,* 232.

40. Arendt's critique of the trial has invited many responses, the most remarkable of which is Jacob Robinson's *And the Crooked Shall be Made Straight* (Philadelphia: Jewish Publication Service, 1965), a four-hundred-page book devoted to rebutting, point by point, Arendt's every criticism (as well as laying bare the mistakes in both her research and her analysis). As noted, Robinson, an eminent authority on international law, had worked as a special consultant to Jackson at Nuremberg and served as an adviser to the Eichmann prosecution. For an assessment of Robinson's critique, see Walter Lacqueur, "Footnotes to the Holocaust in Hannah Arendt," in *The Jew as Pariah,* ed. Ron H. Feldman (New York: Grove, 1978), 252–59. A useful compilation of other views concerning Arendt's work is found in *Die Kontroverse: Hannah Arendt und die Juden* (Munich: Nymphenburger, 1964). For recent reconsideration of the Arendt controversy, see "Hannah Arendt and *Eichmann in Jerusalem,*" a special issue of *History & Memory* 8, no. 2 (Winter 1996).

41. Originally by law, the trial would have been conducted by the president of the Jerusalem court, Benjamin Halevi. As noted later in the text, Halevi had presided over the Kasztner libel trial in 1954, a case which raised sensitive issues concerning the alleged collaboration of leaders of the Hungarian Jewish community with the Nazis. Halevi's controversial handling of this trial (deciding that a published claim that the Jewish leadership had paved the way to murder was not libelous) was widely criticized in Israel, and many within the legal and political communities demanded that Halevi recuse himself from the Eichmann trial. Halevi refused, and as a result the Knesset amended the Nazis and Nazi Collaborators law of 1950 to require that a member of the Supreme Court preside over the district court in any trial arising under the statute. Landau, a member of the Israeli Supreme Court, was thus appointed president of this specially empaneled court.

Halevi, the regular president of the Jerusalem District Court, remained second in seniority to Landau. Raveh was a judge of the Tel Aviv District Court. All three had emigrated to Palestine in 1933. Landau, originally from Danzig, had completed his studies of law in London; Halevi grew up in the Saxon town of Weißenfels and had studied in Berlin; and Raveh, originally from Aurich, studied in Berlin and Halle. See *Der Spiegel* 15, no. 16 (1961): 20–32, 30. Indeed, virtually all the principals associated with the trial would have been more comfortable conducting the proceedings in German than in the official language of the trial, Hebrew. And just as Hausner dispensed with Hebrew to examine Ada Lichtmann in Yiddish, the court at times addressed questions to the defense and the accused in the language they all shared as a mother tongue.

42. The defense team consisted of Servatius and Dieter Wechtenbruch, a lawyer from the Munich bar. The costs of the defense were paid by the Israeli government.

43. Ben-Gurion quoted in Telford Taylor, "Large Questions in the Eichmann Case," *New York Times Sunday Magazine,* January 22, 1961, 23; Sneh quoted in Segev, *The Seventh Million,* 333.

44. See Berel Lang, "Holocaust Memory and Revenge: The Presence of the Past," *Jewish Social Studies* 3 (1996): 8.

45. See Segev, *The Seventh Million,* 260–62.

46. Despite common misconceptions, neither crimes against humanity nor genocide, as a statutory matter, is equivalent with mass murder.

47. The 1950 law defined "crimes against the Jewish people" as "any of the following acts, committed with intent to destroy the Jewish people in whole or in part: 1. killing Jews; 2. causing serious bodily or mental harm to Jews; 3. placing Jews in living conditions calculated to bring about their physical destruction; 4. imposing measures intended to prevent births among Jews; 5. forcibly transferring Jewish children to another national or religious group; 6. destroying or desecrating Jewish religious or cultural assets or values; 7. inciting to hatred of Jews." The offense of crimes against the Jewish people thus essentially tracks the statutory language for genocide (which also was adopted into Israeli law), applying it specifically to acts committed against the Jewish people. See Robinson, *And the Crooked Shall Be Made Straight,* 89.

48. By explicitly arguing that genocide was meant to apply prospectively, while crimes against the Jewish people was intended to apply retrospectively, Minister Rosen, in effect, admitted that the post hoc quality of the law was structured into the definition of the offense. The genocide bill was also adopted by the Knesset and became the Law on the Prevention of and Punishment of the Crime of Genocide 5710–1950.

49. This point found support in the position taken by the noted constitutionalist Herbert Wechsler, who argued, "Israel as a state in the international commu-

nity has no right to employ its law to condemn and punish crimes 'against the Jewish people.'" See Herbert Wechsler, "Adolf Eichmann and the Law," *New York County Bar Association Bulletin* 19, no. 3 (Jan.–Feb. 1962), 101.

50. Taylor, "Large Questions in the Eichmann Case," 22.

51. Other critics have observed that the notion of crimes against the Jewish people was *by design* a rejection of moral universalism. See Osiel's more recent argument that the charge of crimes against the Jewish people was "willfully and unabashedly antiliberal." *Mass Atrocity, Collective Memory, and the Law*, 62. Osiel's argument, in turn, is based upon Pnina Lahav's "The Eichmann Trial, the Jewish Question, and the American Jewish-Intelligentsia," *Boston University Law Review* 72 (1992): 555–75, and Michael Keren's "Ben-Gurion's Theory of Sovereignty: The Trial of Adolf Eichmann," in *David Ben-Gurion: Politics and Leadership in Israel*, ed. Ronald Zweig (London: Frank Cass, 1991). Both of these pieces argue that Ben-Gurion was convinced that the Holocaust had demonstrated the dangers of assimilationist liberalism. Nazi genocide, he was convinced, had to be understood as an attack on the Jewish people in specific and not against humanity in abstract.

52. As to the question of impartiality, Hausner likened such a prosecution to a treason trial in which questions of judicial objectivity may be similarly raised. Regarding the alleged political pressures placed upon the court, Hausner offered familiar arguments about the institutional independence of the judiciary. Concerning the claim that Eichmann was illegally delivered to the court by agents of the state, the prosecution cited authority suggesting "firstly that it does not make any difference how a person is brought within the area of jurisdiction; secondly that it does not make any difference whether this was done by private individuals or by an official arm of the government." *TAE* 1:19.

53. The trial itself offered numerous moments that poignantly reminded one of the youth of the Israeli legal institutions. Early in the proceeding, for example, the court directed questions to Avner Less, an Israeli police officer who described the circumstances of Eichmann's interrogation:

Q: Under what circumstances [did you first see the Accused]?
A: It was together with Nizav Mishne [Lt.-Colonel Hofstädter] in the interrogation room of the *Iyar* camp when the Accused was brought in.
PRESIDING JUDGE: Which room?
WITNESS LESS: The *Tishul* interrogation or investigation room.
ATTORNEY GENERAL: *Tishul* is a derivative from the word *she-elah* [question], Your Honour.
PRESIDING JUDGE: This is a new term that I have not heard of. [1:129]

It is, of course, well known that the transformation of Hebrew from a dead language of religious meaning into a living language of secular practice required the creation of many neologisms, and so one can understand Hausner's momentary shift from prosecutor to etymologist, as he teaches the judges the names of the very branches of the police responsible for investigating the cases they decide.

Chapter 5. The Court v. the Prosecution

1. See, in particular, Leon Wells, *The Death Brigade* (New York: Holocaust Library, 1978). This book was published in France in November 1961 shortly before the court delivered its judgment in the Eichmann trial. It was published in the United States in 1963 under the title *The Janowska Road.* According to Hausner, the prosecution preferred to call witnesses who had given statements at Yad Vashem or had published accounts of their experiences because the memories of such witnesses could be more easily refreshed by their previous statements. The prosecution also "found that writers were usually equipped with good powers of observation and carefully checked their facts before publishing them." Hausner, *Justice in Jerusalem*, 296.

2. Chaim Gouri, *Face à la Cage de Verre: Le Procès Eichmann, Jerusalem, 1961* (Paris: Éditions Tirésias, 1995). Gouri repeated this observation to me in conversation.

3. At this point in Wells's testimony, however, his "voice broke and his black skullcap toppled from his head." *New York Times,* May 2, 1961, 12.

4. Lawrence Langer, *Holocaust Testimonies: The Ruins of Memory* (New Haven: Yale University Press, 1991), 165.

5. See Edward W. Cleary et al., *McCormick on Evidence* (St. Paul: West Publishing, 1984), 919–45.

6. Again, as noted, the IMT received evidence indicating the important role he played in the implementing of the final solution.

7. Like Article 8 of the Nuremberg charter, the Nazis and Nazi Collaborators Law of 1950 specifically precluded a defense based on superior orders.

8. The first four counts detailed crimes against the Jewish people; counts 5, 6, and 7 involved crimes against humanity concerning Eichmann's activities as head of Section IVB4; count 8 enumerated war crimes committed by Eichmann; counts 9–11 discussed crimes against humanity associated with Eichmann's function as the official responsible for "evacuating" citizens; count 12 described crimes against the children of Lidice, Czechoslovakia, in connection with Eichmann's functions in the Gestapo in Berlin; the final three counts dealt with Eichmann's membership in organizations declared criminal by the IMT in 1946.

9. Peter Brooks, "The Law as Narrative and Rhetoric," in *Law's Stories,* ed. Brooks and Gewirtz, 19.

10. Brandt's testimony, however, was not without its difficulties, particularly as it concerned his memory of Eichmann's alleged promise to blow up the

Auschwitz gas chambers as a term for their "trucks for Jews" negotiations. *TAE* 3:1064–65.

11. A provocative and prescient fictional treatment of this problem is found in Ida Fink's "The Table," in *Scraps of Time and Other Stories,* trans. Madeline Levine and Francine Prose (New York: Pantheon, 1987). It is perhaps worth noting that Fink, a prominent Israeli novelist, first participated in Yad Vashem's project of recording oral testimony of Holocaust experiences directly in the wake of the Eichmann trial.

12. G. M. Gilbert, "The Mentality of ss Murderous Robots," *Yad Vashem Studies on the Jewish Catastrophe and Resistance* 5 (1963): 35–41, 36.

13. Cleary et al., *McCormick on Evidence,* 33.

14. In fact, Dinur was not the author's original name. Born Yehiel Feiner, the author changed his name to Dinur (Hebrew for "From the Fire") shortly after his emigration to Israel. See Segev, *The Seventh Million,* 4.

15. Several of Dinur's books specifically address his struggles to establish psychic distance from the Holocaust; most noteworthy — and bizarre — is his hallucinatory memoir *Shivitti: A Vision* (San Francisco: Harper and Row, 1989), which documents his attempt to heal his debilitating obsession with the past through an LSD treatment administered by a Dutch psychiatrist.

16. Tom Segev argues that Dinur's collapse was occasioned not by his anguished contact with the unspeakable, but by the "confession" in which he publicly acknowledged, for the first time, that he was the writer known only as Katzetnik. It was the impossibility of publicly reconciling his quotidian self with his fugitive existence as survivor that led to the crisis on the stand, a crisis that Segev believes is paradigmatic of deeper conflicts within Israeli national identity. Segev, *The Seventh Million,* 11.

17. Telling in this regard is the fact that in its lengthy judgment, the court quotes from the testimonies of the survivor witnesses relatively infrequently and then only in short passages. By far the longest quotation from an eyewitness comes not from the testimony of a Jewish survivor, but from the Gerstein Report, a detailed account by a former ss officer of "what he saw with his own eyes " at the Belzec extermination camp. *TAE* 5:2150–51. See the discussion of Gerstein in chap. 9.

Chapter 6. Didactic Legality and Heroic Memory

1. Hausner's defense of the trial as a display of legal self-sufficiency powerfully echoed in this regard Ben-Gurion's views. The Israeli statesman, for example, dismissed out of hand the suggestion that Eichmann should be handed over to an international tribunal, with the following argument: "This is perhaps the first case in human history of historical justice, where a small people, whose enemies and persecutors are so numerous, was afforded the opportunity to place on trial, in its

sovereign country, one of the chiefs of its oppressors for atrocities committed against hundreds and thousands of its children." Ben-Gurion, quoted in Michael Keren, "Ben-Gurion's Theory of Sovereignty: The Trial of Adolf Eichmann," in *David Ben-Gurion: Politics and Leadership in Israel,* ed. Ronald W. Zweig (London: Frank Cass, 1991), 40. Thus the Eichmann trial can partially be understood as a robust defense of the principle of sovereignty, the very principle that compromised the Nuremberg trial's effort to do justice to the crimes of the Holocaust.

2. Arendt, *Eichmann in Jerusalem,* 239.

3. Hannah Arendt, *The Human Condition* (Chicago: University of Chicago Press, 1958), 240–41. Arendt's argument implicitly questions the coherence of submitting Eichmann's crimes to legal punishment, for she notes that in the case of "radical evil," "we can neither punish nor forgive such offenses that . . . transcend the realm of human affairs and the potentialities of human power." Such an argument thus revives her critique of the Nuremberg trial (see part 1). Arendt, *The Human Condition,* 241.

4. Jean Hampton, "The Retributive Ideal," in *Forgiveness and Mercy,* ed. Jeffrie Murphy and Jean Hampton (Cambridge: Cambridge University Press, 1988), 137.

5. Lang, "Holocaust Memory and Revenge," 17. Lang describes how Abba Kovner, before his emigration to Israel and years before his testimony at the Eichmann trial, had organized a group of former Vilna partisans devoted to exacting revenge on the German population. The most spectacular plan of this group, the poisoning of the water supplies in Hamburg, Frankfurt, Munich, and Nuremberg, was aborted after Kovner was arrested by British authorities during a trip to Palestine to obtain the necessary poisons. See Lang, "Holocaust Memory and Revenge," 4–6.

6. Ibid., 8.

7. Langer, *Holocaust Testimonies,* 165, 204.

8. Bauman, *Modernity and the Holocaust.* Also of note are Raul Hilberg's discussion of the Jewish councils in *The Destruction of the European Jews* (an account that has often been erroneously associated with Arendt's argument — probably because Arendt frequently cites Hilberg's work) and Isiah Trunk, *Judenrat: The Jewish Councils in Eastern Europe under Nazi Occupation* (New York: Macmillan, 1972).

9. Arendt, *Eichmann in Jerusalem,* 125. For a discussion of the claim as a counterfactual, see Richard J. Bernstein, *Hannah Arendt and the Jewish Question* (Cambridge: MIT Press, 1996), 161–65.

10. Segev, *The Seventh Million,* 258. For a discussion of the trial and affair, see also Yehuda Bauer, *Jews for Sale?: Nazi-Jewish Negotiations, 1933–45* (New Haven: Yale University Press, 1994), and Yechiam Weitz, "The Herut Movement and the Kasztner Trial," *Holocaust and Genocide Studies* 8, no. 3 (1994): 349–71.

11. Pnina Lahav, *Judgment in Jerusalem: Chief Justice Simon Agranat and the Zionist Century* (Berkeley: University of California Press, 1997).

12. Segev, *The Seventh Million,* 308.

13. Halevi later expressed regret for having expressed this formulation. For a general discussion of Halevi's conduct, see Leora Bilsky, "Judging Evil in the Trial of Kastner," *Law and History Review* (forthcoming, 2000).

14. See the discussion in chapter 4, n. 41.

15. "Eichmann Trial Is Interrupted Twice by Spectators' Outcries," *New York Times,* May 26, 1961, 1.

16. "Death Camp Survivor Explains Why Jews Did Not Resist," *Times* (London), May 2, 1961, 10.

17. It is instructive to compare Hausner's treatment of the witnesses with Halevi's, who, consistent with his behavior during the Kasztner trial, often seemed dissatisfied with the survivors who appeared before the court. In the case of one early survivor witness, Noach Zabludowicz, Halevi basically interrupted Hausner's examination to accuse the witness of having been a collaborator (*TAE* 1:340–41); later in the trial Halevi apologized to the attorney general and the court for the "misunderstanding" (ibid., 3:1156). Thus Halevi's question to Ya'akov Gurfein, a survivor originally from Galicia: "Tell me, at the railway station when they packed you into the train going to Belzec [extermination camp], . . . why didn't you resist, why did you board the train?"—expressed greater skepticism about the behavior of survivors than did similar questions posed by Hausner. Ibid., 1:333.

18. For a discussion of the history and memorializing logic of Yom Hazikkaron, see Young, *The Texture of Memory,* 265–72.

19. Primo Levi, *Moments of Reprieve,* trans. Ruth Feldman (New York: Summit Books, 1986), 10.

20. Even Eichmann, it seems, looked forward to the trial as an opportunity to unburden himself. Thus during his lengthy pretrial interrogation by a special section of the Israeli police, Eichmann declared, "Within my inner self, I have been prepared for a long time already, for this general statement, but only I did not know when fate would place me in the position of making this statement" (*TAE* 1:140–41). At the end of his lengthy time on the stand, he declared, "I am even happy that the cross-examination took so long. I did at least have the opportunity here to separate the truth from the untruth which was heaped on me over fifteen years" (ibid., 4:1812–13).

21. For a discussion of the structure of survivor testimonies, see Annette Wieviorka, "On Testimony," in *Holocaust Remembrance: The Shapes of Memory,* ed. Geoffrey Hartman (Oxford: Blackwell, 1994), 23–32.

22. According to the trial, only three persons survived Chelmno, and all testified for the prosecution: Srebrnik, Michael Podchlewnik, and Mordecai Zurawski.

Lanzmann's *Shoah* describes Srebrnik and Podchlewnik as the only survivors of Chelmno. The *Encyclopedia of the Holocaust*, ed. Israel Gutman (New York: Macmillan, 1990), 283–86, lists the total number of survivors of Chelmno as five.

23. Claude Lanzmann, *Shoah: The Complete Text of the Film* (New York: Pantheon, 1985), 3, 4.

24. Lanzmann, *Shoah*, 7. For a discussion of Podchlewnik's silence, see Felman, "The Return of the Voice" in *Testimony*, ed. Felman, 224–25.

25. *New York Times*, May 9, 1961, 16.

26. In her attack on the coherence of the charging statute, Arendt writes, "The Nazis and Nazi Collaborators (Punishment) Law of 1950 is wrong, it is in contradiction to what actually happened, it does not cover the facts (*Eichmann in Jerusalem*, 249). This prompted Jacob Robinson to comment, "How can a law be "in contradiction to what actually happened"? Laws are not narratives of the past history; they simply prescribe the rules according to which the court measures the facts" (*And the Crooked Shall Be Made Straight*, 88). Thus in attacking Arendt, Robinson offers a restatement of the very ideas of legal formalism that one finds both Arendt and the court defending in the trial against the prosecution's didactic approach.

27. Arendt, *Eichmann in Jerusalem*, 246.

28. She does, however, praise the court for recognizing in its judgment the key principle of administrative massacre: that one's responsibility is inversely related to one's proximity to the killings.

29. Ibid., 252. Here Arendt revives the controversy over the meaning of "humanity" in "crimes against humanity." Arendt's capacious view of a crime "against mankind in its entirety" thus can be seen as an attempt to revive an understanding partially articulated but never fully embraced at Nuremberg.

30. Ibid., 250.

31. Arendt acknowledges that the Eichmann trial contributed to other litigations but dismisses this as a mere by-product of the case.

32. Lotte Kohler and Hans Saner, eds., Robert Kimber and Rita Kimber, trans., *Hannah Arendt–Karl Jaspers: Correspondence 1926–1969* (New York: Harcourt Brace Jovanovich, 1992), 410.

33. Ibid.

34. Ibid., 413.

35. As I noted in the introduction, a number of recent works have compared the utility of trials and truth commissions as responses to traumatic history. See, for example, Nino, *Radical Evil on Trial;* Osiel, *Mass Atrocity, Collective Memory, and the Law;* Teitel, *Transitional Justice;* Naomi Roht-Arriaza, ed., *Impunity and Human Rights in International Law and Practice* (New York: Oxford University Press, 1995); Michael Ignatieff, *The Warrior's Honor: Ethnic War and the Modern Conscience* (London: Chatto and Windus, 1998).

36. Hausner, *Justice in Jerusalem,* 291.

37. Levi, *The Drowned and the Saved,* 36–69, 40, 37, 43.

38. Arendt, *Eichmann in Jerusalem,* 253.

39. As other commentators have noted, the phrase "banality of evil" appears only once in Arendt's book: as the concluding, italicized words of the main text commenting on Eichmann's characteristically trite words as he prepared himself for his execution: "It was as though in those last minutes he was summing up the lessons that this long course in human wickedness had taught us — the lesson of the fearsome, word-and-thought-defying *banality of evil,*" (ibid., 231). Arendt's argument seems to differ importantly from her response to the Nuremberg trial (see part 1). There her image of Nazi genocide was of radical evil; in *Eichmann in Jerusalem* the evil of Nazi genocide is comprehended in terms of its banality. David Luban has argued that the ostensible shift actually does not represent a substantive change in Arendt's thinking, as "radicalness" describes the nature and magnitude of the crimes, whereas "banality" describes the motives and psychology of the perpetrators. See David Luban, "What the Banality of Evil Is Not," (manuscript). Luban's position, in turn, builds upon Richard Bernstein's treatment of the question; see Bernstein, *Hannah Arendt and the Jewish Question,* 137–53.

40. This position closely resembles Ohlendorf's response to a similar question at Nuremberg. See the discussion of Ohlendorf's testimony in chapter 3.

41. See Raul Hilberg, *The Politics of Memory: The Journey of a Holocaust Historian* (Chicago: Ivan R. Dee, 1996), 148. Unfortunately, Arendt is not consistent in her stance. After all, the main thrust of her position is that the bureaucratic killer "commits his crimes under circumstances that make it well-nigh impossible for him to know or feel that he is doing wrong" (*Eichmann in Jerusalem,* 253) — not that the bureaucratic killer serves out of a positive sense of the justice of his acts.

42. *Eichmann in Jerusalem,* 254.

43. Ibid., 253.

44. Levi, *The Drowned and the Saved,* 37.

Chapter 7. Retrials and Precursors

1. Lest one prematurely conclude that the age of Holocaust perpetrator trials has altogether passed into history, the recent French trial of Maurice Papon for complicity in crimes against humanity is a reminder that the perpetrators and their helpers have not altogether disappeared from the scene. See Annette Wieviorka, "France and Crimes Against Humanity," in *Lives in the Law,* ed. Austin Sarat, Lawrence Douglas, and Martha Umphrey (Ann Arbor: University of Michigan Press, 2001).

2. Binder, "Representing Nazism," 1322.

3. Rousso, *The Vichy Syndrome,* 201.

4. Ibid.

5. Quoted in Tom Teicholz, *The Trial of Ivan the Terrible: State of Israel v. John Demjanjuk* (New York: St. Martin's Press, 1990), 269. The prosecutorial team consisted of Blatman, the state attorney; Michael Shaked, supervisor of the Criminal Division of the Jerusalem District Attorney's Office; Michael Horowitz, deputy district attorney of the Central District; and Dafna Bainvol, senior deputy district attorney of Jerusalem.

6. Admittedly some commentators were less than convinced by Blatman's argument. "The trial will not be much of an educational experience," opined the *Jerusalem Post.* "Since Eichmann, awareness of the Holocaust by the Israeli post-Holocaust generation needs no such boost, while people who deny the Holocaust will keep denying it." Teicholz, *The Trial of Ivan the Terrible,* 81.

7. *Criminal Case (Jerusalem) 373/86, The State of Israel v. Ivan (John) Demjanjuk* (Tel Aviv: Israel Bar Association, 1991), 39 [hereafter cited as *The Demjanjuk Trial*].

8. Leila Sadat Wexler, "The Interpretation of the Nuremberg Principles by the French Court of Cassation: From Touvier to Barbie and Back Again," 32 *Columbia Journal of Transnational Law* 289 (1994): 331

9. Wexler, "The Interpretation of the Nuremberg Principles," 319.

10. Robert H. Miller, "The Convention on the Non-Applicability of Statutory Limitations to War Crimes and Crimes Against Humanity," *American Journal of International Law* 65 (1971): 479.

11. The common designation "the trial of the guards" is something of a misnomer, as the twenty-two defendants included everything from two camp adjutants to two dentists and a doctor.

12. Though German authorities began preparing a case in 1958, it was the Eichmann trial that helped create the legal and social impetus for the prosecution, as the German nation began the painful and often grotesque process of confronting the crimes that had been sponsored in its name. The trial did not end until 1965.

13. Adalbert Rückerl, *NS-Verbrechen vor Gericht: Versuch einer Vergangenheitsbewältigung* (Heidelberg: C. F. Müller Juristischer Verlag, 1984), 126.

14. Devin Pendas, "Displaying Justice: Nazis on Trial in Postwar Germany" (Ph.D. diss., University of Chicago, 2000); see also Rebecca Whitman, MS, 3.

15. Hannah Arendt, "Introduction" to Bernd Naumann, *Auschwitz: A Report on the Proceedings Against Karl Ludwig Mulka and Others Before the Court at Frankfurt* (New York: Frederick A. Praeger, 1966), xxi–xxii.

16. See "NS-Verbrechen: Verjährung," *Der Spiegel* Nr.11/1965, 30–44.

17. Rückerl, *NS-Verbrechen vor Gericht,* 207.

18. Miller, "Non-Applicability of Statutory Limitations," 483.

19. "Für Völkermord gibt is keine Verjährung: *Spiegel*-Gespräch mit dem Philosophen Professor Karl Jaspers," *Der Spiegel,* Nr. 11/1965, 53–71, 60.

20. Wexler, "The Interpretation of the Nuremberg Principles," 321–22.

21. See Miller, "Non-Applicability of Statutory Limitations," 476–77.

22. Bassiouni, *Crimes Against Humanity in International Law,* 235.

23. Wexler, "The Interpretation of the Nuremberg Principles," 318, 333.

24. See Leila Sadat Wexler, "Reflections on the Trial of Vichy Collaborator Paul Touvier for Crimes Against Humanity in France," *Law and Social Inquiry* 20, no. 1 (1995): 191–220; and the essays in Golsan, ed., *Memory, the Holocaust, and French Justice.*

25. Barbie was German; it was not until the trial of Paul Touvier in 1994 that a Frenchman stood trial for crimes against humanity arising from wartime atrocities.

26. Continental jurisprudence linguistically distinguishes between *Verfolgungs-verjährung,* prescriptive periods placed on prosecutions, and *Vollstreckungsver-jährung,* statutes requiring that the punishment be imposed within a specific period following the rendering of judgment. See Miller, "Non-Applicability of Statutory Limitations," 479.

27. Wexler, "Interpretation of the Nuremberg Principles," 337.

28. Ibid., 338.

29. Ibid.

30. Ibid., 339.

31. Finkielkraut, *Remembering in Vain,* 20.

32. Ibid.

33. Wexler, "Interpretation of the Nuremberg Principles," 342.

34. Ibid., 343.

35. 6(c), as we recall, defined crimes against humanity as persecutions on political as well as racial or religious grounds.

36. This issue was revisited in both the Touvier and Papon trials.

37. Wexler, "Interpretation of the Nuremberg Principles," 343.

38. Indeed, this is now the generally accepted position in international law. Genocide, by contrast, is not defined in terms of state practices.

39. Binder, "Representing Nazism," 1338.

40. "*Spiegel*-Gespräch mit Karl Jaspers," 58.

41. Although the decision of the Cour de Cassation meant that the killings of Jewish children and members of the resistance both constituted crimes against humanity, the two crimes were not treated altogether identically. Here the court made its final notable distinction, concluding that when Barbie tortured members of the resistance to obtain military secrets, he committed war crimes. It was only when he deported resistance members to concentration camps, the court argued, that he acted at the behest of Nazi hegemonic ideology and thus committed crimes against humanity.

42. Binder, "Klaus Barbie," 1341.

43. Finkielkraut, *Remembering in Vain,* 20.

44. Quoted in ibid.

45. Karl Marx, "The Eighteenth Brumaire of Louis Bonaparte," in *The Marx-Engels Reader,* ed. Robert Tucker (New York: Norton, 1978), 594.

46. Teicholz, *The Trial of Ivan the Terrible,* 49.

47. In 1979, the investigation and prosecution of Nazi war criminals was transferred to the newly established division of the Justice Department, the Office of Special Investigations (OSI).

48. Such deportations often occur as a form of extradition, so the accused can stand trial in the country in which his chief crimes were committed. Feodor Fedorenko, who was investigated by the INS in tandem with its investigation of Demjanjuk, was, roughly at the time of Demjanjuk's extradition to Israel, extradited to the Soviet Union, where he was tried and executed in 1986. The legal aspects of Fedorenko's denaturalization proceedings are treated in *United States v. Feodor Fedorenko,* 455 F.Supp 893 (Southern District of Florida, 1978); and *Fedorenko v. United States* 449 U.S. 490 (1981).

49. See Teicholz, *The Trial of Ivan the Terrible.*

50. At trial, the prosecution was able to submit the original Trawniki card.

51. The second suspect was Fedorenko.

52. *TAE* 3:1214–15.

53. *Criminal Appeal 377/88 Ivan (John) Demjanjuk v. The State of Israel: Judgment of the Supreme Court of Israel* (Jerusalem: Supreme Court, 1993), 44 [hereafter cited as *Judgment of the Supreme Court*].

54. As the trial court itself observed, "The witness . . . appeared as if he were there and was undergoing the entire shocking experience a second time." *The Demjanjuk Trial: District Court,* 50.

55. Ibid., 381.

56. Yoram Sheftel, *Show Trial: The Conspiracy to Convict John Demjanjuk as 'Ivan the Terrible,'* trans. Haim Watzman (London: Victor Gollancz, 1994), 43, 45.

57. Teicholz, *The Trial of Ivan the Terrible,* 274.

58. Sheftel, *Show Trial,* 225.

59. At the time of the Eichmann trial, as noted in chap. 4, n. 41, the Knesset passed a law requiring that trials of Nazis and Nazi Collaborators be conducted by a three-judge panel headed by a sitting member of the Supreme Court.

60. *The Demjanjuk Trial: District Court,* 2.

61. Sheftel, *Show Trial,* 112.

62. Ibid., 198.

63. *The Demjanjuk Trial: District Court,* 11.

64. Ibid., 2.

65. Ibid., 13.

66. Ibid., 12.

67. Ibid., 10.

68. Ibid., 93.

69. Ibid., 199.

70. The defense's first choice was Elizabeth Loftus of the University of Washington, perhaps the most renowned expert on memory problems. Loftus, however, decided not to testify apparently out of respect to members of her own family who had survived the Holocaust.

71. Wagenaar's critique of this conclusion and his attack on the identification parades can be found in Willem Wagenaar, *Identifying Ivan: A Case Study in Legal Psychology* (Cambridge: Harvard University Press, 1988).

72. *The Demjanjuk Trial: District Court*, 199.

73. Teicholz, *The Trial of Ivan the Terrible*, 278.

74. *The Demjanjuk Trial: District Court*, 263–64.

75. Gitta Sereny explained Demjanjuk's refusal to admit that he had served as a guard, though not at Treblinka, in terms of both his fear of extradition to the Ukraine and his unwillingness to reveal himself as a liar to his family. Gitta Sereny, "John Demjanjuk and the Failure of Justice," *New York Review of Books*, October 8, 1992, 32–34.

76. These included the suicide of Dov Eitan, who had joined the defense team to help prepare the appeal, and an attack upon Sheftel, who had acid thrown in his face by a fanatic.

77. Sheftel, *Show Trial*, 322. Adding to the confusion was the fact that Demjanjuk had originally stated that his mother's maiden name was Marchenko, a common Ukrainian surname.

78. For a discussion of the mistakes made by the Office of Special Investigations, see *Demjanjuk v. Petrovsky*, 10 F.3rd 339 (Sixth Cir., 1993).

79. *Judgment of the Supreme Court*, 41.

80. Binder, "Representing Nazism," 1350–51.

81. Teicholz, *The Trial of Ivan the Terrible*, 269.

82. Rousso, *The Vichy Syndrome*, 211.

83. Note the additional irony that "for diametrically opposed reasons, both Vergès and the resistance lawyers wanted the Resistance to figure in the [trial]." Ibid., 213.

84. Quoted in Binder, "Representing Nazism," 1355.

85. Ibid., 1362.

86. Ibid.

87. Ibid., 1363.

88. Sheftel, *Show Trial*, 102.

89. *Judgment of the Supreme Court*, 7.

90. Sheftel, *Show Trial*, 342.

Chapter 8. "Did Six Million Really Die?"

1. See Manuel Prustchi, "The Zundel Affair," in Alan Davies, ed., *Antisemitism in Canada: History and Interpretation* (Waterloo, Ontario: Wilfred Laurier Univ. Press, 1992), 255.

2. Lipstadt, *Denying the Holocaust,* 158.

3. Richard Harwood [alias Richard Verrall], "Did Six Million Really Die?" (Toronto: Samisdat, n.d.), 21.

4. Harwood [alias], "Did Six Million Really Die?" 4.

5. Quoted in Leonidas E. Hill, "The Trial of Ernst Zundel: Revisionism and Law in Canada," in *Simon Wiesenthal Center Annual* (Chappaqua, N.Y.: Rossel Books, 1989).

6. Harwood [alias], "Did Six Million Really Die?" 5, 20.

7. Zundel was also indicted under section 177 for publishing *The War, the West, and Islam,* an anti-Zionist pamphlet; this charge, however, played a marginal role in the trial, and Zundel was acquitted of this charge.

8. R.S.C. (Revised Statutes of Canada), chap. C-34 § 177 (1st Supp. 1970).

9. For a more complete text of the law, see Stephen J. Roth, "Denial of the Holocaust: An Issue of Law," *Institute of Jewish Affairs Research Reports,* no. 2 (1994): 5.

10. The full text of the statute appears in ibid., 4.

11. The United States also has not been a site of perpetrator trials because there, as noted in chap. 7, crimes against humanity does not exist as an incrimination in domestic federal law.

12. Quoted in Gerald Tishler, "Holocaust Denial and Group Libel: Comparative Perspectives," *Boston College Third World Law Journal* 8 (1988): 65–90, 71.

13. While the "First Amendment recognizes no such thing as a 'false' idea" (*Gertz v. Robert Welch, Inc.,* 418 U.S. 323 (1974), 339), it does recognize that there is such a thing as a false fact, and the Supreme Court continues to maintain that "false statements of fact" deserve no constitutional protection as "they interfere with the truth-seeking function of the marketplace of ideas" (*Hustler Magazine v. Falwell,* 485 U.S. 46 (1988), 52). Thus inasmuch as a statement denying the mass extermination of Jews during the World War II constitutes a false statement of fact, and that such a statement will usually be made in reckless disregard of the truth, then it seems that civil actions such as "intentional infliction of emotional distress" might offer a constitutionally permissible response to Holocaust denial.

14. Lipstadt, *Denying the Holocaust,* 1–29.

15. Geoffrey Hartman, "Introduction: Darkness Visible," in *Holocaust Remembrance,* ed. Hartman, 11.

16. Lipstadt, *Denying the Holocaust,* 2.

17. The German Democratic Republic, during its existence, engaged in a less

substantial struggle with the Nazi past and, by extension, with the issue of Holocaust denial. For a nuanced discussion, see Jeffrey Herf, *Divided Memory: The Nazi Past in the Two Germanys* (Cambridge: Harvard University Press, 1997).

18. See Eric Stein, "History Against Free Speech: The New German Law Against the 'Auschwitz' — and Other — 'Lies,'" *Michigan Law Review* 85 (1986): 277–324.

19. 75 *BGHZ (Entscheidungen des Bundesgerichtshofes in Zivilsachen)* 160; 33 *NJW (Neue juristiche Wochenschrift)* 45 (1980); see also Stein, "History Against Free Speech," 301–05.

20. 75 *BGHZ* 160, 166.

21. Decision of 30 January 1985, OLG (Oberlandsgericht) Celle, No. 1 Ss 126/84 — 10 Js 228/80 Sta; see also Stein "History Against Free Speech," 304.

22. 75 *BGHZ* 160, 162.

23. Ibid., 162–63. Translation by the author.

24. Passed as "Einundzwanzigstes Strafrechtänderungsgesetz" [Twenty-first law modifying the criminal law] on 13 June 1985.

25. Juliane Wetzel, "The Judicial Treatment of Incitement against Ethnic Groups and the Denial of National Socialist Mass Murder in the Federal Republic of Germany," in *Under the Shadow of Weimar: Democracy, Law, and Racial Incitement in Six Countries,* ed. Louis Greenspan and Cyril Levitt (Westport, Conn.: Praeger, 1993), 99. See also Wetzel, "Die Leugnung des Genozids im internationalen Vergleich," in *Die Auschwitzleugner,* ed. Brigitte Bailer-Galanda, Wolfgang Benz, Wolfgang Neugebauer (Berlin: Elefanten Press, 1996).

26. Daniel Beisel, "Die Strafbarkeit der Auschwitzlüge," *NJW* 1995, Heft 15, 999.

27. In this way, the law reconciled the contradictory decisions handed down by the Bundesgerichtshof (Federal court of justice) and the Bundesverfassungsgericht (Federal constitutional court) earlier in 1994. The Bundesgerichtshof is the nation's highest appellate court in cases of civil and criminal law. The Bundesverfassungsgericht, by contrast, decides constitutional questions and is the only court with the authority to declare laws unconstitutional under the Basic Law. In its decision in the *Irving* case, the Bundesverfassungsgericht had resolved a free speech claim involving an act of prior restraint. Notified that the revisionist historian David Irving (see discussion of Irving's role in the Zundel trial in chap. 9) was slated to address a rightist rally in Munich, city administrators instructed the organizers to bar or interrupt the delivery of "punishable speeches" (strafbare Redebeiträge). *NJW* 1994, Heft 28, 1779. Confronted with a challenge to the constitutionality of the city's acts, the constitutional court addressed the question, "Is Holocaust denial an opinion?" (See Horst Meier, "Das Strafrecht gegen die 'Auschwitzlüge,'" *Merkur* 48, no. 12 (1994): 1128–32, 1130). While recognizing that "the delineation between the expression of an opinion and the statement of fact

can admittedly be difficult," the court insisted that the denial of the Holocaust constituted a "proscribable untruth": "the proscribed utterance, namely, that there was no persecution of the Jews in the Third Reich, constitutes a factual claim that has been proven untrue in countless eyewitness reports and documents, in the judgments of numerous criminal trials and the determinations of professional historians" *NJW* 1994, Heft 28, 1780. Here the court specifically distinguished Holocaust denial from denials of German culpability for the outbreak of the Second World War. This latter claim, which, as we recall, the Allies treated as provable fact at Nuremberg, involved complex judgments ("komplexe Beurteilungen") which could not be reduced to factual claims. Holocaust denial, by contrast, involved the denial of an event, not its interpretation.

The Bundesgerichtshof, however, seemed to reach a contradictory conclusion in its decision in the *Deckert* case. The head of the rightist National Democratic Party, Günter Deckert, had been convicted of "sympathetically translating" a public speech delivered by Fred Leuchter, a well-known American negationist and self-styled gas chamber expert. Though convicted, Deckert had seen his one-year sentence suspended by a lower court impressed by the defendant's "responsible personality" and "distinct principles." The prosecution appealed (as did Deckert), and the high court concluded that evidence that the defendant had published "bare denials of the Holocaust" (bloße Ableugen) did not suffice to support a conviction of racial incitement. This decision, however, found little support in the constitutional court's conclusion that denial constituted a "proscribable untruth," and the change in the law of incitement passed at the end of 1994 in effect supplanted the high court's decision. Now "mere denial" suffices to support a conviction. In 1995, Deckert was arrested on charges of inciting racial hatred.

28. See, for example, Meier, "Das Strafrecht gegen die 'Auschwitzlüge.'"

29. See the discussion of Benjamin in Jacques Derrida, "Force of Law: The 'Mystical Foundation of Authority,'" in *Deconstruction and the Possibility of Justice,* ed. Drucilla Cornell, Michael Rosenfield, and David Gray Carlson (New York: Routledge, 1992), 3–64.

30. Rousso, *The Vichy Syndrome,* 4.

31. Indeed, these circumstances remind one of the limits of the metaphor of dramaturgy for describing the legal process, as the decision to stage a trial is often less fashioned and more the outcome of extraordinary pressures.

32. *Transcript of Her Majesty the Queen v. Ernst Zundel,* unpublished (Toronto: The Court House, 1985): 2311 [hereafter cited (often parenthetically in the text) as *TEZ-1985* followed by page number].

33. See the discussion in Hill, "The Trial of Ernst Zundel," 179–82.

34. Inasmuch as the elements of the offense required the state to prove that Zundel knew of the falsity of the statements he had published, taking judicial notice of the Holocaust still would have left the prosecution in the position of hav-

ing to submit evidence about the accused's intentions and mindset. On the other hand, insofar as the standard of judicial notice is based on a reasonableness standard, then taking notice of the Holocaust would presumably have branded the accused as, by definition, unreasonable, if not mendacious.

35. Warren Kinsella, *Web of Hate: Inside Canada's Far Right Network* (Toronto: HarperCollins, 1995), 83. Christie's clients included, among others, James Keegstra, a teacher convicted under the hate crimes statute for spreading anti-Semitism and Holocaust negationism; and Imre Finta, the first man ever to be charged under the war crimes section of the Canadian Criminal Code.

36. *Nazi Concentration Camps* was originally submitted at Nuremberg precisely to rebut such claims.

Chapter 9. Historians and Hearsay

1. Such relaxed standards did not impeach the quality of justice rendered at these trials, I have argued. Often considered a norm necessitated by the quirks of the jury system, the hearsay rule arguably has less application in a bench trial, as was the case in both the Nuremberg and Eichmann proceedings.

2. In the second trial, however, Christopher Browning cited evidence indicating that Dachau's gas chamber probably had become operational shortly before the camp's liberation.

3. Levi, *The Drowned and the Saved,* 83.

4. Saul Friedlander, *Kurt Gerstein: The Ambiguity of Good* (New York: Alfred A. Knopf, 1969), 228.

5. Harwood [alias], "Did Six Million Really Die?" 6, 5.

6. Ironically, the term "revisionist," first prominently used in a juridical context to describe those who agitated for a revision of the verdict against Alfred Dreyfus, is now used as an appellation for Holocaust deniers. See Robert L. Hoffman, *More Than a Trial: The Struggle Over Captain Dreyfus* (New York: Free Press, 1980).

7. Marvin E. Frankel, "The Search for the Truth: An Umpireal View," *University of Pennsylvania Law Review* 123 (1975): 1032.

8. As a related matter, revisionists in the United States have mastered the technique of dressing up their arguments in the rhetoric of the First Amendment, claiming that they seek not to silence or foreclose dialogue but to subject the historical understanding of the Holocaust to "robust scrutiny" and "open debate" — the very catchphrases that lie at the heart of liberal defenses of free speech. Even if these appeals fundamentally misstate the doctrinal commitments of the First Amendment (false statements of fact, uttered in reckless disregard of the truth, hardly enjoy robust constitutional protection), they remain rhetorically effective. Deborah Lipstadt, for example, has described how numerous American univer-

sity newspapers believed that they were obligated to run advertisements paid for by the Institute for Historical Review — accepting, as they did, the institute's argument that the refusal to do so would have constituted censorship of an unpopular viewpoint. Lipstadt, *Denying the Holocaust,* 183–208.

9. In 1998, Christian Gerlach, a German scholar, described a recently discovered note by Himmler as establishing the existence of such an order, but this discovery has hardly settled the matter. Alan Cowell, "Hitler's Genocide Order," *New York Times,* January 21, 1998, A4.

10. Pierre Vidal-Naquet, *Assassins of Memory: Essays on the Denial of the Holocaust,* trans. Jeffrey Mehlman (New York: Columbia University Press, 1992), 21–24.

11. Kaltenbrunner had testified at Nuremberg that "special treatment" referred to the unusually pleasant conditions that awaited Jews sent to concentration camps.

12. He was, as noted, acquitted on the second count relating to the publication of the *The War, the West, and Islam.*

13. Quoted in Prutschi, "The Zündel Affair," 269.

14. Quoted in Gabriel Weimann and Conrad Winn, *Hate on Trial: The Zundel Affair, the Media, Public Opinion in Canada* (Oakville: Mosaic Press, 1986), 30.

15. Ibid., 78.

16. Prutschi, "The Zündel Affair," 252.

17. Weimann and Winn, *Hate on Trial,* 103; Faurisson's claim that there were no gas chambers in Nazi Germany is a perfect example of negationists' rhetorical strategies, as Faurisson based his point on Martin Broszat's work. Broszat, one of Germany's best-known Holocaust scholars, observed, in a paper published in the 1960s, that all the gas chambers had been located outside of Germany proper (for example, in Poland). Ignoring for the moment the factual accuracy of Broszat's assertion (I have noted the controversies about the Dachau facility), one can see how Faurisson misappropriates the historian's point to make a very different kind of claim.

18. During voir dire, Christie sought to ask each prospective juror a number of offensive questions, including, "Do you believe the Holocaust happened as depicted in the media . . . ?" *Regina v. Zundel,* 31 Canadian Criminal Cases (3d) 97 (Ontario Appeal Cases, 1987), 130 [hereafter cited as 31 CCC followed by page number]. Though the appellate court concluded that Judge Locke properly had refused the questions as framed, it held that the "fundamental right to a fair and proper trial" obligated Locke to permit Christie to rephrase the proposed questions. His failure to permit this compromised the defense's right to challenge for cause and thus eroded the overall fairness of the proceeding. One of the elements of the offense, the trickiest from the standpoint of the Crown, required the prosecution to prove that Zundel had published false statements with full knowledge

of their falsity. In his charge, Locke had asked the jurors to consider whether Zundel had published "Did Six Million Really Die?" "with no honest belief in the essential truth" of its claims (31 CCC, 156). Such a formulation obviously equated knowledge of falsity with the absence of "honest belief." While this may sound unproblematic, the appellate court reasoned that a person might act recklessly with regard to the truth or falsity of a claim — and therefore lack an honest belief in its truth — yet still not have positive knowledge of its falsity. Section 177, however, "requires proof of actual knowledge of falsity . . . recklessness . . . is insufficient" (ibid., 157). Here, again, the court concluded that the trial judge's error had prejudiced the defense.

19. *In the District Court of Ontario: Her Majesty the Queen v. Ernst Zundel* (Toronto: The Court House, 1988), unpublished transcript, "Rulings on Pre-Trial Motions," 18 [hereafter cited as *TEZ-1988* followed by page number].

20. Lipstadt's characterization of Irving as a Holocaust denier led the British historian to bring a libel suit; the trial of *Irving v. Lipstadt and Penguin Books* resulted in Justice Charles Gray's emphatic dismissal of Irving's claim.

21. *Regina v. Zundel*, 75 Canadian Criminal Cases (3d) 449 (Supreme Court Reports, 1992), 456 [hereafter cited as 75 CCC followed by page number].

22. Prutschi, "The Zündel Affair," 253.

23. Buttressed by Faurisson's testimony, Christie insisted that Gräbe himself had fled Germany in the 1960s to avoid possible indictment for having committed perjury about his own wartime activities. See, "Bewegtes Leben," *Der Spiegel* Nr.53/1965, 26–28.

24. Yet when Christie demanded to know whether any Holocaust survivor had ever been subjected to cross-examination, it was pointed out that the witnesses at the Demjanjuk trial, under way at the same time in Jerusalem, had indeed been so "validated" (*TEZ-1988*, 3919).

25. Hilberg was declared an unavailable witness. His earlier statement was admissible, as it had been thoroughly cross-examined.

26. Christopher Browning, "The Revised Hilberg," *Simon Wiesenthal Center Annual* 3 (1986): 294.

27. Maier, *The Unmasterable Past*, 95.

Chapter 10. The Legal Imagination and Traumatic History

1. Jorge Luis Borges, "The Witness," in idem, *A Personal Anthology*, ed. Anthony Kerrigan (New York: Grove Press, 1967), 178.

2. Whether such an obligation is truly binding as a normative matter or merely perceived as such is largely moot. Indeed, whether one believes, as I do, that this model of legal obligation is proper, or whether one maintains, as a votary of critical legal studies might, that it is a mere fetishization of law, is beside the point: for

prosecutors and judges — particularly those presiding over extraordinary trials — will tend, as a descriptive matter, to perform their institutional roles in an attempt to fulfill its terms.

3. I do not, however, mean to suggest that there is a legal obligation to initiate such prosecutions. Cf. Diane F. Orentlicher, "Settling Accounts: The Duty to Prosecute Human Rights Violations of a Prior Regime," *Yale Law Journal* 100, no. 8 (June 1991): 2537–2615.

Index

Italicized page numbers indicate photographs and illustrations.